POCOSIN WETLANDS

An Integrated Analysis of Coastal Plain Freshwater Bogs in North Carolina

Edited by

Curtis J. Richardson
Duke University

with the assistance of

Mary L. Matthews
Stephen A. Anderson
Duke University

Hutchinson Ross Publishing Company

Stroudsburg, Pennsylvania

Library of Congress Catalog Card Number: 81-7158
ISBN: 0-87933-418-5

83 82 81 1 2 3 4 5
Manufactured in the United States of America.

Library of Congress Cataloging in Publication Data

Main entry under title:

Pocosin wetlands.

Proceedings of a conference, held Jan. 3-4, 1980, at the Duke University Marine Laboratory, Beaufort, N.C.; sponsored by Integrated Case Studies Program in Natural Resource Analysis of the Duke University School of Forestry and Environmental Studies, and others.

Includes index.

1. Wetland ecology—North Carolina—Congresses. 2. Bog ecology—North Carolina—Congresses. 3. Wetlands—North Carolina—Congresses. 4. Bogs—North Carolina—Congresses. I. Richardson, Curtis J. II. Duke University. Marine Laboratory. III. Duke University. School of Forestry and Environmental Studies. IV. Title: Coastal plain freshwater bogs in North Carolina.

QH105.N8P6 333.91'8'09756 81-7158
ISBN 0-87933-418-5 AACR2

Distributed world wide by Academic Press, a subsidiary of Harcourt Brace Jovanovich, Publishers.

Proceedings of

POCOSINS:

A Conference on Alternative Uses of the Coastal Plain Freshwater Wetlands of North Carolina

January 3-4, 1980

Duke University Marine Laboratory
Beaufort, North Carolina

Sponsored by:

Integrated Case Studies Program in
Natural Resource Analysis
Duke University School of Forestry and Environmental Studies

and

Coastal Energy Impact Program
Office of Coastal Management
North Carolina Department of
Natural Resources and Community Development

in cooperation with

Duke University Marine Laboratory

and

Water Resources Research Institute
The University of North Carolina

Chairman of the Conference:

Curtis J. Richardson
School of Forestry and Environmental Studies
Duke University

Conference Coordinator:

Stephen A. Anderson
School of Forestry and Environmental Studies
Duke University

Conference Planning Committee:

Stephen A. Anderson, Nonindustrial Section Chairman
School of Forestry and Environmental Studies
Duke University

David Carr, Conference Logistics
School of Forestry and Environmental Studies
Duke University

Frank Convery, Resource Economics Section Chairman
School of Forestry and Environmental Studies
Duke University

Benjamin Jayne, Industrial Section Chairman
School of Forestry and Environmental Studies
Duke University

Ed Kuenzler, Resource Ecology Section Chairman
Department of Environmental Sciences and Engineering
The University of North Carolina at Chapel Hill

Jack Royer, Law and Policy Section Chairman
School of Forestry and Environmental Studies
Duke University

Pocosin Field Trip Leaders:

Dick Barber, Marine Laboratory, Duke University
Norm Christensen, Department of Botany, Duke University
Henry Wilbur, Department of Zoology, Duke University

Panel Discussion Leader:

John R. Clark
National Wetlands Technical Council and The Conservation Foundation

Panel Members:

Dick Barber, Marine Ecologist, Marine Laboratory, Duke University
Vincent Bellis, Sierra Club
Richard Campbell, Forestry, Weyerhaeuser Company
Wendell Gilliam, Soil Scientist, North Carolina State University
Bill Hyde, Resource Economist, School of Forestry and Environmental Studies, Duke University
Ed Kuenzler, Wetlands Ecologist, Department of Enviromental Sciences and Engineering, University of North Carolina
Doug Nelson, Office of Coastal Management, North Carolina Department of Natural Resources and Community Development

Keynote Speaker:

Eugene Odum, Institute of Ecology, University of Georgia

To Carol and John and to the people who first understood the value of pocosins—the American Indian.

Table of Contents

SECTION III. INDUSTRIAL VALUES

SECTION IV. RESOURCE ECONOMICS

SECTION V. LAW AND POLICY

CONFERENCE CRITIQUE

Preface

Pocosins are freshwater wetlands, their name taken from an Algonquin Indian word meaning "swamp-on-a-hill." They occur on the southeastern coastal plain from Virginia to north Florida and once covered more than two million acres in North Carolina. Most of the natural stands of timber were harvested years ago but pocosins generally have been viewed as having marginal potential for development.

Recently, however, spurred by soaring prices for wood products, food, energy and minerals, intensive development and management are taking place in many pocosin areas. Timber production, agriculture and peat extraction are a few of the uses. Extensive draining, clearing, diking, burning, and other activities are often carried out on pocosins without a clear understanding of either local ecosystem response or external effects.

We chose to focus on pocosins because their development potential is still a matter of speculation and management alternatives are not yet being discussed in the atmosphere of confrontation. The pocosins conference is viewed as the first step in understanding the benefits, costs and risks associated with the conversion of large tracts of North Carolina wetlands and in developing integrated management guidelines for these threatened and valuable natural resources.

From the start, we recognized that exploration of the full ramifications of pocosin utilization alternatives goes far beyond the expertise of a few academicians. Participants from varied resource disciplines were invited to discuss the present knowledge of the effects of alternative uses of coastal plain freshwater wetlands from a number of different perspectives. At the conference, background information was presented on the ecology and hydrology of pocosins. Succeeding sessions examined pocosins for their nonindustrial values, including fish and wildlife and recreation; and their industrial values, including forest management, peat mining and coastal fisheries. Another session focused on economics, including the economics of peat utilization, intensive forestry, agriculture, and pocosin preservation. Law and policy issues for pocosin management, including the political economy, the legal framework for management, and preservation policy, were discussed in the last session.

Throughout the conference, we tried to address a number of questions regarding pocosins. How will development alter the inherent character of these wetlands? And, how will changes in the wetland resource system affect neighboring ecological systems? What is the present distribution of these lands and what is their rate of conversion? What values do they possess in their present state? What social and economic effects will development have on local communities? What additional impacts will be felt at the state and national levels?

For any wildland area or wetland type, questions such as these must be addressed openly by all interested parties to provide a sound basis on which to establish a coherent usage policy. Natural and social scientists can play a vital role as advisors in this decision-making process, by laying out clearly what we do and do not know about the environmental, economic and social systems under study.

The conference and its proceedings should not be the culmination of our efforts on pocosins. Having brought the interested parties together, we must address major questions such as: What are the total costs and benefits of pocosin conversion? How much of this wetland resource should we develop? What are the effects (positive and negative) of development on adjacent ecosystems? Who regulates the use of pocosins? What more must be learned about pocosins to determine potential repercussions of their development? But which questions are the most important to answer and who will answer them? We hope that this volume will help guide managers concerned with pocosins, that it will identify a few of the critical unknowns, and that its readers will be moved to seek integrated solutions through future mutual endeavors.

Curtis J. Richardson
William A. Thompson
Co-directors, Integrated Case Studies in Natural Resource Analysis

Acknowledgments

Steve Anderson's perspectives, organizational skills, and dedication were indispensable in making the conference on pocosin wetlands and this volume a success. Steve, along with William Thompson, gave invaluable assistance by reviewing early manuscript drafts and by arranging for outside reviewers for papers in sections two and four, respectively. Jack Royer greatly aided in work on section five.

Five preconference planning sessions were held over a nine-month period in 1979. Consultation with persons in industry, state, local and federal government, universities, and conservation groups was vital in the identification of conference participants who could provide the breadth and depth essential to this undertaking. We are grateful to the many persons who gave their time and advice. Graduate students in the Duke School of Forestry and Environmental Studies played a valuable role, gathering voluminous data on pocosins and working to make the conference a success. A special note of thanks goes to Dennis Adrian, Andrea Ayvazian, David Carr, Sally De Becker, Sara Fried, and Roland Zitzman for background work on conference materials and handling of the conference logistics. We thank John Costlow, director, and the staff of the Duke University Marine Laboratory for providing conference facilities and aiding us with the meeting.

Special thanks is extended to the Office of Coastal Management, who served as conference cosponsor, and Jim Smith of the Coastal Energy Impact program, who saw the value of this effort. Sincere thanks is extended to the scientists who contributed papers to the proceedings and worked patiently with us during the review process. We gratefully acknowledge the efforts of the forty-six reviewers who worked so conscientiously to provide us with papers of the highest professional standards. We also thank Mary Elizabeth Robinson who retyped many of the manuscripts.

Finally, we especially thank the foundation whose support made this effort possible and kept the price of this volume affordable to the user community.

Curtis J. Richardson
Conference Chairman

Mary L. Matthews
Publications Coordinator

Conference Speakers (S), Section Moderators (M), and Paper Authors (A)*

Andrew B. Allen (S), First Colony Farms, Route 1, Box 201, Creswell, North Carolina 27978

Steve Anderson (M), School of Forestry and Environmental Studies, Duke University, Durham, North Carolina 27706

Ray Ashton (S,A), North Carolina State Museum of Natural History, Post Office Box 27647, Raleigh, North Carolina 27611

Steve Barnes (S,A), First Colony Farms, Route 1, Box 201, Creswell, North Carolina 27978

Edward Bergman (S), Department of City and Regional Planning, University of North Carolina, Chapel Hill, North Carolina 27514

David Brower (S,A), Center for Urban and Regional Studies, University of North Carolina, Chapel Hill, North Carolina 27514

Rebecca Burchell (A), Department of Botany, Duke University, Durham, North Carolina 27706

R. G. Campbell (S,A), Weyerhaeuser Company, Post Office Box 1391, New Bern, North Carolina 28560

Robert N. Campbell, Jr. (A), First Colony Farms, Route 1, Box 201, Creswell, North Carolina 27978

David Carr (A), School of Forestry and Environmental Studies, Duke University, Durham, North Carolina 27706

Norm Christensen (S,A), Department of Botany, Duke University, Durham, North Carolina 27706

John Clark (M), The Conservation Foundation, 1717 Massachusetts Avenue, N.W., Washington, D.C. 20036

Frank Convery (M), School of Forestry and Environmental Studies, Duke University, Durham, North Carolina 27706

Arthur Cooper (S,A), 3020 Biltmore Hall, Department of Forestry, North Carolina State University, Raleigh, North Carolina 27611

Charles C. Daniel III (S,A), U.S. Department of the Interior, Geological Survey, Post Office Box 2857, Raleigh, North Carolina 27602

*Three papers (by Lilly, Gilliam and Skaggs, and Ingram and Otte), were added to the original proceedings to provide the readers of this volume with additional information on pocosin systems.

Rhonda Evans (A), School of Forestry and Environmental Studies, Duke University, Durham, North Carolina 27706

J. W. Gilliam (A), Department of Soil Science, North Carolia State University, Raleigh, North Carolina 27611

H. J. Harwood (S,A), Research Triangle Institute, Post Office Box 12144, Research Triangle Park, North Carolina 27709

Milton S. Heath, Jr. (S,A), Institute of Government, 232 Knapp Building, 0524, University of North Carolina, Chapel Hill, North Carolina 27514

J. H. Hughs (A), Weyerhaeuser Company, Post Office Box 1391, New Bern, North Carolina 28560

Roy Ingram (A), Department of Geology, University of North Carolina, Chapel Hill, North Carolina 27514

Benjamin Jayne (M), School of Forestry and Environmental Studies, Duke University, Durham, North Carolina 27706

Edward Kuenzler (M), Department of Environmental Sciences and Engineering, 131 Rosenau Hall, University of North Carolina, Chapel Hill, North Carolina 27514

Annette Liggett (A), School of Forestry and Environmental Studies, Duke University, Durham, North Carolina 27706

Paul Lilly (A), Department of Soil Science, North Carolina State University, Raleigh, North Carolina 27611

William Lindenmuth (S,A), School of Forestry and Environmental Studies, Duke University, Durham, North Carolina 27706

Joseph McClees (A), North Carolina Department of Natural Resources, and Community Development, Division of Marine Fisheries, Morehead City, North Carolina 28557

Philip McMullan, Jr. (A), Research Triangle Institute, Post Office Box 12144, Research Triangle Park, North Carolina 27709

Tom Monschein (S,A), North Carolina Wildlife Resources Commission, New Bern, North Carolina 28560

Nancy Noneman (A), Center for Urban and Regional Studies, University of North Carolina, Chapel Hill, North Carolina 27514

Eugene Odum (S), Institute of Ecology, University of Georgia, Athens, Georgia 30601

Lee Otte (A), Department of Geology, University of North Carolina, Chapel Hill, North Carolina 27514

Stephen Peters (S), Department of Sociology, Duke University, Durham, North Carolina 27706

Joseph A. Phillips (S), Division of Soil and Water Conservation, Raleigh, North Carolina 27611

Sandra Postel (S,A), INTASA, Inc., 1030 Curtis Street, Menlo Park, California 94025

Curtis J. Richardson (S,A), School of Forestry and Environmental Studies, Duke University, Durham, North Carolina 27706

Chuck Roe (S,A), Department of Natural Resources and Community Development, Post Office Box 27687, Raleigh, North Carolina 27611

Jack Royer (M), School of Forestry and Environmental Studies, Duke University, Durham, North Carolina 27706

Ellen Simms (A), Department of Botany, Duke University, Durham, North Carolina 27706

R. W. Skaggs (A), Department of Soil Science, North Carolina State University, Raleigh, North Carolina 27611

Michael Street (S,A), Division of Marine Fisheries, Post Office Box 769, Morehead City, North Carolina 28557

John Taggart (S,A), Department of Natural Resources and Community Development, Post Office Box 27687, Raleigh, North Carolina 27611

William Thompson (S,A), School of Forestry and Environmental Studies, Duke University, Durham, North Carolina 27706

Michael Vasievich (A), USDA Forest Service, S.E. Forest Experiment Station, Duke University, Durham, North Carolina 27706

Brooks M. Whitehurst (S), Texasgulf, Inc., Post Office Box 48, Aurora, North Carolina 27806

Henry Wilbur (S,A), Department of Zoology, Duke University, Durham, North Carolina 27705

Dennis Whigham (S,A), Chesapeake Bay Center for Environmental Studies, Smithsonian Institution, Post Office Box 28, Edgewater, Maryland 21037

Integrated Case Studies in Natural Resource Analysis

The complexities of today's world demand a holistic approach to natural resource problem analysis and policy formulation. Established by a private foundation grant, the Integrated Case Studies in Natural Resource Analysis Program works to develop such an approach. The program, housed in Duke University's School of Forestry and Environmental Studies, operates under a broad charter to: (1) develop holistic and innovative approaches to natural resource management and problem solving, and (2) improve the training of natural resource professionals.

Five objectives provide a framework of operation:

1. Development of integrated methods for resource and environmental problem solving;
2. Cooperative involvement of professionals (in public and private sectors), students, and faculty in the examination and analysis of real world natural resource and environmental issues;
3. Development and utilization of alternatives to traditional educational methods;
4. Establishment of a nonpartisan forum in which to analyze complex resource problems;
5. Dissemination of products and methods into academic and professional practice.

The program meets its objectives by means of an integrated case study approach. Within the scope of the program, "integrated" refers to a methodology which incorporates a number of disciplines and is holistic in design, problem analysis, and execution. "Case study approach" refers to an in-depth analysis of a specific issue. The program seeks to bring together team members trained in many disciplines (multidisciplinary) to interact with each other in the examination of a problem such that their combined efforts equal more than the sum of the individual parts (holism). The research team uses the case study approach in its investigation of issues surrounding past, current, or recurrent natural resource and environmental problems and uses the data and information assembled to formulate a number of alternative solutions. The intent of a case study lies in the in-depth examination of a problem and the generation of realistic solutions, not in the advocacy of a single solution.

Pocosins: A Conference on Alternative Uses of the Coastal Plain Freshwater Wetlands of North Carolina and this volume are examples of the Integrated Case Studies approach.

Background

Pocosins: An Ecosystem in Transition

Curtis J. Richardson, Rhonda Evans, and David Carr

ABSTRACT

Pocosins are evergreen shrub bogs found on the southeastern coastal plains of the United States. They comprise more than 50% of North Carolina's freshwater wetlands. Their dominant vegetation of *Pinus serotina, Cyrilla racemiflora, Magnolia virginiana, Persea borbonia, Ilex glabra, Myrica heterophylla* and *Smilax laurifolia* grows on waterlogged, acid, nutrient poor, sandy or peaty soils. The typical pocosin usually covers thousands of acres, is removed from large streams and is subject to periodic burning. In 1962, natural pocosins covered 2,243,550 acres (907,933 hectares [ha]) in North Carolina, nearly 70%, of the nation's pocosins. By 1979 as a result of forestry and agricultural development, only 695,000 acres (281,000 ha) remained undisturbed. As of 1980, 33% of pocosin wetlands surveyed were totally developed, 36% were under partial or potential development status and 31% remained in their natural state. Less than 5% of pocosins are under protection from development by federal or state agencies. Major timber companies, large agricultural corporations, and federal and state forestry agencies control approximately 44%, 21%, and 18%, respectively, of the pocosin land. The major shift in ownership patterns from 1962 has been the transfer of nearly 500,000 acres (202,000 ha) to corporate farm operations. Major users of pocosin lands drain, burn, and carry out extensive site preparation. These developmental activities on pocosins have resulted in changes in hydrologic regime, outputs of fresh water and nutrients (e.g., phosphorus) to estuarine areas, extensive smoke damage and air pollution problems. In order for resource managers to develop appropriate management guidelines for the remaining pocosins, an integrated analysis of the resource must be completed.

Key Words: pocosins, Carolina bays, maps, ownership patterns, development trends, land use, impact analysis

INTRODUCTION

Freshwater wetlands comprise nearly 90% of the total area of wetlands in the United States (Council on Environmental Quality, 1971) and, in 1962, accounted for 72% of the 5,885,600 acres (2,377,540 hectares [ha]) of wetlands reported for North Carolina (Wilson, 1962).

Only recently have the values of natural wetlands become evident (Good et al., 1978; Greeson et al., 1979). Values most often listed are: (1) biological productivity, (2) water storage, (3) flood protection, (4) aquifer recharge, (5) nutrient and sediment removal, (6) wildlife habitat, (7) habitat for unique and endangered species, (8) carbon storage, (9) nursery area for fisheries, (10) detritus output for aquatic life, (11) recreation, and (12) aesthetics (visual and cultural). Not all of these attributes are present in every wetland, and for many wetland ecosystems, none of these values have been verified.

Drained, some wetlands can take on new value in terms of food, fiber, and energy production. In a highly altered state, they are no longer considered wetlands but are classified as wet soils by the Soil Conservation Service (Dideriksen et al., 1979). Has society benefited by converting wetlands to wet soils? How much wetland area has been converted? How much remains? Is wetland conversion irreversible?

Using North Carolina pocosins as a regional case study, this and the following papers address these major questions. A working definition for pocosins, their geographic range, wetland conversion trends, ownership patterns, and the values and potential impacts of development are presented for this major freshwater wetland type in the southeastern coastal plains of the United States.

DEFINITION AND CLASSIFICATION OF POCOSIN TYPES

The word pocosin is an Algonquin Indian term that means "swamp-on-a-hill" (Tooker, 1899). In 1875, Kerr defined pocosins as "... flatwoods with no natural drainage ways, different from swamps in that they are not alluvial, occurring on divides between rivers and sounds and frequently elevated above streams of which they were the source." In 1899, Tooker further described pocosins as marshy or boggy areas where water backs up during rainy seasons or with spring freshets. Harper in 1907 characterized a pocosin as an "... extensive, flat damp, sandy or peaty area usually remote from large streams, supporting a scattered growth of pine (mostly *Pinus serotina*) and a very dense growth of shrubs, mostly evergreen, giving the whole a decided heath-like aspect. ..." The most holistic definitions of pocosin were proposed by Wells (1928), Woodwell (1958), and Kologiski (1977). Wells described them as being primarily restricted to the southeastern coastal plain, occurring in broad, shallow basins, in drainage basin heads, and on broad, flat uplands. These areas have long hydroperiods, temporary surface water, periodic burning, and soils of sandy humus, muck or peat. The dominant vegetation consists of broadleaf, evergreen shrubs (*Cyrilla racemiflora, Magnolia virginiana, Persea borbonia, Ilex glabra, Myrica heterophylla, Smilax laurifolia*) and pines (*Pinus serotina*). Woodwell (1958) also stressed that pocosins are a successional stage maintained by fires, composed of a combination of pocosin pine (*P. serotina*), a dense shrub layer and peat soil. The soils are acidic and may be flooded up to several inches for long periods. Fire naturally occurs every fifteen to twenty years. Kologiski added that common synonyms for pocosin include bay, bayland, bayhead, xeric shrub bog, and evergreen shrub bog.

In the 1956 national survey of wetlands types (Shaw and Fredine, 1956), pocosins were classified as Type VIII (bogs) and given the lowest waterfowl rating, nationwide, of all the twenty wetland classifications. In the new wetland classification system by the United States Fish and Wildlife Service (Cowardin et al., 1979), pocosins are classified as: System: Palustrine; Class: Scrub-shrub; Subclass: Broad-leaved evergreen; Water regime: Saturated; Water chemistry: Fresh-acid; Soil: Medisaprist.

Unfortunately, the term "pocosins" has been viewed and defined differently by scientists in various disciplines—e.g., botanists, geologists, hydrologists, and soil scientists—which results in confusion in the literature as to the wetland type, origin, and successional stage of the ecosystem being compared. From a vegetational perspective, there appears to be a consensus that pocosins are usually covered in a dense tangle of evergreen and deciduous shrubs and vines (see Christensen, this volume). The geology of wetland ecosystems often labeled vegetatively as pocosins can be quite different (i.e., large pocosin tracts vs. bays) (see Daniel, Campbell and Hughes, this volume).

Geologically, very large pocosin tracts covering thousands of acres are found on flat, clay based soils, in shallow basins on divides between ancient rivers and sounds. The process of paludification, i.e., bog expansion caused by a gradual rising of the water table as peat accumulates, has proceeded for several thousand years with vegetation and undecomposed peat blocking natural drainage (Dansereau and Segadas-Vianna, 1952; Heinselman, 1970; Whitehead, 1972; Daniel, this volume). Pocosin areas initially developed as primary mire systems (i.e., wetlands formed in basins or depressions). Most have succeeded through the secondary mire stage (i.e., wetlands which develop beyond the physical boundaries of the depression with the peat acting as a water reservoir) and into the present tertiary mire system (i.e., wetlands which develop above the physical limits of the ground water with the peat acting as a reservoir holding water by capillarity above the level of the main groundwater mass draining through the landscape) (Moore and Bellamy, 1974). Thus, hydrologically, tertiary pocosin systems act as a perched water table and receive water primarily from rainfall.

Carolina bays, as wetlands having pocosin type vegetation, are of unknown origin, variable in size (a few acres up to several thousand), are most often found on sandy soils, and are elongated, elliptical depressions on a northwest-southeast axis, with a high sand rim to the southeast (see Ingram and Otte, this volume). The North Carolina Heritage program further classifies bays into four subtypes: (1) bays with clay based substrata found typically in the inner coastal plain, (2) "humate" bays or bays with a sandy soil and water perching, spodic soil horizon, (3) peat filled bays with shrubby vegetation centered in Bladen County, and (4) water filled bays or bay lakes. Approximately 400,000, or 80% of the total number, are found in the Carolinas (Carolina Bay Workshop, unpublished data, Heritage Program, 1981; also Daniel, this volume).

Soil scientists report both mineral (sandy-humus) and organic mucks and peats (Histosols) for pocosins (see Barnes, this volume for specific classification). The deep organic soils are deficient in available nutrients, and in most cations (except H+), exchange of hydrogen ions for cations results in low soil pH (Dolman and Buol, 1967). The organic constituents are preserved by the anaerobic conditions and acidity (pH < 4.0) of the poorly drained peats (Maki, 1974; Snyder, 1978). The soils are saturated or shallowly flooded primarily during the cool seasons (Daniel, Gilliam and Skaggs, this volume). On the raised organic soils, precipitation is virtually the only source of plant nutrients. As a result, nutrients are scarce and the ecosystem is referred to as ombrotrophic (i.e., nutrient poor). Drainage waters from natural pocosins tend to be low in nutrients, conductivity, and pH, but high in humic acids and color (Kuenzler et al., 1977; Kirby-Smith and Barber, 1979). But, dramatic differences in nutrient output have been found for pocosins with mineral versus organic soils and developed versus natural pocosins (see Gilliam and Skaggs, this volume). The differences in pocosin ecology, geology, areal extent, soils, and nutrient output emphasize the problem of developing broad management guidelines for all pocosins. Specific pocosin types need to be defined, analyzed, and best management practices developed for each.

For the purpose of including all of North Carolina's coastal bog ecosystems in this volume, a broad vegetational definition of pocosins as described by Wells (1928), Woodwell (1958), and amplified by Kologiski (1977) *is used. This definition excludes bottomlands, wooded swamps, and marshes,* but does represent more than 53% of freshwater wetlands and 38% of all fresh and salt water wetlands in North Carolina (Wilson, 1962). Wilson reported that 95% of North Carolina's wetland area (2,377,540 ha) was located in the coastal plain.

In summary, the typical pocosin ecosystem in North Carolina is characterized by the vegetation previously mentioned, growing on waterlogged, acid, nutrient poor, sandy or peaty soils located on broad, flat topographic plateaus, usually removed from large streams and subject to periodic burning. However, pocosin vegetation as previously noted is also found in areas of geologically different origin (e.g., bays) or is found in locations which are drier, not subject to as intense a fire regime, or which are less isolated from mineral-rich ground waters.

GEOGRAPHIC RANGE AND DEVELOPMENT TRENDS FOR NORTH CAROLINA POCOSINS

Wilson's 1962 survey of North Carolina wetlands was used as a reference base for the range and area of pocosins. He defined pocosins as bogs with moist to waterlogged soils that are often flooded in the winter and confined his study to forty-one counties that lie within 40 mi (64 km) of coastal waters. His list of typical vegetation resembles those of Wells (1928), Woodwell (1958), Kologiski (1977), and Christensen (this volume). Total pocosin acreage reported for North Carolina represents nearly 70% of the nation's pocosins (Shaw and Fredine, 1956) and in 1962 covered 2,243,550 acres (907,933 ha), nearly 16% of the entire land area of the forty-one coastal counties studied (Figure 1). In many coastal counties, pocosin wetlands comprised the largest single land area type (e.g., Dare 55.7%; Tyrell: 54.2%; Hyde: 53.4%; Jones: 42.7%; Pender: 36.1%; and Carteret: 34.7%). See Table 1 for total acreage in each county. Acreage figures included only natural ombrotrophic pocosins (i.e., undrained areas that receive nutrients entirely

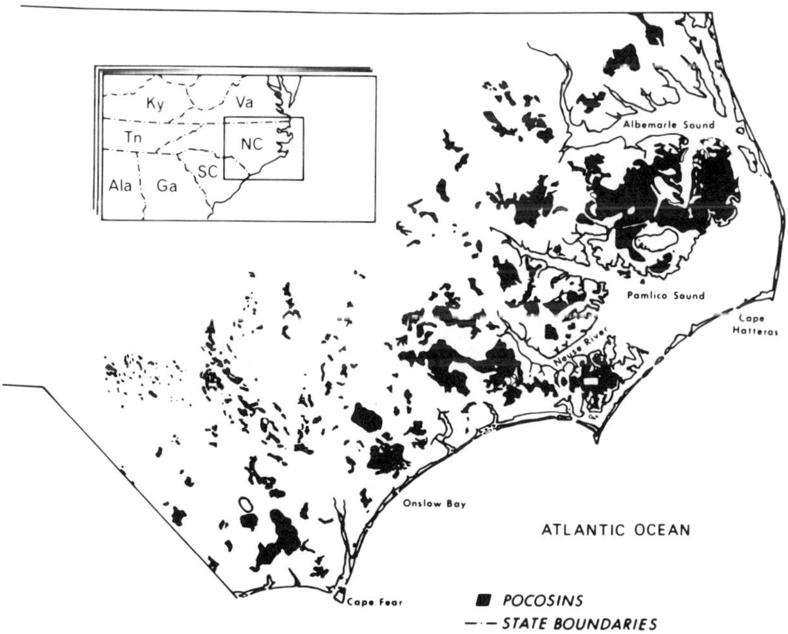

FIGURE 1. *Natural pocosin wetlands in coastal North Carolina as of 1962 (reassembled from Wilson, 1962).*

TABLE 1. *Natural Pocosin Acreage by County in North Carolina (Adapted from Wilson, 1962)*

County	Pocosin (acres)	Total (acres)	Percent of county
Beaufort	119,700	531,840	22.5
Bertie	57,300	443,520	12.9
Bladen	135,400	562,560	24.1
Brunswick	107,100	558,720	19.2
Camden	28,900	152,960	18.9
Carteret	118,300	340,480	34.7
Chowan	10,150	115,200	8.8
Columbus	81,800	600,960	13.6
Craven	126,000	464,000	27.2
Cumberland	31,300	423,040	7.4
Currituck	13,750	174,720	7.9
Dare	138,200	248,320	55.7
Duplin	89,300	526,080	17.0
Edgecombe	4,300	327,040	1.3
Gates	-0-	219,520	-0-
Greene	10,500	172,160	6.1
Halifax	250	462,080	0.05
Harnett	-0-	387,840	-0-
Hertford	-0-	227,840	-0-
Hoke	10,700	264,960	4.0
Hyde	216,700	405,760	53.4
Johnston	1,450	508,800	0.28
Jones	127,500	298,880	42.7
Lenoir	23,300	250,240	9.3
Martin	43,700	307,840	14.2
Nash	-0-	353,280	-0-
New Hanover	6,000	124,160	4.8
Northampton	-0-	345,600	-0-
Onslow	120,700	483,840	24.9
Pamlico	40,300	218,240	18.5
Pasquotank	27,200	146,560	18.6
Pender	198,000	548,480	36.1
Perquimans	18,850	167,040	11.3
Pitt	30,000	419,840	7.1
Robeson	69,500	604,160	11.5
Sampson	30,600	616,320	5.0
Scotland	4,100	202,880	2.0
Tyrrell	138,500	255,360	54.2
Washington	61,200	215,040	28.5
Wayne	3,000	355,200	0.85
Wilson	-0-	238,720	-0-
	2,243,550	14,270,080	15.72[1]

1. Pocosins comprise 15.72% of total land area in the 41 counties studied.
2. Note: 1 acre = 0.4047 hectares.

from rainfall and lose water primarily by evapotranspiration) and partially drained bogs that maintained pocosin type vegetation (Wilson, personal communication, 1980). These data excluded pocosins altered for cropland and forest plantations and the acreage thus cannot be considered the extent of North Carolina's original pocosin land.

A complete record of wetlands prior to 1962 is not available for the entire state but total pocosin conversion had probably not exceeded 10% by this time (see Lilly, this volume). One example of an area already totally developed for agriculture by 1962 is shown as an open rectangle (clear area surrounded by black) in Carteret County on Figure 1. In the ten years prior to 1962, an estimated 100,000 acres (40,469 ha) of pocosin in the four-county area north of Pamlico Sound were also cleared and drained for agricultural purposes (Wilson, 1962).

Wilson's 1962 pocosin maps by county were compared to 1979 Landsat imagery to obtain an estimate of the extent of conversion of pocosin land during the seventeen-year period, 1962 to 1979. Landsat imagery (slides made from color composite positives) were projected onto North Carolina Department of Transportation county maps (1 in = 2 mi). Natural areas of pocosin as delineated by Wilson were transferred to the county maps and compared with the 1979 acreage. Additional aerial imagery (United States Geological Survey quadrangle maps), low elevation flights and ground-truthing were also used to confirm 1979 estimates. The accuracy of our total acreage figures is within 10%. For example, our estimate of 1962 pocosin acreage as recalculated from photocopies of Wilson's county maps was 2.1 million acres compared to his reported 2.24 million acres (Table 1). Acreage figures are reported directly from Wilson but are rounded off to the nearest thousand in our 1979 estimates.

Using these procedures, we determined that 1,503,000 acres (608,464 ha) of natural or slightly altered pocosins remained by 1979. Seven hundred and forty thousand acres (299,467 ha) of pocosin identified as natural in 1962 are now *totally developed* (figures 2A, B, and C). *Totally developed* is defined here as wetlands that have been drained and ditched, their natural vegetation removed, their soils prepared for agriculture, forestry or industry, etc., and that are clearly depicted on Landsat imagery or other photos. On a statewide basis, total conversion by 1979 represented nearly 33% of Wilson's 1962 acreage for pocosin land. The total conversion was more than 40% in Washington County and as low as 5% in Dare County (Figure 2A).

The acreage for pocosin that has had no drainage or human disturbance is, however, considerably less than 1,503,000. For example, closer analysis of the largest expanse of pocosin in the state, the Albemarle–Pamlico region, reveals that most of the area has extensive drainage systems (Daniel, 1978 and this volume). Thus, a second category, *in transition*, was established to denote those pocosin areas that were either partially altered (drained, cleared, or cut), planned for development by their owners (personal communication with owners), and/or disturbed to the point where native vegetation and ecosystem processes (e.g., hydrologic flux) were changed. Thirty-six percent of the original 2.24 million acres (808,000 acres; 327,000 ha) of pocosin area may be classified as in transition. Only 31%, or 695,000 acres (281,000 ha), still exists in its *natural* state.

The six largest natural areas of pocosin remaining in North Carolina are found in the northern part of the coastal plain in Dare and Pasquotank counties; in Carteret, Craven and Jones counties in the central part of the region; and in Pender, Duplin, and Brunswick counties in the southern portion (figures 2A, B, C). Numerous smaller natural areas (i.e., bays) are found throughout Bladen, Sampson, Cumberland and Robeson counties. Our survey does not include accurate detail on small (2 to 5 acre) bays and

FIGURE 2A.

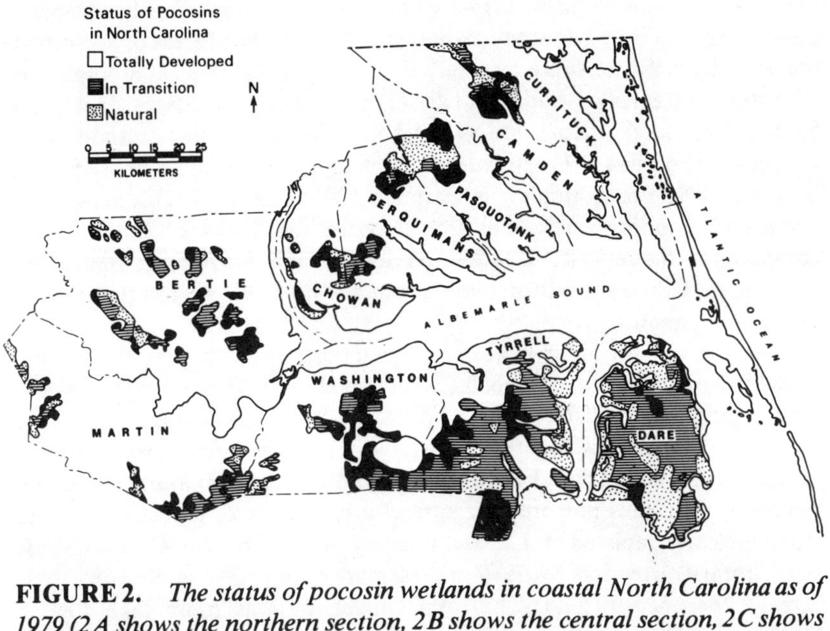

FIGURE 2. *The status of pocosin wetlands in coastal North Carolina as of 1979 (2A shows the northern section, 2B shows the central section, 2C shows the southern section). These maps are based on Wilson's 1962 survey and were determined from Landsat photo analysis, North Carolina fire map surveys, industrial use maps, and field checks by Rhonda Evans, David Carr, Randy Bournique, and C. J. Richardson, Duke University. See text for a description of the three categories: totally developed, in transition, and natural. (NOTE: A larger [more accurate scale], complete version of these maps is available for $5 from the School of Forestry and Environmental Studies Publications Office, Duke University, Durham, N.C. 27706.)*

FIGURE 2B.

FIGURE 2C.

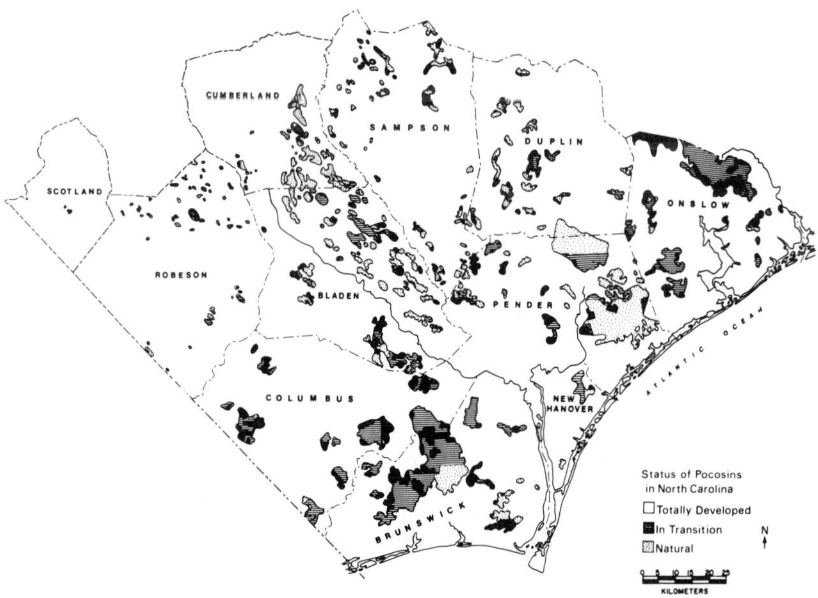

pocosins. Several counties—Wayne, Greene and Edgecombe—were not covered by Landsat imagery but these counties contained less than 18,000 acres of pocosins. Surveys of areas under protection and areas being considered for preserves are listed by Taggart (this volume) and Roe (this volume).

Doucette and Phillips (1978) provide another estimate of wetland acreage (all wetland types) and drainage patterns in North Carolina. Their data summarize a survey of the seventeen Soil Conservation Service districts that account for 92% of the coastal zone of North Carolina. Wet soil groups (Dideriksen et al., 1979) were correlated to wetland types (assuming that the indicator plant community is present) and a total land area was determined (Table 2). Their data show that approximately 32% of wetlands has been drained for farmland and agriculture, 33% is potentially drainable (our "in transition" category), and 35% is not drainable, because it is coastal marsh or government owned land under some protection status (Table 2). These

TABLE 2. *An Estimate[1] of Wetland[2] Drainage for Agriculture and Forestry in Seventeen Coastal Counties in North Carolina, Adapted from Doucette and Phillips (1978)*

Category and land use	Acres	Hectares	Percent of all wetland
Converted wetlands (drained)			
1. Farmland			
a. Extensively drained	59,000	23,836	3.3
b. Partially drained	171,000	69,084	9.5
2. Forestland			
a. Partially drained	337,000	136,148	18.8
Total	567,000	229,068	31.6
Wetlands potentially drainable			
1. Farmland	7,000	2,828	0.4
2. Forestland	483,000	195,132	27.1
3. Miscellaneous	107,000	43,228	6.0
Total	597,000	241,188	33.5
Wetlands not drainable	625,000	252,500	34.9
Total coastal wetland area	1,789,000	722,756	100.0

1. Source: "Coastal Land Drainage Questionnaire," April, 1978. North Carolina State University, Department of Soil Science, Raleigh.
2. Wetland areas were estimated based on soil associations as described in Soil Associations of the Coastal Management Area (N.C. Division of Earth Resources, 1977) and correlated to wetland types of Fish and Wildlife Circular 39, using Soil Conservation Service Memorandum, N.C. 4, November 4, 1977 (USDA, 1977).

results are comparable to our categorical analyses: 33% developed, 36% in transition, and 31% natural.

Technically, most undeveloped pocosins are drainable. Little of this land is in government ownership or preserves, and current management practices indicate that the present owners will carry out extensive draining in order to capitalize on their investment. It is apparent that pocosins will be subject to continued destruction and conversion. While it is true that over 100,000 acres of pocosin (>40,000 ha) are now receiving some degree of protection (Taggart, this volume), it is also true that a large proportion of this land had already been drained and logged prior to receiving protected status. The percentage of pocosins now receiving some protection is low, although protected acreage has probably doubled since 1962. Major additions to acreage under protection status are the designated Rare II tract of pocosin in the Croatan National Forest and the Nature Conservancy holdings in the Green Swamp (Taggart, this volume).

From our data and that of Doucette and Phillips (1978), it would appear that nearly 740,000 acres (299,000 ha) of pocosins have been completely altered and that an additional 808,000 acres (326,000 ha) will be drained in the near future. The remaining natural pocosin (695,000 acres or 31% of the original total area) is society's only real option for the future existence of this ecosystem type.

POCOSIN OWNERSHIP PATTERNS

Land ownership patterns give some additional insight into development and management trends, investment trends and the potential for preservation. Major timber company, large corporate farm, and state and federal ownerships comprise 83% of the area (Figure 3). This is close to the 85% ownership of wetlands in North Carolina that was reported for the same three groups in 1962 by Wilson. The only major shift in ownership patterns within the group is the transfer of nearly 500,000 acres (202,000 ha) of corporate forestland to large-scale agriculture since 1970 (Carter, 1975). The actual percentage of major timber company holdings on pocosin wetlands is unknown (as indicated by the broken line on Figure 3). These companies often have timber options on private lands and data on recent purchases are not yet available. Data for the other three categories shown in Figure 3 and a preliminary survey of county tax offices suggest that timber interests own 40% to 50% of all pocosin land.

The North Carolina Forest Service estimates that there were 1,333,687 acres (539,723 ha) of bays and wet pocosin in North Carolina in 1975 (Knight and McClure, 1975). Their definition of bays and wet pocosins is "... large low wet forested land recesses with peaty soils and boggy conditions." They also report an additional 5,008,837 acres (2,027,001 ha) of dry pocosin and flat woods. It is impossible to separate the dry pocosin and flatwood sites in their report to obtain a total pocosin acreage figure. For the bays and wet pocosins, they reported 26% owned by the forest industry, 17% under governmental ownership, and the remaining 57% under farmer and miscellaneous private ownership. These data indicate that timber companies have purchased a smaller percentage of the bays and deep, wet, peat pocosins. This is due to the unproductive nature of these areas without intensive site preparation (see Campbell and Hughes, this volume).

In summary, better estimates of ownership patterns by pocosin type are badly needed if we are to develop realistic management alternatives and best management practices for these areas.

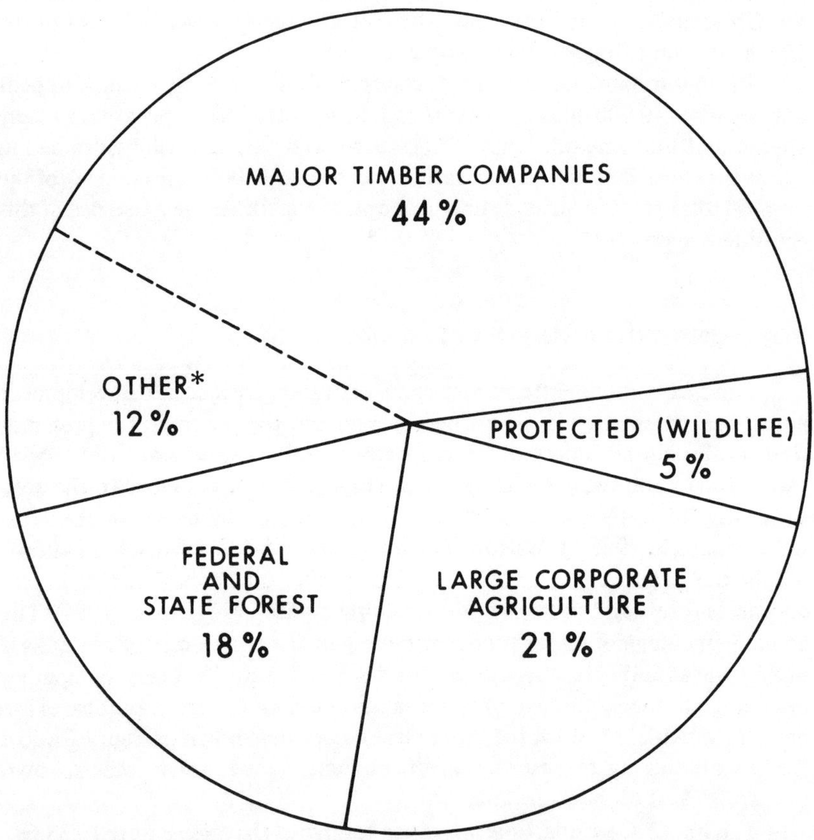

FIGURE 3. *General estimate of ownership patterns (by percent) of North Carolina pocosins. Calculations are based on a survey of coastal tax office maps, industrial use maps, and state maps during 1979 and 1980. (*This category includes small, private landowners. Their land may be in forestry, agriculture, or its natural state.)*

DEVELOPMENT ACTIVITIES AND POTENTIAL IMPACTS OF POCOSIN ALTERATIONS

Prior to development of pocosins for agriculture and forestry, removal of vegetation, placement of drainage ditches, burning of debris, scraping, surface preparation, and road building must occur. These activities are discussed in detail in the industrial section, this volume.

The search for new energy sources has created additional incentive to alter pocosins. Pocosins make up the vast majority of peatlands in the state (Otte and Ingram, 1979). Researchers estimate that energy reserves have been overestimated, but that 540 metric tons of moisture-free peat are available on 0.6 million acres (243,000 ha) of harvestable peatlands in North Carolina (Ingram and Otte, this volume). The potential benefits of peat mining are discussed by Campbell (this volume), but the related environmental impacts are unknown.

To date, phosphate mining has not occurred directly in pocosins of North Carolina. Dumping of process wastes and the development of slime ponds has, however, affected wetlands adjacent to mines. Release of phosphate from this industry to estuarine systems may also have severe adverse impacts on the regional nutrient balance (Richardson, this volume). In addition, the daily pumping of millions of gallons of water from the Castle Hayne aquifier by phosphate mining operations has resulted in a significant drop in the freshwater level near well heads and may affect the entire regional water system (Heath, 1975). A review of phosphate mining maps indicates that rich deposits lie directly under some pocosins. Before these areas could be mined, pocosins would have to be removed as overburden, thus altering thousands of additional acres of natural wetlands. The effects of pocosin development and landscape alterations on regional hydrology are significant (Daniel, this volume) and must be researched in greater detail before best management practices can be utilized.

A summary matrix for pocosin utilization and development activities reveals that all uses of these wetlands, except for nature preserves, will result in some alterations (Table 3). Almost all development requires draining. Ditching does not, however, necessarily result in the total loss of pocosin vegetation unless ditching is followed by scraping and surface removal, burning, and water pumping. Peat soils have low hydraulic conductivity and the maintenance of lowered water tables over 100 m from drainage canals is nearly impossible (Maki, 1974; Daniel, this volume).

Significant effects of pocosins development on adjacent ecosystems have already become evident for the coastal plain region. Drainage of fresh water from these ecosystems may adversely affect estuarine biota (Street and McClees, Richardson, this volume). Severe dust and particulate problems following drainage have already been reported for a number of coastal counties. Military bombing and the resulting uncontrollable fires were responsible for burning 30,000 acres (12,000 ha) and 28,000 acres (11,000 ha) of

TABLE 3. *Interaction Matrix for Pocosin Utilization and Development Activities in North Carolina*

Use	Activity												
	Draining and ditching	Burning and smoke production	Scraping and surface removal	Deep mining	Aquifer pumping	Reforestation and planting	Fertilization	Road building	Liquid waste disposal	Solid waste disposal	Spraying	Dredging and filling	Creation of holding ponds
Agriculture (crops & animals)	X	X	X		X	X	X	X	X	X	X		X
Forestry	X	X	X			X	X	X			X		
Parks/Recreation	X	X	X			X		X	X	X	X		X
Peat Mining	X	X	X					X					X
Phosphate mining	X[1]		X[1]	X[1]	X			X[1]	X	X		X	X
Natural preserve		X[2]											
Bombing		X	X										X

1. Effects if future mining activities occur directly in pocosin ecosystems.
2. Dependent on management guidelines.

pocosin in 1971 and 1980, respectively. Smoke from fires used in land clearing activities has resulted in school closings, highway accidents, and localized health problems. Complaints have reached such porportions that the North Carolina Forestry Association plans to propose legislation to regulate burning activities (Green, Acting Director, Division of Forest Resources, North Carolina Department of Natural Resources and Community Development, personal communication, 1980).

It is evident that the consequences of inadequate management guidelines for the alteration and use of pocosin ecosystems have resulted in environmental problems, both within pocosins and to adjacent systems.

SUMMARY

Hopefully, we have given some idea of what a pocosin is and is not, where it occurs, how much land is involved, and what the trends and potential for development might be. We have highlighted some of the activities that take place when pocosins are placed under intensive management. To develop appropriate management guidelines for future pocosin utilization, we now need to address specific problems with a holistic analysis of the resource system.

From the chapters that follow, it should become evident that the pocosin resource is viewed quite differently by each special interest group. For example, pocosins with deep peats are not of interest to forestry because of low economic return (i.e., poor tree growth), while these acres are of highest priority to the peat mining interests. Preservationists and hunters view natural pocosins as a unique refuge for plants and animals, but industry and the general public, for the most part, view these wetlands as wastelands ready for development. Scientists have not studied these areas in enough detail to be able to give sound predictions on the response of these ecosystems to major alterations or give society the "real value" of these natural ecosystems. Up to the present, pocosins have generally been neglected by policy makers.

In 1980, we can still debate over remaining natural pocosins. The resource, and its future, hopefully can be better managed with the information in this volume.

LITERATURE CITED

Carter, L. J., 1975. Agriculture: A new frontier in coastal North Carolina. Science, 189:271-275.

Council on Environmental Quality, 1971. Environmental quality: The second annual report. Washington, D.C., pp. 235-238.

Cowardin, L. M., V. Carter, F. C. Golet, and E. T. LaRoe, 1979. Classification of wetlands and deepwater habitats of the United States. Fish and Wildlife Service. U.S. Department of the Interior, PWS/OBS-79/31, 103 pp.

Daniel , C. C., 1978. Land use, land cover, and drainage on the Albemarle–Pamlico peninsula, eastern North Carolina, 1974. U.S. Geological Survey Water Resources Investigation, pp. 78-134.

Dansereau, P., and F. Segadas-Vianna, 1952. Ecological study of the peat bogs of eastern North America. Structure and evolution of vegetation. Can. J. Bot., 30:490-520.

Dideriksen, R. I., A. R. Hidlebaugh, and K. O. Schmude, 1979. Wet soils for crop production in the United States, pp. 632-641. In: Greeson, P. E., J. R. Clark, and J. E. Clark, eds., Wetland functions and values: The state of our understanding. Amer. Water Res. Assoc., Minneapolis, Minn., 674 pp.

Doucette, W. H., and J. A. Phillips, 1978. Overview: Agricultural and forest land drainage in North Carolina's coastal zone. Center for Rural Resource Development, Report No. 8, North Carolina State University, Raleigh, N.C.

Dolman, J. D., and S. W. Buol, 1967. A study of organic soils (Histosols) in the tidewater region of North Carolina. Tech. Bul. No. 180, N.C. Agricultural Experiment Station, Raleigh, N.C.

Good, R. E., D. F. Whigham, and R. L. Simpson, eds., 1978. Freshwater wetlands: Ecological processes and management potential. Academic Press, New York, N.Y., 378 pp.

Greeson, P. E., J. R. Clark, and J. E. Clark, eds., 1979. Wetland functions and values: The state of our understanding. Amer. Water Res. Assoc., Minneapolis, Minn., 674 pp.

Harper, R. M., 1907. A midsummer journey through the coastal plain of the Carolinas and Virginia. Bull. Torrey Bot. Club, 34:351-377.

Heath, R. C., 1975. Hydrology of the Albemarle–Pamlico region, North Carolina. USGS Water Resources Investigation, 9-75, 98 pp.

Heinselman, M. L., 1970. Landscape evolution, peatland types, and the environment in the Lake Agassiz Peatlands Natural Area, Minnesota. Ecol.. Monogr., 40:235-261.

Kerr, W. C., 1875. Physical geography, resume, economical geology. Geological Survey of North Carolina, Vol. 1, Raleigh, N.C., 120 pp.

Kirby-Smith, W. W., and R. T. Barber, 1979. The water quality ramifications in estuaries of converting forest to intensive agriculture. Report No. 148, Water Resources Research Institute of the University of North Carolina, Raleigh, N.C., 70 pp.

Knight, H. A. and J. P. McClure, 1975. North Carolina's timber. USDA For. Ser. Res. Bull., SE-33, 52 pp.

Kologiski, R. L., 1977. The phytosociology of the Green Swamp, North Carolina. Tech. Bull. No. 250, N.C. Agri. Exp. Sta., Raleigh, N.C., 101 pp.

Kuenzler, E. J., P. J. Mulholland, L. A. Ruley, and R. P. Sniffen, 1977. Water quality in North Carolina coastal plain streams and effects of channelization. Report No. 127, Water Resources Research Institute of the University of North Carolina, Raleigh, N.C., 160 pp.

Maki, T. E., 1974. Factors affecting forest production on organic soils. In: Aandahl, ed., Histosols: Their characteristics, classification and use. Soil Sci. Soc. of America.

Moore, P. D. and D. J. Bellamy, 1974. Peatlands. Springer-Verlag, New York, 221 pp.

Otte, L. J., and R. L. Ingram, 1979. Peat resources of North Carolina. Quarterly report to North Carolina Energy Institute.

Shaw, S. P., and C. G. Fredine, 1956. Wetlands of the United States: Their extent and their value to waterfowl and other wildlife. Fish and Wildlife Serv., U.S. Department of the Interior, Circ. 39.

Snyder, J. R., 1978. Analysis of vegetation in the Croatan National Forest, North Carolina. Master of Arts Thesis, Department of Botany, University of North Carolina, Chapel Hill, 126 pp.

Tooker, W. W., 1899. The adapted Algonquin term "Poquosin." Am. Anthropol., Jan.: 162-170.

Wells, B. W., 1928. Plant communities of the coastal plain of North Carolina and their successional relations. Ecol., 9:230-242.

Whitehead, D. R., 1972. Developmental and environmental history of the Dismal Swamp. Ecol. Mono., 42:301-315.

Wilson, K. A., 1962. North Carolina wetlands: Their distribution and management. N.C. Wild. Res. Comm., Raleigh, N.C., 169 pp.

Woodwell, G. M., 1958. Factors controlling growth of pond pine seedlings in organic soils of the Carolinas. Ecol. Mono., 28:219-236.

A History of Swamp Land Development in North Carolina

J. Paul Lilly

ABSTRACT

Development of North Carolina swamp lands began as early as 1700, first for timber production and later for agriculture. Swamp lands were considered more fertile than upland soils and agricultural successes at Lake Phelps and Lake Mattamuskeet in the early 1800s caused the state to drain swamp land to raise money for public education. Canals were dug at considerable expense but little land was sold. The Civil War halted swamp land development but by the 1880s intense logging had begun and timber companies were acquiring much land. The 1909 drainage act enabled landowners to fund areawide drainage projects and greatly accelerated development. In the 1930s paper companies began buying timber company land, Croatan National Forest and Hofmann Forest were formed, and the remaining state owned swamp lands were preserved for wildlife. Nearly all the swamp land in the state has been logged and drained for forestry or agriculture. Land is currently considered a good investment, and it is likely that most privately owned nonpaper company land will be developed for agriculture or forestry.

Key Words: swamp land development, history, drainage, timber companies, lake drainage, agricultural development

INTRODUCTION

The recent increased rate of swamp land development in eastern North Carolina (Richardson et al., this volume) has captured the attention of the public, many of whom perceive this as a new activity. However, efforts to "reclaim" swamp land for agriculture date back to at least the early 1700s. Essentially all the swamp lands in the state have been logged at least once and have had some drainage imposed, either for agricultural development or to aid logging and reforestation. The dark surfaced farmland of the lower coastal plain–tidewater area was once swamp land, and some of it has been in cultivation for well over 200 years. Thus it should be recognized that much of the swamp land has been converted to other uses and that which remains has been extensively modified.

The term "swamp land" as used in this paper refers to all poorly drained lands in the state. It includes the areas known as swamps, bays, bogs, marshes, wetlands and, of course, pocosins. Historically, citations of state owned swamp lands include even salt marsh, since early state laws included all wetlands.

Because of the difficulty in distinguishing between some of these wetland types, no attempt was made to limit this discussion to pocosins alone. Also, from a development standpoint, such classifications are not particularly important. The mineralogy of the underlying soil and the character of the organic material when drained and matured are more relevant than landscape position or present vegetation. For these reasons all areas requiring drainage for development will be called swamp lands. The major areas of such land in North Carolina are shown in Figure 1.

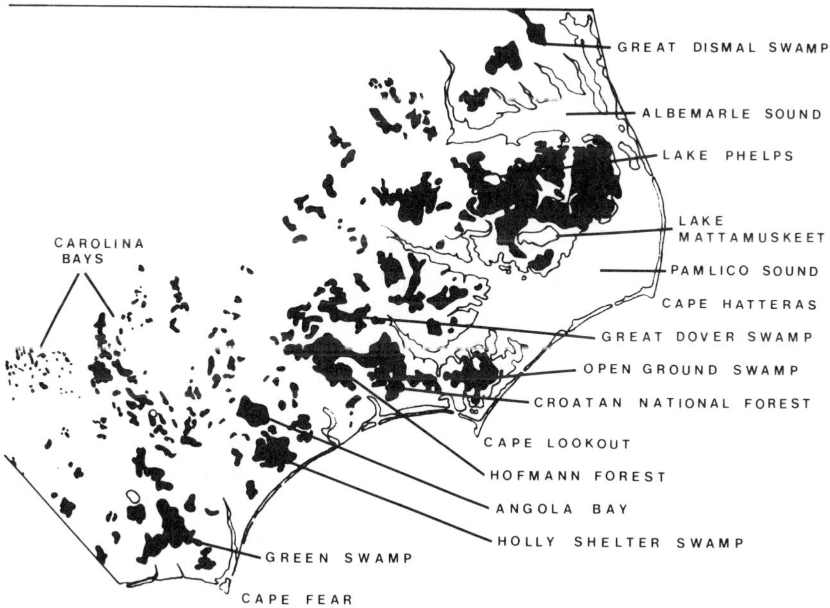

FIGURE 1. *Major freshwater wetlands of North Carolina. Adapted from Wilson (1962) by R. K. Evans, School of Forestry and Environmental Studies, Duke University.*

FIRST SETTLEMENTS

The first English settlement in North America was on Roanoke Island, North Carolina, in 1584, but it failed as did the next two attempts. The North Carolina swamp lands were visited by Europeans for the first time during this period. Englishmen from Ocracoke on a punitive expedition raided and burned an Indian village in present-day Hyde County in 1585 and discovered Lake Mattamuskeet (Sharpe, 1958). This began nearly four centuries of exploration, exploitation and development of the swamp lands.

After the failure of the colonies on Roanoke Island, effort shifted to the Chesapeake Bay and, in 1607, the first permanent English settlement was established at Jamestown, Virginia. Appropriately enough, Jamestown was located on swampy ground. The site of the first fort is believed to have been lost to the James River and its exact location is unknown (Noel Hume, 1963).

The Virginia settlement grew slowly and no further attempts were made to colonize North Carolina from the sea. Few records have survived, but it is likely that within a few years the more adventurous frontiersmen were entering North Carolina from the north. The earliest hard evidence of actual settlement is a map dating from 1657 showing settlers in North Carolina (Lefler and Newsome, 1973). By 1663 twenty-nine grants totaling 26,123 acres (10,572 ha) had been recorded, and North Carolina had a population of over 500.

Settlement of the Albemarle and Pamlico Sounds Area

Settlement of the Albemarle and Pamlico sounds area proceeded quite rapidly, largely because of the diminished influence of the Indians of the region. Conflicts with the settlers, and European diseases (especially small pox), had reduced their numbers in Virginia from about 18,000 to 2,000 by 1700 (Noel Hume, 1963). A similiar situation probably occurred in North Carolina. Settlers had appeared throughout the Pamlico Sound area by 1700, and Bath was established as the first incorporated town in North Carolina in 1706. At about the same time, in 1709, a Swiss colony was being established at New Bern, and settlements were appearing in the Cape Fear River valley. The last serious Indian trouble was the Tuscarora War fought from 1711 through 1715 in the area just west of New Bern. After the Tuscarora Indian threat was removed, settlers rapidly moved westward.

It had taken a hundred years for the frontier to reach as far west as the heads of the coastal sounds but in the next one hundred years the frontier would move beyond the Mississippi River. During this time, the east was being thoroughly settled, farmed, and even urbanized. Pressure for land was intense, and the population surpluses of the east caused the frontier to continue to expand. The population of North Carolina was about 36,000 in 1729, more than 50,000 in 1752, up to 120,000 by 1765 and was estimated at 345,000 by 1775 (Lefler and Newsome, 1973).

THE GREAT DISMAL SWAMP IN THE 1700s

During the 1700s there was much activity around the coastal swamp lands, although the swamps were more often considered a hindrance than an asset (Merrens, 1964). The first area to be utilized was the Great Dismal Swamp because of its accessibility. The swamps were exploited primarily for timber, especially cypress and white cedar, both highly prized for their resistance to decay.

The earliest more or less objective descriptions of the Great Dismal Swamp are provided by Colonel William Byrd who led a survey party through it in 1728 when the disputed line between the colonies of Virginia and North Carolina was being resolved (Boyd, 1929). He is also credited with being the first to propose that it be drained. It was realized quite early that the swamp was higher in the center than at the edges and it was asserted that a canal leading from the swamp would drain it easily by gravity and make land available for agriculture. In the meantime, considerable logging activity took place with wooden pathways being built for horses and canals dug for small barges (Brown, 1970). In 1763 George Washington and five associates, self-styled as "Adventurers for Draining the Great Dismal Swamp," acquired 40,000 acres (16,188 ha) of rich timberland in the swamp. This group was chartered by the Virginia Assembly in 1764 as the Dismal Swamp Land Company. A canal, called the Washington Ditch, was dug to Lake Drummond to facilitate logging, primarily for cypress shingles, and is now believed to be the oldest canal still in use in the United States (Brown, 1970).

The plan to farm the swamp failed, and in 1795 Washington sold his share in the company after becoming dissatisfied with the management. However, the company continued to thrive for many years as a timber company.

DEVELOPMENT OF SHALLOW SWAMPS BEFORE 1800

While the deeper peat swamps were being used only by timber companies, the shallower, more easily drained swamp lands were being developed for agriculture. Hyde County, the oldest surviving county in North Carolina, was named in 1711 and became a county in 1738 (Sharpe, 1958). The area near Englehard was apparently settled soon after 1700. A reservation of 10,240 acres (4,144 ha) for the Machapunga Indians was established at Lake Mattamuskeet in 1724 (Pomeroy and Yoho, 1964), indicating that there was land pressure in the area by that date. Governor George Burrington reported in 1734 ". . . that all the plantable land along navigable streams had been taken up" (Pomeroy and Yoho, 1964). Fort Landing in Tyrrell County was settled about 1700, Gum Neck about 1750 (Heath, 1975) and the Kendrick's Creek area of Washington County was settled about 1732 (Sharpe, 1961). Much of the settled land in Washington County was naturally well drained, but much of Hyde and Tyrrell counties was swamp land requiring drainage, as indicated by Captain Collet's map (1770) of North Carolina.

POST REVOLUTIONARY WAR LAND DEVELOPMENT

After the Revolutionary War, a number of factors combined to create the first real boom in swamp land development. There was considerable interest in land in general, and in the east, the swamp lands were the only lands available. Investors were attracted to land because there was no industry and slaves were about the only other investment alternative (Pomeroy and Yoho, 1964). Another factor favoring swamp development was the interest in rice growing. Rice was cultivated throughout the coastal zone from Virginia south. Also, it was believed at the time that malaria was caused by swamp gases, and swamp drainage was thought to improve the public health. In addition, the successful use of peatlands for agriculture by the Europeans had not gone unnoticed. England and the continent had experienced land pressure and loss of woodlands sometime earlier, and peatlands were used for fuel and farming by 1800. William Aiton, writing in 1811, indicates that so-called moss earth had been receiving considerable attention for some years in England and Scotland.

All of these factors caused two major projects to be launched in the American swamp lands at about the same time in the 1780s. The first of these was the Dismal Swamp Canal and the second was the Collin's Plantation on Lake Phelps. These two projects moved development off the edges of the swamps and into their interiors.

Dismal Swamp Canal

A canal connecting Chesapeake Bay with Albemarle Sound was proposed in 1784 and a commission was appointed to study it (Brown, 1970). There were no good ports in Albemarle Sound, partly because the sound was shallow in spots and partly because there were no reliable inlets through the Outer Banks (Collet, 1770). In 1787 the Virginia Assembly approved the canal, and in 1790 the North Carolina Assembly followed suit. Digging began in 1793 (Brown, 1970) and the canal was completed but had no locks by 1805. When the canal was begun, it was believed that the route would be essentially level. However, by the time the necessary locks were completed about 1812, 19 ft of lift were in the system. The canal provided a means of transport for agricultural products from the Albemarle area, but forestry products comprised by far the greater portion of the traffic.

The Dismal Swamp Canal had a profound effect on the entire swamp since the canal spoil bank and the road on it created a dam. Consequently, water was deepened to the west of the canal and land was drained to the east (Ruffin, 1861). Much of the drained land soon was being farmed, with the better land and the most extensive development on the North Carolina end of the canal (Ruffin, 1861). Estimation of the extent of development in the Great Dismal Swamp is difficult because of discrepancies in the various estimates of the original area. Shaler (1890) wrote that the area of the swamp was about 2,200 sq mi (5,698 sq km), or 1,408,000 acres (569,804 ha), of which 700 sq mi (1,813 sq km) had been drained, while Brown (1970) says the swamp originally covered 600 to 1,000 sq mi (1,554 to 2,590 sq km) and that two-thirds of that had been reclaimed. Steward (1979) also states that only about one-third of the swamp remains. Lewis and Cocke (1929) estimated that the swamp remaining at that time probably did not exceed 700 sq mi (1,813 sq km). The present size is estimated at 400 to 750 sq mi (1,036 to 1,943 sq km) (Cahill, 1974). Shaler's figure probably includes a great deal of shallow swamp or dark surfaced mineral soils, and the disagreements are likely caused by the lack of a common definition for "swamp land." Nevertheless, it is apparent that a large part of the Great Dismal Swamp has been developed, and that the portion remaining has been severely modified. Whitehead said, ". . . hence it appears that as a natural area the northernmost of the great cypress-gum swamps is doomed" (Whitehead, 1972).

Lake Phelps and Somerset Place

The other major development was specifically for agriculture on Lake Phelps. Lake Phelps (sometimes called Lake Scuppernong) was not discovered by white men until about 1755, even though it was only a few miles from areas that had been settled for a number of years (Tarlton, 1954). It was eventually established that the lake was considerably higher than the nearest waterway, the Scuppernong River, and it was proposed that the lake be drained so that the bottom could be farmed. However, before the plan was implemented, a group of Edenton businessmen led by Josiah Collins saw the advantage of the lake for rice production. In 1784 the North Carolina General Assembly authorized them to proceed and gave them seven years in which to complete the project (Tarlton, 1954). They formed "The Lake Company" and acquired a total of nearly 110,000 acres (44,516 ha) of land. Collins also privately owned 60,000 acres (24,281 ha) lying to the east on Alligator River. These lands, covering about 170,000 acres (68,797 ha) must have included much of Washington and Tyrrell counties south of the high ground along Albemarle Sound.

The project was quite successful overall. Slaves were brought from Africa, a canal dug from Lake Phelps to the Scuppernong River, land cleared, and rice planted. Because of the differences in elevation, the rice fields could be flooded and drained at will, and water power was available to drive a sawmill and other machinery. The land was covered with large cypress trees (Ruffin, 1839) which were processed at the sawmill to provide a large part of the farm income. Rice culture was abandoned after a few years, allegedly because of disease problems with the slaves (Tarlton, 1954), and attention turned mostly to corn.

Collins gained full control of the plantation, called Somerset Place, and his success attracted other developers. The most notable were the Pettigrews on their neighboring plantation, Bonarva. When Edmund Ruffin visited the area in 1839, he found an estimated 5,000 acres being farmed by five or six proprietors (Ruffin, 1861). When Ruffin revisited the area in 1857, he found evidence that at least 3 ft. of organic surface had been lost in places (Ruffin, 1861), indicating that this development was in deep organic swamp. None of the original organic surface remains, but the underlying mineral soil is being farmed quite successfully today.

The lake plantation continued to prosper until the Civil War, when the freeing of the slaves caused both loss of labor and loss of capital. Most of the assets of a plantation were tied up in its slaves, and Somerset Place was no exception. In 1860 the plantation had 328 slaves valued at $325,000, but in 1869 the remaining 4,428 acres (1,792 ha) of the plantation proper were sold to settle a debt of $10,000 (Sharpe, 1961).

The property has been divided and redivided and has belonged to many different people over the years. Immediately after the Civil War, much of the land was farmed by tenants. In 1937, as a result of the depression of the 1920s and '30s, the Federal Farm Security Administration acquired the land from a bank and incorporated it into the Scuppernong Farms settlement project (Tarlton, 1954). The state acquired the Somerset house and part of Bonarva in 1939 for a state park (Sharpe, 1965). The resettlement project failed and all lands were auctioned off in 1945 (Tarlton, 1954). Today, the area is a prosperous community of family farmers.

EARLY SETTLERS AT LAKE MATTAMUSKEET

The area around Lake Mattamuskeet was developed by individuals, with only a few large landowners. Draining and development proceeded quietly but steadily in the isolated area, and by 1839 it was estimated that 32,000 acres were in cultivation (Ruffin, 1861). The development was concentrated on the higher ground of the lake rim and extended toward the Pamlico Sound to the south and southeast. Ruffin (1861) described the Mattamuskeet lands as "the most extensive and important of all the drained and cultivated swamp lands on the Atlantic coast, and also the oldest of such improvements . . . ." Lake Mattamuskeet was originally estimated to be 20 mi (32.2 km) long and about 7 mi (11.3 km) wide, with the outlet to Wysocking Bay being dammed at Lake Landing to provide water power (Ruffin, 1861). In 1836 the lake overflowed; Ruffin reported that all crops were destroyed and water stood nearly to the doors of the dwellings on the highest ground. As a consequence, in 1838 the state provided money to dig a canal 7 mi (11.3 km) long from the lake to Wysocking Bay and the water level was lowered by 3.5

ft (1.1 m). The size of the lake was reduced to 16 mi (25.7 km) long by 5 mi (8 km) wide and the sandy bottom was laid bare for widths varying from one-half to 3 mi (.8 to 4.8 km). Lake Mattamuskeet is approximately the same size today, and the former lake bottom is partly forested and partly farmed. The attempt to drain the lake for agriculture in the early 1900s will be discussed later.

RICH SOILS

Ruffin and other authors of the 1800s write at length about the richness of the swamp soils and their continuing productivity for more than seventy years. This was in sharp contrast to North Carolina's better drained mineral soils which were routinely abandoned to forest when they became unproductive after only a few years. The main reason for the enduring fertility of the swamp lands was the release of nutrients, especially phosphorus, from the organic matter as it decayed and the land subsided. This was before the time of commercial fertilizers and plant nutrition was poorly understood. The main cropping pattern on the swamp lands was corn intercropped with peas, and hogs were fattened on the peas and waste corn. Thus the corn received its nitrogen from the pea crop and its phosphorus and probably some potassium from mineralization of organic matter. Some nutrients would have been provided by the hog manure as well. This was apparently sufficient nutrients for the relatively low-yielding corn of the time.

All swamp lands were not as productive and the reasons were not understood. As late as 1896 it was written that "The character of the Hyde County soil has never been understood. The cause of its fertility has never been explained . . ." and, "Lands in Hyde County, cultivated for a period of one hundred years continuously in corn, without the application of manure, show no apparent loss of fertility" (State Board of Agriculture, 1896). Soils research begun in the early 1900s has since placed Blacklands agriculture on a firm scientific foundation (Lilly, 1981).

SWAMP LAND DEVELOPMENT BY THE STATE

In the early 1800s the swamp lands began to be perceived as a valuable resource and the state actively began to encourage their development. The success of the farmers around Lake Mattamuskeet and Lake Phelps had much to do with the interest. In 1819 the Board of Internal Improvements was established and was active until 1826 in promoting the drainage of swamp lands and construction of railroads, plank roads, and turnpikes (Pomeroy and Yoho, 1964). Archibald D. Murphey is generally credited with first proposing the drainage of swamp lands (Murphey, 1819). He referred to the "noxious exhalations" of the swamps and advocated they be drained to improve the public health, and incidentally to reclaim them for agriculture.

The most important act affecting swamp lands occurred in 1825, however, when the State Literary Fund was established. Monies from various sources, including sale of swamp lands, were to go into this fund to support public education. At the same time, all swamp lands not already granted were ruled to be state property and were turned over to the Literary Fund. The board was authorized to raise money for development by lottery and was directed to survey the swamp lands. In his report of 1827, Mr. Nash, state engineer, estimated the state owned swamp land at 1,500,000 acres (607,035 ha) and said nearly all of it was of excellent quality and acceptable for drainage (Kerr, 1867). Also, in 1827 it was first suggested that the bottom of Lake Mattamuskeet be farmed but the suggestion was rejected in 1837. Mr. Nash estimated the area of Open Ground Swamp and White Oak Swamp at 180,000 acres (72,844 ha) in 1827, and said the land had reverted to the state because of nonpayment of taxes. The state essentially gave up on the Dismal Swamp lands because the local people claimed the lands had all been surveyed and patented earlier. In 1837 reorganization placed responsibility for reclamation work with the Literary Board for the first time (Pomeroy and Yoho, 1964). Little probably would have been done except for a windfall the state had received from the federal government in 1836.

North Carolina received $1,433,757.39 as its share of revenues from sale of public lands. The public debt was retired with $400,000; $100,000 was set aside for current expenses; and the Literary Fund suddenly found itself with total assets of about $1,700,000 and an unknown amount of swamp land of unknown value (Pomeroy and Yoho, 1964). In an attempt to utilize the swamp lands, the board set aside $200,000 for development, a truly large sum of money for the time. This began a long period of attempts to develop the swamp lands for sale which lasted until the early part of this century.

It was decided to follow up the success at Lake Phelps by digging canals to drain other lakes in the state. From 1838 to 1842, canals were dug at Lake Mattamuskeet, Alligator Lake, and Pungo Lake (Kerr, 1867). An area estimated at 60,000 to 70,000 acres (24,281 to 28,328 ha) was drained at Alligator Lake and Pungo Lake at a cost of $170,000, and in 1841 the best land was offered for sale. No bids whatsoever were made, and over the next ten years the board actively tried to sell land. In that time, only some desirable timber land was sold at very low prices (Kerr, 1867).

The Open Ground Swamp was partially drained in 1855 by a canal dug to the center of the tract from Ward's Creek. A square mile (2.6 sq km) was ditched around to create two blocks of land each one mile by one-half mile (1.6 by .8 km). Edmund Ruffin visited the land in 1856 and proclaimed it totally worthless for agriculture (Ruffin, 1861). He described the area, bare of large trees for many years, as ". . . a singular and remarkable scene of desolation and solitude." Again, there were no successful land sales.

W. C. Kerr (1867) attributed the poor response to incomplete drainage, fear of swamp disease, lack of access roads, and lack of clear title to the lands.

Soon after the board began trying to sell land, various groups began to press their prior claims. The North American Land Company of Pennsylvania claimed much of Hyde County; the Albemarle Swamp Land Company claimed the land around Pungo Lake; and over 500,000 acres (202,345 ha) of Carteret, Craven, Onslow, and Jones counties were being claimed by persons professing to have purchased the estate of David Allison, as well as by the University of North Carolina under a state law giving it title to unclaimed estates.

The great effort by the state to develop swamp lands for agriculture essentially ended in 1860, although some interest continued into the 1880s. Edmund Ruffin's important book on swamp lands, commissioned by the state, was published in 1861. Also, Ebenezer Emmons, state geologist, in his report on swamp land agriculture published in 1860, was enthusiastic about the potential of the swamp lands for agriculture. The Civil War ended active promotion of the swamp lands, however, and some people were coming to the conclusion that the deeper swamps were perhaps not suited for agriculture after all.

The lack of success with deep swamps does not mean there were no successes, however. Private landowners had continued to do quite well in draining shallower swamps. For example, Emmons (1860) reported that General Blount of Beaufort County, who owned over 50,000 acres (20,234 ha) was a ". . . successful pioneer in subjugating the swamps." He also mentioned some agriculture in the swamps of Onslow and Jones counties, referred to Dover Swamp, and mentioned one canal cut through the "White Oak desert" to a distance of 1 mi (1.6 km) and providing 12 ft (3.7 m) of fall for water power. Holly Shelter, Angola Bay, and Green Swamp were essentially untouched at that time, although dams were backing water into the Green Swamp and probably changing its character.

AGRICULTURE IN THE POST CIVIL WAR PERIOD

In 1867 W. C. Kerr, state geologist, wrote a report reviewing all the activities of the Literary Board (after the Civil War, the State Board of Education). He concluded that more than $200,000 had been spent with not enough income to defray current expenses. Mr. Kerr stated: "The inevitable conclusion . . . is that the swamp lands are simply vast beds of peat, the only portions of them having any agricultural value consisting of a few belts and ridges . . ." (Kerr, 1867). This report, along with reports by Walter Gwynn, engineer, W. G. Lewis, agent, and Thomas Allen, surveyer, was republished in 1883 by the State Board of Education in response to continuing requests for information on the swamp lands (Scarborough, 1883). W. G. Lewis (1867) reported that a canal had been cut from Slocum's Creek to Lake Ellis in Craven County. The lake was drained and 500 acres (202 ha) of rice planted in 1867 and 1868. He also reported that a field of 100 acres (41 ha) had been cleared in White Oak Swamp and corn grown successfully. Thomas Allen reported on the White Oak Swamp in 1869, giving its size as 85,532 acres (34,614 ha).

The Civil War had bankrupted the University of North Carolina and the Literary Fund and it was urged that the state sell off the swamp land to which it had uncontested title, estimated at 500,000 acres (202,345 ha). There was a considerable amount of land speculation after the Civil War, and North Carolina actively tried to attract outside capital as a way of stimulating the state's economy (Lefler and Newsome, 1973).

LOGGING IN THE LATE 1800s

By the 1880s emphasis in the swamp lands was shifting from agriculture to forestry south of Albemarle Sound. Loggers had been active in the Great Dismal Swamp for many years and the original forests were nearly depleted (Shaler, 1890). White cedar was scarce but some cypress remained in the more inaccessible areas (Hale, 1883). The two largest companies were the Richmond Cedar Works and the Roper Lumber Company, both primarily interested in cypress and white cedar. The Dismal Swamp Land Company was still active on its 40,000 acres (16,188 ha), which were sold to the John L. Roper Company in 1899, and by them to Camp Manufacturing Company (Union-Camp Corporation) (Livermore, 1939). Until 1882 much of the juniper or white cedar was taken out of the swamps by hand, a process called "bull hunching" (Hanlon, 1970).

The 1880s saw the more extensive use of logging railroads and other mechanical aids. Roper Lumber Company established a large sawmill at Lee's Creek (now Roper) about 1885 and built a railroad south to log the swamps of Washington and Beaufort counties (Hanlon, 1970). The Albemarle Land and Timber Company had been operating out of Pantego, logging 120,000 acres (48,563 ha) of land obtained from the Josiah Collins estate in 1840, but was stopped by the Civil War. The Roper Lumber Company dominated the western part of the Albemarle peninsula and logged in other areas as well. By 1907 this company owned 600,000 acres (242,814 ha) of land and had cutting rights on 200,000 (80,938 ha) more (Hanlon, 1970). The other dominant company was the Richmond Cedar Works which had extensive holdings in Tyrrell and Dare counties and other areas. Richmond Cedar Works cut over more than an estimated 1 million acres (404,690 ha), and perhaps as much as 2 million (809,380 ha) (Hanlon, 1970). It still owned 165,000 acres (66,774 ha) as late as 1952 and was the source of much of the land eventually owned by West Virginia Pulp and Paper Company and later First Colony Farms in Tyrrell and Dare counties.

In 1883 Hale published a survey of the eastern forest lands in which he said Duplin and Pender counties had the largest known bodies of cypress timber east of the lower Mississippi valley. Out of an estimated 206 sq mi (534 sq km), the state owned 174 (451 sq km). This was primarily in Holly Shelter Swamp and Angola Bay, which had remained in state ownership. Ashe in 1894 surveyed the timberlands in all the eastern counties. He reported that Brunswick County still had 4,000 acres (1,619 ha) of white cedar and 20,000 acres (8,094 ha) of cypress and loblolly pine that had never been lumbered. This included land in the Green Swamp area which amounted to 166,000 acres (67,179 ha), much of which had been logged and the timber rafted to mills at Georgetown, South Carolina. The Nelson-Clark Company of Sheboygan, Wisconsin, purchased 80,000 acres (32,375 ha) in the Green Swamp in 1890 and operated a mill at Bolton for many years (Hanlon, 1970). Ashe (1894) said large quantities of white cedar had also been taken out of Columbus County. Pender County had 15,000 acres (6,070 ha) of cypress, one-third of which had been cut, and the county had a total swamp area of 160,000 acres (64,750 ha). Onslow County had over 100,000 acres (40,469 ha) of swamp but only 4,000 acres (1,619 ha) of cypress. The White Oak River drainage had been cut over but logging had just begun in the rest of the county. Pamlico County had 3,000 acres (1,214 ha) of white cedar, partially logged, and 7,000 acres (2,833 ha) of cypress, over half lumbered. By 1894, some cypress was left in Beaufort County but it was rapidly being depleted, according to Ashe (1894).

The great remaining timber resource at the turn of the century was on the Albemarle peninsula consisting of Hyde, Dare, Tyrrell, and Washington counties. It was estimated that over 1 million acres (404,690 ha) of swamp with 40,000 acres (16,188 ha) of white cedar still remained (Ashe, 1894) but the cypress was being depleted and the land converted to agriculture. The area north of Albemarle Sound was nearly depleted with only 8,000 acres (3,238 ha) out of the original 65,000 acres (26,305 ha) remaining.

The late 1880s and 1890s began a period of about fifty years of heavy logging activity in the eastern swamp lands. When logging began, land was cheap and often poorly surveyed. Much of it was considered worthless after the timber was removed since the logging was exploitative and reforestation was essentially unknown. However, the state had never totally lost its interest in draining swamp land for agriculture and a number of land companies were trying to make a profit off cheap land. Later the timber companies themselves began to promote their logged-over lands for agricultural development.

AGRICULTURAL DEVELOPMENT, EARLY 1900s

In 1891 the General Assembly created the Geological and Economic Survey to examine the natural resources of the state, including forests and soils (Pomeroy and Yoho, 1964). The State Board of Agriculture, also promoting the eastern swamp lands, described them as ". . . a resource of inestimable value in time, perhaps not distant . . ." in 1896. The swamp lands of Jones County were described as being " . . . as rich as the Mississippi Valley," and those of Beaufort County as ". . . equal in fertility to the bottomlands of the Nile." This type of exaggeration tended to stimulate interest in the swamp lands, and the canals cut by the timber companies were making drainage possible over larger areas.

In 1909 the state passed legislation which enabled groups of landowners to set up drainage districts and support areawide projects through assessments against land (Pratt, 1909). The drainage act was of utmost importance in swamp development and very shortly, a number of projects were under way, including drainage of 70,000 acres (28,328 ha) around Lake Mattamuskeet and 4,000 acres (1,619 ha) at Angola Bay (Pratt, 1909). Pratt estimated that 4,505 sq mi (11,668 sq km) of swamp land in the entire state of North Carolina were reclaimable. By 1911, fifty-three drainage districts had been established or were being organized, covering over 700,000 acres (283,283 ha) (Pratt, 1912).

Among the first projects completed was the one covering the Terra Cecia area of Beaufort County and other lands near Belhaven. Drainage was started there about 1907 by the Wilkinson brothers on a 10,000-acre (4,047 ha) tract and, by 1910, three canals had been dug in the area, each draining from 8,000 to 14,000 acres (3,238 to 5,666 ha) (Pratt, 1911; Pomeroy and Yoho, 1964). By 1928 it was estimated that over half a million acres (202,345 ha) of swamp in the coastal plain had been drained as a result of the 1909 act (Thompson, 1928).

The high interest in swamp lands resulted in an agricultural research farm being established in Wenona in 1912 (N.C. Dept. of Agriculture, 1962). By this time, the Roper Lumber Company was a subsidiary of the Norfolk and Southern Railroad, which donated the land for the Blacklands Test Farm. The John L. Roper Company had at one time operated its own experimental farm at Elmhurst to promote land development (Sharpe, 1961). When the state research farm was moved from Wenona in 1943, it was relocated on land including the Elmhust farm, and, now known as the Tidewater Research Station, it is still located there. The Roper Company and the Norfolk and Southern Land Company also established the Carolina Meadows development south of Lake Phelps and offered 80-acre (32 ha) tracts for sale. Only a few were sold and the development failed (Heath, 1975).

In 1916, a company known as the Virginia-Carolina Farms Company obtained title to Open Ground Swamp, intending to develop it for colonization, but World War I prevented the plan and title passed to the East Coast Land Company and later to the University of Chicago (Dachnowski-Stokes and Wells, 1929). A drainage district was formed in 1923 but abandoned in 1926.

Lake Mattamuskeet Development

By far the most ambitious project begun in the early 1900s was the draining of Lake Mattamuskeet. This had been proposed as a way to help the economy of Hyde County since it was believed that the soil of the lake bottom was fertile. The first attempt made in 1913 (Sharpe, 1958) failed. After another unsuccessful attempt, the project was acquired by August Heckscher in 1925. A pumping district of 100,000 acres (40,469 ha) (49,000 acres or 19,830 ha in the lake) was established and a station capable of pumping 1 million gallons (3,785.4 kl) per minute was built (Thompson, 1928). The project attracted a great deal of attention but ultimately failed because of excess water, crop pests, poor pump design and poor soil conditions. Only two of the pumps could be run at the same time because of excess vibration, and water from the surrounding swamp land was not controlled. Also, the soil proved to be almost pure sand and tended to refill the drainage ditches. The lake was turned over to the federal government in 1934 and it was allowed to refill.

OTHER SWAMP LAND TRANSFERS OF THE 1930s

At about the same time Lake Mattamuskeet was acquired by the federal government, various other swamp lands were changing hands. First of all, the North Carolina Forestry Foundation bought the White Oak Swamp in 1934, a total of 78,000 acres (31,566 ha) (Pomeroy and Yoho, 1964). This was later renamed the Hofmann Forest. Secondly, the Croatan National Forest was established and land acquisition began in 1936 (Pomeroy and Yoho, 1964) with 152,351 acres (61,655 ha) in federal ownership. The federal resettlement program at Bladen Lakes failed and the land passed into state control in 1939. The remaining lands of the State Board of Education, a total of 68,000 acres (27,519 ha) at Holly Shelter, Angola Bay, Goose Creek and Gull Rock (Pomeroy and Yoho, 1964), were turned over to the Wildlife Resources Commission.

The most important shifts in ownership and management, however, were those brought about by the land acquisition of the paper companies. As the virgin forests were being depleted and timber companies were encountering stiff competition from west coast woods, the demand for paper was increasing. The paper companies could use second growth pine quite well and cutover forest lands were relatively cheap. As a result, much of the land owned by lumber companies was bought by paper companies.

RECENT DEVELOPMENT AND CURRENT STATUS

Since World War II there has been steady development of swamp lands for agriculture and forestry. It was found that successful production of pine trees on poorly drained soils required drainage, and paper companies began extensive canaling and ditching. By the 1960s most of the swamp land not in public ownership belonged or had belonged to paper companies. In recent years, pressure for land has increased again and large acreages are being developed for agriculture (Richardson et al., this volume). Land ownership patterns were included in Wilson's work in 1962 but important changes have taken place since then.

Great Dismal Swamp

As much as 80% of the Great Dismal Swamp may have been developed with 400 to 750 sq mi (1,036 to 1,945 sq km) remaining (Cahill, 1974) out of an original 2,200 sq mi (5,698 sq km) (Shaler, 1890). In 1973 Union Camp Corporation presented 49,000 acres (19,830 ha), including much of the former lands of the Dismal Swamp Land Company, to the Department of the Interior through The Nature Conservancy (Thomas, 1976). This land is being operated as the Great Dismal Swamp National Wildlife Refuge. The Department of the Interior plan was to add an additional 67,400 acres (27,276 ha) to the refuge for a total of 116,400 acres (47,106 ha), or about one-half the swamp as it now exists (Craig, 1973; Cahill, 1974). Since then the acreage in the refuge has been increased to 97,000 acres (39,255 ha) with plans to increase it to about 107,000 acres (43,302 ha). In addition, the North Carolina Parks Department owns about 14,300 acres (5,787 ha) in the swamp but has no plans for the land.

Albemarle–Pamlico Peninsula

Most of the swamp lands in this area are in private ownership. The Air Force has recently acquired 40,000 acres (16,188 ha) in Dare County for use as a bombing range. The other land in public ownership includes 12,287 acres (4,972 ha) at Pungo Lake acquired in 1963 and operated as Pungo National Wildlife Refuge, and 15,501 acres (6,273 ha) in the Swan Quarter National Wildlife Refuge, much of it salt marsh (Pomeroy and Yoho, 1964). The Lake Mattamuskeet National Wildlife Refuge totals 50,177 acres (20,306 ha), over 40,000 acres (16,188 ha) of which are under water. Smaller tracts are at Pea Island and Gull Rock.

First Colony Farms owned about 376,000 acres (152,163 ha) at its peak in the mid-1970s (Carter, 1975) but has since sold several tracts of land. The company owns much of mainland Dare County (with the exception of the bombing range), with large acreages in Tyrrell and Washington counties and some in Hyde. The remaining swamp lands of the peninsula belong to other private individuals or companies (Figure 2, Richardson et al., this volume).

Pamlico–Neuse Peninsula

Essentially all the land on this peninsula is in private ownership. The major swamp lands are Gum Swamp, Bay City Pocosin, Light Ground Pocosin, and Big Pocosin. Together they cover over 50,000 acres (20,235 ha). Much of the land not owned by paper companies is being cleared for agriculture. There are few large landowners.

Open Ground Swamp, Croatan National Forest, Hofmann Forest

About 40,000 acres (16,188 ha) of the Open Ground Swamp are being developed for agriculture, out of an original estimated 50,000 acres (20,234 ha) (Dachnowski-Stokes and Wells, 1929) to 87,680 acres (35,483 ha) (Kerr, 1867). Most of the remainder belongs to paper companies. The Croatan National Forest consists of 152,351 acres (61,655 ha) in federal ownership (Pomeroy and Yoho, 1965) and includes most of the swamp land. The Forestry Foundation owns the 78,000-acre (31,566 ha) Hofmann Forest (Pomeroy and Yoho, 1964) which had an original estimated acreage of 85,532 acres (34,614 ha) (Allen, 1869). This land is managed for educational purposes and timber production. Some land around the margins is being developed for agriculture.

Holly Shelter and Angola Bay

The 1827 survey indicated 58,240 acres (23,569 ha) claimed by the state in Holly Shelter (Kerr, 1867). In 1939, however, the state transferred only 38,500 acres (15,581 ha) in Holly Shelter to the Wildlife Resources Commission to form the Holly Shelter Wildlife Management Area (Pomeroy and Yoho, 1964). Its acreage is given as 48,470 acres (19,615 ha) by Powell (1968). The additional acreage is apparently private in-holdings acquired at a later date (Pomeroy and Yoho, 1964). In 1827 Angola Bay was surveyed to have 50,000 acres (20,234.5 ha) in state ownership. The Wildlife Resources Commission, however, was assigned only 21,134 acres (8,553 ha) in Angola Bay in 1942 (Pomeroy and Yoho, 1964).

Green Swamp

Green Swamp is estimated to cover about 90,000 acres (36,422 ha) (Powell, 1968) and is part of a 1795 grant of 170,120 acres given to three men. In about 1938, Reigel Paper Company purchased it as part of a 130,000-acre (52,610 ha) tract obtained from Waccamaw Lumber Company (Pomeroy and Yoho, 1964). In 1977, the state obtained 13,850 acres (5,605 ha) in Green

Swamp for preservation from Federal Paper Board Company through The Nature Conservancy. Most of the swamp belongs to paper companies.

CONCLUSION

At the present time, land investment is seen as a desirable hedge against inflation and there is considerable competition for available land. A significant amount of swamp land is in public ownership and is not available for development. Large amounts belong to paper companies and likely will remain forested though highly modified as a result of current forest management practices. The area of most intense development is the Albemarle peninsula, also the area with the smallest proportion of land in public ownership. Land clearing has not proceeded as rapidly as Heath (1975) projected, but it is likely to be as extensive eventually. It is quite likely that the swamp lands in private ownership will be cleared and drained for agriculture and forestry as long as current investment opportunities exist.

LITERATURE CITED

Aiton, W., 1811. On the origin, qualities, and uses of moss earth. Farmers Magazine, Edinburgh. Reprinted: Edmund Ruffin, ed., 1837. Farmers Register. Petersburg, Va., Vol.V, No. 8, pp. 462-477.

Allen, T. H., 1869. Report on White Oak Swamp. In: Scarborough, John C., ed., 1883. Reports on the swamp lands of North Carolina belonging to the State Board of Education, pp. 79-81. State Board of Education, Ashe and Gatling, Raleigh, N.C.

Ashe, W. W., 1894. The forests, forest lands, and forest products of eastern North Carolina. North Carolina Geol. Sur. Bul. 5, J. Daniels, Raleigh, N.C., 128 pp.

Boyd, W. K., ed., 1929. William Byrd's histories of the dividing line betwixt Virginia and North Carolina. The North Carolina Historical Commission, Raleigh, N.C., 341 pp.

Brown, A. C., 1970. The Dismal Swamp Canal. Norfolk County Historical Society, Chesapeake, Va., 234 pp.

Cahill, C., 1974. The Great Dismal Swamp Plan. American Forests, American Forestry Association, 80(12): 18-21.

Carter, L., 1975. Agriculture: A new frontier in coastal North Carolina. Science, Vol. 189, No. 4199, pp. 271-275.

Collet, J. A., 1770. A complete map of North Carolina. In: W. P. Cummings, 1962. The Southeast in early maps. Univ. of North Carolina Press, Chapel Hill, 284 pp.

Craig, J. B., 1973. Dismal's bright future. American Forests, American Forestry Association, 79(5):10-11.

Dachnowski-Stokes, A. P., and B. W. Wells, 1929. The vegetation, stratigraphy, and age of the "Open Land" peat area in Carteret County, North Carolina. Jour. Wash. Acad. Sci., 19:1-11.

Emmons, E., 1860. Report of the N. C. Geological Survey, 1852-1863, Agriculture; Containing descriptions, with many analyses, of the soils of the swamp lands. W. W. Holden, Raleigh, N.C., 95 pp.

Gwynn, W., 1867. Report on the swamp lands. In: Scarborough, J. C., ed., 1883. Reports on the swamp lands of North Carolina belonging to the State Board of Education, pp. 25-64. State Board of Education, Ashe and Gatling, Raleigh, N.C.

Hale, P. M. (compiler), 1883. Woods and timber of North Carolina. P. M. Hale, Raleigh, N.C., 272 pp.

Hanlon, H. A., 1970. The bull hunchers. McClain Publishing Co., Parsons, W. Va., 352 pp.

Heath, R. C., 1975. Hydrology of the Albemarle–Pamlico region, North Carolina, a preliminary report on the impact of agricultural developments. U. S. Geol. Survey, Water-Resources Investigations, No. 9-75, 107 pp.

Kerr, W. C., 1867. Report on the swamp lands. In: Scarborough, John C., ed., 1883. Reports on the swamp lands of North Carolina belonging to the State Board of Education, pp. 5-24. State Board of Education, Ashe and Gatling, Raleigh, N.C.

Lefler, H. T. and A. R. Newsome, 1973. The history of a southern state: North Carolina, third ed. Univ. of North Carolina Press, Chapel Hill, 807 pp.

Lewis, I. F. and E. C. Cocke, 1929. Pollen analysis of Dismal Swamp peat. J. Elisha Mitchell Sci. Soc., 45: 37-38.

Lewis, W. G., 1967. Report on the swamp lands. In: Scarborough, John C., ed., 1883. Reports on the swamp lands of North Carolina belonging to the State Board of Education, pp. 65-78. State Board of Education, Ashe and Gatling, Raleigh, N.C.

Lilly, J. P., 1981. The Blackland soils of North Carolina, their characteristics and management for agriculture. N. C. Agri. Exp. Sta. Tech. Bull. 270, 70 pp.

Livermore, S., 1939. Early American land companies. Oxford Univ. Press, London, 327 pp.

Merrens, H. R., 1964. Colonial North Carolina in the eighteenth century. Univ. of North Carolina Press, Chapel Hill, 293 pp.

Murphey, A. D., 1819. Memoirs on the internal improvements contemplated by the legislature of North Carolina; and on the resources and finances of that state. In: Hoyt, W. H., ed., 1914. The papers of Archibald D. Murphey. North Carolina Historical Commission, Vol. II, pp. 103-195. E. M. Uzzell & Co., state printers, Raleigh, N.C.

Noel Hume, I., 1963. Here lies Virginia. Alfred A. Knopf, New York, 316 pp.

North Carolina Department of Agriculture, 1962. Tidewater Research Station, 1912-1962, 50th anniversary program. N. C. Dept. of Agriculture, Raleigh, 4 pp.

Pomeroy, K. B. and J. G. Yoho, 1964. North Carolina lands. The American Forestry Association, Washington, D.C., 372 pp.

Powell, W. S., 1968. The North Carolina Gazeteer. Univ. of North Carolina Press, Chapel Hill, 561 pp.

Pratt, J. H., 1909. Drainage of North Carolina swamp lands. Elisha Mitchell Sci. Soc. J., 25:158-163.

Pratt, J. H., 1911. Proceedings of the third annual drainage convention (1910). North Carolina Geological and Economic Survey, E. M. Uzzell & Co., Raleigh, N.C., Economic Paper No. 21, 67 pp.

Pratt, J. H., 1912. Proceedings of the fourth annual drainage convention (1911). North Carolina Geological and Economic Survey, Edwards and Broughton, Raleigh, N.C., Economic Paper No. 26, 45 pp.

Ruffin, E., 1839. "Jottings down" in the swamps. Farmers Register, Edmund Ruffin, publisher, Petersburg, Va., Vol. VII, No. 11, pp. 698-733.

Ruffin, E., 1861. Sketches of lower North Carolina and the similar adjacent lands. Institute for the Deaf and Dumb, Raleigh, N.C. , 296 pp. N. C. State Univ. Microfiche No. 17,243-17,246a.

Scarborough, J. C., ed., 1883. Reports on the swamp lands of North Carolina belonging to the State Board of Education. Ashe and Gatling, Raleigh, N.C., 81 pp.

Shaler, N. S., 1890. General account of the freshwater morasses of the United States with a description of the Dismal Swamp region of Virginia and North Carolina. U. S. Geol. Survey, Annual Report, Part 1, Vol. 10, pp. 255-339.

Sharpe, B., 1958. A new geography of North Carolina, Vol. II. Sharpe Publishing Co., Raleigh, N.C., pp. 887-907.

Sharpe, B., 1961. A new geography of North Carolina, Vol. III. Sharpe Publishing Co., Raleigh, N.C., pp. 1615-1640.

Sharpe, B., 1965. A new geography of North Carolina, Vol. IV. Sharpe Publishing Co., Raleigh, N.C., pp. 2121-2140.

State Board of Agriculture, 1896. North Carolina and its resources. M. I. and J. C. Stewart, Raleigh, N.C., 413 pp.

Stewart, P. C., 1979. Man and the swamp: The historical dimension. In: Kir, Paul W., Jr., ed., 1979. The Great Dismal Swamp, pp. 57-73. Univ. Press of Virginia, Charlottesville.

Tarlton, W. W., 1954. Somerset Place and its restoration. N. C. Dept. Cons. and Dev., Div. of State Parks, Raleigh, N.C., offset printed report, 141 pp.

Thomas, B., 1976. The swamp. Norton, New York, 222 pp.

Thompson, H. T. 1928. A study of the physiographic history of swamp lands in relation to the problem of their drainage. Unpublished M. A. Thesis, University of North Carolina, Chapel Hill, 48 pp.

Whitehead, D. R., 1972. Development and environmental history of the Dismal Swamp. Ecological Monographs, 42(3):301-305.

Wilson, K. A., 1962. North Carolina wetlands: Their distribution and management. N.C. Wildlife Resources Commission, Raleigh, N.C., 169 pp.

Section I.
Resource Ecology

The Structure and Development of Pocosin Vegetation

Norman L. Christensen, Rebecca Bea Burchell, Annette Liggett, and Ellen L. Simms

ABSTRACT

Shrub dominated communities inhabit a variety of wetland situations on the coastal plain, including poorly drained interstream areas, Carolina bays, swales in stabilized dune fields, and seeps and stream margins. Shrubs vary in height from 0.5 to 4 m with *Cyrilla racemiflora*, *Lyonia lucida*, *Ilex glabra*, and *Zenobia pulverulenta* being the most abundant species. Emergent trees of *Pinus serotina*, *Acer rubrum*, *Magnolia virginiana*, *Gordonia lasianthus*, and *Chamaecyparis thyoides* are common. Aboveground biomass (minus tree boles) varies from 1200 to 1800 g m^{-2} in nutrient poor ombrotrohpic areas to 3300 to 4700 g m^{-2} in more eutrophic situations. Evergreen sclerophylous species are common and their success appears to be related to their high nutrient use efficiency, particularly with respect to nitrogen and phosphorus. Fire has been a prominent force in the evolution of most pocosin plants as is evidenced by the production of serotinous cones by pond pine and the capacity to sprout from subterranean organs found in nearly all pocosin plants. Vegetational patterns within and among pocosins are discussed and fire effects on vegetation and environment are described.

Key Words: fire, life history characteristics, nutrient cycling, pattern, succession, vegetation analysis

> All the people in the Neighbourhood floct . . . to behold such Rarieties as they fancied us to be. The men left their belov'd Chimney Corners, the good women their Spinning Wheels, and some, of more Curiosity than Ordinary, rose out of their sick Beds, to come and stare at us. They lookt upon us as a Troop of Knight Errants, who were running this great Risque of our Lives; and some of the gravest of them question'd much whether we were not all Criminals, condemned to this dirty work for Offences against the State. "Ye have little reason to be merry, My Masters," said one of them, with a very

solemn Face, "I fancy the Pocosin you must struggle with to-morrow will make you change your Note, and try what Metal you are made of. Ye are, to be sure, the first of Human Race that ever had the Boldness to attempt it, and I dare say will be the last. If, therefore, you have any Worldly Goods to dispose of, My Advice is that you make your Wills this very Night, for fear you die Intestate to-Morrow."

William Byrd, 1728

INTRODUCTION

Pocosins or evergreen shrub bogs represent perhaps the least studied and least understood vegetation type on the Atlantic coastal plain. Their limited economic value, impenetrable character, and alleged dense populations of venomous or otherwise malevolent critters have successfully repelled ecologists for the past fifty years. Added to this is a considerable measure of confusion over the features that unify this ecosystem type, the factors that limit its productivity and diversity, the impact of natural and man-caused disturbance within it, and its successional status relative to other coastal plain ecosystems.

Pocosins are often characterized as ombrotrophic bogs which are dominated by evergreen shrubs. The assemblage of species which characterizes such bogs also forms physiognomically similar communities in other hydrologic situations (and has also been termed pocosin) (Harper, 1914; Wells, 1928, 1946; Wells and Shunk, 1931; Woodwell, 1956). Furthermore, over half of the shrub species that occur in shrub bogs, including several dominants, are quite deciduous.

Woodwell (1956) suggested that pocosin vegetation occurred in at least three hydrologically dissimilar situations: flat interstream areas on lower coastal plain terraces, Carolina bays, and ridge and bay areas. To these we add the shrub bogs surrounding springs and steam heads of the upper coastal plain, particularly the sandhills region.

The formation of shrub bogs in flat interstream areas is discussed by Daniel (this volume) and has also been described by Whitehead (1972). Slow runoff, often coupled with poorly drained substrata, leaves these areas saturated with water year-round (and truly ombrotrophic). Included among such pocosins are the Great Lake pocosin of Croatan National Forest as well as the extensive swamp lands in northeastern North Carolina.

The elliptical depressions or Carolina bays which characterize the lower and middle coastal plain often support shrub bog vegetation. The theories regarding the origin of these southeast-northwest oriented features are numerous and, in some cases, bizarre (Cooke, 1933; Grant, 1945; Odum, 1952; Prouty, 1934; Shriever, 1955). The most convincing theories suggest that these areas were formed and oriented by strong prevailing winds in at least two episodes during the late Pleistocene epoch (Watts, 1979; Whitehead, personal communication). The bays are quite varied vegetationally, appearing in many cases to be undergoing typical hydrarch successions (Clements, 1916) from lakes to bogs. Wells and Boyce (1953) questioned this interpretation, however, suggesting instead that lakes were created by fires burning deep into peat-filled depressions. In many cases where such bays present continuous shrub cover, one finds that the pocosin is actually a floating mat.

Ridge and bay pocosins occur in the swales in now-stabilized dune fields on the lowest coastal plain terraces (Colquhoun, 1969). These areas are fed by gound water as well as rain water.

Pocosin vegetation is also characteristic of seeps, springs, and margins of slow-flowing streams in the sandhills region. These areas are fed primarily by ground water and often occur mid-slope where subsoil clay horizons approach the surface (Wells and Shunk, 1931).

GENERAL VEGETATIONAL FEATURES

The typical pocosin vegetation is dominated by a shrub understory with scattered emergent trees. The shrub cover varies in height from 0.5 m to over 4 m and usually includes a mixture of evergreen and deciduous species. Indeed, deciduous species may actually dominate some shrub bogs. The most common tree species is pond pine, *Pinus serotina*, although other pines, such as *P. taeda* (loblolly pine), and *P. palustris* (longleaf pine), may also occur, particularly in drained areas. These last two pines and slash pine, *Pinus elliotii*, have been planted extensively in pocosins under silivicultural management. Atlantic white cedar (*Chamaecyparis thyoides*) and cypress (*Taxodium* spp.) also occur in some pocosins. Hardwood trees, such as red maple (*Acer rubrum*), sweet bay (*Magnolia virginiana*), and loblolly bay (*Gordonia lasianthus*), are common in most areas. These trees vary in stature from being part of the shrub cover to over 10 m tall.

Aboveground biomass varies considerably among shrub bogs depending on time elapsed since burning and productivity. In the very nutrient-poor ombrotrophic areas, aboveground biomass (minus the mass of tree boles) is approximately 1200 to 1880 g m^{-2} whereas, in more eutrophic situations, 3300 to 4700 g m^{-2} is characteristic (Wendel et al., 1962). Such areas are often distinguished as low and high pocosins, respectively, and representative sites are illustrated in Figure 1. The proportion of this aboveground material which is living decreases as these communities develop. No estimates exist of below-ground biomass; however, our observations in the low pocosins of the Croatan National Forest reveal that living roots and lignotubers are concentrated in the upper 30 cm of peat.

Although peat mosses (*Sphagnum* spp.) occur in most shrub bogs, their importance varies considerably. Wherever shrub cover becomes continuous

FIGURE 1A

FIGURE 1B

FIGURE 1. *A. Low pocosin vegetation from Croatan National Forest, Craven Co., N.C. Standing crop = ca. 1500 g m*$^{-2}$*. B. High pocosin vegetation from the Green Swamp, Brunswick Co., N.C. Standing crop = ca. 3000-4000 g m*$^{-2}$*. Both areas had been unburned over 20 years at the time the photographs were taken.*

and productivity is high, they are limited to light gaps and small disturbances (L. E. Anderson, personal communication). However, in ombrotrophic low pocosins they may contribute greatly to total community production and peat formation.

The southeastern coastal plain is climatically transitional between subtropical Florida and eastern Mexico and cold-temperate New England. A similar transition is apparent in the flora. Several species with tropical affinities reach their northernmost extent in pocosins. Included in this group are *Cyrilla racemiflora*, *Persea borbonia*, and *Gordonia lasianthus*. Other species, especially members of the Ericaceae and Aquifoliaceae, are of more northern extraction.

PHYSIOLOGICAL CHARACTERISTICS OF POCOSIN PLANTS

As mentioned previously, the most prominent components of pocosin communities are shrubs which may vary from being completely winter deciduous to evergreen. Even those shrubs which retain leaves through the winter do so with varying intensity. For example, *Cyrilla racemiflora* and *Kalmia angustifolia* lose their leaves gradually through the winter whereas *Lyonia lucida* and *Ilex glabra* maintain their leaves through two growing seasons.

In addition to being evergreen, many shrubs are also sclerophyllous, having leaves with thickened cuticles and structurally reinforced with lignin. Evergreen sclerophyllous vegetation is often associated with areas of drought and the abundance of such plants in shrub bogs has attracted much attention and speculation. Schimper (1898) proposed that anaerobic conditions in the rooting zone prevent water uptake and the plants experience "physiological drought." However, Caughey (1945) and Schlesinger and Chabot (1977) showed that these plants were not unusually drought stressed compared to nonsclerophyllous plants in other habitats. This has also been verified for bog plants of northern bogs (Marchand, 1975; Small 1972b).

The nutrient deficient environments of most raised bogs have led some workers to suggest that sclerophylly in these ecosystems may be an adaptation to conserve nutrients. This increased conservation of nutrients could come about as a consequence of the regulation of litter fall and decomposition (Monk, 1966) or as a result of a prolonged period of mineral accumulation and use (Monk, 1971; Schlesinger and Chabot, 1977; Small, 1972a, c). It has been proposed that sclerophylly provides necessary structural support and defense against herbivory for longer lived leaves. However, Loveless (1961, 1962) proposed that sclerophylly is a direct response to mineral deficiencies rather than evergreenness. Indeed, some deciduous pocosin plants, such as *Lyonia mariana* and *Zenobia pulverulenta*, also have sclerophyllous leaves.

Small (1972c) found that photosynthetic yields per unit of nitrogen were highest in evergreen plants in northern bogs. Schlesinger and Chabot (1977), working in Okefenokee Swamp (Georgia) estimated that nitrogen use efficiency might be 30% higher in *Lyonia lucida* (evergreen sclerophyllous) than in *Clethra alnifolia* (deciduous). By their calculations, deciduous species would need a photosynthetic rate 50% greater than evergreen species in order to compete in an area with an eight-month growing season. Because direct measurements of photosynthesis in pocosin shrubs have not been made and direct measurements of nutrient use efficiency are wanting, the relative costs and benefits of deciduousness and evergreenness among pocosin shrubs are far from resolved and deserve a thorough comparative study.

Another aspect of the leaves of some pocosin shrubs which has some practical importance is their content of secondary chemicals. Shrubs, such as *Persea borbonia*, *Myrica cerifera*, and *Ilex glabra*, are known to contain large quantities of aromatic compounds (Komarek, 1974). Indeed, ether extractives in the leaves of *Ilex glabra* may account for 40% of leaf dry weight (Shafizadeh et al., 1977). As a consequence of high levels of aromatic compounds, the leaf tissues of pocosin shrubs have comparatively high caloric values (Hough, 1969). The adaptive significance of these compounds is uncertain, but they likely have a role in defense against herbivores. They also have the effect of increasing shrub flammability and fire intensity (Christensen, 1980).

Not unexpectedly, Woodwell (1958) found that pond pine could tolerate the nutrient deficiencies of pocosin peats better than species that did not naturally occur in pocosins. He attributed this in part to the ability of pond pine to utilize ammonium nitrogen. Barnes and Naylor (1959) showed that pond pine could directly incorporate many forms of organic nitrogen. The advantages of such uptake in the reducing environment of peat bogs is clear and it seems likely that many pocosin species share this ability.

Insectivorous plants, particularly *Sarracenia flava*, *S. purpurea*, and *Drosera* spp., are often found scattered in shrub bogs, particularly where shrub stature is low. The role of insects as alternative nutrient sources for these plants has long been suggested (Plummer, 1963) and it has been demonstrated that insects can ameliorate deficiencies of nitrogen and phosphorus in these plants (Christensen, 1976).

Nutrient relationships in *Sphagnum* are worthy of some mention. Peat mosses function best in low pH environments with low ionic strength. Indeed, they regulate the pH of their surroundings by ion exchange but cannot do so in water buffered by high cation content (Clymo, 1963, 1964). An almost immediate result of nutrient addition or drainage in pocosins is the disappearance of these plants.

LIFE HISTORY CHARACTERISTICS OF POCOSIN PLANTS

The life histories of most pocosin species center on fire. Not only are they tolerant of fire, but many plants seem to require fire to complete their life cycle. The relationship between fire cycles and the evolution of life-history characteristics is best exemplified by pond pine. Established trees are quite resistant to fire, sprouting from the root as well as from epicormic buds along the bole. Only the most severe fires completely kill these trees. Furthermore, pond pine produces moderately serotinous cones which remain closed after seed maturation for two to ten years (Fowells, 1968). The heat of the fire stimulates cone opening and seed release at the time when the probability of successful seedling establishment is highest (Christensen, 1980; Woodwell, 1958). Because cones eventually open without fire, some seeds are being released each year while a reservoir of seeds is retained on the tree. Thus, seeds from a particular tree may establish in nearby burned areas or other disturbance situations.

All of the shrubs that occur in pocosins sprout vigorously after fire; however, little is known regarding their germination requirements. None of these shrubs has yet been shown to have heat-stimulated germination such as is found in the western chaparral (Mooney and Dunn, 1970), and those which have been tested germinate freely after stratification (Hughes, 1964). Nevertheless, successful germination and establishment rarely occur in pocosins which have not been recently burned, with the exception of low pocosin areas where occasional seedlings can be found (Christensen, unpublished data).

Although herbs are not a major component of pocosin ecosystems in interfire years, they may become quite abundant immediately following fire. Some species, such as *Andropogon virginicus* and members of the Asteraceae, are dispersed into recently burned areas and are eventually eliminated as the shrub cover regenerates. It is likely that some herb species produce seeds which lie refractory in the peat from fire to fire, although this has not been established. Plants, such as *Woodwardia virginica*, *Arundinaria gigantea*, and *Carex walteriana*, are perennial inhabitants of pocosins and their postfire abundance is simply a consequence of rapid vegetative growth. Sexual reproduction is rare in these species (Hughes, 1951, 1966), but vegetative stalks and fronds can nearly always be found in most pocosins.

VEGETATIONAL PATTERNS AMONG POCOSINS

To date, the most extensive vegetational analysis of pocosins is that done by Woodwell (1956). In this unpublished master's thesis, Woodwell classified pocosins into three associations based on dominant shrub species: *Cyrilla racemiflora*, *Lyonia lucida*, and *Zenobia pulverulenta*. Based on Woodwell's field notes, Christensen (1979) published a quantitative listing of constancy and average cover for each species in each association. Wells (1946) studied vegetation of Holly Shelter Bay and his data were also summarized by Christensen (1979).

Woodwell (1976) found that associations dominated by *Cyrilla racemiflora* and *Lyonia lucida* were segregated geographically. In central and northeastern North Carolina, *Cyrilla* is the chief dominant, whereas to the

TABLE 1. *Pocosin Classification according to Kologiski (1977)*

PINE-ERICALEAN Community Class

Pinus serotina/*Cyrilla racemiflora-Zenobia pulverulenta* community type

Characteristic of deep peats, long hydroperiods, and frequent fires. Low productivity and low pine density. "Low pocosin"

Pinus serotina/*Gordonia lasianthus-Lyonia lucida* community type

Characteristic of elevated areas ("islands") within the above type. Apparently formed by accumulation of litter and *Sphagnum* around the tree boles and stumps

Pinus serotina/*Cyrilla racemiflora-Lyonia lucida* community type

Intermediate to deep peats with moderate to long hydroperiods. Longer fire return times. "High pocosin"

CONIFER-HARDWOOD Community Class

Pinus serotina/*Cyrilla racemiflora-Lyonia lucida-Acer rubrum-Nyssa sylvatica* var. *biflora* community type

Shallow organic soils with shorter hydroperiods. *Sphagnum* may be present, but no deep peat. Mature trees are taller and less deformed than in Pine-Ericalean pocosins.

Pinus serotina-Taxodium ascendens/*Acer rubrum-Cyrilla racemiflora-Lyonia lucida-Nyssa sylvatica* var. *biflora* community type

Similar to above, but with a larger component of swamp forest species. Clearly successional to swamp forest.

south, *Lyonia lucida* is more abundant. Both Woodwell and Wells agreed that *Zenobia pulverulenta* is indicative of recent disturbance, particularly by fire. Often associated with *Zenobia* were *Clethra alnifolia*, *Kalmia angustifolia* var. *caroliniana*, *Ilex glabra* and *Cassandra calyculata*. Woodwell suggested that on favorable sites, *Zenobia* is overtopped by *Cryilla* and *Lyonia* within five years.

More recently, Kologiski (1977) completed a phytosociological study of the Green Swamp. He divided pocosin vegetation in this area into two community classes, each encompassing several community types. The Pine–Ericalean community class is codominated by *Pinus serotina* and various shrub species, whereas the Conifer–Hardwood community class is dominated by either pine or cypress with intermediate-sized hardwood trees. The community types and their respective environmental correlates are described in Table 1. The Pine–Ericalean community class is typical of most raised bog situations, whereas the Conifer–Hardwood community class seems to be more characteristic of fen-like conditions. Kologiski speculated that this latter class was a successional stage in the development of swamp forest. Quantitative correlations between vegetation and environment were not made in this study and the suitability of this classification system outside of the Green Swamp has yet to be determined.

RELATIONSHIP BETWEEN VEGETATIONAL COMPOSITION AND ENVIRONMENT

In an attempt to understand more specifically the relationship between environment and vegetational variations in pocosins, we reanalyzed Woodwell's original data for fifty-eight pocosins sampled throughout North and South Carolina. On the assumption that vegetational composition is a reflection of the particular environment of a pocosin, we ordinated these stands using reciprocal averaging ordination (Hill 1973, 1974). Ordinations were performed on these data using estimated cover values for each species. The data were double standardized (Bray and Curtis, 1957) and log-10 transformed. Only species occurring in three or more stands were used in the ordination. In this procedure, stands are ranked along axes based on variation in species composition. Each successive axis accounts for successively less variation. One of the advantages of reciprocal averaging is that it simultaneously ordinates species and stands and thus allows characterization of species distributions.

The arrangements of stands and species for the first two axes are shown in Figure 2 for shrubs. This graphical approach provides a means of quantitatively evaluating Woodwell's (1956) classification. *Zenobia* dominated stands had high first and second axis scores, *Lyonia lucida* dominated stands had intermediate first axis and low second axis scores and the *Cyrilla* dominated stands had low first axis scores. Although Woodwell's categories do not fall into three discrete groups, they do tend to dominate particular portions of the ordination. This reaffirms the view that the vegetation varies in a continuous fashion and that any classification scheme is arbitrary.

Using Woodwell's field notes, we were able to determine the pocosin type (bay, flat, or ridge and bay), age since burning, depth of peat, depth to water table, and substrate type (clay, silt or sand). These data were compared to stand scores from the above ordinations using Spearman's Rank Correlation Analysis with the following results. The first axis in the shrub ordination showed no significant correlations with any of the above environmental variables but was significantly correlated with shrub diversity ($R= .65$, $P<0.0001$). Thus, stands with high first axis scores (*Zenobia* dominated stands) are more diverse than stands with low scores. Woodwell (1956) noted that diversity was inversely related to productivity and age since fire. In more productive bogs *Cyrilla* and *Lyonia* tend to dominate quickly, excluding other species. This generalization is supported by comparatively low first axis scores of *Lyonia* and *Cyrilla*. Deciduous shrub species tend to have higher first axis scores than evergreen shrubs with some notable exceptions (e.g., *Lyonia mariana*). The second axis is positively correlated with peat depth ($R= .35$, $P<0.0005$). This relationship was most clear on sites with clay substrate

($R = .45$, $P < 0.02$) and showed no significant relation for sites with sandy substrata ($R = .25$, $P < 0.15$). Shrub axis 2 shows a slight negative correlation ($R = -.33$, $P < 0.01$) with species diversity, with the most diverse stands occuring in the lower right part of this ordination. There is a tendency for bay pocosins to have higher first and second axis scores than either flats or ridge and bay areas but this was not statistically significant.

Perhaps the most significant lesson we can extract from such data analysis is that we know relatively little about the causes of variations among pocosins. There is clearly need for a much more thorough comparative study of pocosin vegetation over a broad geographic area.

VEGETATIONAL PATTERNS AND STRUCTURE WITHIN POCOSINS

Relatively few data are available regarding the spatial patterns of vegetation within pocosins. Given the apparent homogeneity of pocosin areas, one wonders whether spatial patterning plays a significant role in the coexistence of pocosin shrubs. Although quantitative data are few, some generalizations regarding species distributions within bogs can be made.

It should first be emphasized that the environmental monotony of pocosins is more apparent than real. In many areas, peat moss (*Sphagnum* spp.) accumulates in hummock-hollow patterns reminiscent of bogs of the Lake States (Lane, 1980; Vitt, Crum, and Snider, 1975). *Sphagnum cuspidatum* occurs in moist swales, oftentimes with *Zenobia pulverulenta*. Such

FIGURE 2. *Reciprocal averaging ordinations of pocosins sampled by Woodwell (1956). Stands and species are arranged in two-dimensional statistical space based on compositional similarities. In the stand ordination, C =* Cyrilla-*dominated stands, L =* Lyonia lucida-*dominated stands, and Z =* Zenobia-*dominated stands (Woodwell's classification). In the species ordinations acronyms refer to species names as follows: LYMA =* Lyonia mariana, *CYRA* = Cyrilla racemiflora, *MYCE* = Myrica cerifera, *LYLU* = Lyonia lucida, *GOLA* = Gordonia lasianthus, *NYBI* = Nyssa sylvatica *var.* biflora, *ILGL* = Ilex glabra, *ILCO* = Ilex coriacea, *CLAL* = Clethra alnifolia, *ZEPU* = Zenobia pulverulenta, *PEBO* = Persea borbonia, *ITVI* = Itea virginica, *MAVI* = Magnolia virginiana, *FOGA* = Fothergilla gardenii, *VACO* = Vaccinium corymbosum, *VACC = unidentified* Vaccinium *species, SOAR* = Sorbus arbutifolia, *ACRU* = Acer rubrum, *LYLI* = Lyonia ligustrina, *SMLA* = Smilax laurifolia, *KACU* = Kalmia cuneata, *KAAN* = Kalmia angustifolia *var.* caroliniana, *GAYL* = Gaylussacia *spp., CACA* = Cassandra calyculata. *E, SD, and D refer to evergreen, semideciduous, and deciduous, respectively. All nomenclature is according to Radford et al. (1968).*

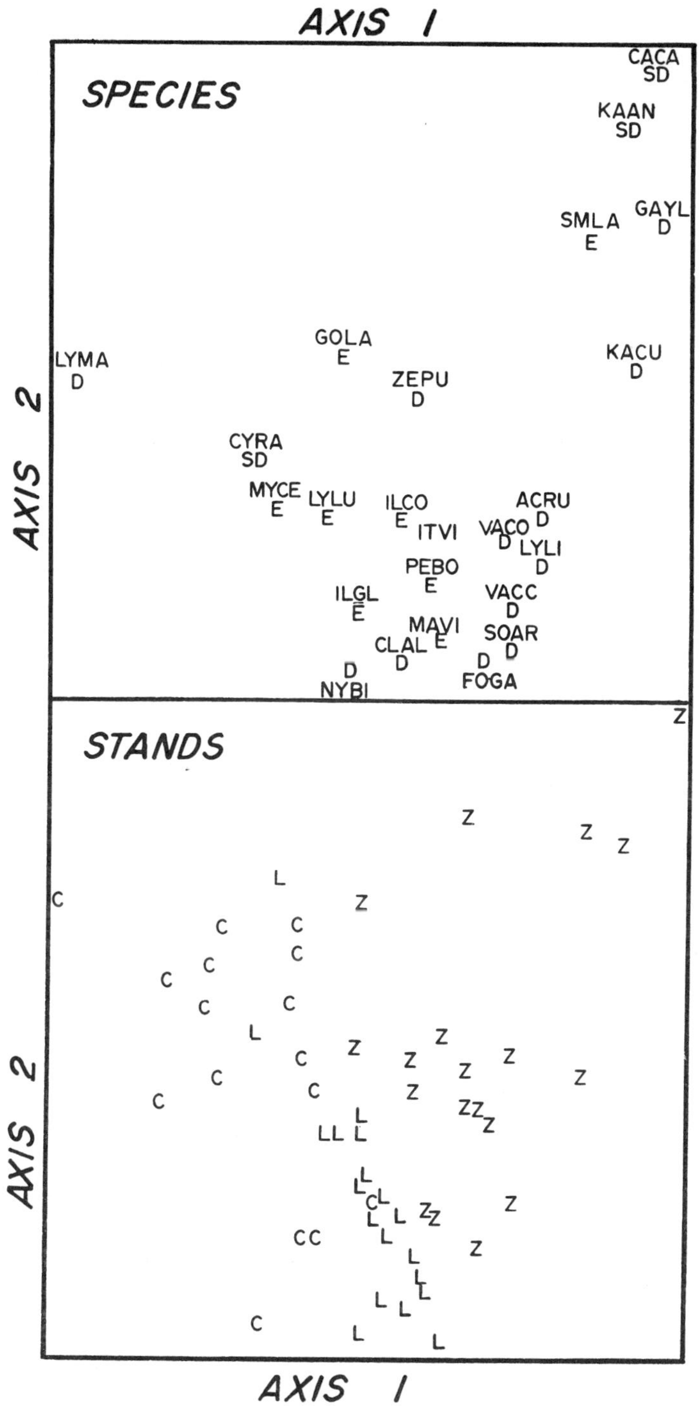
AXIS I
SPECIES
STANDS
AXIS 2
CACA SD
KAAN SD
SMLA E
GAYL D
GOLA E
LYMA D
KACU D
ZEPU D
CYRA SD
MYCE E
LYLU E
ILCO E
ACRU D
ITVI
VACO D
LYLI D
PEBO E
ILGL E
VACC D
MAVI E
SOAR D
CLAL D
D NYBI
D FOGA

depressions often represent localized areas where considerable peat has burned away during fire. In many cases the level of the peat is below the mean water table. Plant growth in these depressions is quite slow and shrub stature stunted. Intermediate areas are characterized by *Sphagnum magellanicum* with *Sphagnum bartelettianum* forming the hummocks (Lane, 1979). The hummocks are often associated with the bases of shrubs. Intermediate-sized trees, such as *Gordonia lasianthus*, *Acer rubrum*, and *Magnolia virginiana*, often occur in raised areas or "islands" (Kologiski, 1977; Wells, 1946) although the causes of these islands are unclear.

DeBecker (unpublished data), using nearest neighbor methods, found that pond pine trees had a highly regular pattern in low pocosin areas of the Croatan National Forest. Gill (1975) observed the same pattern among pitch pines in the New Jersey pine barrens. Gill attributes this distribution to concentrated seed predation; however, competition for limited nutrients seems a more plausible explanation (Woodwell, 1958).

As Woodwell pointed out, species richness in shrub bogs is often highest in areas with low production. This is true to some extent within a given pocosin with the exception of "hollow" or swale areas which, though unproductive, may support only *Zenobia pulverulenta*.

SPATIAL AND SUCCESSIONAL RELATIONS TO OTHER COMMUNITIES

In areas where drainage patterns become more definite or where pocosins are around lakes or ponds, shrub bogs give way to swamp forest vegetation. This change is often gradual and characterized by decreasing shrub diversity and increasing tree diversity. Peat depth decreases, and nutrient availability and productivity increase along this gradient (Kologiski, 1977; Daniel, this volume).

At the other end of the moisture gradient, shrub bogs give way to savannas and flatwoods. These areas are dominated by longleaf, loblolly, and slash pines and often have a diverse herbaceous understory. On heavier soils, understory trees and shrubs may be important components of these communities. The ecotone between savannas and pocosins may be quite sharp, even though the moisture gradient is more gradual. This is largely a consequence of high fire frequency in the savannas. Fires in savannas tend to burn up to the pocosin margin, being extinguished by the moisture content of the shrubs. Only during drought periods do such fires carry into adjacent pocosins. In areas where fire has been excluded from savannas, the line between these communities is far less clear (Christensen, 1980).

Penfound (1952) considered that shrub bogs were part of a successional sere leading to swamp forest dominated by white cedar. Wells (1928, 1942) and Kologiski (1977) also described pocosins as successional or fire disclimaxes. Descriptions by Ashe and Pinchot (1897) seem to indicate that many present-day pocosins were indeed white cedar swamps prior to settlement. The presence of white cedar logs beneath the shallow peats of parts of the Holly Shelter and Green swamps (Wells, 1946; Kologiski, 1977) and the invasion of white cedar into many of the Carolina bays support this notion. A superficial reading of these observations might lead one to conclude that pocosins have been created by chronic human disturbance of swamp forests. Although this is undoubtedly true in some areas, there is abundant evidence that most of the extensive moor-like or raised bogs have not been altered significantly in several millenia (Daniels et al., 1977; Daniel, this volume; Whitehead, 1972). Daniels et al. found white cedar stumps at the base of 1 to 2 m of peat in the Hofmann Forest. Radiocarbon dates suggest that this area was a white cedar swamp at the close of the Xerothermic period, 5,000 to 7,000 years B.P. It has since been inhabited by shrub bog.

Except at their margins, the extensive upraised shrub bogs show very little sign of succeeding to swamp forest; i.e., species that typify swamps, such as cypress, Atlantic white cedar, and tupelo, are virtually absent. Even in the long-term absence of fire (if such is possible), these truly ombrotrophic pocosins appear quite stable. The importance of fire in maintaining pocosin vegetation increases greatly as one moves towards more fen-like (i.e., areas receiving nutrients from adjacent ecosystems) or otherwise more productive situations. Thus, rather than creating pocosins *de novo*, human disturbance has extended their boundaries. As one moves toward the pocosin–swamp ecotone (i.e., areas that correspond to Kologiski's Conifer–Hardwood community class) fire or other chronic disturbance becomes more essential to maintenance of shrub bog vegetation (Christensen, 1980; Wells and Whitford, 1976).

We should note here that the question of what pocosins would become in the absence of fire is basically moot. Changes in relative amounts of dead versus living aboveground biomass, coupled with the accumulation of peat above the mean water table and the flammability of the shrubs, virtually guarantee that these areas will eventually burn. Thus, once pocosins are established, the very character of the vegetation favors a fire regime which tends to perpetuate that vegetation.

EFFECTS OF DISTURBANCE ON POCOSIN VEGETATION

One of the most significant human impacts on pocosins is the draining of areas to increase production or facilitate use of pocosins for agriculture or silviculture. The impacts of such drainage on pocosin communities have not been thoroughly studied, although it is clear that productivity is greatly stimulated by this treatment. Because this topic will be discussed elsewhere in this volume, we wish only to reiterate one potentially negative aspect of this increased productivity—that is the reduction in species diversity.

Undoubtedly the most frequent disturbance in pocosins is fire. There is abundant evidence that this has been true since the close of the last ice age (see Christensen, 1980, for review). However, aside from a few almost anecdotal accounts, relatively little information is available regarding the effects of fire in pocosins.

That species diversity (both richness and equitability) is highest in shrub bogs immediately following fire is well known (Christensen, 1980; Garren, 1943; Wells, 1946; Woodwell, 1956) and has already been emphasized in this paper. Furthermore, successful establishment from seed in most pocosin species is usually confined to immediate postfire years. What is largely unknown is how fire affects plant environments so as to effect these changes.

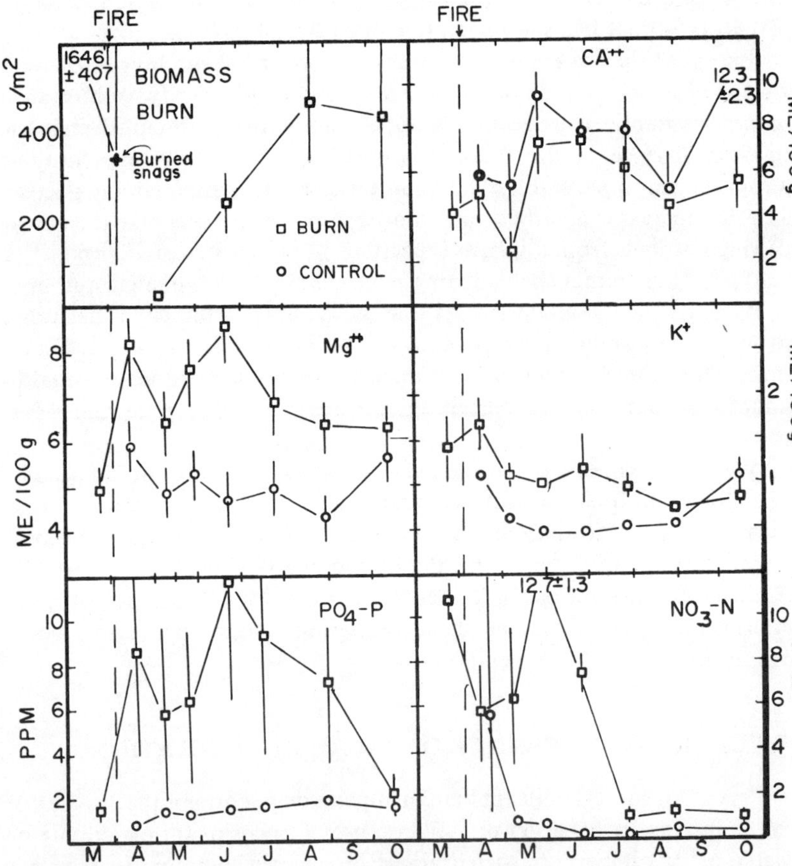

FIGURE 3. *Changes in biomass and soil nutrients (top 5 cm of peat) following prescribed fire in the Great Lake Pocosin, Croatan National Forest. Each point in the nutrient data is the mean of 20 samples. Biomass data are the means of harvests of 10 m x m plots except for October, which is the mean of 15 such plots. Vertical lines are 95% confidence limits.*

We have initiated an intensive study of fire response in pocosins of the Croatan National Forest and will report some of our findings here.

The vegetation and changes in several extractable nutrients (upper 5 cm of peat) associated with a prescribed burn in 1979 are graphed in Figure 3. This pocosin had not been burned for twenty-five years. The pocosin regained nearly 25% of its prefire biomass in the first growing season. The concentrations of most nutrients are increased by burning with these concentrations returning to their prefire levels by the end of the first growing season. Although ammonium levels were rather variable in both the burned and unburned areas, nitrate levels were consistently higher in the burned area. This suggests that fire may stimulate nitrification, an interesting result considering the low pH of these soils (3.5 to 4.0). Calcium was consistently lower in the burned peat.

Woodwell (1958) showed that most pocosin peats are deficient in available N and P. Our own bioassays with pond pine confirm his observations and suggest that available Mg and Fe may also limit growth in unburned pocosins. Burning results in these elements (NO_3-N, PO_4-P, Mg, and Fe) being temporarily increased, reducing these deficiencies (Burchell and Christensen, unpublished data).

One important impact of fire that is often overlooked is its effect on environmental heterogeneity. This effect is seen in the broad statistical confidence limits characterizing the means of some of the burned peat nutrient data. Some localities within a particular pocosin are clearly more nutrient enriched than others. It takes only a casual walk through a recent burn to appreciate that fires do not burn evenly. In some areas, fire may smolder into the peat as deep as 50 cm, leaving behind a residue of white ash and a depression which may be well below the mean water table. Other areas are only lightly burned or spared completely. Thus, fire adds heterogeneity to an otherwise monotonous landscape and its potential role in maintaining species diversity can not be overemphasized.

The effects of fire on microclimate and water availability are perhaps as important as the effect on nutrients and far less studied. Radiation is increased at the soil surface, not only increasing available light, but also heating the now-blackened peat surface so that temperatures in excess of 50° C in the upper centimeter of peat are common. Consequently, the upper 5 to 10 cm of peat dry out nearly completely between rains during the growing season. One result is very little germination or seedling establishment of shrubs or pond pine in these areas. Successful establishment is confined to areas where peat has burned to near the water table and moisture is readily and consistently available. Thus, localized variations in fire intensity may determine patterns of reproduction and patterning within pocosins long after the direct effects of the fire have disappeared.

Fire should be viewed as a highly cyclical phenomenon in pocosins and its frequency and intensity are largely governed by changes inherent in the development of the vegetation (Christensen, 1980.) As the pocosin regenerates following a fire, the amount of dry dead fuel increases as does the likelihood that the pocosin will carry a fire. In such situations, fire seems almost inevitable and the absence of fire may represent more of a disturbance than even the most intense inferno.

A point should be made regarding the relative impacts of prescribed fire versus wildfire. Prescribed fires are likely to be set when they can be most easily controlled, whereas the opposite is true of wildfires. Thus, prescribed fires rarely burn deeply into the peat. In areas where burning is intended simply to create a fuel break (such as in the Croatan National Forest), this fact is of little concern. But if fire is being prescribed to facilitate regeneration from seed or to preserve natural diversity (as in natural reserves), it may be a poor replacement for wildfire.

ACKNOWLEDGMENTS

We are greatful to Sally DeBecker for assistance in gathering some of the data reported here. We thank C. W. Ralston and George Woodwell for making available their original research notes and Dr. Ralston for many beneficial discussions. We also wish to thank Claude Hood, superintendent of Bladen Lakes State Forest, and Brad Jenkins, Phil Kromer, and Lynn Young (superintendent) of Croatan National Forest, not just for their continuing cooperation, but for educating us in many pocosin matters. Drs. Mark M. Brinson and William H. Schlesinger read an early draft of this paper and made many helpful suggestions. We very much appreciate the financial support provided by the USDA Forest Service, although the views expressed here are our own and do not necessarily reflect Forest Service policy. We also thank the Duke University Graduate School and University Research Council for their financial aid.

LITERATURE CITED

Ashe, W. W., and G. Pinchot, 1897. Timber trees and forests of North Carolina. North Carolina Geol. Surv. No. 6, 227 pp.

Barnes, R. L., and A. W. Naylor, 1959. Effect of various nitrogen sources on growth of isolated roots of *Pinus serotina*. Physiol. Planta, 12:82-89.

Byrd, W., 1728. Histories of the dividing line betwixt Virginia and North Carolina, facsimile ed. Dover Publications, New York, 340 pp.

Bray, J. R., and J. T. Curtis, 1957. An ordination of the upland forest communities of southern Wisconsin. Ecol. Monogr., 27:325-349.

Caughey, M. G., 1945. Water relations of pocosin or bog shrubs. Plant Phys., 20:671-689.

Christensen, N. L., 1976. The role of carnivory in *Sarracenia flava* L. with regard to specific nutrient deficiencies. J. Elisha Mitchell Sci. Soc., 92:144-147.

Christensen, N. L. 1979. Shrublands of the southeastern United States, pp. 441-449. In: R. L. Specht, ed., Heathlands and Related Shrublands of the World, A. Descriptive Studies, Elsevier, Amsterdam.

Christensen, N. L., 1980. Fire regimes in southeastern ecosystems. In: H. A. Mooney, T. Bonnicksen, N. L. Christensen, W. A. Reiners, and J. Lotan, eds., Fire regimes and ecosystem properties. USDA For. Serv., Gen. Tech. Report, Washington, D.C. (In press).

Clements, F. E., 1916. Plant succession: An analysis of the development of vegetation. Carnegie Inst. Pub. 242, 512 pp.

Clymo, R. S., 1963. Ion exchange in *Sphagnum* and its relation to bog ecology. Ann. Bot. Lond. n.s., 27:309-324.

Clymo, R. S., 1964. The origin of acidity in *Sphagnum* bogs. Bryologist, 67:427-431.

Colquhoun, D. J., 1969. Geomorphology of the lower coastal plain of South Carolina. Div. of Geology, State Development Board. Ms-15, Columbia, S.C., 36pp.

Cooke, C. W., 1933. Origin of the so-called meteorite scars of South Carolina. Washington Acad. Sci. J., 23:569-570.

Daniels, R. B., E. E. Gamble, W. H. Wheeler, and C. S. Holzhey, 1977. The stratigraphy and geomorphology of the Hofmann Forest pocosin. Soil Sci. Amer. J., 41:1175-1180.

Fowells, H. G., 1968. Silvics of forest trees of the United States. USDA, Agriculture Handbook No. 271, 762 pp.

Garren, K. H., 1943. Effects of fire on vegetation of the southeastern United States. Bot. Rev., 9:617-654.

Gill, D. E., 1975. Spatial patterning of pines and oaks in the New Jersey pine barrens. J. Ecology, 63:291-298.

Grant, C., 1945. A biological explanation of the Carolina bays. Sci. Monthly, 61:443-450.

Harper, R. M.,1914. The "pocosin" of Pike County, Alabama, and its bearing on certain problems in succession. Bull. Torrey Bot. Club, 41:209-220.

Hill, M. O., 1973. Reciprocal averaging: An eigenvector method of ordination. J. Ecol., 61:237-249.

Hill, M. O., 1974. Correspondence analysis: A neglected multivariate method. J. Royal Stat. Soc. Ser. C., 23:340-354.

Hough, W. A., 1969. Caloric values of some forest fuels of the southern United States. USDA Forest Service Res. Note, SE-120, 6 pp. Southeastern For. Exp. Sta., Asheville, N.C.

Hughes, R. H., 1951. Observations of cane (*Arundinaria*) flowers, seed, and seedlings in the North Carolina coastal plain. Bull. Torrey Bot. Club, 78:113-121.

Hughes, R. H., 1964. Some observations on germination of gallberry seed. USDA Forest Service Res. Note, SE-17, 3 pp. Southeastern For. Exp. Sta., Asheville, N.C.

Hughes, R. H., 1966. Fire ecology of canebrakes. Tall Timbers Fire Ecology Conference, Tallahassee, Fla., 5:149-157.

Kologiski, R. L., 1977. The phytosociology of the Green Swamp, North Carolina. North Carolina Agric. Exp. Sta. Tech. Bull. no. 250, 101 pp.

Komarek, E. V., Sr., 1974. Effects of fire on temperate forests and related ecosystems: Southeastern United States, p. 251-277. In: T. T. Kozlowski and C. E. Ahlgren, eds., Fire and ecosystems. Academic Press, New York, N.Y.

Lane, D. M., 1980. Ecology of the coastal plain *Sphagnum* of North Carolina. Veroff. Geobot. Inst. ETH, Stiffung Rubel, Zurich, 68:114-120.

Loveless, A. R., 1961. A nutritional interpretation of sclerophylly based on differences in the chemical composition of sclerophyllous and mesophytic leaves. Ann. Bot., n. s. London, 26:168-184.

Loveless, A. R., 1962. Further evidence to support a nutritional interpretation of sclerophylly. Ann. Bot., n.s. London, 26:551-561.

Marchand, P. J., 1975. Apparent ecotypic differences in the water relations of some northern bog Ericaceae. Rhodora, 77:53-63.

Monk, C. D., 1966. An ecological significance of evergreenness. Ecology, 47:504-505.

Monk, C. D., 1971. Leaf decomposition and loss of ^{45}Ca from deciduous and evergreen trees. Amer. Midland Natur., 86:379-384.

Mooney, H. A. and E. L. Dunn, 1970. Convergent evolution of Mediterranean-climate evergreen sclerophyll shrubs. Evolution, 24:292-303.

Odum, H. T., 1952. The Carolina bays and a Pleistocene weather map. Amer. J. Sci., 250:263-270.

Penfound, W. T., 1952. Southern swamps and marshes. Bot. Rev., 18:413-446.

Plummer, G. L., 1963. Soils of the pitcher plant habitats in the Georgia coastal plain. Ecology, 44:727-734.

Prouty, W. F., 1934. "Meteor craters" of the Carolinas. J. Elisha Mitchell Sci. Soc., 50:48, 59-60.

Radford, A. E., H. E. Ahles, and C. R. Bell, 1968. Manual of the vascular flora of the Carolinas. University of North Carolina Press, Chapel Hill, N.C., 1183 pp.

Schimper, A.F.S., 1898. Pflanzengeographies auf physiologischen Grundlage. Fischer, Jena.

Schlesinger, W. H. and B. F. Chabot, 1977. The use of water and minerals by evergreen and deciduous shrubs in Okefenokee Swamp. Bot. Gaz., 138:490-497.

Shafizadeh, F., P.P.S. Chin and W. F. DeGroot, 1977. Effective heat content of green forest fuels. Forest Sci., 23:81-89.

Shriever, W., 1955. Were the Carolina bays oriented by gyroscopic action? Science, 120:806.

Small, E., 1972a. Ecological significance of four critical elements in plants of raised *Sphagnum* peat bogs. Ecology, 53:498-503.

Small, E., 1972b. Water relations of plants in raised *Sphagnum* peat bogs. Ecology, 53:726-728.

Small, E., 1972c. Photosynthetic rates in relation to nitrogen recycling as an adaptation to nutrient deficiency in peat bog plants. Can. J. Bot., 50:2227-2233.

Vitt, D. H., H. Crum, and J. Snider, 1975. The vertical zonation of *Sphagnum* species in hummock-hollow complexes in northern Michigan. Mich. Bot., 14:190-200.

Watts, W. A., 1979. Late Quaternary vegetation history of White Pond on the inner coastal plain of South Carolina. Quat. Res., 13:187-199.

Wells, B. W., 1928. Plant communities of the coastal plain of North Carolina and their successional relations. Ecology, 9:230-242.

Wells, B. W., 1942. Ecological problems of the southeastern United States coastal plain. Bot. Rev., 8:533-561.

Wells, B. W., 1946. Vegetation of Holly Shelter Wildlife Management Area. North Carolina Dept. Cons. and Develop. Bull. 2, 40 pp.

Wells, B. W. and S. G. Boyce, 1953. Carolina bays: Additional data on their origin, age and history. J. Elisha Mitchell Sci. Soc., 69:119-141.

Wells, B. W. and I. V. Shunk, 1931. The vegetation and habitat factors of the coarser sands of the North Carolina coastal plain: An ecological study. Ecol. Monogr., 1:466-520.

Wells, B. W. and L. A. Whitford, 1976. History of stream head swamp forests, pocosins, and savannas in the Southeast. J. Elisha Mitchell Sci. Soc., 92:148-150.

Wendel, G. W., T. G. Storey, and G. M. Byram, 1962. Forest fuels on organic and associated soils in the coastal plain of North Carolina. USDA Forest Service, Southeastern Exp. Station Paper No. 144, Asheville, N.C.

Whitehead, D., 1972. Developmental and environmental history of the Dismal Swamp. Ecol. Monogr., 42:301-315.

Woodwell, G. M., 1956. Phytosociology of coastal plain wetlands of the Carolinas. Unpublished M. A. Thesis, Duke University, 50 pp.

Woodwell, G. M., 1958. Factors controlling growth of pond pine seedlings in organic soils of the Carolinas. Ecol. Monogr., 28:219-236.

Pocosin Fauna

Henry M. Wilbur

ABSTRACT

Pocosins now serve two important functions in the maintenance of the diversity of species in the coastal plain of the Carolinas. These are the natural habitat of several endemic species which have always been restricted to pocosins. They are also refuges for native species which once ranged widely but are now confined to pocosins because they are among the last habitats to be destroyed by human activity. Very little is known about the life histories and geographic distribution of suspected pocosin endemics. The role of pocosins as refuges for black bear and other game species is clear. Recent developments in the theory of island geography may offer guidelines for the planning of natural areas that could assist in the maintenance of threatened species as other pocosins areas are developed.

Key Words: biogeography, endemics, fauna, *Hyla andersoni*, natural areas

INTRODUCTION

Pocosins have been a natural history curiosity since the first naturalist traveled through the Carolinas. John Lawson in his 1709 book, *A New Voyage to Carolina*, mentioned pocosins (percoarson, perkosan) several times, and they have figured prominently in all succeeding natural history accounts. Most of this attention has been paid by botanists who discovered many endemic plants in the pocosins. Subsequent studies, including some detailed vegetation analyses (Kologiski, 1977; Allen et al., 1979), have resulted in a fairly detailed floristic knowledge of this community type (Wells, 1967). Zoologists have not made faunistic surveys to complement these floristic studies and the study of ecosystem processes has just begun in the last decade.

Unfortunately, this paper cannot review a long history of faunistic studies that parallel our development of knowledge of the floristics of pocosins. Pocosin communities contain many unique species that are adapted to life in this peculiar habitat. These species have evolved in close association with pocosins and the destruction of pocosins certainly will lead to their local extinction. Pocosins are also refuges for species that once ranged over habitats now disrupted by human activities.

ENDEMIC POCOSIN SPECIES

A large number of plants, especially evergreen shrubs of the families *Aquifoliaceae* and *Ericaceae* (the hollies, laurels, fetterbushes, blueberries and huckleberries) are adapted to pocosins. These evergreen shrubs give pocosins their characteristic aspect. The bamboo brier (*Smilax laurifolia*) and other vines that are associated with this dense vegetation make pocosins impenetrable. Fears of canebreak rattlesnakes (*Crotalus horridus atricaudatus*), water moccasins (*Agkistrodon piscivorous*), bears (*Ursus americanus*), and persistent rumors of panthers (*Felis concolor*) further discourage natural history studies of the pocosin fauna.

Surely the plants that are specialized for the exploitation of pocosins are themselves a resource for an assemblage of specialized insects. Two such examples are well known. The large, conspicuous swallowtail (*Papilio palamedes*) feeds as a larva on red bay (*Persea borbonia*), a plant which is also attacked by an aphid that makes a characteristic gall on the leaf margins. The second example is the butterfly, Hessel's Hairstreak (*Mitoura hesseli*), a species of "special concern" to conservationists (Cooper et al., 1977) because its larval food plant, Atlantic white cedar (*Chamaecyparis thyoides*), has suffered a drastic reduction in range due to overcutting and habitat destruction. Even short term studies of pocosin insects are sure to uncover unknown associations between insects and endemic pocosin plants.

To my knowledge only one extant vertebrate can be called a pocosin endemic, the pine barrens treefrog (*Hyla andersoni*); and this declaration stretches the definition of pocosin. *Hyla andersoni* is always associated with pocosin vegetation (e.g., *Magnolia*, *Vaccinium*, *Gaylussacia*), but it is not known to occur in the large flat shrub bogs of the outer coastal plain. Its range in the Carolinas is centered in the sandhills region where the shrubs associated with the term pocosin (see Christensen, this volume) grow along seepage areas and the edges of small branches in Richmond, Moore, Lee, Harnett, Johnston, Wayne, Lenoir, Jones, Onslow, Pender, Bladen, Robeson, Scotland, Hoke, Cumberland and Sampson counties, North Carolina, and into adjacent counties in South Carolina (Martof et al., 1980). *Hyla andersoni* also occurs in the pine barrens of southern New Jersey and in a small area in Okaloosa and Walton counties in the Florida panhandle.

Because of its rarity and spotty distribution, *Hyla andersoni* has been considered as threatened with extinction throughout its range. Those interested in management or development of pocosins within the potential range of this species should be aware of its threatened status and its habitat requirements.

Only the broad outline of the biology of this species is known from one study in New Jersey (Noble and Noble, 1923) and another in Florida (Means and Longden, 1976). In the course of my community studies of amphibians in

Scotland and Richmond counties, North Carolina, I have observed a number of breeding aggregrations and I have collected eggs and tadpoles of *Hyla andersoni*. My observations are in substantial agreement with the general statement of habitat requirements made by Means and Longden. The essential requirement appears to be shrub bog vegetation close to a suitable breeding site. Eggs and tadpoles have been collected only from clear, highly acidic water with rich growths of *Sphagnum*. Breeding sites are usually small pools in seepages on hillsides or in roadside ditches.

The current fragmentation of the species range may have occurred during a warm, dry period that followed the Wisconsin glaciation. The northward expansion of its range into New Jersey is almost certainly a post-Wisconsin event. Populations of *Hyla andersoni* should be looked for throughout the southeastern coastal plain wherever suitable habitat is known. Special care should be taken to avoid confusion with *Hyla cinerea*, a related species with a similar call.

The spotted turtle, *Clemmys guttata*, is widespread in the Northeast and upper Midwest (Conant, 1975), but in North Carolina it is virtually restricted to the coastal plain where it is rarely found far from white cedar bogs (personal observation). This is an example of a species which specializes on pocosins in North Carolina but has a broader ecological distribution in other parts of its range.

Pocosins may also play a somewhat cryptic role as important secondary habitats of species endemic to the pine savannahs or sand ridges adjacent to pocosins. For example, the endangered eastern diamondback rattlesnake (*Crotalus adamanteus*) is endemic to long-leaf pine wiregrass flatwoods, but its principal food, rabbits, may depend on pocosins for food and cover in North Carolina. I do not know of links with pocosins of two other pine flatwoods endemics: Backman's sparrow (*Aimnophila aestivatis*) and the red cockaded woodpecker (*Dendrocopos borealis*).

Pocosin endemics are important because as long as a politically potent segment of the American public maintains that government has the responsibility to protect species threatened with extinction, there will be a need to study the habitat requirements and population biology of species specialized for unique habitats. *Hyla andersoni* and other rare species may well become the focus of tension between habitat conservers and habitat disturbers. Vertebrate biologists in the Carolinas soon will be asked questions about these species that we cannot answer.

POCOSINS AS REFUGES

The second point that I wish to stress is that in addition to being the only habitat of specialized species of plants and animals, pocosins are now the refuge habitat of once more widely distributed species. The continuing development of well-drained soil types for use by agriculture, silviculture, and real estate development has meant that pocosins, as a difficult-to-exploit habitat, have become increasingly different from surrounding areas. Once widespread species have sought cover or have been confined to these natural wetlands (see Richardson et al., this volume, for pocosin development practices).

The importance of pocosins to fish and game animals is the subject of T. D. Monshein's contribution in this volume. I hope to consider a somewhat more abstract result of this history of progressive restriction of species ranges from continuous distributions to fragmentation into isolated pockets of pocosins.

Pocosin endemics may be the focus of emotional debate and the legal justification for preserving pocosins as natural areas; however, the overall importance of pocosins may be as nature refuges rather than as nature preserves. That is, species such as whitetailed deer and black bear, which once roamed freely throughout the coastal plain, are now concentrated in pocosins, not because pocosins are necessarily the best habitat, but because they tend to be the last area cleared for human land use.

The result of this refuge effect is that the once continuous geographic range of species has been fragmented into a mosaic of refuges with various degrees of isolation from one another. Figure 2 (Richardson et al., this volume) illustrates this point. In North Carolina, species that once had as their range a complex of habitats, each with its own costs and benefits with respect to food and cover, now see their range as an archipelago of relatively safe islands of pocosin in a sea of hostile, human-dominated habitats. The truth of this extreme view needs to be tested. Biologists now have the biochemical and genetic tools to determine the extent of fragmentation of the gene pools of native species. We can, without great difficulty, estimate the degree of genetic difference between populations inhabiting neighboring pocosin islands.

The amount of isolation will depend on the animal studied. The pocosins are closely enough packed that birds are probably not inhibited from flying among patches in search of endemic holly plants, blueberries and other shrubs that produce animal dispersed seeds encased in nutritious fruits. Some large mammals such as deer use the pocosin islands as cover and move into more open habitats to forage. Other large mammals such as bobcat and bear are probably less inclined to move between patches. Some endemic insects probably rarely move from patch to patch.

This fragmentation can have important demographic and genetic effects. Different patches can support isolated populations which may grow or decline independently of populations in other patches. This is important for both management and conservation decisions. If patches do have dynamically independent populations with a low level of migration, then the populations may be considered independent evolutionary units. If the populations are small, say tens rather than hundreds of individuals, and migration is low, less than one individual per generation, then the population will be susceptible to the process of genetic drift, in which genetic variability is reduced as chance effects eliminate rare genes. This inbreeding reduces the capacity of the population to respond to changes in the environment. Loss of genetic flexibility can be a road to eventual extinction (e.g., Dobzhansky et al., 1977; Futuyma, 1979).

A more important process is that of genetic differentiation among isolated populations. If migration is low between populations, then evolutionary change can proceed independently as each population adapts to its specific environment (e.g., Ehrlich and Raven, 1969). What was once a genetically continuous population is now fragmented into an ensemble of genetically independent populations, a population of populations, a metapopulation. This metapopulation has greater genetic variability than the original population. Such a long-term process does not affect the fauna on a ten-year time scale, but the elimination of every patch accelerates these effects. The process will be obvious on a hundred-year time scale. We need to know more about this process. It is being studied intensively by theoretical population geneticists and some experimentalists, but we still know very little about the genetic structure of natural populations.

PLANNING POCOSINS NATURAL AREAS

The most important point that a theoretical ecologist may have for the land use planner may be in the area of guidelines for planning natural areas. In the last decade there has been an attempt by ecologists to evolve a new field called applied biogeography in which island or patch size, island topography, and position with respect to other islands are related to the number of species that the island can support as an equilibrium community. Any island has some characteristic rate of arrival of new species and some rate of random extinction of established species. These two opposing forces can balance one another to yield an equilibrium number of species which will be changing in taxonomic composition while remaining relatively constant in magnitude.

The two most important determinants of the number of equilibrium species are the island and its distance from the nearest source of colonists. The species to area relationship is well known (e.g., MacArthur and Wilson, 1967):

$$\log S = a + Z \log A$$

where A is area, S is the number of species and a and Z are fitted constants. The constant Z varies with the group of animals being studied and the distance of the island from the nearest source of colonists. Common sense says that larger islands close to mainland should have more species than small remote islands, but with some background information, island biogeography should be able to estimate how many more. That is, we should be able to make economic decisions about how many more species we should expect per hundred thousand dollars invested in additional land acquisition to enlarge an existing refuge. Typically, Z lies between 0.2 and 0.4. Therefore, for a tenfold increase in the size of an area, we can expect roughly a doubling of the number of species it will support.

This basic theory has been elaborated in several directions, and it has been subjected to several experimental and comparative tests (MacArthur, 1972; MacArthur and Wilson, 1967; Wilson and Willis, 1975), but it has been strongly criticized by Gilbert (1980). Several guidelines that have emerged from this work should be considered in the creation and management of natural areas.

1. Individual preserves should be as large as possible. The stochastic extinction of species becomes less likely if population sizes are large and if the population is divided into several subpopulations. Large species, especially carnivores, have large home ranges and must be supported by large prey populations. Specialized species may require a large area in which to seek their peculiar resource.
2. Clusters of preserves will support more species than widely spaced patches of equal area. Extinction has a random component independent of habitat quality. It is therefore possible to set up a cluster of preserves in which reciprocal intercolonization among patches maintains global species diversity even though local extinction is an expected occurrence. The cluster effect can be enhanced by corridors of suitable habitat that permit safe passage of colonists from one patch to another. In the coastal plain, river swamps and creek bottoms form the natural corridors between patches of pocosin.
3. Peninsular faunas tend to behave as island faunas; therefore regular shapes with a high area to perimeter ratio will support more species than a patch of equal area but irregular outline.

Maintenance of high biological diversity should be the primary goal of natural areas. The protection of conspicuous, endangered species may be a politically and aesthetically attractive rationale for habitat preservation, but we must not get hung up on single species. As the population biology of threatened and endangered species is studied, at least equal effort should be made to understand the community ecology and ecosystem processes of threatened and endangered habitats.

I searched *Ecology*, *Ecological Monographs*, *The American Midland Naturalist*, and *The Journal of the Elisha Mitchell Scientific Society* looking for papers on the community ecology and population biology of pocosin animals. My conclusion is that the study of nongame species is an open area for research even at the most descriptive level. The filling of this void must begin before we can make intelligent recommendations to land use planners and conservationists.

LITERATURE CITED

Allen, C., M. Corcoran, L. McDade, J. Travis, and D. Wheeler, 1979. An ecological survey of selected inland Dare County sites, with evaluation for conservation potential. Unpublished report to North Carolina Natural Heritage Program, 53 pp.

Conant, R., 1975. A Field Guide to Reptiles and Amphibians of Eastern and Central North America. Houghton Mifflin, Boston, 429 pp.

Cooper, J. E., S. S. Robinson, and J. B. Funderburg, eds., 1977. Endangered and threatened plants and animals of North Carolina. North Carolina State Museum of Natural History, Raleigh, N.C., 444 pp.

Dobzhansky, T., F. J. Ayala, G. L. Stebbins, and J. W. Valentine, 1977. Evolution. Freeman, San Francisco, 572 pp.

Ehrlich, P. R., and P. H. Raven, 1969. Differentiation of populations. Science, 165:1228-1232.

Futuyma, D. J., 1979. Evolutionary biology. Sinauer, Sunderland, Mass., 565 pp.

Gilbert, F. S., 1980. The equilibrium theory of island biogeography: Fact or fiction? J. Biogeography, 7:209-235.

Kologiski, R. L., 1977. The phytosociology of the Green Swamp, North Carolina. N.C. Agricult. Exp. Sta. Tech. Bull. No. 250, 101 pp.

Lawson, J., 1709. In: Lefler, H. T., ed., 1967. A new voyage to Carolina. Univ. North Carolina Press, Chapel Hill.

MacArthur, R. H., 1972. Geographical Ecology. Harper and Row, New York, 269 pp.

______, and E. O. Wilson, 1967. The Theory of Island Biogeography. Princeton Univ. Press, Princeton, N.J., 203 pp.

Martof, B. S., W. M. Palmer, J. R. Bailey, and J. R. Harrison III, 1980. Amphibians and Reptiles of the Carolinas and Virginia. Univ. North Carolina Press, Chapel Hill.

Means, D. B., and C. J. Longden, 1976. Aspects of the biology and zoogeography of the pine barrens treefrog (*Hyla andersoni*) in northern Florida. Herpetologica, 32:117-130.

Noble, G. K., and R. C. Noble, 1923. The Anderson treefrog (*Hyla andersonii* Baird); observations on its habits and life history. Zoologica, 2:416-455.

Wells, B. W., 1967. The natural gardens of North Carolina. Univ. North Carolina Press, Chapel Hill, 458 pp.

Wilson, E. O., and E. O. Willis, 1975. Applied biogeography, pp. 522-534. In: M. L. Cody and J. M. Diamond, eds., Ecology and Evolution of Communities. Belknap, Cambridge, Mass.

Hydrology, Geology, and Soils of Pocosins: A Comparison of Natural and Altered Systems

Charles C. Daniel III

ABSTRACT

Peat accumulation on the lower coastal plain of eastern North Carolina and southeastern Virginia began in drainage lows or other depressions by 8,900 years B.P. (before present). As these peatlands grew they eventually mantled interstream uplands creating the broad elevated topography typical of pocosins. Pocosins, like other wetlands, provide abundant retention stroage and act as storm buffers by attenuating flood peaks. Runoff from unaltered wetlands has little effect on receiving waters because the low peak runoff and diffuse nature of the discharge over a broad margin or shoreline is assimilated without causing rapid fluctuations in water quality. Water budgets and flow-duration curves show that the construction of drainage channels in wetlands without further changes in land use or land cover results in increased peak flows and low flows at the expense of mid-range flows; there is little change in total runoff. However, drainage modifications coupled with a radical change in vegetation, as in conversion of swamp forest to agriculture, can increase total runoff by reducing both interception losses and the residence time that water in the watershed can be returned to the atmosphere by evapotranspiration. In brackish or salty coastal streams, rapid influxes of fresh water from outfall canals can flush out the saline water. Agricultural practices also increase the amount of sediment, nutrients, and dissolved minerals leaving the land. Compared to natural swamp drainage, average concentrations of calcium, magnesium, sulfate, and bicarbonate were four to ten times higher in farm drainage waters on the Albemarle–Pamlico peninsula during 1977 to 1979. Total nitrogen was 50% higher, apparently due to nitrate; there was little or no difference in phosphorus.

Key Words: pocosins, swamps, freshwater wetlands, hydrogeology, hydrologic budget, streamflow, duration curves, water quality, channelization, canals, land reclamation, drainage systems, drainage effects, Albemarle–Pamlico peninsula, Great Dismal

Swamp, East Dismal Swamp, North Carolina, Virginia, coastal plain

INTRODUCTION

Although this paper will focus on pocosins, the "swamp-on-a-hill" is only one of a variety of freshwater wetlands on the lower coastal plain of North Carolina and adjacent coastal states. In this region, the typical freshwater wetlands can be grouped into several categories, including those along the flood plains of streams, in depressions between dunes and beach ridges (ridge and swale topography), in depressions such as Carolina bays, on hillsides and other slopes where the water table intersects the land surface, and those mantling broad upland areas. The pocosins technically belong to the last group.

All of these wetlands are characterized to greater or lesser extent by having similarities of vegetation, varying thicknesses of organic soils, and a high water table much or all of the year. Mcreover, it should be emphasized that these wetlands exist because of the interaction of favorable climatic, geologic, and hydrologic conditions. In order to better understand the hydrogeologic processes that are at work in natural pocosin succession or are later altered by man, some climatic, hydrologic, and geologic information about all these different wetland types will have to be interrelated.

Consequently, this discussion will center on a variety of natural and altered wetlands on the southeastern coastal plain, many of which might loosely be referred to as pocosin-type wetlands. (See Christensen and Richardson et al., this volume, for more specific pocosin definitions.) Information from studies of pocosin-type wetlands of southeastern Virginia is included because they are, in part, contiguous and contemporaneous with similar wetlands on the North Carolina coastal plain. Additionally, much research in Virginia, particularly in the Great Dismal Swamp, provides insight into the origin and development of pocosins in North Carolina.

In order to present a more comprehensive description of pocosin hydrology and hydrologic properties, it also will be necessary to draw information from a number of other sources, particularly from northern Europe and Asia. Research on freshwater wetlands with deep organic soils—peatlands—has been limited in North America, certainly not on the scale of research in northern Europe and the Soviet Union where the combined area of peatlands represents nearly 77% of the world's total exploitable peatlands (U.S. Department of Energy, 1979).

In North America, pressures to develop wetlands and peat resources have increased in conjunction with the rapid growth in population since World War II. The demand at first was for timber production, then for agricultural use, and most recently for fuel production. At the same time, an increased environmental awareness has raised concerns about the impacts of altering wetlands as their importance becomes known and it is realized that these are not useless lands as previously thought. This increased interest is particularly noticeable in North Carolina where so-called super farms

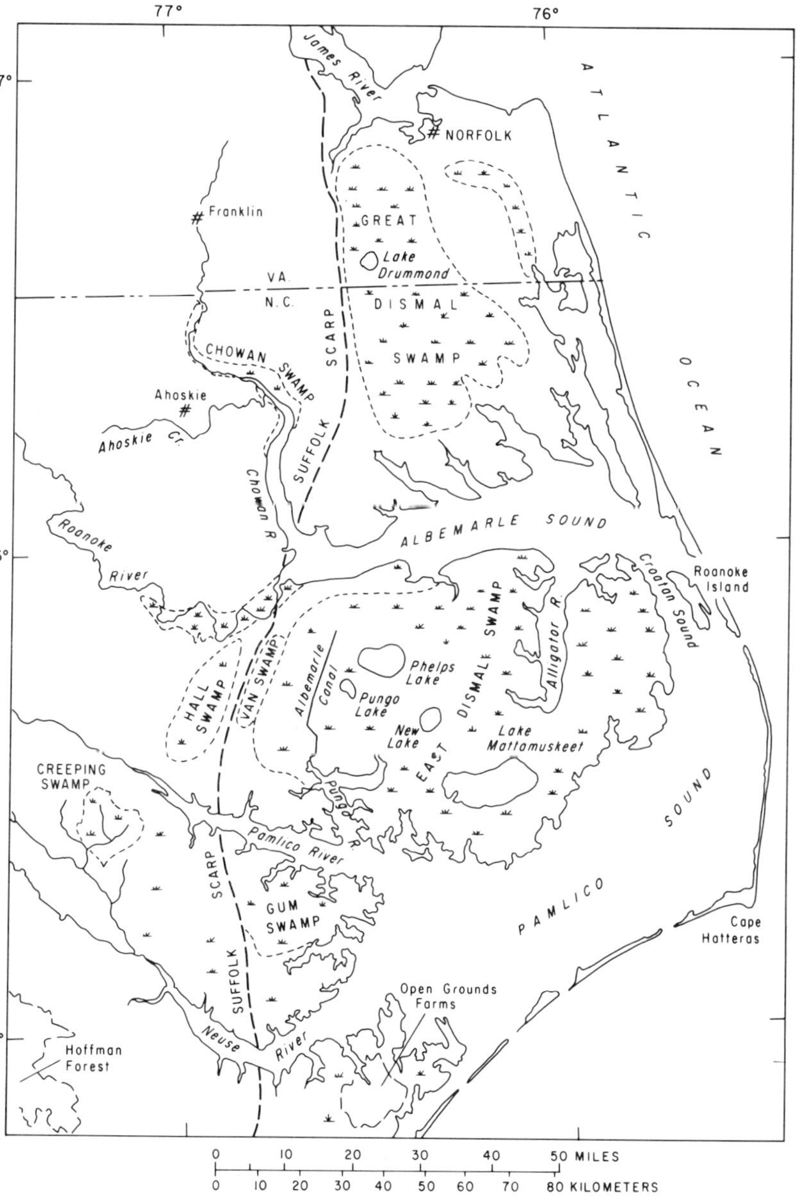

FIGURE 1. *Regional setting of coastal waters and wetlands of northeastern North Carolina and southeastern Virginia.*

(Carter, 1975) have been developing large areas for agricultural use. Out of this concern comes a necessity for a better understanding of the role that wetlands play in the environment as storm buffers to attenuate flood peaks, as filters to trap sediment and remove other constituents from water, as wildlife habitat, as nursery areas for marine organisms along the coastal fringe, as an influence on groundwater and surface water supplies, and as a special environment that supports a number of unique plants and animals.

Figure 1 presents the regional setting of coastal waters and wetlands of northeastern North Carolina and southeastern Virginia and shows specific areas to be discussed in this paper. Among the more important are the Ahoskie Creek and Creeping Swamp basins, the Great Dismal Swamp, and the Albemarle–Pamlico peninsula which includes the East Dismal Swamp and Van Swamp.

Items of particular interest for discussion include the origin and natural development of pocosins, their water budgets, characteristics of runoff rates, water table levels and fluctuations, and the hydrologic properties of soils beneath pocosins. Water quality data for undeveloped areas are also presented. This information is compared with data from pocosin areas that have been cleared and drained for agricultural use or channelized to improve surface runoff. This control basin technique provides a means for determining the hydrologic changes that take place as well as evaluating the magnitude of these changes.

Data Collection on the Albemarle–Pamlico Peninsula

Because of concerns about the impacts of large-scale land clearing and drainage on the hydrology of freshwater wetlands, including peatlands, and the surrounding coastal waters of the Albemarle–Pamlico peninsula, the United States Geological Survey, in cooperation with the North Carolina Department of Natural and Economic Resources, began a study of the region in 1974. The rapid pace of development at that time and projected plans for future development led Heath (1975) to describe the regional hydrology and make a preliminary evaluation of the impact of agricultural developments.

In order to quantify and evaluate in detail the changes actually taking place on the peninsula, three watersheds were identified and instrumented beginning in 1976. These three watersheds, Van Swamp, Albemarle Canal, and the Pungo Refuge, shown in Figure 2, were chosen because they are representative of the broad range of soil types, vegetation, and stages of development found on the peninsula. The data collection program included construction and instrumentation of gauging stations to measure runoff and monitor water temperature and specific conductance. A monthly sampling program was initiated to collect water samples for determination of concentrations of major and minor inorganic constituents, nutrients, sediment, and

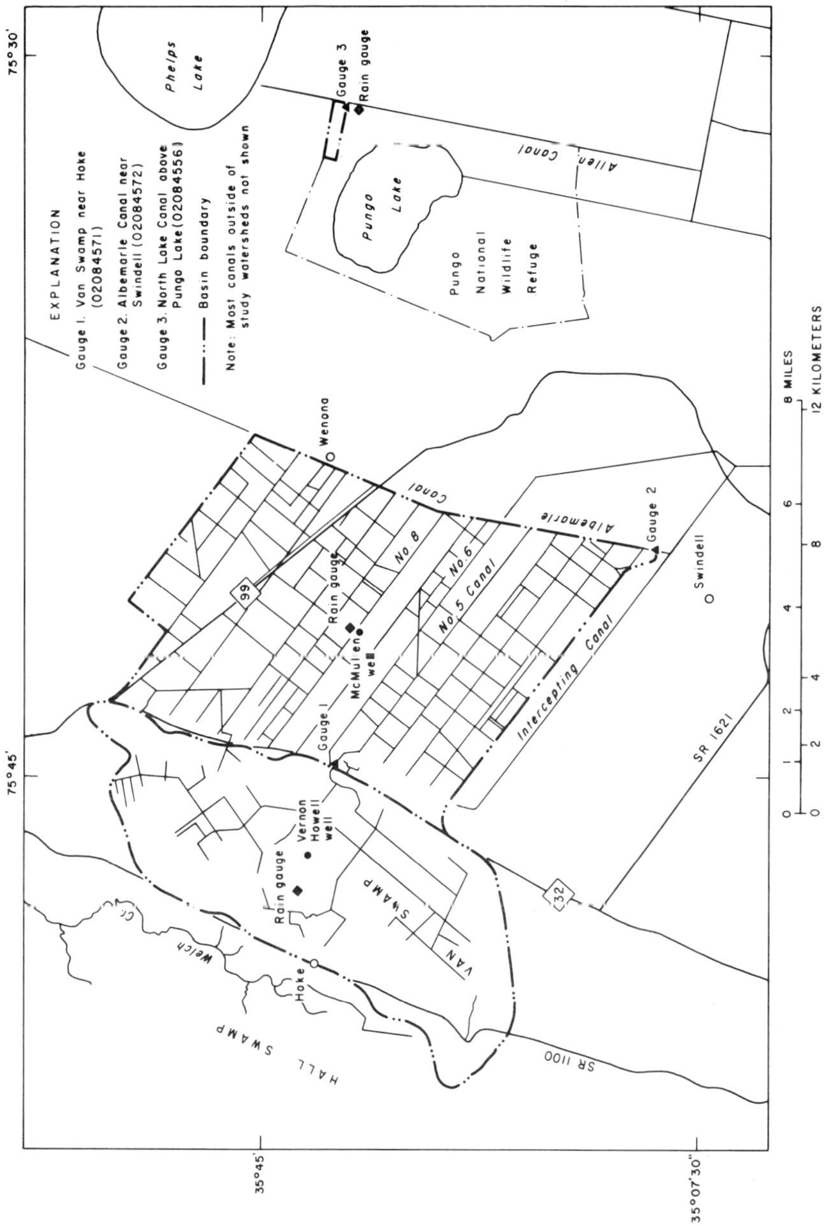

FIGURE 2. *Location of three watersheds under investigation on the Albemarle–Pamlico peninsula, 1976 to 1979 (drainage after Daniel, 1978).*

organic components and to make measurements of biological and physical characteristics. Once or twice a year, samples were collected for determination of herbicides and pesticides. Rain gauges and wells were also constructed in each of the three watersheds, as near the geographic center of the watersheds as possible (Figure 2). In the small watershed northeast of Pungo Lake, numerous wells were installed to monitor in detail the behavior of groundwater levels in both the deep organic soil and underlying mineral soil of that watershed.

Van Swamp, which drains 23 sq mi (60 km^2), remains primarily a forested wetland although some timbering and agricultural development is taking place along the higher ground on the eastern and western borders. A few dirt roads and canals have been built into Van Swamp by forestry interests to provide access and fire control. Van Swamp lies in an elongated topographic flat between a low sand ridge to the east and a scarp to the west that rises to an altitude of 50 ft (15.2 m). Hall Swamp lies on the broad upland west of the scarp. The Vernon Howell well, near the center of the densely forested part of Van Swamp, is more than one-half mile north of the nearest large canal. The land surface at the site is covered by forest litter and the upper 2 ft of soil is sandy with a humate-rich zone at the top. Beneath the soil zone the well penetrates 13 ft (4.0 m) of silt, silty sand, and grey clay with scattered bits of shell.

Albemarle Canal, part of the extensive artificial drainage system that has been created on the Albemarle–Pamlico peninsula, was mapped by the author based on photography taken during 1974 to 1976 (Daniel, 1978). It is one of several major drainage canals that ultimately empty into the Pungo River. The flow in Albemarle Canal includes the discharge from Van Swamp which lies 6 mi (9.6 km) to the west and drains through two canals, known as Number 5 and Number 6, to Albemarle Canal. The 45 sq mi (117 km^2) of land lying between Albemarle Canal and Van Swamp is highly developed agricultural land. Although the gauging station on Albemarle Canal, near Swindell, measures runoff from 68 sq mi (176 km^2), it is estimated that the total drainage area at the mouth of the canal is twice as large, and most of this additional drainage area is agricultural land. Only a few forested remnants of the East Dismal Swamp remain, nearly all having been timbered and ditched between 1956 and 1973 (Heath, 1975, figures 4 and 5).

The McMullen Farm well is located at the edge of a field near the center of the highly developed and well-drained farmland that lies between Van Swamp and Albemarle Canal. The well is 320 ft (98 m) southwest of a large drainage ditch, Number 8 canal, that empties into Albemarle Canal 3 mi to the southeast. The soil and underlying sediment to a depth of 14 ft (4.3 m) is composed of silt and clay. At 15 ft (4.6 m) the well bottoms in a layer of shells and shell hash. Any organic soil or humate that may have been present at this site prior to land clearing has since been removed by oxidation. Both the Vernon Howell and McMullen Farm wells were installed to monitor changes in the water table.

The small watershed located between Pungo Lake and Phelps Lake is in the northeast corner of the Pungo Wildlife Refuge and drains 0.29 sq mi (0.75 km^2) of pocosin-type wetland. This watershed was once part of a much more extensive area of wetland extending east-west along the axis of the peninsula; however, much of this land is now extensively drained by a system of canals and drainage ditches (Daniel, 1978). Even though the Pungo study area is itself bordered by canals, the deep organic soil and vegetation, consisting of pond pine, evergreen bay and shrubs, within the watershed is relatively undisturbed.

Runoff from the Pungo watershed is isolated from the surrounding drainage by earthen dams and low banks of spoil taken from the canals. Canals on the north and east are outside the spoil banks, and canals on the west and south are inside the spoil banks. Drainage and runoff within the watershed moves to the west and south where it is routed eastward through North Lake Canal. Discharge from North Lake Canal is measured at a gauge on the southwest corner of the watershed before it discharges into Allen Canal. The two canals carrying runoff from this watershed are not maintained and have been allowed to become partially filled with sediment and aquatic vegetation.

Within the Pungo Refuge study site as much as 12 ft (3.7 m) of woody peat and muck overlie a mineral soil of sand, silt, and clay. Because of the low permeability of the peat, the ground water within the mineral soil is confined and under artesian pressure. Consequently, a number of wells have been installed to monitor changes in both the water table, which is in the peat, and the potentiometric surface of the underlying artesian system. The stratigraphy of the Pungo Refuge study site, which is much more complicated than described here, will be discussed in some detail in the next section because it provides insight into the formation and development of peatlands on the lower coastal plain.

GROWTH AND DEVELOPMENT OF FRESHWATER PEATLANDS ON THE SOUTHEAST ATLANTIC COASTAL PLAIN

Landscape Development

Any discussion of present day pocosins and related freshwater wetlands on the Atlantic coastal plain must begin with a brief description of the geologic processes that have shaped the coastal plain surface over the last million years of the earth's history. During this time, sea level has ranged from as much as 200 ft (61 m) above to several hundred feet below its present level. These fluctuations are attributed to the expansion and contraction of the polar ice caps. This process has not been a continuous one, for the broad surface of the coastal plain was shaped by these past seas into a sequence of complex terraces (Oaks, 1965) offset by scarps and sand ridges (Daniels et al., 1972). These latter features apparently indicate temporary pauses in the change of sea level and thus mark former marine shorelines.

When the last of several great expansions of polar ice began about 75,000 years ago, sea level was 45 to 50 ft (13.7 to 15.2 m) higher than at present (Oaks and Coch, 1973) and the shoreline was along a feature now referred to as the Suffolk Scarp (Figure 1). For several thousands of years, sea level slowly fell. Then about 35,000 years ago, sea level fell below its present level as the expansion of polar ice began to accelerate. During the Wisconsin Ice Age, approximately 15,000 years ago, the sea level was as much as 400 ft (122 m) below its present level.

As sea level declined, large areas of the continental shelf were exposed as dry land and streams crossing the coastal plain were rejuvenated. Stream velocities increased and erosion extended stream valleys onto the continental shelf. As part of this rejuvenation, complex drainage patterns were carved into the coastal plain surface. In some cases, such as the buried channels found by Riggs and O'Connor (1974, Figure 11) beneath Croatan Sound and Roanoke Island, deposition of more recent inorganic sediments and reworking by coastal processes has removed any surficial topographic evidence of these features. In others the accumulation of fine-grained organic sediments and peat deposits has been sufficient to obscure the presence of this ancient drainage system.

By about 14,000 years ago the ice had retreated from central Wisconsin and by about 10,000 years ago Michigan's Upper Peninsula and the Great Lakes had been exposed. For the last several thousand years sea level has been rising, and modern records of sea level over the last fifty years (Milliman and Emery, 1968) indicate that the ocean is still rising at a rate of more than a foot a century.

The rising sea level has brought about a major change in the hydrologic regime of the coastal plain. Streams that had been eroding and deepening their channels became drowned by rising ocean water. Stream velocities declined, channels became clogged with sediments that could no longer be carried in suspension, and aquatic vegetation began to grow and accumulate along these spreading estuaries and their sluggish tributaries. As the climate has become milder since the end of the Wisconsin Ice Age, there has also been a gradual, apparently "unidirectional" (Whitehead, 1972), vegetational change from boreal spruce/pine forests during the period of maximum ice advance to hardwood dominated forests containing many of the species now found in northeastern North Carolina and southeastern Virginia by the early post-glacial period. Although a precise climatic reconstruction is not possible, the climate of this region during the peak of glaciation was probably comparable to present-day northern New England.

In the southeastern United States, forested swamps that include extensive peatlands are common. Many border rivers like the Chowan and lower Roanoke whereas others, like the Dismal Swamp, mantle more extensive upland areas of low relief. On some of the broad uplands, the swamp forests have given way to expanses of cane, grasses, sedges, evergreen bay, pond pine, and other vegetation typical of a savannah environment. Even though there is a tendency toward vegetational succession as a peatland grows, there usually is considerable floral diversity within any given peatland at any given time in its history. This change in vegetation, as well as diversity of vegetation, is due in part to changes in the quantity and quality of water entering the peatland.

Growth of Peatlands on the Coastal Plain

Any comparison between the peatlands that now mantle the broad interstream uplands and other peatlands on the coastal plain is perhaps best viewed in the context that these wetlands represent different successional stages in a process of wetland development. Not only are there peatlands on the interstream divides, there are large areas of peatland in floodplains and other drainage lows. There are also peatlands in the topographic lows, called swales, between relic beach and dune ridges; and large areas of peatland are found within the unique elliptical depressions called Carolina bays (Prouty, 1952).

Perhaps the most significant influence on peatland formation and peatland evolution in the lower coastal plain has been the postglacial rise in sea level and associated climatic changes. Not only did the rise in sea level inundate stream valleys, it also reduced the water table gradients that had existed between the interstream uplands and the rapidly flowing streams of an earlier time. The decrease in gradient and the accompanying rise in the water table would have been most pronounced near depressions or adjacent to drainage lows and least pronounced under the interstream uplands. But even in the upland areas, an increase in precipitation and sluggish drainage would raise water tables and cause the bottoms of depressions to become damper for longer periods of the year, perhaps sufficient to support a bog or formation of a lake. As water tables rose, the soil would become damper and vegetation changes would begin to take place with species adapted to drier conditions giving way to more water tolerant species.

Thus it is not too surprising that several peatland studies (Whitehead, 1965, 1972; Oaks and Coch, 1973) have found that the earliest pollen and plant remains occur in topographic lows in the pre-peat surface. Often the lowest part of this organic accumulation is an organic mud or gel, suggesting deposition in open water. The earliest peats also tend to be fine grained, with little evidence of woody materials, and the pollen residues contain a high proportion of pollen from aquatic vegetation. This suggests that the rise in the water table along with the decrease in stream velocity in coastal valleys favored temporary ponding.

Geology and Soils

On the basis of exploratory coring, Oaks and Coch (1973) clearly demonstrated that the surface on which the Great Dismal Swamp developed possesses a subtle but well-developed dendritic drainage pattern with shallow, branching valleys and corresponding interstream drainage divides or "highs." The presence of this pre-peat drainage had been suspected much earlier by Shaler (1890) who, after probing part of the Dismal Swamp peat with sharpened poles, proposed that "there may be a number of stream valleys so encumbered by accumulation of vegetable matter that they are no longer evident to the eye." In contrast to the pre-peat surface, the present surface of the swamp is relatively flat and undissected by stream valleys. North of Lake Drummond the swamp is 10 to 11 mi (16.1 to 17.7 km) wide, east to west, and its surface slopes gently eastward at 1 ft per mile from an altitude of 25 ft (7.6 m) at the toe of the Suffolk Scarp to 15 ft (4.6 m) at the eastern limit of the peat soil.

The available radiocarbon dates indicate the earliest organic sediments in the Great Dismal Swamp were formed about 8,900 $\pm$160 years ago (Oaks and Coch, 1973). However, according to Harrison et al. (1965), both younger and older freshwater peats were encountered in borings for the Chesapeake Bay Bridge Tunnel near the present mouth of Chesapeake Bay at depths between 56 and 95 ft (17.1 and 29.0 m) below present sea level. The earliest of these peats, recovered from a depth of 89 ft (27.1 m), has been dated at 15,280 $\pm$200 years B.P. and has a full-glacial pollen profile containing abundant spruce pollen. Two other samples taken at approximately minus 82 ft (25.0 m) were dated at 10,340 $\pm$130 years B.P. and 11,590 $\pm$150 years B.P. and contained a late-glacial pine/spruce pollen profile that is comparable to the pollen profile of the inorganic sediments immediately beneath the deepest Dismal Swamp peat. Another sample from minus 70 ft (21.3 m) was dated at 8,135 $\pm$160 years B.P. and contained an oak/hickory pollen assemblage generally associated with the fine grained fibrous peat that occurs in the lower half of the thicker Dismal Swamp profiles between the organic clays below and the forest peat above.

Thus the radiocarbon dates from the Dismal Swamp profiles and the Chesapeake Bay peats place the deposition of the earliest organic clays and part of the overlying fibrous peat between 10,340 $\pm$130 and 8,135 $\pm$160 years B.P. while sea level was still 70 ft (21.3 m), or more, below present mean sea level. Even though sea level was still many feet below the level of the Dismal Swamp drainage system, the abundance of pollen from aquatic vegetation, plus grasses and sedges in the pollen profile, suggests the presence of standing water and the ponding of water in low areas.

Once peat began to be formed in the drainage lows on the east side of the swamp, it continued to increase in depth and area by spreading inland up the valleys and laterally mantling the interstream divides (Whitehead, 1972). Thus a progressive change took place from a regional mineral soil to a peat soil as hardwood forests on the stream divides were replaced by a cypress/gum swamp. As through-flowing drainage channels in the swamp became filled with peat, the discharge of streams from the west was forced to spread out over the swamp surface. During the wet winter and spring months, standing water still accumulates along the west side of the swamp below the Suffolk Scarp before slowly discharging eastward across the swamp surface as sheet flow. Today, the presence of drainage canals has worked to reduce the period that standing water remains on the swamp floor (Carter et al., 1977).

The thickest accumulation of organic sediment found by Whitehead (1972) was 11.5 ft (3.50 m) at a point 2.5 mi (4.0 km) north of Lake Drummond. Oaks and Coch (1973) report a somewhat thicker section (12.8 ft, 3.90 m) from the southern part of the swamp in North Carolina. Where the organic section is thickest over the old drainage lows, there is a general progression from inorganic sediments, commonly a white, fine to medium sand, presumably of fluvial origin, overlain by a soft, light blue clay, to organic clays (gel-mud), fine-grained clayey peats, and eventually forest peat. A tangled layer of logs, stumps and roots occurs about 3 ft (0.9 m) below the surface through much of the western part of the swamp (Oaks and Coch, 1973).

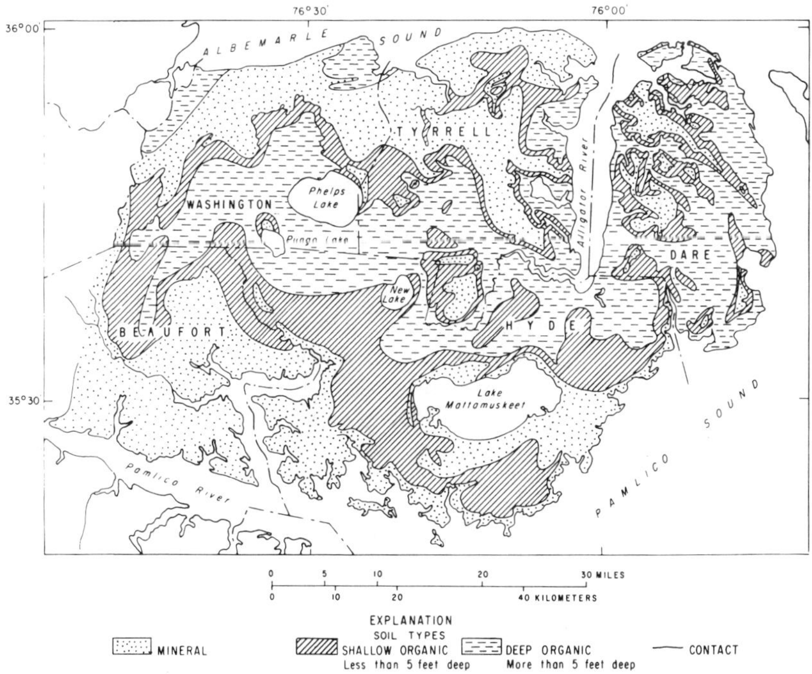

FIGURE 3. *Generalized soils map of the Albemarle–Pamlico peninsula (modified from Heath, 1975).*

The occurrence and developmental history of peat on the Albemarle–Pamlico peninsula has many similarities to the peat in the Great Dismal Swamp. Aided by interpretation of peat cores, one can look at a soils map of the peninsula (Figure 3) and envision the outlines of a branching pre-peat drainage system that flowed from the west end of the peninsula eastward to the southern end of the Alligator River. The axis of this drainage apparently passed between the current positions of Pungo Lake and Phelps Lake. The present land surface in this area, at 15 to 17 ft (4.6 to 5.2 m), is the highest altitude in the central part of the peninsula (Daniel, 1978, Figure 2), whereas the surface levels of both Phelps Lake and Pungo Lake are approximately 10 ft (3.0 m) above sea level. Prior to the recent land development and construction of drainage canals, the natural drainage divide between Albemarle Sound to the north and the Pamlico River to the south passed between these lakes.

Coring of the peat northeast of Pungo Lake by the author has identified a peat-filled channel (Figure 4) whose axis trends generally in a north-south direction and was probably a tributary to the main central stream of the pre-peat drainage. It is interesting to note that the peat filling this channel is among the thickest deposits on the peninsula.

The inorganic sediment immediately beneath the peat is a coarse sand or silty sand that is thickest along the former drainage low (Figure 4C) and is probably of fluvial origin. The thickest section of organic sediment is 12.1 ft (3.69 m) at well 3, however, the thickness of organics at all wells between 7 and 4 (Figure 4B) is about 12 ft (3.7 m). Immediately above the sands at the bottom of the channel is 3.5 ft (1.07 m) of fine-grained fibrous peat and organic ooze (perhaps equivalent to the gel-mud of Whitehead, 1972) that contains few woody remains. Immediately above this is a layer of very fine-grained inorganic grey clay that contains a few interbedded lenses of clean, well-sorted sand. This bed of clay thickens somewhat to the east where it apparently intertongues with brown organic clay and sandy peat, all of which rest unconformably on the pre-peat surface. The extent or character of this clay unit to the west side of the channel is not known, although it may extend to the basal contact with the pre-peat surface. It is possible that this clay was partly derived from the mineral soil west of the former channel.

The presence of the grey clay with interbedded sand lenses is indicative of a quiet open water phase during which parts of the peninsula were sometimes subject to storms that brought in sand or winnowed the sand from the clay by wave action. The deposition of clay may have been initiated by an increase in precipitation, the rise in sea level, or local ponding caused by differential growth and accumulation of peat. Above the grey clay is a sandy peat which grades upward through a coarse fibrous peat into a forest peat. As in the Great Dismal Swamp, an extensive layer of stumps and logs underlies the peat surface to a depth of about 3 ft (0.9 m) (for current soils characteristics see Barnes, this volume).

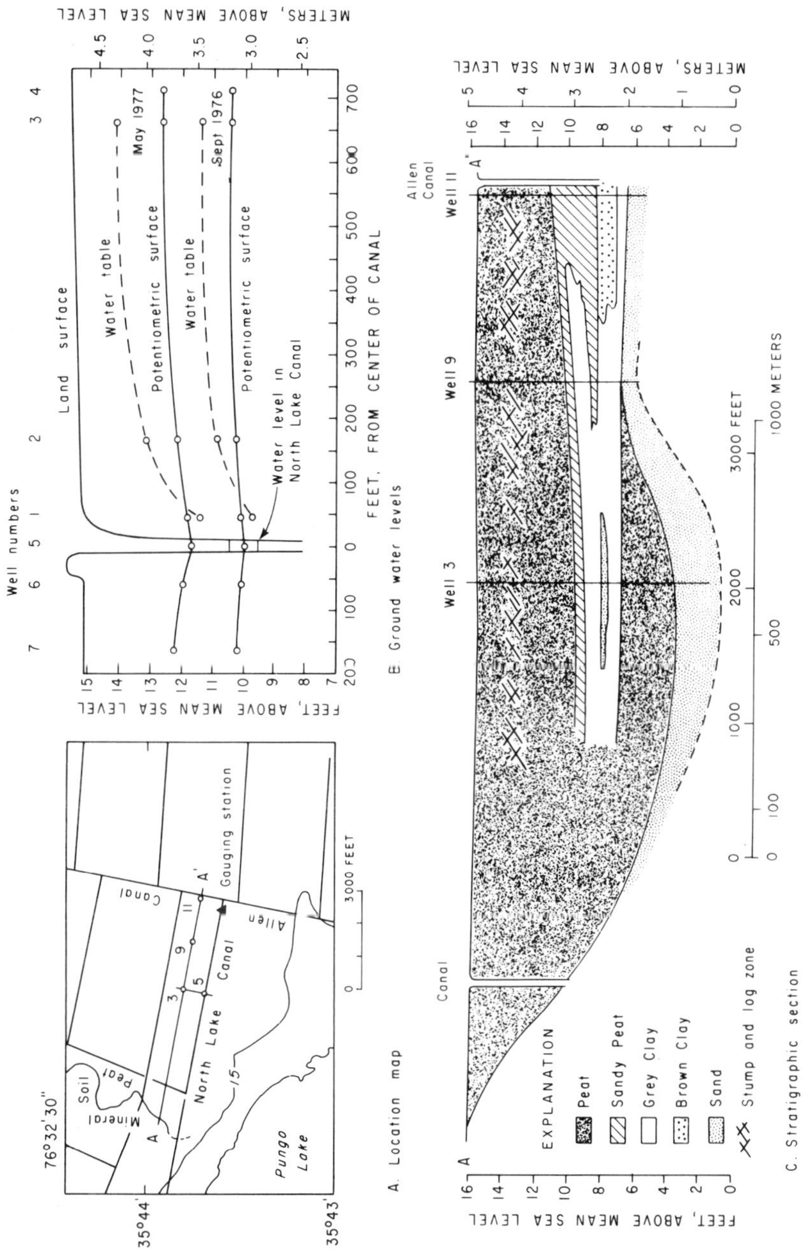

FIGURE 4. *Location map (A), water level profiles (B), and stratigraphic section (C) of the Pungo Refuge study site.*

By the time that the deposition of the upper part of the fibrous peat began to give way to the lower part of the forest peat, the substratum was becoming significantly more peaty and probably dried out during a portion of the year. Radiocarbon dates from the Dismal Swamp show that much of the forest peat in that area developed from 3,500 years ago to the present. The eventual transition to a true swamp forest with accumulation of forest peat, the presence of a distinct stump layer, as well as deterioration of pollen preservation indicates that periodic drying of the peat surface and accelerated oxidation were taking place.

Several factors may have contributed to this change in the regional hydrology: (1) continued accumulation of organic sediment over the surface, (2) changes in the rate of sea level and water table rise, and (3) a decrease in precipitation. The accumulation of organic sediment alone would contribute to this condition, even if the water table continued a slow rise; however, the transition to swamp forest quite likely reflects some interaction of these factors. There is evidence of a distinct slackening in the rise of sea level between 6,000 to 4,000 years ago (Milliman and Emery, 1968). This was probably associated with a general climatic shift to much drier conditions during this time. A general decrease in precipitation is supported by evidence from Volo Bog, Illinois, where McComas et al. (1972) found evidence of much lower water levels in streams and lakes about 6,000 years B.P. There the maximum water table decline, based on radiocarbon dates on organic silts and marls, is placed at $6{,}529 \pm 97$ years B.P. Afterwards precipitation increased and filling of northern lakes and bogs with peat has been nearly continuous to the present.

On the basis of the previous discussion, it appears that several large areas of peatland that now mantle the broad interstream uplands of the coastal plain of northeastern North Carolina and southeastern Virginia are the most recent stage of an evolving wetland morphology that started as swamps and marshes along drainage lows or in other depressions where high water tables and abundant water during much of the year favored the accumulation of plant remains. The evidence also suggests that many peatlands in the lower coastal plain that began in earlier drainage systems have tended to migrate inland keeping pace with rising sea level. Thus, when allowed to remain in an undisturbed state, peatlands will normally accumulate organic debris, change their vegetation, and grow in depth and lateral extent.

HYDROLOGY OF NATURAL AND ALTERED PEATLANDS

Water and Nutrient Availability and Peatland Development

The favorable interaction of water, climate, and landforms is necessary for the formation and development of peatlands. The water may be derived directly from precipitation (rainfall and snow) or indirectly from ground water, streamflow, or overland flow (that part of rainfall or snow melt that travels over the soil surface to the nearest stream or lake). In peatlands where the accumulation of plant remains has created a land surface that is higher than the surrounding landforms, most or all of the water and nutrients will come from precipitation (ombrotrophic), but peatlands in depressions and river flood plains will receive water and nutrients from some combination of these sources (minerotrophic).

Even when an appreciable amount of water is available, there is no guarantee that water alone will lead to the formation of organic soils, thus the importance of climate and landforms. The configuration of the land surface has a major influence on the movement and availability of water. Flat topography contributes to low rates of surface runoff. Closed depressions like the prairie potholes of the upper Mississipi Valley, ice block depressions in the glaciated area in the north-central and northeastern states, or Carolina bays of the southern Atlantic coastal plain, often contain ponds or lakes from which surface outflow is limited. Forested wetlands and bogs surround most of these bodies of water. In many others the inward growth of vegetation and accumulation of plant remains have slowly filled the open water areas. In the majority of Carolina bays there are no ponds, any past ponds having already been filled, or there never were ponds because the accumulation of peat and organic sediment was able to keep up with the rising water table.

Once peat begins to accumulate in a depression or on a hillside, ground water tends to enter the peatland at the uphill edge, because the peat acts as a dam to regional groundwater flow. Where ground water enters at the edge of a peatland, dissolved minerals will be depleted by cation exchange and plant consumption as the water moves farther and farther away from its source. This is usually marked by a gradual change in vegetation community from one that requires a mineralized water (minerotropic) to one that can survive on mineral-poor water (ombrotrophic). The result can be a transition from swamp forest near the source of ground water to scrub land at some distance away from the source. Thus it is not unusual for the vegetation in depression-filling peatlands such as Carolina bays and ice block depressions in glaciated terrain to be concentrically zoned with forested swamp around the outer perimeter grading inward to scrub and other low-growth vegetation. Below bluffs and on hillside slopes, the vegetation zoning may take the form of bands that roughly parallel the physiographic feature.

Some apparent zoning is present in the Dismal Swamp that is related to the Suffolk Scarp (Carter et al., 1977; Shaler, 1890), although timbering, drainage, and fire have subsequently resulted in the encroachment of scrub land into the once extensive swamp gum/cypress forests that covered much of the west side of the swamp below the scarp. On the Albemarle–Pamlico peninsula, extensive swamp forests were also once present on the wetlands east of the Suffolk Scarp. Today only remnants of these former forests remain in Van Swamp and on the northwest corner of the peninsula south of

Plymouth (Daniel, 1978). To the east of these swamp forests where the organic soils are thicker and the vegetation is further removed from the source of nutrients and minerals, the swamp forests give way to pond pine, evergreen shrubs, and sedges.

The availability and seasonal fluctuation of water also will contribute to vegetational diversity on the peatland surface. Slightly elevated topography within the peatland that has periodic drying of the root zone will support vegetation such as pines or pond pine whereas portions of the peatland that are flooded much or all of the year will tend to support other species such as cypress and swamp gum. On the east side of the Dismal Swamp and in the elevated peatlands between Phelps Lake and Pungo Lake, the somewhat shorter hydroperiod and the seasonal fluctuation of the water table, like the reduced availability of nutrients, has contributed to the formation of scrub land (see Christensen, this volume, for information on the vegetational patterns).

Water Movement in Peatlands

The high water content of organic soils common to wetlands is both the product and the cause of several interesting hydrologic phenomena. It is not uncommon for organic soils to have water contents higher than 80% when saturated, indicating a high total porosity. The nature of this porosity and the related ability to transmit water is affected, however, by the degree of decomposition of the organic remains. Eggelsmann (1975) demonstrated that conductivity is also related to the type of organic remains. This relationship shows a rather wide range of conductivity when the peat is in a loose condition and relatively constant conductivity when it is in a denser condition. This indicates that as decomposition becomes more complete, the size of the pore spaces decreases and the water in these pores is not easily drained.

Hydraulic conductivities as great as 120 ft per day (37 m/d) have been reported (Boelter and Verry, 1977) for undecomposed peats. On the other hand, hydraulic conductivities are much smaller in well-decomposed peats. For example, a vertical conductivity of 0.097 ft per day (0.030 m/d) was determined by the Hantush-Jacob method (Lohman, 1972) from a pumping test at the Pungo study site, thus illustrating that as degree of decomposition increases, hydraulic conductivity can decrease by a factor of more than a thousand.

The vertical conductivity determined at the Pungo site represents the average conductivity of the entire 12-ft (3.7 m) thickness of peat; and it is apparent from soil samples and observations of seepage into test holes that the conductivity of the near-surface peat is greater than that of peat several feet below the surface. Test holes were dug in the upper 6 ft (1.8 m) of the peaty soil on several occasions during wet and dry periods of the year. The uppermost part of the soil profile consists of the poorly decomposed remains of shrubs, leaves and roots; but at increasing depth, decomposition is more complete. During winter and spring when the water table is usually close to land surface, at a depth of 1.5 to 2 ft (0.46 to 0.61 m), test holes rapidly fill with water to the water table elevation. On the other hand, holes dug during late summer and fall, when the water table is as much as 4 to 5 ft (1.2 to 1.5 m) below land surface, take several days to fill to the water table elevation. The differences in rates of infiltration illustrate the decrease in conductivity with depth, and thus it is likely that the conductivity of the deeper peat is even less than the average value of 0.097 ft per day (0.030 m/d).

Groundwater and Nutrient Relationships

In growing peatlands, accumulated organic remains tend to isolate the wetland from the influence of the regional groundwater system. Where the accumulation of plant remains is sufficient to form a regionally elevated surface, the water table within the peat will tend to become slightly elevated above the regional groundwater system and isolate itself from the chemical influence of the ground water in the underlying mineral soils. Once the water level within the peat is higher than the water level in the underlying mineral soil, the driving force (head difference) is present to cause downward movement of water through the peat and into the underlying sediments. Although recharge will take place under these conditions, rates of recharge can be very low because of the small hydraulic conductivity of the peat and the usually small difference between the water levels.

Water levels measured at the Pungo Refuge study site northeast of Pungo Lake provide an interesting example of this relationship (Figure 4B) and illustrate the impact of canal construction on groundwater levels. Water levels in wells tapping the sandy mineral soil (Figure 4C) beneath the peat rise well above the contact with the less permeable overlying peat; thus they are accurately called artesian wells, and the level to which the water rises is a potentiometric surface. Water levels in the number 5 well (Figure 4B), which was driven through the bottom of North Lake Canal and into the mineral soil, rise above the water level in the canal. During construction of the number 5 well, a casing segment was driven to within one-half foot (0.15 m) of the canal surface and water was observed to overflow from the well into the canal.

Water levels in water table wells at sites 1, 2 and 3 generally remained 1 to 1.5 ft (0.30 to 0.46 m) above water levels in the deeper artesian wells. During the four years (1976 to 1979) that water levels were measured at the Pungo Refuge, only at the number 1 site did the water table periodically fall below the potentiometric surface. This occurred during dry periods when the combination of drainage and evaporation of soil moisture from the canal bank exceeded the rate of decline of the artesian head due to upward movement of water through the bottom of the canal.

Prior to construction of North Lake Canal and other canals between Pungo Lake and Phelps Lake, it is likely that the relationship of the water table to the potentiometric surface observed in the center of the Pungo study site extended over the entire central part of the peninsula. Consequently, the water table in the peat would have been higher than the level in the underlying mineral soil over the entire area, and the vegetation on the surface would have been isolated from the influence of the underlying mineral soil.

The impact of canal drainage on water levels is evidenced by the symmetrical decline in water levels toward the canal (Figure 4B). Not only does the canal drain the organic layer, the canal is also a line of discharge from the underlying mineral soil. Decline in the water table occurs by a combination of drainage to the canal plus soil moisture evaporation and transpiration from the canal banks. It is interesting to note that the greatest drawdown of water levels occurs close to the canal and this effect does not appear to extend too far from the canal. In the case of the number 2 well site,

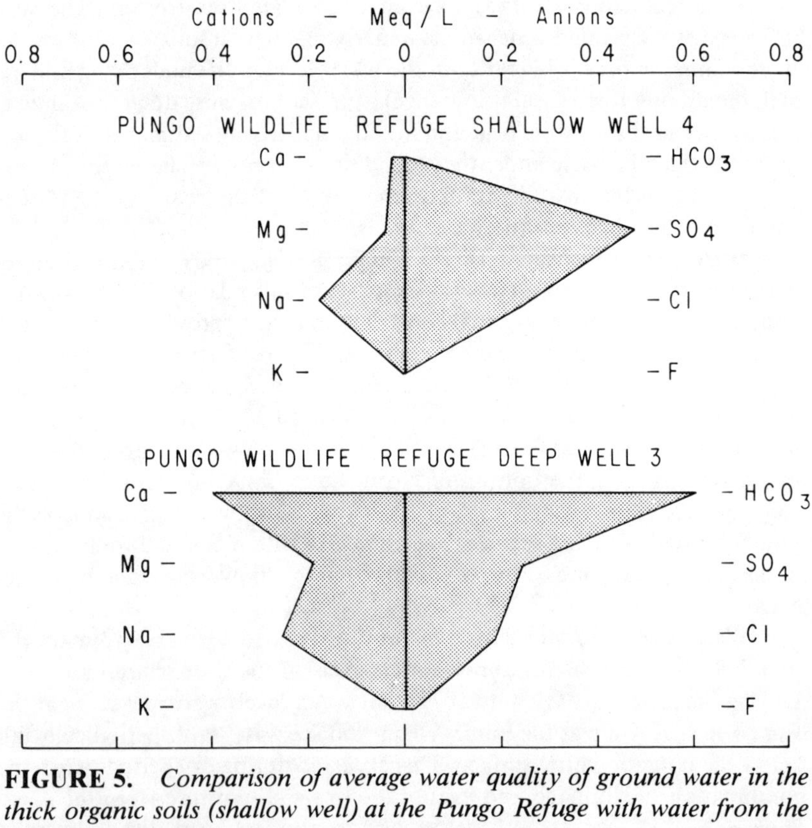

FIGURE 5. *Comparison of average water quality of ground water in the thick organic soils (shallow well) at the Pungo Refuge with water from the underlying mineral soil (deep well), 1977 to 1979 water years (diagram modeled after Stiff, 1951).*

165 ft (50 m) north of North Lake Canal (Figure 4B), the water table was never lower than the potentiometric surface during 1976 to 1979 and the level of the water table was not much lower than at the number 3 site in the center of the drainage block. Obviously, the very low hydraulic conductivity of the peat prevents rapid lateral drainage to the canal and the principal cause of rise and fall of groundwater levels is precipitation and evapotranspiration. With this being the case, the sense of movement for water within the peat is essentially vertical.

The impact of this head relationship on groundwater chemistry in the Pungo Refuge area is shown on Figure 5. The concentrations of the major dissolved cations are much lower in water from the organic soils than in the underlying mineral soils. This is particularly important with respect to calcium which has been linked to the presence or absence of forested peatland (Boelter and Verry, 1977). The presence of calcium is important because it reacts with the carbonic acid (H_2CO_3) in rain to form calcium bicarbonate ($Ca[HCO_3]_2$)and this dissociates in water to form bicarbonate ions (HCO_3^-).

Bicarbonate ions are responsible for most buffering systems in natural waters and sufficient amounts of bicarbonate yield pH values close to neutral. Environments with near neutral pH values contain more of the available plant nutrients. The low concentration of bicarbonate in the shallow groundwater system reflects the low pH and the low buffering capacity of these organic soils. Consequently, once the accumulation of peat had effectively isolated the swamp forest from groundwater and surface-water sources of nutrients and minerals, rainfall became the principal source of these constituents.

Thus when trees in the earlier swamp forest were destroyed by fire, disease, or man's activities, regeneration of these trees was not favored because of the lower availability of nutrients and minerals; and more tolerant vegetation, such as the pond pine/evergreen shrub community generally associated with pocosins and Carolina bays, established itself.

Seasonal Fluctuations of Groundwater Levels

Water table fluctuations are influenced by the hydraulic properties of the soil and underlying strata, the seasonal pattern of evapotranspiration, and fluctuations in the supply of water to the goundwater system. Raised wetlands have a greater amount of water table fluctuation due to seasonal changes in evapotranspiration and the variability of precipitation inputs than do wetlands fed by ground water or associated with streams and bodies of open water.

Water level records from four wells in watersheds on the Albemarle–Pamlico peninsula (Figure 6) exhibit surprisingly similar long-term patterns of water level fluctuation despite differences in soil type, plant cover, and degree of development. Moreover, these watersheds display considerable seasonal variation in the water level hydrographs.

Changes in the potentiometric surface shown by Pungo Deep Well 3, which is screened in the sandy mineral soil beneath the peat, nearly mimic water table changes in the overlying peat as shown by Shallow Well 3. This is attributed to a loading phenomena; that is, changes in the amount of water within the water table aquifer cause pressure changes in the artesian system that are reflected by changes in the potentiometric surface. An interesting example of this effect is seen on recorder charts soon after the beginning of a storm. The onset of precipitation will be followed by an almost immediate rise in the potentiometric surface only to be followed later by a rise in the

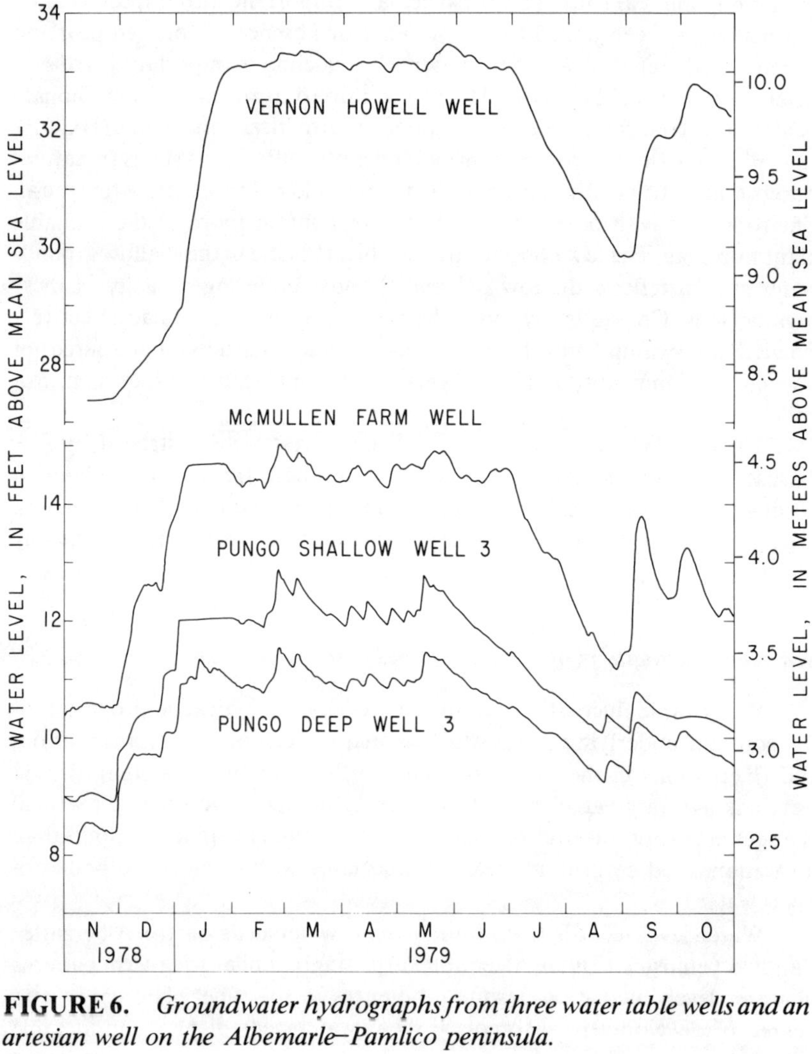

FIGURE 6. *Groundwater hydrographs from three water table wells and an artesian well on the Albemarle–Pamlico peninsula.*

water table. Apparently, the weight of the rain water will cause pressure changes in the artesian system at the same time that the rain is infiltrating the unsaturated zone above the water table. Consequently, the water table will continue to rise after a storm is over, whereas the potentiometric surface will remain relatively constant until both water levels begin to fall under the influence of drainage and evapotranspiration.

The considerable influence of evapotranspiration on water levels can be seen by the fact that water levels remain near land surface during the winter and early spring when evapotranspiration is low and rainfall tends to exceed evapotranspiration. The water levels decline to greater depths during the summer months in response to increased evapotranspiration, at the same time continuing to fluctuate in response to precipitation. In contrast to water levels in these upland swamps (and former swamps), the water table in the Chowan Swamp, where much of the land surface is less than 2 ft (0.6 m) above sea level, fluctuated by less than a foot throughout 1975. On occasion, the fluctuation of the water table coincided with high water levels in the nearby Chowan River which is tidally affected (Daniel, 1977). Similarly, narrow ranges of water table fluctuations are shown by Boelter and Verry (1977) for two groundwater-fed wetlands in northern Minnesota.

An interesting feature of the water level hydrographs from the Albemarle–Pamlico peninsula is the tendency of the water levels to remain fairly constant, fluctuating only over a narrow range, from January through May or June. This suggests that there is some limiting level to which the water table will rise and that any further recharge from precipitation will be rejected to become surface runoff.

Surface Water

Streamflow is the net effect of all the processes that influence the hydrologic cycle of a watershed. Although the watersheds of many enclosed peatlands contain upland areas devoid of peat, the streamflow from these watersheds can still be analyzed to evaluate the effect that peat deposits have as water storage areas and regulators of streamflow. In raised swamps or pocosins, measuring runoff has proved to be much more difficult because surface runoff usually does not exit the watershed through a single outlet. Heavy storms often result in sheet flow across the swamp surface, and even when the swamp surface is not flooded, a great deal of water can move through the very porous tangle of roots and organic debris that comprises the uppermost part of the soil profile. Thus storm runoff may not be routed to a single outlet but will slowly move in a diffuse layer out of the peatland to discharge over a broad reach of shoreline along a bordering stream or other body of water. This characteristic has a significant stabilizing influence on the chemical quality of adjacent bodies of water and, as will be seen, is perhaps the most easily altered facet of wetland hydrology.

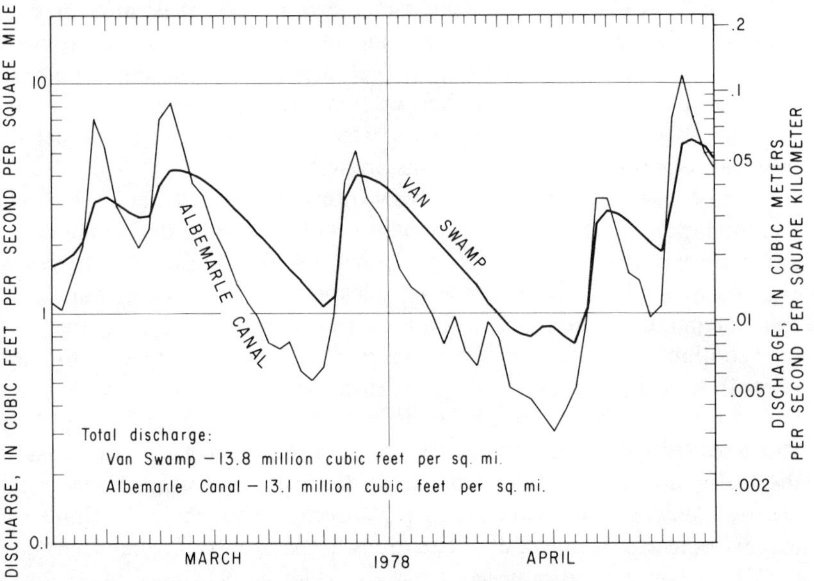

FIGURE 7. *A comparison of discharge hydrographs from a forested swampland and a formerly forested swamp after its conversion to agricultural use.*

One of the important hydrologic functions of swamps, marshes, and other wetlands is to provide retention storage for storm waters by spreading the water over a wide area of generally flat land underlain by porous soils. The result is a decrease in the velocity of runoff and a tendency to desynchronize the peaks of tributary streams. In this way wetlands function as storm buffers to reduce the flood peak and lengthen the duration of the flood.

This effect is dramatically illustrated in Figure 7, which shows discharge hydrographs from the forested Van Swamp watershed and the intensely farmed Albemarle Canal watershed. The March and April record shows five floods and none of the Van Swamp peaks were as high, or the recessions as low, as those from Albemarle Canal. Yet, the total unit runoff from the two watersheds, at 13.8 and 13.1 million cu ft/sq mi (1.51×10^5 and 1.43×10^5 m^3/km^2) for Van Swamp and Albemarle Canal, respectively, is nearly equal. There is about a 5% difference between these values, which is within the error involved in the discharge measurements.

The fact that the total discharges for this two-month period are so close only serves to illustrate that the amount of runoff is strongly influenced by the time of year that rain falls, for on an annual basis the total runoff from Albemarle Canal is greater than from Van Swamp. The seasonal variation in runoff is apparent from the Pungo Refuge records shown in Figure 8. During the winter and spring when evapotranspiration is low, the soil becomes

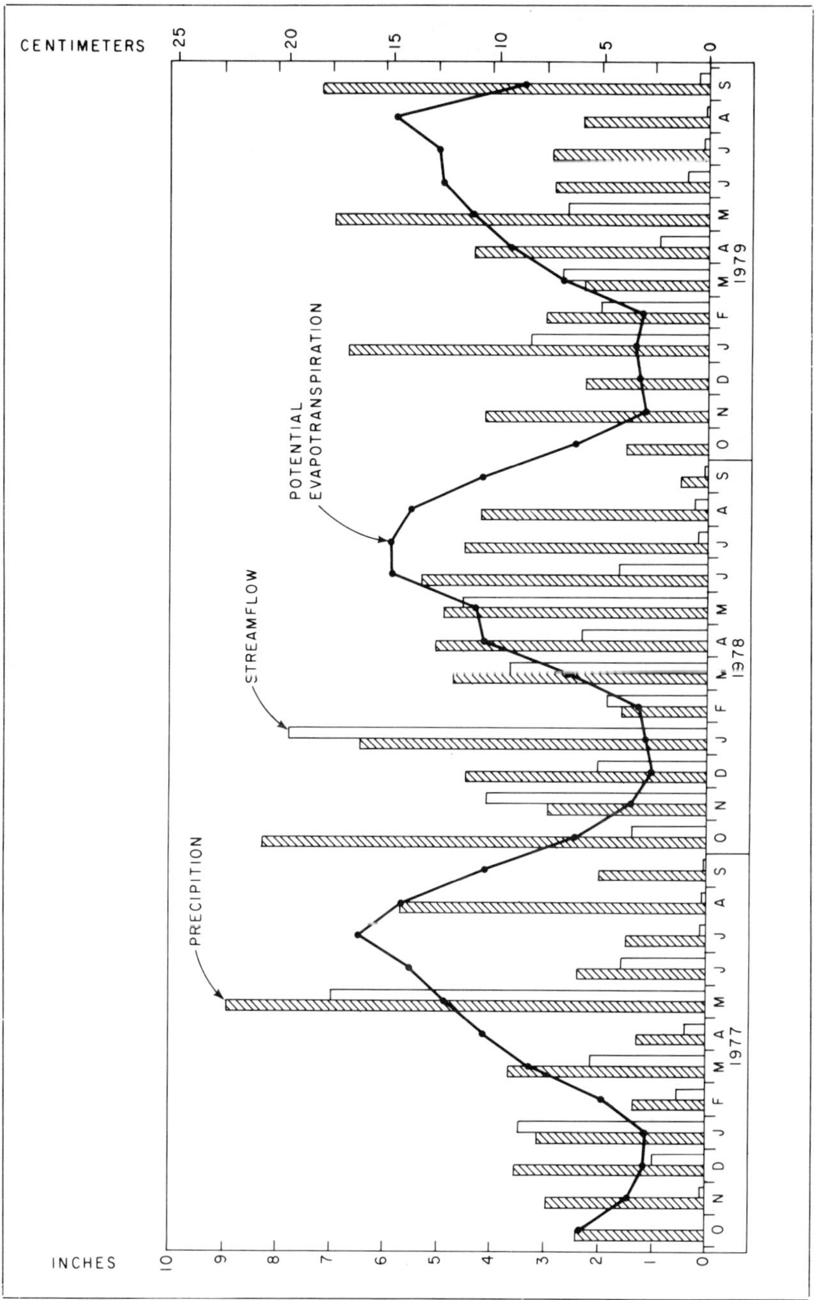

FIGURE 8. *Monthly precipitation, streamflow, and potential evaportranspiration at the Pungo Refuge study site, 1977 to 1979 water years.*

saturated and much of the precipitation runs off the surface of the watershed. As shown in Figure 6, the water table at this time of year is near land surface and this apparently explains the similar March to April discharge shown in Figure 7. On the other hand, during the summer months, soils are saturated only after heavy or prolonged rains and peak runoff rates are greatly reduced.

Thus it becomes apparent that there is a relationship between peak runoff and depth to the water table. The greater the depth to the water table, the more storage capacity that is available to temporarily hold part of the water from a storm. The plot of peak runoff versus storm rainfall at the Pungo Refuge shown in Figure 9 illustrates the impact of water table levels on peak runoff rates for this watershed. However, this relation will probably be somewhat different in watersheds underlain by thin organic soils and mineral soils that have lower porosity than the thick peat soil at the Pungo Refuge. This relation will also be affected by the differences in permeability of peat and mineral soils. The surficial peats are often poorly decomposed and have very high conductivity, greatly in excess of most mineral soils. Therefore, during periods when the water table is high, they can release any additional rainfall inputs more quickly than mineral aquifers. Yet, once the water table falls to levels where the peat is more decomposed and less permeable, the rate at which new rainfall will be lost can be very low, often lower than for mineral soils.

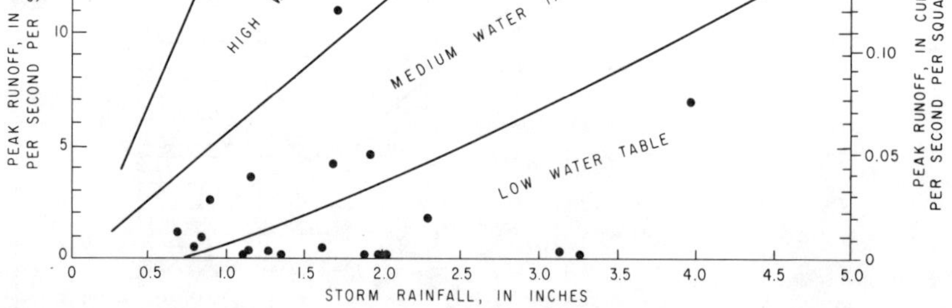

FIGURE 9. *Relation of peak runoff to storm rainfall and water table level at Pungo Wildlife Refuge. (High water table conditions existed when water levels fluctuated between 2.0 and 2.5 ft [0.6 and 0.7 m] below land surface, medium water tables were 2.5 to 4.5 ft [0.7 to 1.4 m] below land surface, and low water tables were more than 4.5 [1.4 m] below land surface.)*

Runoff distribution during the year is also influenced by the source of water. As shown by Boelter and Verry (1977), runoff from predominantly groundwater-fed wetlands is more evenly distributed throughout the year. Groundwater-fed wetlands are surface discharge points for the larger regional groundwater system and this provides a more constant supply of water than precipitation. By slowing the release from storage, the hydraulic properties of the wetlands help regulate groundwater discharge and spread out the inputs from precipitation. In contrast, raised wetlands like those on the Albemarle–Pamlico peninsula exhibit more variability in discharge due to variability of precipitation inputs, and there is usually little discharge after June as evapotranspiration returns most precipitation to the atmosphere.

Water Budget

Water budgets were determined for three watersheds on the Albemarle–Pamlico peninsula during the 1977 to 1979 water years. As shown in Table 1, input consists of precipitation, and water is lost by surface runoff, groundwater recharge, and evapotranspiration. Although the loss to groundwater recharge was estimated from hydrologic properties of the underlying aquifers (Heath, 1975), the magnitude of this value is sufficiently small that errors in the value should not seriously change the computed value of evapotranspiration or any subsequent conclusions based on other items in the budget.

The annual rainfall in the three watersheds averages approximately 50 in (127 cm) per year and the estimates of potential evapotranspiration based on the Penman method (Daniel, 1977) average 39.9 in (101 cm). On the northeastern North Carolina coastal plain, long-term average rainfall as represented by measurements on Roanoke Island and at New Holland south of Lake Mattamuskeet average about 51 in (130 cm) per year (Heath, 1975) and thus are comparable to the rainfall data from the western end of the Albemarle–Pamlico peninsula. An estimate of average potential evapotranspiration by Heath (1975), based on pan evaporation data collected at Hofmann Forest, is 36 in (91 cm) annually.

However, as data in Table 1 show, the actual evapotranspiration from a watershed can be much lower than the potential evapotranspiration. There can also be considerable year-to-year variation in the components of the water budget as well as variation from watershed to watershed in a given year. The year-to-year variation is largely caused by differences in the amounts of precipitation plus the distribution of the precipitation within the year. If most of the precipitation occurs during the winter and spring when evapotranspiration is low, more of the precipitation will be lost as runoff. This was apparently the case in 1978, which was a wet year, and most of the precipitation fell early in the year. On the other hand, if more of the precipitation falls during summer and fall there will be less loss to runoff and more loss to evapotranspiration.

TABLE 1. *Water Budgets for Three Watersheds on the Albemarle–Pamlico Peninsula, 1977 to 1979 Water Years*

	1977		1978		1979	
	Totals (inches)	Percent of rainfall	Totals (inches)	Percent of rainfall	Totals (inches)	Percent of rainfall
	North Lake Canal above Pungo Lake (Pond pine, evergreen shrub swampland; thick peat soil)					
Rainfall	39.03	100.00	53.15	100.00	46.60	100.00
Runoff	15.68	40.17	29.93	56.31	12.17	26.11
Potential ET[1]	42.56		39.74		37.27	
Actual ET	22.85	58.54	22.72	42.75	33.93	72.81
Groundwater loss[2]	.50		.50		.50	
	Van Swamp (Forested swampland; peat and mineral soil)					
Rainfall			48.71	100.00	52.91	100.00
Runoff			30.53	62.68	17.86	33.76
Potential ET			39.74		37.27	
Actual ET			17.68	36.30	34.55	65.30
Groundwater loss			.50		.50	
	Albemarle Canal (Agricultural land, formerly forested swamp; peat and mineral soil)					
Rainfall			53.43	100.00	49.23	100.00
Runoff			33.84	63.33	20.23	41.09
Potential ET			39.74		37.27	
Actual ET			19.09	35.73	28.50	57.89
Groundwater loss			.50		.50	

1. Calculated by Penman method for area of northeastern North Carolina and southeastern Virginia as described by Daniel (1977), pp. 24-28.
2. Estimated for the Albemarle-Pamlico peninsula by Heath (1975), pp. 42-45.

Note: To convert values given in inches to centimeters, multiply by 2.54.

Within a regional setting, the basin-to-basin differences within a given year are controlled primarily by differences in soil types, plant cover, and the degree of development. By inspection of the 1978 to 1979 record of the three watersheds in Table 1, it becomes apparent that in both years the annual runoff, as percent of rainfall, is least at the Pungo Refuge, intermediate out of Van Swamp, and greatest for the Albemarle Canal farm drainage. The inverse pattern holds for actual evapotranspiration. By comparing these data as percent of rainfall, the variability introduced by the year-to-year differences in precipitation can be reduced. The lower proportion of runoff and higher proportion of evapotranspiration at the Pungo site results from the presence of thick organic soil with its very high porosity under the entire watershed in addition to the scrub vegetation on the surface. The organic soil tends to hold the water and subsurface drainage is very slow. In peatland watersheds that are vegetated by scrubs and sedges, the evapotranspiration tends to be greater than in a forested peatland because of higher surface winds and a generally greater biomass of transpiring plants (Boelter and Verry, 1977).

Natural forested peatlands also tend to lose more precipitation by interception losses than do developed peatlands. Interception losses are the part of precipitation that wets and clings to vegetation and is returned by evaporation to the atmosphere without ever reaching the land surface. Losses as high as 6 to 8 in (15 to 20 cm) per year have been reported for closed canopies of black spruce (Boelter and Verry, 1977). Consequently, the actual evapotranspiration from Van Swamp, which is forested, could be expected to be higher than from the Albemarle Canal farm area from which the swamp forest has been removed, even if there had been no hydraulic improvements. But there have been extensive improvements by ditching, canal construction, and grading of the land surface, and this acts to reduce the residence time that water is available within the basin for evapotranspiration. As a consequence of these changes, it is not surprising that more rainfall leaves this watershed as surface runoff than in the other two watersheds, and less is lost through evapotranspiration.

With regard to the formation and growth of elevated peatlands on the coastal plain, it is informative to look at the rainfall and evapotranspiration data for the Pungo Refuge and Van Swamp. In all but the driest years, rainfall exceeds even potential evapotranspiration and in the wetter years when actual evapotranspiration approaches potential, there is still a considerable excess of moisture. A water budget determined for Creeping Swamp by Winner and Simmons (1977) covering the period July 1974 through June 1975 is similar to the 1977 water budget for the Pungo Refuge.

Rainfall in excess of evapotranspiration is necessary to establish and maintain the slightly elevated water table within the peat mass that was described earlier for the Pungo Refuge. Thus the evidence from several sources shows there is at present more than sufficient excess water to maintain and support the growth of elevated peatlands such as pocosins. Apparently this has been the prevailing condition on the southeastern coastal plain for a considerable length of time. Although there is no accurate way to determine for how long, the presence of elevated peatlands and the few available radiocarbon dates would suggest that elevated peatlands have been forming for several thousand years.

Hydrologic Impacts of Peatland Alteration

Following channelization or other forms of land drainage, the most immediate effect on the hydrology of the developed area is seen in changes in streamflow characteristics. The flow duration curve is a convenient means of comparing the flow characteristics of different streams, or the flow characteristics of the same stream for different periods of time. Flow-duration

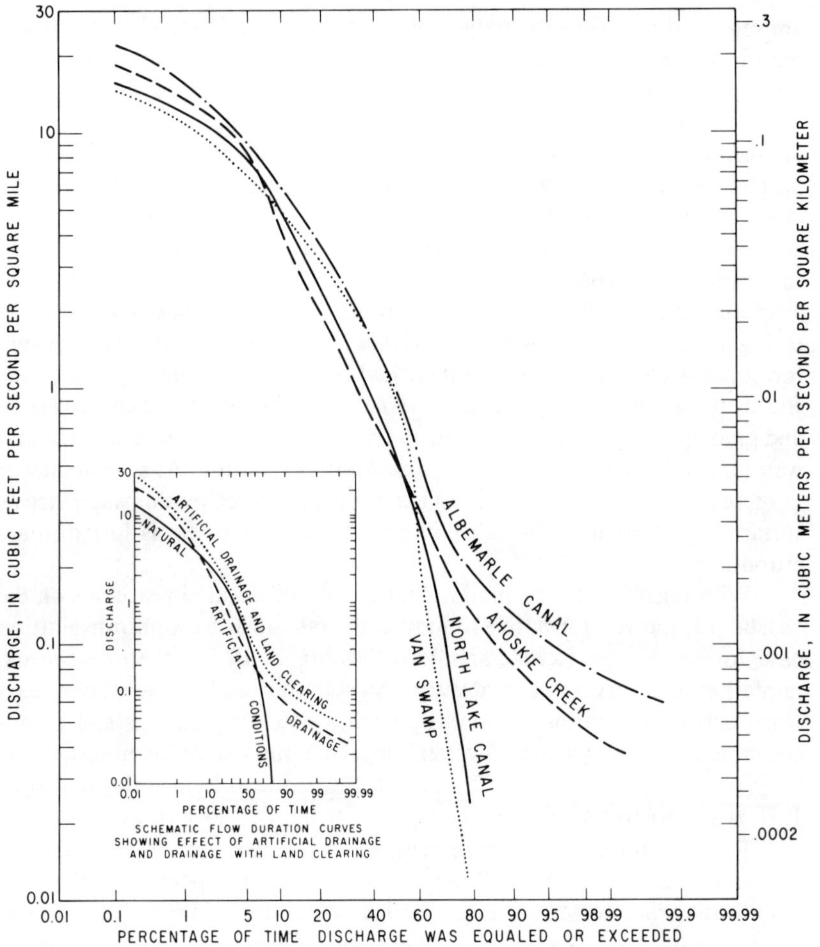

FIGURE 10. *Flow duration curves for Ahoskie Creek, which has been channelized; Albemarle Canal, which drains highly developed agricultural land; and North Lake Canal and Van Swamp, both of which drain essentially natural swampland, 1977 to 1979 water years.*

curves for Van Swamp near Hoke, North Lake Canal above Pungo Lake, Albemarle Canal near Swindell, and Ahoskie Creek at Ahoskie are shown in Figure 10. All of these curves were computed for the water years 1977 to 1979. Drainage areas and land use statistics for these watersheds are shown in Table 2.

The Ahoskie Creek basin is located approximately 30 mi (48 km) northwest of Albemarle Sound. The channels of Ahoskie Creek and many of the tributaries have generally low gradients and are bordered by swamp

TABLE 2. *Comparison of Drainage Areas and Land Use Characteristics for Selected Watersheds in Northeastern North Carolina*

Station and station number	Drainage area mi²	Drainage area km²	Land use—percent of drainage area: Forest	Agriculture	Urban
Albemarle Canal near Swindell (including Van Swamp)[1] 02084572	68	176	38	62	<1
(excluding Van Swamp)[1]	45	117	5	95	0
Van Swamp near Hoke[1] 02084571	23	60	90	10	1
North Lake Canal above Pungo Lake[1] 02084556	0.29	0.75	100	0	0
Ahoskie Creek at Ahoskie[2] 02053500	57	148	51	43	6
Creeping Swamp near Vanceboro[3] 02091970	27	70	89	11	0

Sources of data:
1. Daniel (1978)
2. U.S. Geological Survey (1977a)
3. U.S. Geological Survey (1977b)

forests on essentially all of the flood plain areas. The channels in the Ahoskie Creek watershed were deepened and widened between 1962 and 1964. Land use data in Table 2 show that the percent of the basin in agriculture and forest is about equally divided. The amount of land in agriculture also appears to have remained relatively constant for some time. Certainly there has been no rapid clearing and drainage comparable to that taking place on the Albemarle–Pamlico peninsula.

The duration curves of North Lake Canal and Van Swamp are typical of streamflow from undeveloped or unchannelized wetlands. A nearly identical duration curve for Ahoskie Creek prior to its channelization between 1962 and 1964 is shown by Heath (1975, Figure 39) and this curve in turn is compared by Winner and Simmons (1977, Figure 16) with a similar duration curve from Creeping Swamp to illustrate the similarity in patterns of discharge in both basins prior to channelization.

Perhaps the most obvious feature of the duration curves of undeveloped wetland watersheds is the indication that there are significant amounts of time when there is little or no flow. For example, prior to channelization there was no flow in Ahoskie Creek 8% of the time. During 1971 to 1974 there was no flow in Creeping Swamp about 6% of the time. During 1977 to 1979 North Lake Canal was dry 21% of the time. Interestingly, Van Swamp never completely stopped flowing during 1977 to 1979, although the rate of flow could be extremely low, often less than 0.0004 cu ft per second per square mile (4.4×10^{-6} [m^3/s]/km^2).

The duration curves for Ahoskie Creek and Albemarle Canal in Figure 10 are typical of runoff from channelized and developed wetland watersheds. There are important differences between these two curves with respect to their positions relative to each other and to the curves for the undeveloped watersheds. As shown in the inset, one of the primary effects of channelization is to increase base runoff. This reflects increased groundwater discharge into the deeper channels. By comparision, the channels of most natural wetland drainage systems are much shallower and there does not have to be a large decline in the water table before ground water stops discharging to the channel and streamflow ceases. The other difference is the increased hydraulic efficiency of the improved channels in conveying storm water which is shown by increases in maximum discharges. In other words, during and following storms the rate of runoff is considerably larger through the artificial channels than it would be under natural conditions. This effect on individual floods has already been seen in Figure 7. Inspection of the duration curves shows that, in comparison to discharge from Van Swamp, maximum unit discharges (discharge per square mile) from Albemarle Canal will be more than 40% higher for discharges exceeded about 1% of the time.

In watersheds such as Ahoskie Creek where there have not been significant changes in land use patterns and additional drainage development outside of channelization of existing drainage, the increases in base flow and maximum runoff apparently occur at the expense of mid-range flow (Heath, 1975). This relationship is shown as the artificial drainage curve in the inset in Figure 10. As a consequence, none of the changes in flow results in a significant change in total runoff. This is apparent from a double-mass plot of cumulative rainfall and cumulative runoff in Ahoskie Creek (Figure 11) which shows there has been no change in the slope of the plot after channelization. If there had been an increase in runoff, the slope would have decreased.

Perhaps the most striking impact of land clearing and drainage on former wetlands is shown by the duration curve for Albemarle Canal (Figure 10) and the runoff data in Table 1. The total annual runoff from this watershed was higher than the runoff from two essentially natural watersheds in the same area and it is apparent that this increased runoff is accomplished throughout the entire range of flow, not just in the ranges of base flow and high flow. This is shown schematically by the artificial drainage and land clearing curve in the inset in Figure 10.

Computations based on the data in Table 1 also show that the annual runoff from the Albemarle Canal watershed, as percent of rainfall, was 1% higher than the runoff from Van Swamp in 1978 and 22% higher in 1979. This last value may appear large but apparently is not unreasonable in terms of known values. Mustonen and Seuna (1975) report that when a Finnish

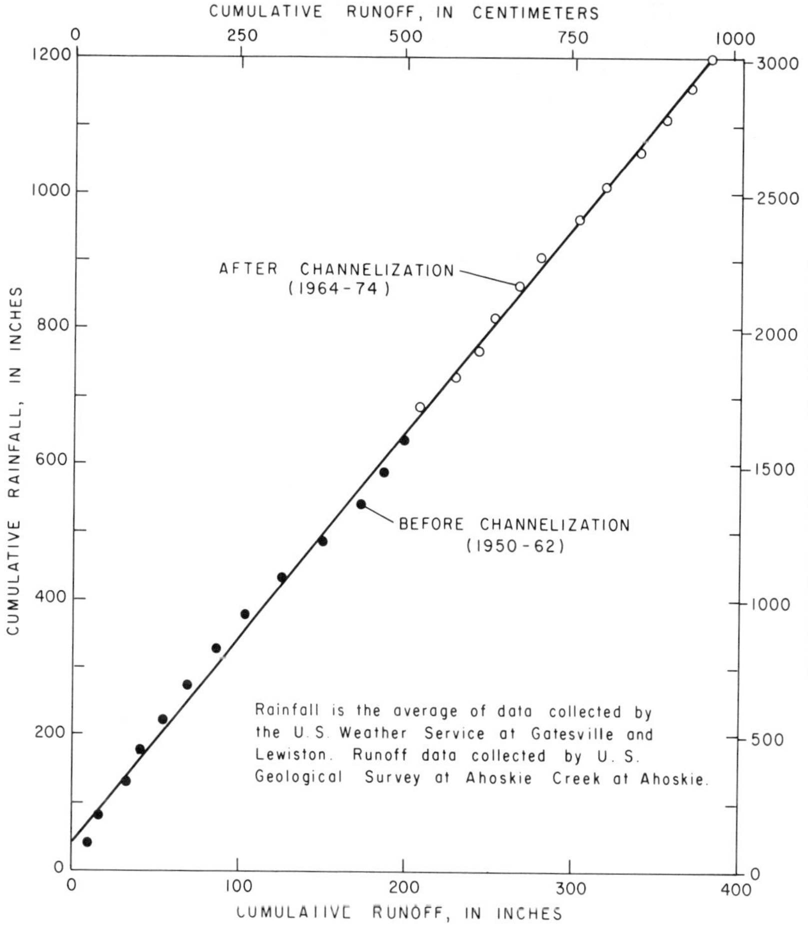

FIGURE 11. *Cumulative rainfall-runoff relation in Ahoskie Creek, 1950 to 1974 (from Winner and Simmons, 1977).*

peatland consisting mostly of open bog and swamp with a poor growth of pine was drained in 1958, transpiration and soil moisture evaporation decreased; maximum runoff increased, and annual runoff increased by 43%.

Several possible reasons for this increase in annual runoff were discussed previously, including the increased hydraulic efficiency of the artificial drainage system, the depth and number of canals, and changes in vegetation. Another factor is the effect of drainage on the hydrologic properties of the drained soils, for the changes that take place will tend to increase surface runoff by reducing infiltration and groundwater storage, particularly in organic and clayey soils. Eggelsmann (1975) found that there is an initial rapid decrease in permeability following drainage, but later the decrease becomes asymptotic to some minimum value (Figure 12). The initial permeability of various peats will depend on the predominant type of vegetable remains involved, and it is apparent from Figure 12 that these differences will persist following drainage. When a peatland is drained, the free water in the larger pores is removed first. This is usually accompanied in organic soils and muds by a reduction in size of the large pores to micropores. Gravity drainage of the micropores is very slow or does not take place at all, and further removal of interstitial water is by soil evaporation or extraction by plants. The reduction in drainable porosity results in lower permeability, higher bulk density, and consolidation of the soil.

As noted earlier, artificial drainage systems generally collect and funnel surface runoff to a few discrete discharge points. When this is coupled with the increased annual runoff and increased peak discharges that also come with construction of the artificial channels, conditions are created that can result in considerable impact on associated hydrologic systems. This is particularly true of receiving waters such as coastal streams and bays that

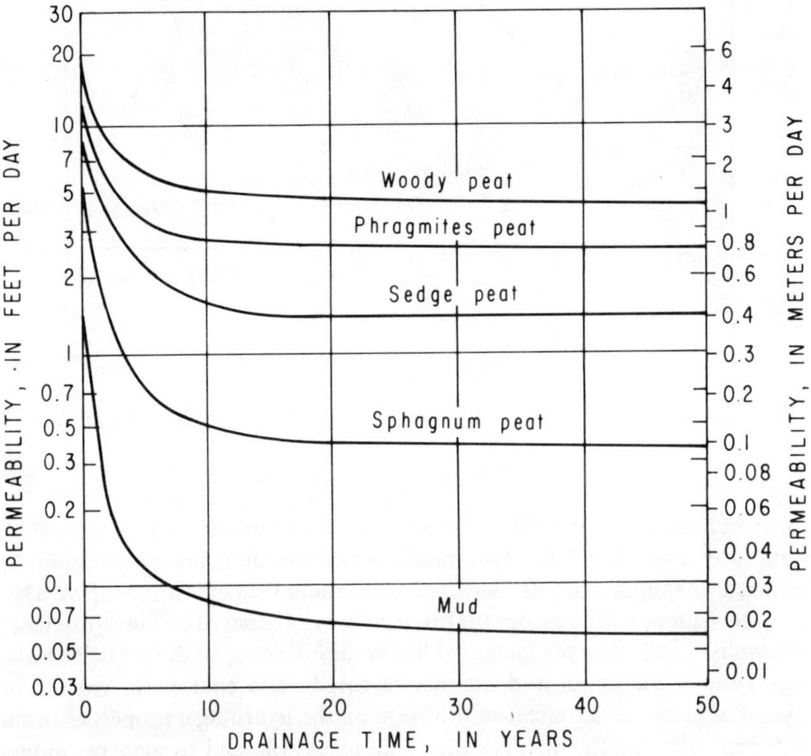

FIGURE 12. *Decrease of peat and mud permeability with time following drainage (after Eggelsmann, 1975).*

contain saline water and support marine life. In natural systems the influx of fresh water to these systems is slowed and diffused by the broad wetlands and marshes that border these waters. The receiving waters have time to assimilate the fresh water without rapid and drastic fluctuations in water quality. Once an artificial drainage system is connected to a coastal stream, however, much of the benefit of this buffering capacity is lost. As shown by Kirby-Smith and Barber (1979), rapid influxes of fresh water will dilute and flush out the saline water and bring in other constituents such as nutrients derived from the areas of developed land. In their study, Kirby-Smith and Barber (1979) found a distribution of nutrients along the main axis of the South River showing increasing concentrations of nutrients with decreasing salinity; the lowest salinities and highest concentrations of nutrients were found near the mouth of the outfall canal from Open Grounds Farm (Figure 1). In the sense that the introduction of large amounts of fresh water can reduce the salinity and generally alter the chemistry of coastal waters to the detriment of the organisms originally living there, then the fresh water itself can be considered a pollutant (see Street and McClees, this volume).

Water Quality of Runoff from Natural and Altered Wetlands

The chemistry of water draining wetlands reflects the source of the water, whether from direct precipitation, surface inflow, or gound water, in some cases the mixing of water from these different sources, and almost certainly some degree of modification by the vegetation and interaction with the organic and mineral components of the soil. As exemplified by the water quality of North Lake Canal and Van Swamp in Table 3, the water leaving natural elevated peatlands and swamp forests will be low in dissolved solids, have a low or acidic pH, be highly colored by organic compounds and carry low concentrations of suspended sediment. In wetlands where ground water is a major contributor to the water budget, the pH of runoff water tends to be somewhat higher and dissolved solids are higher.

After a wetland is cleared and drained for agricultural use or improved reforestation, certain chemical modifications are made to improve the condition of the soils for these uses. Because organic soils are characteristically quite acid, the excessive acidity is reduced by application of lime, as much as 5 to 6 tons per acre (11,200 to 13,400 kg/ha) in the case of the more organic soils on the Albemarle–Pamlico peninsula (Carter, 1975). Nutrients available to plants are also low in organic soils and these deficiencies must be overcome by applications of fertilizer. But not all of these materials are used by the growing plants or remain in the soil. Surface runoff will remove some of the soluble fertilizer and lime from the fields, and downward leaching by ground water will eventually carry additional quantities of these dissolved components to the drainage canals. The surface drainage from plowed and disturbed

TABLE 3. *Summary of Physical Properties, Total Dissolved Solids, and Suspended Sediment for Three Watersheds on the Albemarle–Pamlico Peninsula, 1977 to 1979 Water Years*

	North Lake Canal (Swamp)		Van Swamp (Swamp)		Albemarle Canal (Agricultural land)	
	Mean	Range	Mean	Range	Mean	Range
Color (platinum-cobalt units)	429	150-880	265	70-750	163	50-350
pH (pH units)		2.2-6.6		2.5-5.7		4.4-6.7
Specific conductance (micromhos)	91	60-150	89	50-142	270	110-550
Temperature (° C)	18.2	5.0-34.5	16.5	6.5-27.5	18.9	6.5-30.0
Dissolved solids (Residue at 180° C, mg/l)	147	108-171	103	54-223	245	105-439
Dissolved solids (Sum of constituents, mg/l)	60	42-94	50	30-108	178	66-346
Suspended sediment (mg/l)	14	2-32	16	1-62	42	6-494

Note: Dissolved solids (residue at 180° C) is the total dissolved material in the sample as determined by evaporation and includes both inorganic and organic components; dissolved solids (sum of constituents) is the sum of the major inorganic cations and anions determined analytically.

ground will also carry increased quantities of suspended sediment and particulate organic matter (see Gilliam and Skaggs, this volume).

As a consequence, farm drainage like that from Albemarle Canal in Table 3 has a higher pH, higher dissolved solids, and higher suspended sediment concentrations than runoff from natural wetland watersheds. The total dissolved solids represent the aggregate of many dissolved chemical species and the concentrations of a number of ions are compared in the milliequivalents diagrams in Figure 13. It is apparent that the quality of water from Van Swamp and North Lake Canal is similar and that the concentrations of inorganic constituents are quite low, particularly when compared to the water quality of Albemarle Canal. The most obvious increases are in calcium, magnesium, bicarbonate and sulfate, increases which are attributed to application of lime to the soil. On the average, concentrations of calcium and bicarbonate are about ten times higher in the canal draining the farmland than in the essentially natural waters, magnesium is about six times higher, and sulfate is about four times higher. Concentrations of sodium and chloride are approximately doubled; the increases in sodium and chloride are also attributed to application of fertilizer since these elements are commonly part of the chemical compounds used in formulating fertilizer.

Because of potential eutrophication problems in downstream ecosystems (Hobbie, 1974), it is important to compare the average concentrations of several species of nitrogen and total phosphorus in runoff from the same

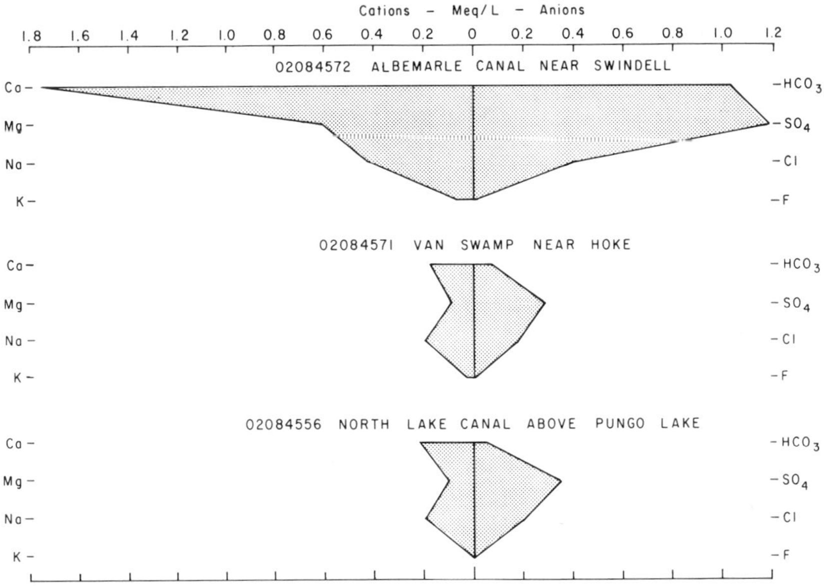

FIGURE 13. *Differences in chemical character between average water quality of runoff in a canal draining farmland on a former swamp forest and two essentially natural wetlands, 1977 to 1979 water years (diagram modeled after Stiff, 1951).*

three watersheds on the Albemarle–Pamlico peninsula (Figure 14). The water quality of Van Swamp and North Lake Canal is quite similar except for a slightly higher amount of total nitrate nitrogen in Van Swamp. The higher nitrate nitrogen may be the result of some of the farming operations that have started on the edges of the swamp. However, most of the total nitrogen in Van Swamp and North Lake Canal is in the form of dissolved organic nitrogen (Figure 14). The amount of dissolved organic nitrogen in Albemarle Canal is only slightly higher than in Van Swamp and North Lake Canal.

The most obvious difference between Albemarle Canal and the other two watersheds is the higher concentration of total nitrogen, which is nearly doubled, and nitrate nitrogen which is several times higher. The difference in total nitrogen amounts to about 1 mg/ 1, approximately the same difference that exists for nitrate nitrogen. It is concluded that the higher total nitrogen in Albemarle Canal is due almost entirely to nitrate nitrogen in the farm runoff.

The amount of total phosphorus leaving all three watersheds is low, although the amount in Albemarle Canal is somewhat higher than in runoff from the other two sites. The average concentration of total phosphorus, as P, in Albemarle Canal was 0.06 mg/ 1 for the study period and the average for dissolved phosphorus was less than 0.02 mg/ 1, suggesting that most of the

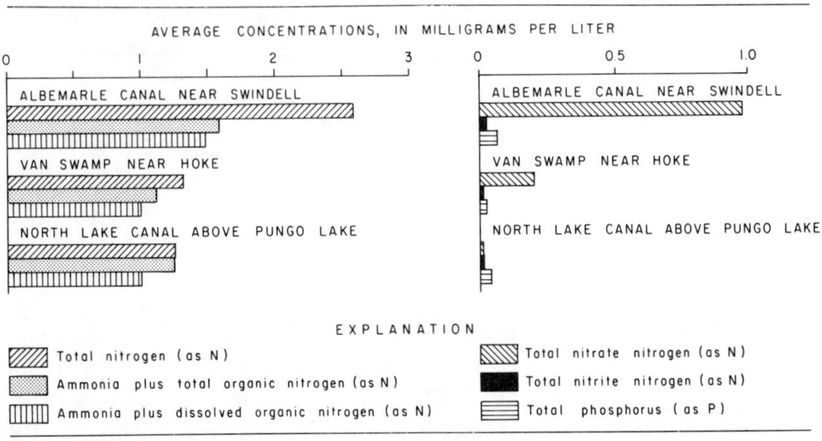

FIGURE 14. *Average concentrations of various forms of nitrogen and phosphorus in runoff from three watersheds on the Albemarle–Pamlico peninsula, 1977 to 1979 water years.*

phosphorus leaving the farmland is in particulate form either as phosphate grains or bound to the suspended sediment. This finding is in general agreement with the findings of Kuenzler et al. (1977) and Ellis et al. (1978). The study of two small watersheds by Ellis et al. (1978) showed that the heavy application of phosphorus fertilizer resulted in the soil water containing many times the phosphorus found naturally. Additionally, phosphorus has also moved deeply into the soil profile. Yet, very little of this phosphorus was being lost in runoff. The soil in these two watersheds was predominantly a fine sandy loam, and in mineral soils where the absorption sites are not saturated, any phosphorus not used by growing plants tends to be tied up on the inorganic mineral grains and is only slowly leached out by ground water. Much of the southern end of the Albemarle Canal watershed, the part of the basin nearest the sampling station, is underlain by mineral soils or thin organic soils with a high mineral content, and this would account for the low amounts of phosphorus found in the runoff. (For further information on phosphorus runoff from coastal wetlands see Gilliam and Skaggs and Richardson, this volume.)

From the above discussion it is apparent that drainage and development of wetlands, particularly wetlands underlain by deep organic soils, will result in some rather substantial changes in water quality. When the increased amounts of nutrients, sediment, and other dissolved constituents are rapidly carried by canal runoff to coastal waters, the resulting drop in salinity and increases in nutrients can result in algal growth, eutrophication (Hobbie, 1974), and ultimate disruption of the marine habitat along the coastal fringe.

CONCLUSION

Pocosins are one of several forms of freshwater wetlands found on the North Carolina coastal plain that are characterized by acidic organic soils and communities of vegetation tolerant of abundant water that is low in nutrients and dissolved minerals. Diversity and zoning of vegetation communities on these wetlands is often the product of differences in the quantity and quality of water that comes into them. Wetlands that are fed by ground water or other sources of water with relatively abundant dissolved minerals, particularly calcium, tend to be forested. Wetlands that are supplied primarily by precipitation and water of reduced mineral content tend to be vegetated by evergreen scrub, pond pine, and sedges. Evidence from auger tests, soil maps, radioisotopic age dating, and pollen analysis suggests that pocosins are a late phase of a slowly evolving wetland morphology that began with accumulation of organic remains in drainage lows or other depressions. As the accumulation of peat grew in depth and breadth, it eventually mantled the interstream areas and, in coalescing, created the broad elevated topography typical of pocosins.

Pocosins, like nearly all wetlands, act as storm buffers to attenuate peak rates of runoff because they provide abundant retention storage. Following heavy rains or flooding, storm waters will be spread over a large area of generally flat land. Additionally, the presence of porous organic soils increases the tendency to hold and restrict the flow of storm water from the wetland. Although flood peaks from unaltered wetlands will be lower than from a developed or channelized wetland, the flood flows will tend to remain high for a longer period of time. The amount of runoff is also strongly influenced by the time of year that rain falls because of the influence of evapotranspiration on groundwater levels. During winter and spring when evapotranspiration is low and water tables are high, a larger portion of rainfall will be rejected and cause higher rates of runoff than during the growing season when the water table falls and becomes saturated only after heavy rains. When the water table is low, heavy rains may cause very little runoff.

Runoff from natural pocosins also tends to be spread over a broad margin or shoreline rather than draining through a well-defined drainage network. Consequently, the effect of runoff from unaltered wetlands on receiving waters will be low because the combination of lower peak runoff rates and the diffuse nature of the discharge can be assimilated without causing rapid fluctuations in water quality. This is particularly important in brackish or salty coastal streams where rapid influxes of fresh water will flush out the saline water.

Modification of wetlands to remove excess water, prevent surface ponding, and reduce the water table can cause profound changes in their hydrology.

Drainage modification by channelization or construction of drainage canals will produce decided alterations in patterns of runoff with increases in both peak flows and low flows. Drainage modifications also tend to route runoff to discrete discharge points. Where channelization or canal construction is done without further changing the patterns of land use or land cover in the watershed, the increases in peak flow and low flow occur at the expense of mid-range flows. The net result is that there appears to be little change in total runoff from the watershed. However, in wetlands where there has been a radical change in vegetation, as in conversion of swamp forest to agriculture, there apparently is an increase in total runoff because interception losses have been reduced and the efficiency of an extensive drainage system reduces the residence time that water is available in the watershed to be returned to the atmosphere by evapotranspiration.

Conversion of peatlands to agricultural use requires, in addition to drainage, the application of lime to reduce soil acidity and extensive use of fertilizer to make up for the deficiency in available nutrients. In comparison to the chemical quality of runoff from unaltered wetlands, there are greatly increased amounts of these constituents in the runoff from lands converted to agricultural use. The pH of the water is increased, the amount of dissolved constituents is increased and suspended sediment is increased. Increases in average concentration of four to ten times were observed for calcium, magnesium, sulfate, and bicarbonate in farm drainage waters on the Albemarle–Pamlico peninsula during 1977 to 1979. A 50% increase in total nitrogen, apparently due to nitrate, was also observed, with little or no increase in phosphorus due to the presence of soils with high mineral content.

ACKNOWLEDGMENTS

The United States Geological Survey, with the support and cooperation of the Ground Water Section of the North Carolina Department of Natural Resources and Community Development, the United States Soil Conservation Service, and the United States Agricultural Research Service, began studying the impacts of channelizing coastal plain streams in the early 1970s. This research was expanded in the mid-1970s to evaluate the hydrologic impacts of land development on the Albemarle–Pamlico peninsula, which includes large areas underlain by deep organic soils, including peatlands. The cooperation of the United States Fish and Wildlife Service in the research at the Pungo National Wildlife Refuge has also done much to further the understanding of the hydrology of these deep organic soils.

LITERATURE CITED

Boelter, D. H., and E. S. Verry, 1977. Peatland and water in the northern lake states. USDA For. Ser. Gen. Tech. Rep. NC-31, 22 pp., N. Cen. For. Exp. Sta., St. Paul, Minn.

Carter, L. J., 1975. Agriculture: A new frontier in North Carolina. Science, 89:4199, pp. 271-275.

Carter, V., M. K. Garrett, L. Shina, and P. Gannon, 1977. The Great Dismal Swamp: Management of a hydrologic resource with the aid of remote sensing. Water Resources Bulletin, Amer. Water Resources Assoc., 13: 1, 12 pp.

Daniel, C. C. III, 1977. Digital flow model of the Chowan River estuary, northeastern North Carolina. U.S. Geological Survey Water Resources Investigations 77-63, 84 pp.

Daniel, C. C. III, 1978. Land use, land cover, and drainage on the Albemarle–Pamlico peninsula, eastern North Carolina, 1974. U.S. Geological Survey Water Resources Investigations 78-134, Map Report, 2 sheets.

Daniels, R. B., E. E. Gamble, W. H. Wheeler, and C. S. Holzhey, 1972. Some details of the surficial stratigraphy and geomorphology of the coastal plain between New Bern and Coats, North Carolina. Carolina Geological Society and Atlantic Coastal Plain Geological Association Annual Meeting and Field Trip Guidebook, Oct. 7-8, 1972, 36 pp.

Eggelsmann, R., 1975. Physical effects of drainage in peat soils of the temperate zone and their forecasting, pp. 69-76. In: Hydrology of marsh-ridden areas: Proceedings of the Minsk Symposium, June 1972. UNESCO Press, Paris, 562 pp.

Ellis, B. G., A. E. Erickson, and A. R. Wolcott, 1978. Nitrate and phosphorus runoff losses from small watersheds in Great Lakes basin. EPA Ecological Research Series, EPA-600/3-78-028, 84 pp.

Harrison, W., R. J. Malloy, G. A. Rusnak, and J. Terasmae, 1965. Possible late Pleistocene uplift, Chesapeake Bay entrance. Jour. Geology, 73: 201-229.

Heath, R. C., 1975. Hydrology of the Albemarle–Pamlico region, North Carolina, a preliminary report on the impact of agricultural developments. U.S. Geological Survey Water Resources Investigations 9-75, 98 pp.

Hobbie, J. E., 1974. Nutrients and eutrophication in the Pamlico River estuary, North Carolina, 1971-1973. North Carolina Water Resources Research Institute, Report No. 100, 239 pp.

Kirby-Smith, W. W., and R. T. Barber, 1979. The water quality ramifications in estuaries of converting forest to intensive agriculture. North Carolina Water Resources Research Institute, Report No. 148, 70 pp.

Kuenzler, E. J., P. J. Mulholland, L. A. Ruley, and R. P. Sniffen, 1977. Water quality in North Carolina streams and effects of channelization. North Carolina Water Resources Research Institute, Report No. 127, 160 pp.

Lohman, S. W., 1972. Ground-water hydraulics. U.S. Geological Survey Professional Paper 708, 70 pp.

McComas, M. R., J. P. Kempton, and K. C. Hinkley, 1972. Geology, soils and hydrogeology of Volo Bog and vicinity, Lake County, Illinois. Illinois Geological Survey Environmental Geology Notes, No. 57, 27 pp.

Milliman, J. D. and K. O. Emery, 1968. Sea levels during the past 35,000 years. Science, 162: 1121-1123.

Mustonen, S. E., and P. Seuna, 1975. Influence of forest drainage on the hydrology of an open bog in Finland, pp. 519-530. In: Hydrology of marsh-ridden areas. Proceedings of the Minsk Symposium, June 1972. UNESCO Press, Paris, 562 pp.

Oaks, R. Q., Jr., 1965. Post-Miocene stratigraphy and morphology, outer coastal plain, southeastern Virginia. Ph.D. Dissertation, Yale University, 226 pp. plus appendices. (Available from University Microfilms, Inc., Ann Arbor, Mich.)

Oaks, R. Q., Jr., and N. K. Coch, 1973. Post-Miocene stratigraphy and morphology, southeastern Virginia. Virginia Division of Mineral Resources Bulletin 82, 135 pp.

Prouty, W. F., 1952. Carolina bays and their origin. Bulletin Geological Soc. Amer., 63:167-224.

Riggs, S. R., and M. P. O'Connor, 1974. Relict sediment deposits in a major transgressive coastal system. Sea Grant Publication UNC-SG-74-04, 37 pp.

Shaler, N. C., 1890. General account of the freshwater morasses of the United States, with a description of the Dismal Swamp district of Virginia and North Carolina. U.S. Geological Survey 10th Annual Report, Part 1, pp. 255-339.

Stiff, H. A., Jr., 1951. The interpretation of chemical water analysis by means of patterns. Journal Petroleum Technology, 3(10):15-17.

U.S. Department of Energy, 1979. Peat prospectus. U.S. Dept. of Energy, Div. of Fossil Fuel Processing, Technical Information Document, 79 pp.

U.S. Geological Survey, 1977a. Land use and land cover, 1972, Norfolk, Virginia; North Carolina. U.S. Dept. of Interior, Geological Survey, Open-File 77-789-1 Land Use Series.

U.S. Geological Survey, 1977b. Land use and land cover, 1974, Rocky Mount, North Carolina. U.S. Dept. of Interior, Geological Survey, Open-File 77-613-1 Land Use Series.

Whitehead, D. R., 1965. Palynology and Pleistocene phytogeography of unglaciated eastern North America, pp. 417-432. In: H. E. Wright, Jr., and D. G. Frey, eds., The quaternary of the United States. Princeton University Press, Princeton, N.J.

Whitehead, D. R., 1972. Developmental and environmental history of the Dismal Swamp. Ecological Monographs, 42(3):301-315.

Winner, M. D., Jr., and C. E. Simmons, 1977. Hydrology of the Creeping Swamp watershed, North Carolina, with reference to potential effects of stream channelization. U. S. Geological Survey Water Resources Investigations, 77-26, 54 pp.

Drainage and Agricultural Development: Effects on Drainage Waters

J. W. Gilliam and R. W. Skaggs

ABSTRACT

To determine the effects of drainage and agricultural development upon drainage waters, three paired areas (six sites) of developed and undeveloped land were selected to span the different soils which are likely to be developed in the Blackland area of North Carolina.

Peak runoff rates occurred earlier and were three to four times higher from developed than from similar undeveloped sites. Total annual outflows were about the same from developed and undeveloped sites of the deep organic soil. However, development may cause a small decrease in ET during some years with a consequent increase in annual runoff. The average water table depth at the center of the 130 ha developed deep organic site was about 25 cm deeper than on the undeveloped site for a three-year period.

There was a significant increase in the loss of nutrients to drainage waters from the developed site as compared to the undeveloped site at all three locations. The increase in nitrogen loss from these organic rich soils was small compared to nitrogen losses from most cultivated mineral soils in North Carolina. The sediment loss from the developed soils was very low as compared to cultivated soils further inland. However, P loss from the developed organic soils was greater when compared to undeveloped organic soils and developed mineral soils (10 to 15 kg ha^{-1} yr^{-1} vs. < 1 kg ha^{-1} yr^{-1}). Some other water variables which changed upon development were pH, T.O.C., B.O.D., Ca, K, Cl, and Na.

Key Words: water quality, agricultural drainage, organic soils, hydrology

INTRODUCTION

Drainage and development of swamp land in eastern North Carolina was initiated by the late 1600s and a large-scale drainage project on organic soils occurred in the 1790s (Ruffin, 1861). Since that time there have been periods of clearing and development followed by longer periods of inactivity (Lilly, 1980). The latest period of increased activity which involves the largest land area began about 1973. This period coincided with the large algae bloom problems in the Chowan River and the general awareness that development of any type results in some environmental changes. Consequently, it was natural and appropriate that questions were raised by the scientific community, by various state and federal agencies, and the general public about the effect that massive land changes would have upon the environment. At that time, it was also recognized that there was a void in basic scientific information concerning the effects of land clearing and development on the hydrology and quality of the drainage waters.

This paper gives some preliminary data obtained in a research project initiated in 1975 to determine the effects of drainage and land development on (1) the hydrology of the area, (2) the water table elevations, (3) seepage to underlying aquifiers and soil subsidence, and (4) the water quality variables and total nutrient and sediment load leaving the area.

PROCEDURES

Three paired areas (six sites) of developed and undeveloped land on the property of First Colony Farms in Washington and Tyrrell counties, North Carolina, were selected for study. These study areas were chosen to represent edaphic groups in the region which largely influence development and management patterns. Although modern soil surveys recognize approximately forty different soils in the region, the three sites chosen generally span the full range of the region's potentially developable soils. Physical properties of each site including hydraulic conductivity and soil water characteristics were studied by Badr (1978). The three major edaphic groups represented are:

1. Mineral soils with a histic epipedon (Histic Humaquepts). This group of soils is characterized by having a high organic matter surface horizon which does not extend deep enough in the soil profile ($<$40 cm) for the soils to be classified as organic soils. The mineral contact below the organic horizon may be either sand or clay. In the region being discussed, this type of soil is the easiest to prepare for cultivated land and is the most productive after clearing.
2. Shallow organic soils (Terric Medisaprist). These soils have a high organic matter surface which extends to 40 to 130 cm below the surface before contacting a mineral layer. This is the second most productive group of soils in the region. The percentage of the soils of this type that is cleared for agricultural purposes depends largely upon the amount of buried wood within the profile.

3. Deep colloidal organic (Typic Medisaprist). This group of soils is characterized by having colloidal organic matter horizons that extend deep into the soil profile (>130 cm). These are the least productive of the soils that may be cleared for agricultural production (see Barnes, this volume). They frequently contain large amounts of buried wood, which is a problem both in the initial land preparation and during cultural operations for several years after clearing. Cleared land of this type is most likely to be used for pasture and forage production. Most of the profit that has been made from this land has resulted from sale of the land.

Weirs were installed and calibrated in place at each drainage site and outflow rates were continuously measured by recording the stage on the upstream side of the triangular weirs with type F water level recorders. A semiproportional automatic water sampler was located at each site for the collection of water samples. The stage recorders were serviced weekly, and water samples were collected at the same time for laboratory analyses. Rainfall was also continuously recorded at each site so the drainage response

TABLE 1. *A Summary of the Experimental Sites, Soils and Cropping Sequences in Washington and Tyrrell Counties, North Carolina*

Site no.	Soil	Drainage area monitored (ha)	Crop grown 1976	1977	1978	1979
101	Mineral-histic epipedon	7.4	Natural	Soybeans	Soybeans	Corn
102	Mineral-histic epipedon	7.4	Natural (good stand of pine)	Natural	Natural	Natural
103	Organic—deep colloidal muck	130	Fescue pasture	Fescue pasture	Fescue pasture	Fescue pasture
104	Organic—deep colloidal muck	130	Natural (bush, bayberry, gallberry, pond pine)	Natural	Natural	Natural
106	Shallow organic—50 to 70 cm deep over clay loam	7.4	Corn	Soybeans	Soybeans	Soybeans
107	Shallow organic—50 to 70 cm deep over clay loam	7.4	Natural (moderately good stand of pine)	Natural	Natural	Natural

could be analyzed for either selected events or on a long-term basis. Water table recorders for continuous measurement of water tables were installed in each site. Some characteristics of the study areas are given in Table 1.

Field measurements of conductivity, salinity, dissolved oxygen, temperature, and pH were made on grab samples taken at the weekly sampling times. Laboratory measurements of total P, total N, nitrate nitrogen, total organic carbon, filterable solids, and turbidity were run on the weekly samples. Analyses for Ca, Mg, Na, Cu, Fe, Mn, Cd, and Zn were run on composite samples at monthly intervals. Fecal and total coliforms were run on grab samples taken every two weeks.

HYDROLOGY

The most dramatic effect of agricultural land development on hydrology is the increase in peak outflow rates from field size units. The effects of development on outflow rates from paired sites on deep colloidal muck soil (sites 103 and 104) are shown in Figure 1 for the period May 5, 1977, to July 4, 1977. Although the sites are about 5 km apart and there were considerable differences in the total annual rainfall for 1977 (Figure 2), rainfall patterns were identical on the two sites for the period shown in Figure 1. The flow measurements include both subsurface drainage and surface runoff from the site. In general, peak flow rates were three to four times higher for the developed site (103) than for the undeveloped (104). For example, a 33-mm rain on May 7, 1977, caused a peak outflow rate of 5.9 cmm (3.5 cfs) on site 103 versus 1.7 cmm (1.0 cfs) for site 104. A much larger storm occurred on May 24 (day 144) when 95 mm of rainfall in less than twenty-four hours caused peak runoff rates of 27.7 cmm (16.5 cfs) from the developed site and 8.4 cmm (5.0 cfs) from the undeveloped site. The peak runoff rates on the developed site also occurred about twenty-four hours sooner than on the undeveloped site for both rainfall events.

Another relatively large storm (53 mm) occurred on July 1 (day 182). However, this event was preceded by a dry June (only 31 mm of rain during the month) and the runoff was negligible from both developed and undeveloped sites.

The peak outflow rates are higher and occur earlier on the developed sites because the drainage system installed in these areas provides mostly surface drainage. The fields are sloped to ditches located 90 m apart so water that is not infiltrated moves rapidly to the drainage outlet. The soils are poorly drained internally with shallow water tables and runoff does not usually occur until the water table rises to near the surface. On the undeveloped sites, there is a thick root mat (15 to 45 cm deep, composed of leaves, twigs and both living and dead plant roots) through which surface waters

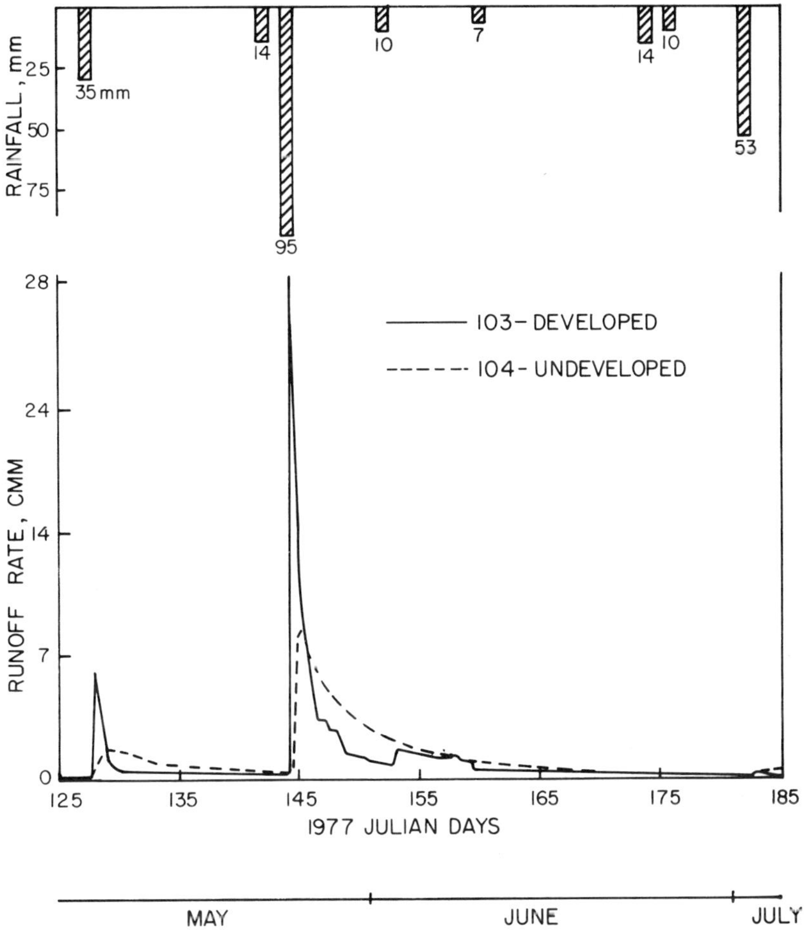

FIGURE 1. *Runoff rates from developed (pasture) and undeveloped (pond pine) deep organic soils during 1977.*

flow in tortuous paths over longer periods of time before finally reaching the drainage outlet. Unlike conventional subsurface flow in soils, flow within the root mat may be concentrated, entering the outlet channel at many distinct points along its length. As water is removed from the root mat and the free surface approaches the interface with the soil mass, the flow process is assumed to gradually change to that which is governed by Darcy's law for flow in porous media. Subsurface flow may continue for long periods as shown by the recession limb of the hydrographs in Figure 1. This flow is derived mostly from bank storage near the open ditches. Even on developed

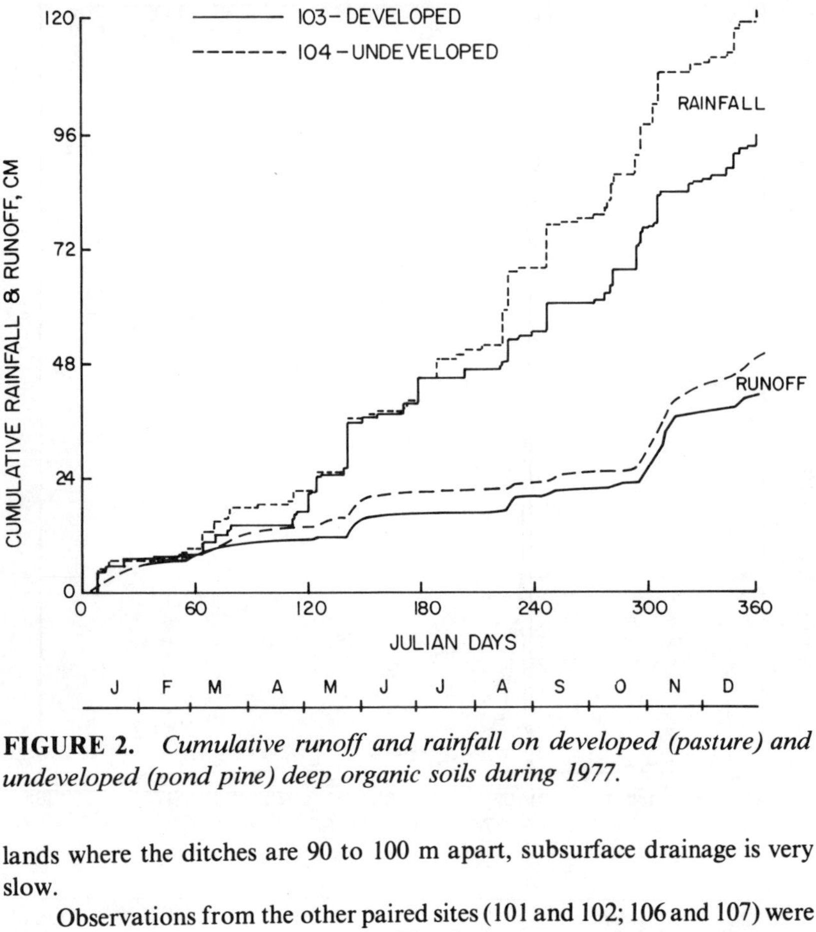

FIGURE 2. *Cumulative runoff and rainfall on developed (pasture) and undeveloped (pond pine) deep organic soils during 1977.*

lands where the ditches are 90 to 100 m apart, subsurface drainage is very slow.

Observations from the other paired sites (101 and 102; 106 and 107) were similar to those shown in Figure 1. The drainage areas for these sites were smaller, 7.4 ha as compared to 130 ha for sites 103 and 104; so peak flow rates occurred earlier and were reduced in magnitude from those given in Figure 1. For example, a 50-mm rainfall resulted in a peak outflow rate of 0.89 cmm (0.53 cfs) for the undeveloped site 102. The peak runoff rates for developed sites 101 and 106 were three to four times those for the respective undeveloped sites 102 and 107.

The observed increase in outflow rates is valid only for situations in which the outlet canal network, including pumping stations, has sufficient capacity to move the drainage water away from the fields. Outlet capacity from our experimental sites was often limited during the months of December through March. Our results show that approximately 50% of the total annual runoff occurs during these months. The main drainage canal system, as currently designed, does not have sufficient capacity to remove water at the rate at which it can flow from developed lands. As a result, the water levels in the canals and field ditches rise and drainage rates from both developed and undeveloped lands are reduced. Under these circumstances, there is very little difference in the runoff rate from developed and natural areas.

While there were relatively large differences between peak runoff rates (Figure 1), there was little difference in total outflow from developed (41.3 cm) and undeveloped (49.2 cm) sites as shown in Figure 2 for sites 103 and 104. Because rainfall at site 104 was 122 cm as opposed to 95 cm at site 103, greater runoff from 104 was expected. Assuming storage of soil water at the beginning and end of the year to be equal and that deep seepage losses are negligible, water lost from each site by evapotranspiration (ET) can be estimated from a water balance by substracting total runoff from rainfall. This procedure gives estimated ET values of 72 cm (28 in) from undeveloped site 104 and 54 cm (21 in) from developed site 103. A monthly water balance showed that the differences in ET occurred during the months of July, August and September when total rainfall on site 104 was 41 cm versus only 24 cm on site 103. The reduced rainfall plus improved drainage on site 103 caused the water table to be deeper (Figure 3) and soil conditions drier than

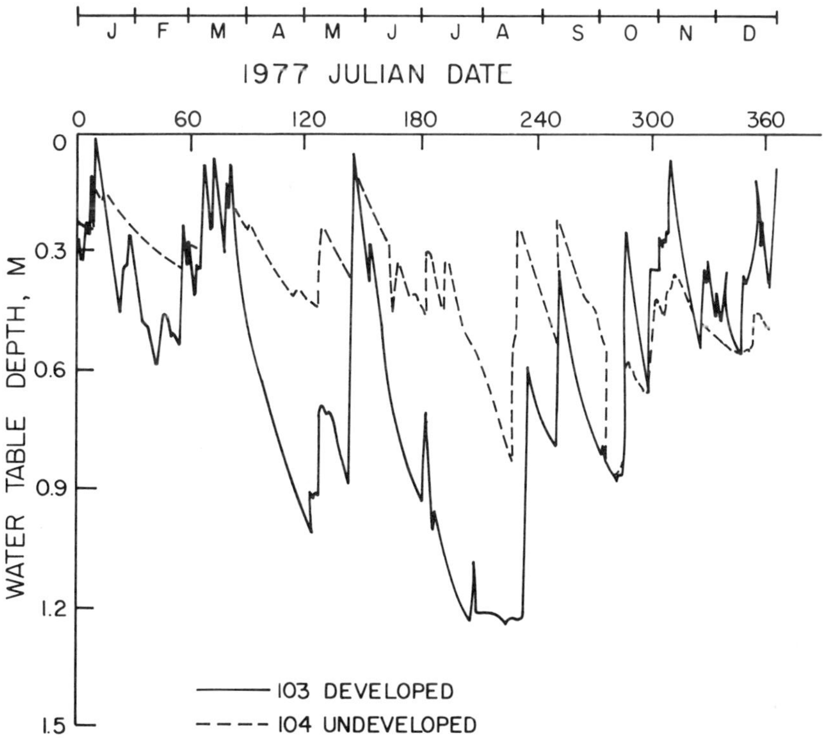

FIGURE 3. *Water table depths near the center of 140 ha developed (pasture) and undeveloped (pond pine) deep organic soils during 1977.*

on the undeveloped site 104. Thus, ET from the developed site was reduced because of limited availability of soil water. Note that rainfall on site 104 exceeded that on 103 by 17 cm during the three months when the lack of soil water reduced ET on site 103 by an estimated 18 cm. Therefore, it may be concluded that the difference in soil water availability, and hence ET, in this case was primarily due to the difference in rainfall rather than to improved drainage on site 103.

Another factor that influences availability of soil water is the depth of the root zone. The unlimed North Carolina organic soils have a low pH (ca. 3.8) and crop rooting depths are limited to the depth of lime incorporation, about 20 cm in most cases. While rooting depths of the native trees and shrubs on natural sites may be somewhat greater than agricultural crops, they are still limited by higher water tables and very acid subsoils. Under the same rainfall conditions, the combination of improved drainage and a shallow root zone may cause a reduction in ET and a consequent increase in outflow from developed soils during some years. This response would occur only during years with dry periods of sufficient length to cause ET to be limited by soil water deficiencies. This will not usually occur in the winter and early spring months when water tables are high and ET is limited by atmospheric variables. Such conditions may develop rather quickly, however, during the early part of the growing season before the rooting systems are established as well as after prolonged drought periods later in the season. The differences in ET for developed and undeveloped conditions would be greater when several such dry periods occur during a season rather than a single drought of longer duration. Because of the relatively small difference in water table depths on developed and undeveloped soils (figures 3 and 4), the difference in ET, and, therefore, in annual runoff, will usually be small.

WATER TABLE DEPTH

The effect on water table depth of the drainage systems currently used in North Carolina organic soils is often misunderstood. A popular misconception is that field drainage ditches, usually placed 90 to 100 m apart, lower the water table to the level of the water in the ditch, approximately 1 to 1.5 m below the soil surface. In fact, the water table elevation in the field changes continuously and rarely falls to the depth of the ditch. The soils are very slowly permeable with subsoil hydraulic conductivities of about 0.02 m/day (Badr and Skaggs, 1978) and the drainage systems installed serve primarily for surface drainage. Drains would have to be placed 10 to 12 m apart to provide subsurface drainage comparable to conventional improved drainage in mineral soils. Even then, the water table would not be drawn down to a constant depth but would vary over time with rainfall and ET.

Water table depths measured near the center of sites 103 and 104 are plotted in Figure 3 for 1977. Similar plots are given in Figure 4 for sites 101

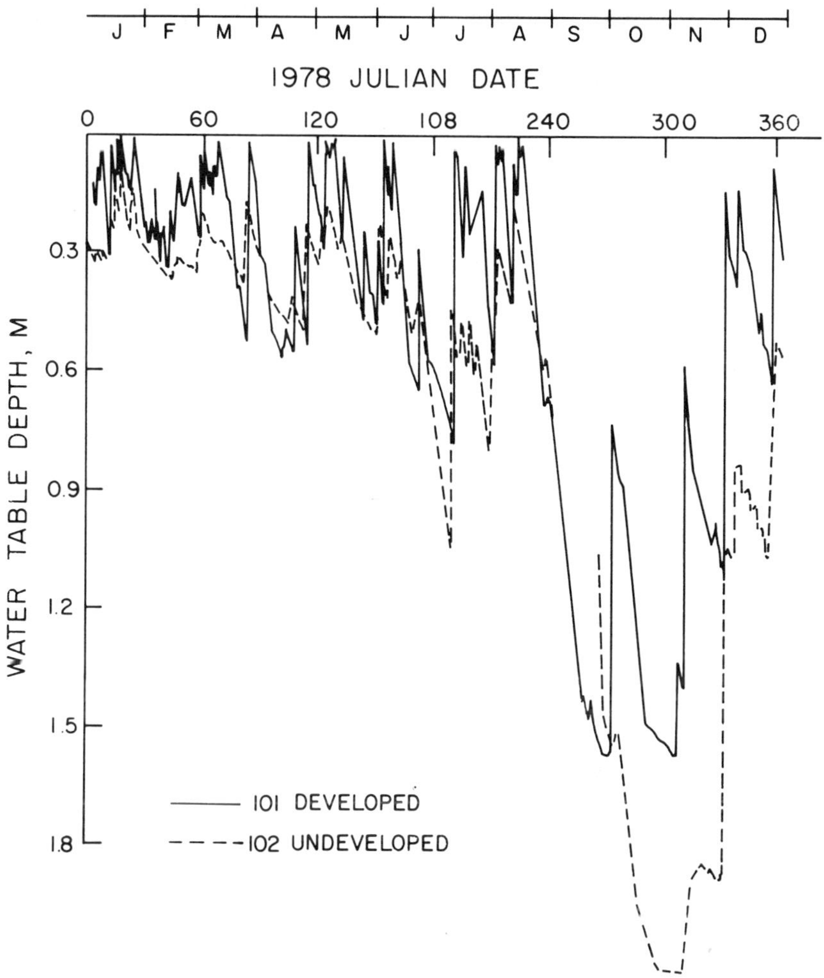

FIGURE 4. *Water table depths at the center of 7.4 ha developed (soybeans) and undeveloped (pine) high organic mineral soils during 1978.*

and 102 during 1978. Note that the water tables on both developed and undeveloped sites are close to the surface during the months of December to March and have varying, but deeper, depths during the summer and fall. On sites 103 and 104 (Figure 3) water table drawdown is primarily due to ET. Good surface drainage on site 103 allows water table drawdown to begin soon after rainfall ceases, whereas surface water on site 104 is removed much more slowly and water table drawdown is delayed. The average water table depth for 1977 on site 103 was 60 cm as opposed to 37 cm for site 104. This 23-cm difference was not entirely due to drainage, however, as site 104 had more rainfall than site 103 during the months of July to September (Figure 2) when the difference in water table depths was greatest.

The average water table depth on the developed site 101 during 1978 was about 20 cm less than that on the undeveloped site 102 (Figure 4). This difference is attributed to the deep root mat (>30 cm deep) on the undeveloped site. Badr (1978) estimated the hydraulic conductivity of the root mat to be 240 m/day. Site 102 is only 90 m wide with ditches on both sides so water moves quickly through the porous mat. The water table rarely rises into the root mat (Figure 4), even during very wet periods when it is coincident with the surface of the developed site. The root mat is removed during the process of development and the hydraulic conductivity of the layer just below the mat is reduced because of compaction (Badr, 1978). Thus, water moves to the lateral ditches much more slowly from within the surface layer of the developed site than from the root mat and surface layer of the undeveloped site. Similar results were observed on sites 106 and 107 where the high conductivity of the root mat again had an effect on increasing the depth to the water table in the undeveloped site.

WATER QUALITY

Nonpoint water contamination from agricultural development is usually caused by nitrogen, phosphorus, and sediments (Richardson, this volume). A large body of evidence indicates water quality problems occur when the concentration or amounts of these variables have increased above some "safe" level. Each of these components is present in drainage water from natural areas, but the quantities are greater in drainage water from cultivated fields. The purpose of this section is to quantify the increase as a result of agricultural development in the high organic matter soils of eastern North Carolina and to compare these increases with those observed in other agricultural soils in North Carolina.

Nitrogen

When severe erosion is not a problem, large losses of nitrogen in drainage water from agricultural fields is in the form of nitrate nitrogen. The loss of nitrate nitrogen from a developed and undeveloped shallow organic soil is shown in Figure 5. All three developed areas (101, 103, 106) in our study lost from 1 to 2 kg of nitrate nitrogen per hectare per year. The average nitrate nitrogen concentration in the drainage water from the three developed areas was less than 1 mg/1. There is an obvious increase (Figure 5) in nitrate lost from these high organic matter soils as a result of development, but this increase is small, particularly when compared to the losses of nitrate from

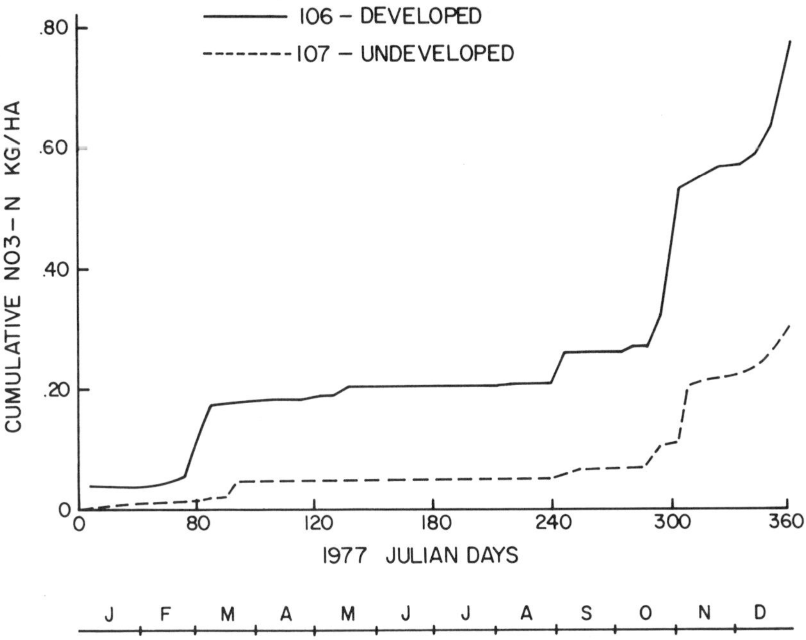

FIGURE 5. *Cumulative loss of nitrate nitrogen in drainage water from developed (soybeans) and undeveloped (pine) shallow organic soils.*

some other agricultural areas and soil types in North Carolina. This comparison is made in Figure 6 which shows nitrate loss measured in a previous study (Gilliam et al., 1979) for a moderately well-drained sandy cultivated soil in the coastal plain and the loss from a field in this study. The large difference in nitrate in drainage water from the two soil types is a result of more denitrification in the poorly drained high organic matter soil (Gambrell et al., 1975).

The effects of development upon the quantities of total Kjeldahl nitrogen moving into the large drainage ditches are shown in Figure 7. Again there is a significant increase due to development. Most of the nitrogen was present as organic nitrogen associated with the sediment because the loss of ammonium nitrogen was less than 1 kg per hectare per year and dissolved organic carbon was relatively low. The availability of this organic nitrogen to microorganisms is relatively low as indicated by low B.O.D. values in the drainage water and the previously measured (Dolman and Buol, 1967) high C/N ratios in the soils. The fact that the ditches require periodic cleaning of sediment indicates that much of the sediment-associated nitrogen is lost from the drainage water before it reaches a stream or estuary. The amount of this reduction would be dependent upon the distance between the field and the outlet and the sediment carrying characteristics of the outlet canal.

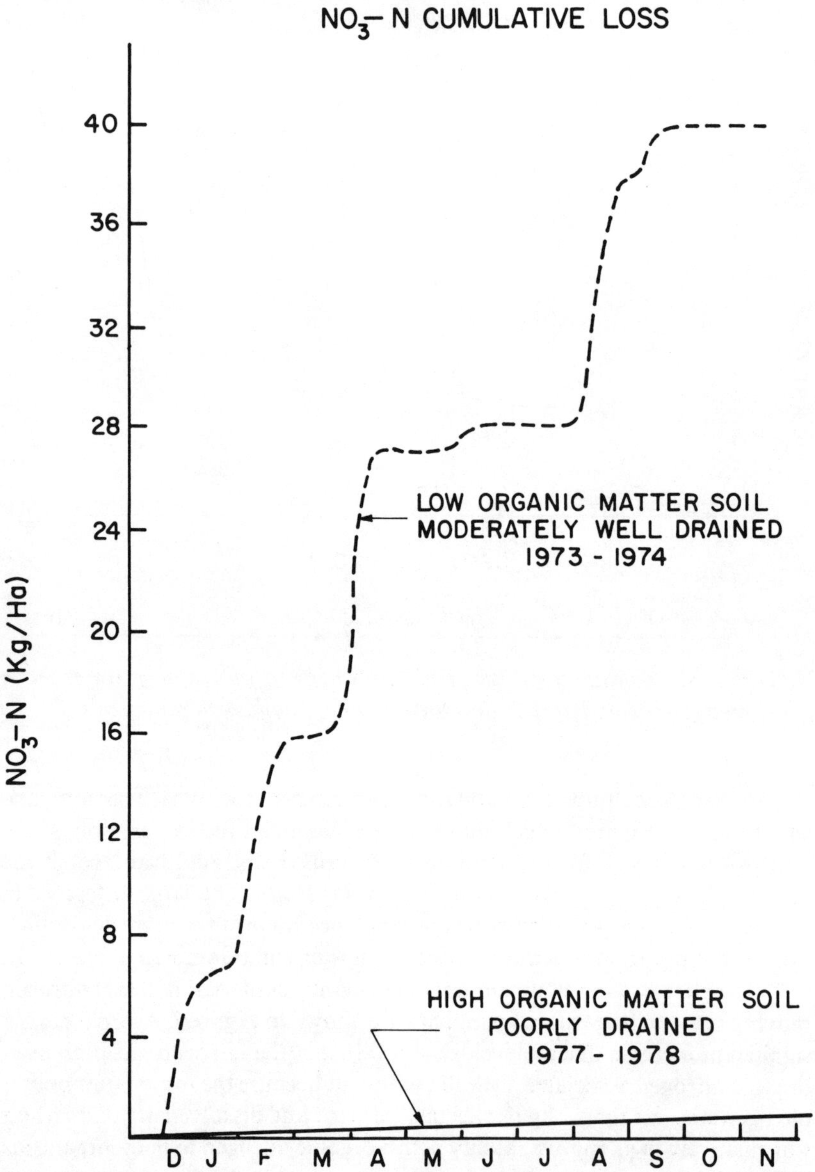

FIGURE 6. *Cumulative loss of nitrate nitrogen in drainage waters from a sandy, moderately well-drained soil and from a high organic matter poorly-drained soil in the North Carolina coastal plains. (Cultivated crops were grown on both areas and both areas had improved drainage systems.)*

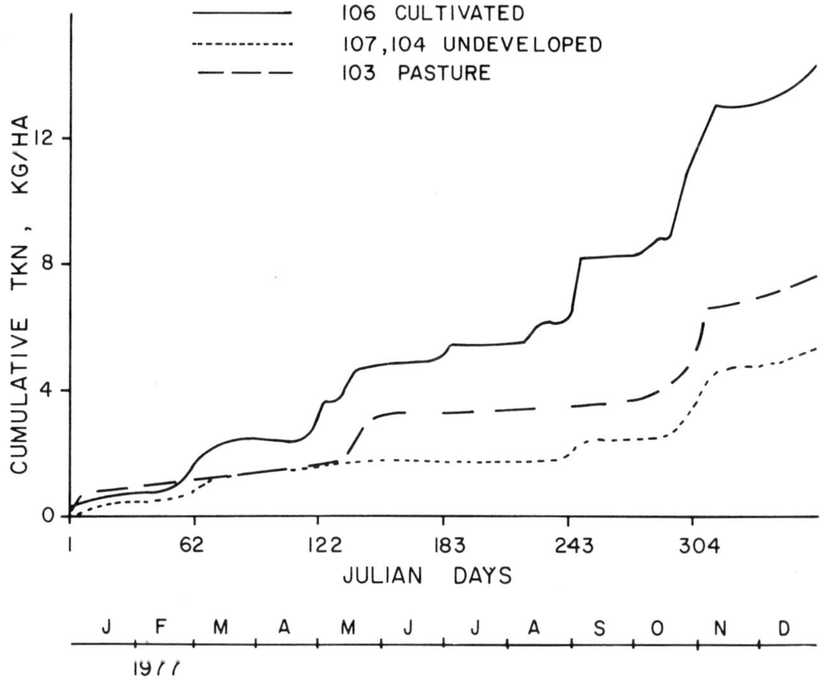

FIGURE 7. *Cumulative loss of total Kjeldahl nitrogen in drainage water from the pasture (deep organic), cultivated (shallow organic) and undeveloped soils.*

Phosphorus

The increase in phosphorus in drainage waters, as a result of development, is very dependent on the type of soil being developed as shown in Figure 8. The shallow and deep organic soils lose ten to twenty times more phosphorus than mineral soils. The amount of phosphorus lost from a developed and fertilized mineral soil is actually slightly less than the amount lost from an undeveloped organic soil. Nearly all of the phosphorus lost from the organic soils is not associated with sediment but is in solution as orthophosphate. Organic matter in soils does not react with phosphorus unless there is sufficient mineral matter to provide aluminum for the exchange sites on the organic matter (Fox and Kamprath, 1971). Thus, significant quantities of fertilizer phosphorus may be lost in drainage waters from acid organic soils as shown in Figure 8.

We cannot make an accurate assessment of the effect that continued clearing and development in the Blacklands area will have upon the quantities

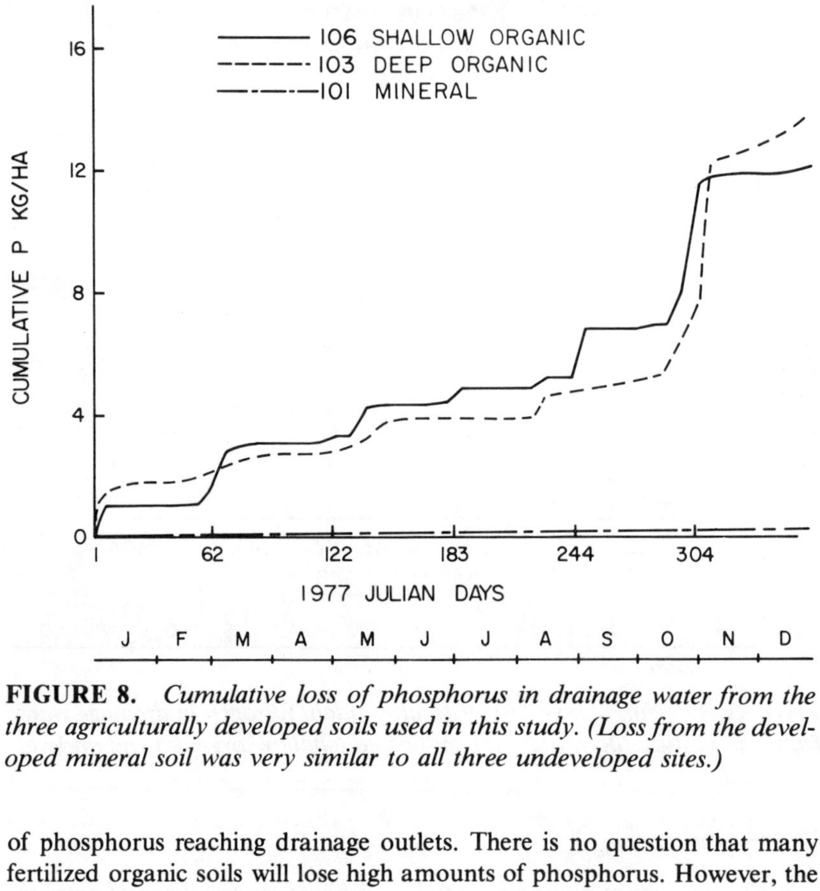

FIGURE 8. *Cumulative loss of phosphorus in drainage water from the three agriculturally developed soils used in this study. (Loss from the developed mineral soil was very similar to all three undeveloped sites.)*

of phosphorus reaching drainage outlets. There is no question that many fertilized organic soils will lose high amounts of phosphorus. However, the true organic soils are not nearly as agriculturally productive under existing technology as mineral soils and, as a result, current agricultural development in the Blacklands places heavy emphasis on mineral soils (organic layer <40 cm thick) (see Barnes, this volume).

Other factors that will influence the quantity of phosphorus reaching outlets is the distance between the field and outlet and the type of sediment or ditch bank between the field and outlet. Mineral sediments in ditches or ditch banks cut into sediments containing shell fragments would readily react with the orthophosphate and remove it from solution. This is almost certainly occurring on Open Grounds Farm in Carteret County where the canals are lined with shell fragments.

Sediments

Because these areas have such a small amount of relief, soil erosion is not an agricultural problem except for sediment deposited in drainage ditches.

TABLE 2. *Average Concentration in Drainage Waters from a Developed (106) and Undeveloped (107) Shallow Organic Soil*

Variable	Developed (soybean)	Undeveloped (pine)
pH	5.6	4.1
D.O. (mg/l)	7.0	6.0
B.O.D. (mg/l)	4.9	1.7
T.O.C. (mg/l)	41	21
Cl (mg/l)	14	8
Na (mg/l)	8.7	5.4
K (mg/l)	1.33	.68
Ca (mg/l)	21.7	4.5
Mg (mg/l)	.02	.01
Cu (mg/l)	.02	.01
Cd (mg/l)	<.01	<.01

However, any time that water flows across a soil area which does not have plant cover, the water will contain more soil particles than water moving over a similar soil with plant cover. Since cultivated soils in the region are sometimes bare and are disturbed during cultural practices, they do lose more sediment than undeveloped areas (340 kg/ha versus 85 kg/ha, respectively). These values are from the shallow organic soil type (106, 107) and are illustrative of and intermediate between the general soil types studied. It should be remembered that most erosion losses are measured in units of tons per hectare and the loss here was approximately 340 kg per hectare. The effect of human activity resulted in a sharp rise in sediment loss during February 1977 as a result of the clearing of the drainage ditch. A small rise was also noted in the spring during planting and cultivation. Much of this sediment will remain in the larger drainage ditch and be placed back on the land during ditch maintenance operations.

Other Water Components

We measured a total of twenty-five different water variables. Many of these are not considered critical in the evaluation of water quality, but we wished to characterize, as well as possible, all changes in drainage water after development. The average concentration of some of these measured variables is given in Table 2 for the shallow organic soil paired sites. This pair was chosen because it was intermediate between the other soil types for most measurements made.

ACKNOWLEDGMENTS

The authors gratefully acknowledge the support of the North Carolina Agricultural Research Service, Water Resources Research Institute of the

University of North Carolina and the United States Environmental Protection Agency in the preparation of this study.

LITERATURE CITED

Badr, A. W., 1978. Physical properties of some North Carolina organic soils and the effect of land development on these properties. M. S. Thesis, N.C. State University, Raleigh, N.C.

Badr, A. W., and R. W. Skaggs, 1978. The effect of land development on the physical properties of some North Carolina organic soils. Paper No. 18-2537. 1978 winter meeting, Am. Soc. Ag. Eng., Chicago, Ill.

Dolman, J. D., and S. W. Buol, 1967. A study of organic soils in the tidewater region of North Carolina. N.C. Agr. Exp. Sta. Tech. Bull. No. 181, 52 pp.

Fox, R. L., and E. J. Kamprath, 1971. Adsorption and leaching of P in acid organic soils and high organic matter soil. Soil Sci. Soc. Am. Proc., 3:154-156.

Gambrell, R. P., J. W. Gilliam, and S. B. Weed, 1975. Denitrification in subsoils of the North Carolina coastal plain as affected by soil drainage. J. Environ. Qual., 4:311-316.

Gilliam, J. W., R. W. Skaggs, and S. B. Weed, 1979. Drainage control to diminish nitrate loss from agricultural fields. J. Environ. Qual., 8:137-142.

Lilly, J. P., 1980. Blackland soils of North Carolina: Their characteristics and management. Technical publication in review in the Soil Science Department at N.C. State University, Raleigh, N.C.

Ruffin, Edmund, 1861. Sketches of lower North Carolina and the similar adjacent lands. Institute for the Deaf and Dumb, Raleigh, N.C. N.C. State University Microfiche No. 17, 17243-17246a.

Peat in North Carolina Wetlands

Roy L. Ingram and Lee J. Otte

ABSTRACT

Peat deposits of North Carolina are of three main geologic types representing the accumulation of organic matter in: (1) pocosins, broad shallow depressions on "uplifted" sea floor; (2) river flood plains; and (3) Carolina bays, elliptical depressions of unknown origin.

The largest pocosin deposits are: (1) Pamlimarle peninsula which has 360 sq mi of peatland and 210 million tons of moisture-free peat (930 sq km, 190 million metric tons), (2) Dismal Swamp which has 100 sq mi of peatland and 60 million tons of peat (260 sq km, 50 metric tons), and (3) Croatan Forest which has 40 sq mi of peatland and 23 million tons of peat (100 sq km, 20 metric tons). These deposits normally range in thickness from 1 to 8 ft (0.3 to 2.4 m).

River flood plain peats of unknown extent occur as lenses in alluvial sands and clays and may attain a thickness of 25 ft (7.6 m). The ash content usually exceeds 10%.

Five to six hundred Carolina bays from 0.2 to 3 mi (0.3 to 5 km) in length are scattered over the coastal plain. Many contain high quality peats up to 15 ft (4.6 m) thick.

Most peats in North Carolina are black, fine-grained, and highly decomposed with ash contents commonly less than 5%. Sulfur contents are low (median 0.2%), and heating values are high (median 10,300 Btu/lb or 24.0 MJ/kg).

North Carolina has an estimated 1000 sq mi (2600 sq km) of peatland containing about 600 million tons (540 metric tons) of moisture-free peat.

Key Words: Carolina bays, Croatan Forest, Dismal Swamp, flood plain, Pamlimarle peninsula, peat, pocosin

INTRODUCTION

Types of Peat Deposits

Peat deposits of North Carolina are of three main geologic types representing the accumulation of organic matter in: (1) pocosins, broad shallow

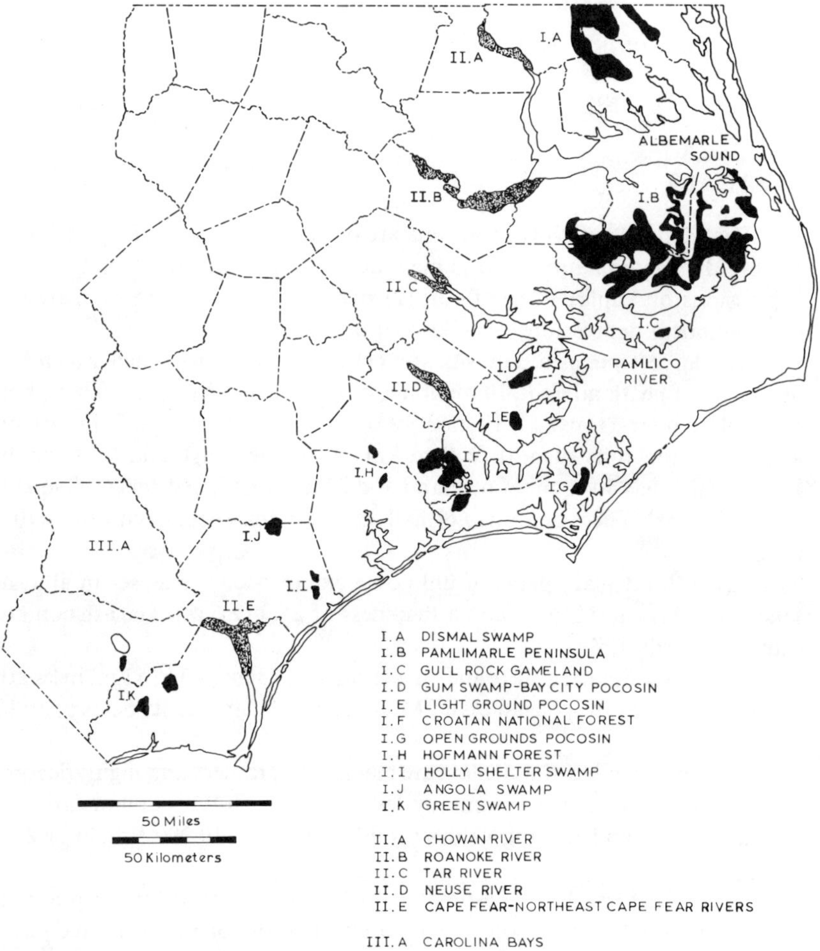

FIGURE 1. *Map showing location of North Carolina peat deposits.*

depressions on "uplifted" sea floor (Type I on Figure 1); (2) river flood plains (Type II on Figure 1); and (3) Carolina bays, elliptical depressions of unknown origin, perhaps meteorite scars (Type III on Figure 1).

Pocosin Deposits

During the Sangamonian interglacial interval about 100,000 years ago, the shoreline of North Carolina was some distance west of the present shoreline (Oaks and Whitehead, 1979). This old shoreline is marked by a sand ridge and eastward-facing scarp, the Suffolk scarp. During the Wisconsin ice age, sea level dropped, reaching a low stand of about 400 ft (120 m) below present sea level about 18,000 years ago. For the past 18,000 years sea level has been rising but has not come back up to the old Suffolk scarp shoreline. The area between the Suffolk scarp and the present shoreline is a relatively flat surface, the Pamlico terrace, sloping from about 15 ft (4.6 m) above sea level to the present shoreline. On this relatively flat surface are many broad, shallow depressions which were dissected by stream channels before peat formation began. About 8,000 to 10,000 years ago peat began to accumulate in these dissected depressions, often building up to form broad, dome shaped surfaces. Early Indians called these areas pocosins, swamp-on-a-hill. North Carolina's major peat deposits are pocosin deposits. (Also see Daniel, this volume.)

Pamlimarle Peninsula Deposits

The largest peat deposits in North Carolina are found in the peninsula between Pamlico River and Albemarle Sound (Pamlimarle peninsula). Most of the peat is found in broad, shallow depressions with thicknesses ranging

TABLE 1. *Estimated Peat Reserves of North Carolina*

Deposit	Area		Weight of moisture-free peat in millions of		Quality of estimate
	mi²	km²	tons	metric tons	
I. Pocosin deposits					
A. Dismal Swamp	100	260	60	54	Good
B. Pamlimarle Peninsula	360	930	210	190	Good
C. Gull Rock	6	16	4	4	Fair
D. Gum Swamp–Bay City	7	18	4	4	Poor
E. Light Ground	9	23	5	5	Excellent
F. Croatan	40	100	23	21	Good
G. Open Grounds	15	40	9	8	Fair
H. Hofmann Forest	10	26	6	5	Fair
I. Holly Shelter Swamp	6	16	4	4	Fair
J. Angola Swamp	20	52	12	11	Poor
K. Green Swamp	10	26	6	5	Fair
II. River flood plains					
A. Chowan	40	100	25	23	Poor
B. Roanoke	50	130	29	26	Poor
C. Tar	10	25	6	5	Poor
D. Neuse	10	25	6	5	Poor
E. Cape Fear	20	50	11	10	Poor
III. Carolina bays	350	900	200	180	Poor
	1063	2737	620	560	

from 1 to 8 ft (0.3 to 2.4 m), but some old channels contain peat up to 19 ft (5.8 m) thick. Most of the peat is moderately to highly decomposed but with much wood. The ash content is usually low (2 to 5%), and the heating value averages over 10,000 Btu/lb (23.2 MJ/kg) on a moisture-free basis. Preliminary work indicates that Pamlimarle peninsula has about 360 sq mi (930 sq km) of peatland containing about 210 million tons (190 million metric tons) of moisture-free peat (Table 1).

Dismal Swamp Deposits

The second largest deposit is found in the Dismal Swamp. The peats are similar to those in the Pamlimarle peninsula except that the ash content is slightly higher. Preliminary work indicates that the Dismal Swamp has about 100 sq mi (260 sq km) of peatland containing 50 to 60 million tons (45 to 70 million metric tons) of moisture-free peat.

Croatan Forest Deposit

The Croatan Forest deposit is the third largest. Preliminary work indicates that the deposit has about 40 to 50 sq mi (100 to 130 sq km) of peatland containing 25 to 30 million tons (23 to 27 million metric tons) of moisture-free peat.

Light Ground Pocosin

The Light Ground Pocosin peat deposit is located in south central Pamlico County, 13 mi (21 km) east of New Bern. Except for a narrow channel 8 to 12 ft (2.4 to 3.7 m) deep, and two small areas of thin peat over highs on the sub-peat surface, the peat lies in a broad, shallow depression and increases in thickness to about 7 ft (2.1 m) in the center. The deposit occupies an area of 9.27 sq mi (24.0 sq km) and has a total of 5.171 million tons (4.691 million metric tons) of moisture-free peat.

The peat lies just to the east of the Arapahoe sand ridge and Suffolk scarp. The normal surface elevation in the area around the peat, the Pamlico terrace or surface, is 15 to 20 ft (4.5 to 6.1 m); however, the surface of the peat is a broad dome reaching an elevation of over 20 ft (6.1 m).

Two main types of peat are present: (1) a brown, decomposed fibrous peat usually restricted to the infilled channels, and (2) a black, fine-grained, highly decomposed humic peat. Stumps and logs of white cedar and cypress are common throughout the black peat.

The moisture content increases with depth from an average of 74% in the top foot to 90% at 9 ft (2.7 m). The bulk density increases from about 180 tons of moisture-free peat per acre-foot (130 kg/cu m) in the top foot to 270 tons

(200 kg/cu m) at 3 ft (0.9 m) and then decreases to 125 tons (90 kg/cu m) at a depth of 9 ft (2.7 m). Within the main body of the peat the ash content is almost always below 10% and is usually below 5%; and the heating value ranges from 9,800 to 10,900 Btu/lb (22.8 to 25.4 MJ/kg) with a median of 10,500 (24.4 MJ/kg). The nitrogen content ranges from 0.9 to 2.0% with a median of 1.4%. The sulfur content ranges from 0.2 to 0.3%.

Other Deposits

The other pocosin deposits (Figure 1) probably contain 1 to 12 million tons each of moisture-free peat (Table 1).

River Flood Plain Deposits

Limited fieldwork has discovered some peat deposits of unknown extent along the lower parts of the Chowan, Roanoke, Neuse, and Cape Fear rivers (Figure 1 and Table 1). The flood plain peats are more difficult to survey than the pocosin peats. Pocosin peats are nearly always found at the surface, but flood plain peats are often covered by several feet of alluvial sand and clay and often grade laterally into inorganic sediments. The flood plain peats are localized and often thick (up to 25 ft or 7.6 m). Ash contents of less than 10% are not common.

Carolina Bay Peats

In North Carolina there are approximately 2,100 Carolina bays. These elliptically shaped depressions over 800 ft (240 m) long are scattered over most of the coastal plain but have a concentration in Bladen County (Prouty, 1952). Of these, about 500 are between 3,000 and 10,000 ft (900 and 3,000 m) long, and about 60 are over 10,000 ft (3,000 m) long. Preliminary work shows that many, but not all, of these bays contain high quality peat up to 15 ft (4.6 m) thick. Ash contents average about 4%, and the heating value averages about 10,000 Btu/lb (23.3 MJ/kg). Very preliminary work indicates that the bays over 3,000 ft (900 m) long have about 350 sq mi (900 sq km) of peatland and contain about 200 million tons (180 million metric tons) of moisture-free peat.

QUALITY OF PEAT

Megascopic Characteristics

Most North Carolina peat is a black, fine-grained, highly decomposed humic to sapric peat. A brown, decomposed fibrous peat is sometimes found but is usually restricted to infilled channels. Stumps and logs of white cedar and cypress are common.

Chemical and Physical Characteristics

Proximate and ultimate analyses of about 260 samples of North Carolina peats were made by the Coal Analysis Laboratory, United States Department of Energy, Pittsburgh, Pennsylvania, following American Society for Testing and Materials (ASTM) recommended procedures. In addition, the moisture and ash contents of about 5,000 samples were determined in our laboratory following ASTM (1979) procedures.

The bulk density (weight of moisture-free peat per unit volume of *in situ* peat) was determined for about 440 samples. Samples of known volumes were collected with Macauley peat samplers and then heated at 105° C to constant weight.

Ash Content

Except for the transition zone between the peat and the underlying mineral sediment and for the edges of the deposits, the ash content is usually less than 10% and commonly less than 5%. Table 2 summarizes the heating values and compositions of the pocosin peats with less than 10% ash.

TABLE 2. *Composition and Heating Value of North Carolina Peats (200 Samples with Less than 10% Ash)*

	Low	Median	High
Btu/lb*	8,700	10,200	11,200
MJ/kg*	20.2	23.7	26.1
% H_2O	70	85 to 90	94
Proximate analysis*			
% Volatiles	52	61	67
% Fixed carbon	26	35	43
% Ash	—	4	—
Ultimate analysis*			
% C	53	60	66
% H	4.1	5.2	6.2
% O	25	29	34
% N	0.9	1.4	2.4
% S	0.1	0.2	0.8
% Ash	—	—	—

* Moisture-free basis

Water Content

The water content ranges from about 70 to 94% with the median being in the 85 to 90% range. The water content in the upper few feet is highly variable and varies seasonally reflecting an adjustment to the balance between precipitation and evapotranspiration (see Daniel, and Gilliam and Skaggs, this volume). In general, peat in the top 2 to 4 ft (0.6 to 1.2 m) has a lower moisture content than the deeper peats where the moisture content is usually in the 90 to 94% range.

Heating Value

Conclusions reached are:

1. The heating value (Btu/lb or MJ/kg) decreases in an almost linear fashion as the ash content increases;
2. Nearly all samples with an ash content of less than 25% have a heating value greater than 8,000 Btu/lb (18.6 MJ/kg);
3. The better peats (less than 10% ash) have heating values ranging from 8,700 to 11,200 Btu/lb (20.2 to 26.1 MJ/kg) with a median value of 10,200 (27.7);
4. The variation in heating values of the better peats is related primarily to the state of decomposition with the more thoroughly decomposed peats (sapric or humic peats) having the higher heating values.

Proximate Analyses

Both the amount of volatile matter and the amount of fixed carbon decrease as the organic matter is diluted with ash materials. The amount of volatile matter in the better peats ranges from 52 to 67% with a median value of 61% (Table 2). The amount of fixed carbon ranges from 26 to 43% with a median value of 35%. The variations in volatile matter and fixed carbon are probably related to the degree of decomposition of the peats.

Ultimate Analyses

The amount of carbon, hydrogen, and oxygen all decrease as the organic matter is diluted with ash materials. The carbon content of the better peats (less than 10% ash) ranges from 53 to 66% with a median value of 60%. The hydrogen content ranges from 4.1 to 6.2% with a median of 5.2%. The oxygen content ranges from 25 to 34% with a median of 29%.

The amount of sulfur is not affected by diluting the organic matter with ash materials. This implies that the sulfur does not come from the organic material. Peats that have been exposed to marine or brackish waters seem to have the highest sulfur contents. The sulfur is very probably of some type of iron sulfide. Of the samples analyzed the sulfur content ranges from 0.1 to 0.8% with a median of 0.2%. On the eastern end of the Pamlimarle peninsula, A. H. Cohen (1979, personal communication) found the sulfur content to range from 0.1 to 3.4% with an average of 0.5%. Compared to coal, North Carolina peat is very low in sulfur. The sulfur content of coal in the United States ranges from about 0.2 to 7.0% with an average of 1 to 2% (Averitt, 1973).

The amount of nitrogen varies from 0.9 to 2.4% with a median of 1.4%.

See Campbell, this volume, for further analysis of North Carolina peats as related to energy development.

Bulk Density

The bulk density (weight of moisture-free peat per unit volume of *in situ* peat) varies with moisture content and with depth.

Except for samples collected in the top few feet, the bulk density varies in an almost inverse linear manner with the moisture content, going from 360 tons per acre-foot (265 kg/cu m) at 75% moisture to 215 tons (158 kg) at 85% moisture to 70 tons (52 kg) at 95% moisture. Within the range of moisture content of 70 to 95%, the equations that fit this relationship are $D = -14.3\,M + 1430$, where D = the bulk density in moisture-free tons per acre-foot, and M =

TABLE 3. *Relation of Bulk Density to Depth of North Carolina Peats*

Depth (Ft.)	Number samples	Bulk density (Tons-MF*/Acre-foot) Low	Median	High	Cum. Avg.
0 to 1	10	130	172	205	172
1 to 2	56	65	190	300	181
2 to 3	86	70	210	435	191
3 to 4	80	70	195	410	192
4 to 5	55	85	162	270	186
5 to 6	46	75	142	250	178
6 to 7	34	75	135	220	171
7 to 8	27	85	115	285	164
8 to 9	17	80	125	340	160
9 to 10	9	80	110	160	155
10 to 11	5	80	115	130	151
11 to 12	5	95	127	160	149
12 to 13	3	90	120	150	147
13 to 14	3	110	120	125	145
14 to 15	3	110	115	135	144

* MF = moisture-free

the per cent moisture; and D = -10.52 M + 1052, where D = the bulk density in kg/cu m.

Although the moisture content is highly variable in the top few feet, the moisture content in general increases with depth. As the moisture content increases, the bulk density decreases. Table 3 shows the relationship between bulk density and depth for 439 samples. The bulk density in the top 4 or 5 ft (1.2 or 1.5 m) is highly variable but is higher for deeper peats. This higher bulk density in the top 4 or 5 ft is probably related to the changing relationship between precipitation and evapotranspiration and the irreversible collapse of capillary openings as water is removed from the peat. Below 5 or 6 ft (1.5 or 1.8 m), the median bulk density remains at about 120 moisture-free tons per acre-foot (88 kg/cu m).

CONCLUSIONS

The best estimate at this time is that North Carolina has about 1,000 sq mi (2,600 sq km) or 0.6 million acres of peatland containing about 600 million tons (540 metric tons) of moisture-free peat (Table 1). Although this estimate is only about one-third of the preliminary estimate of the U.S. Department of Energy (Anon, 1979) of 1,800 million tons, the reserves are significant as 50 million tons will keep a 400 megawatt peat-fired electrical plant operating for about thirty years.

Although peat has not been used in the United States to any great extent, peat has the potential for being used in a variety of ways (Cameron, 1973; Radforth and Brawner, 1977): as organic matter to improve soils; as a fuel for direct combustion; as chemical feedstock to make synthetic gas and gasoline, tars, phenols, benzene, methanol, peat coke, and activated carbon; as an insulating material; and as an absorbent for a variety of substances. (Also see Campbell and Harwood and McMullan, this volume.)

As a fuel for direct combustion, North Carolina peat is of high quality. The ash content is low, usually less than 5 to 10%. The median sulfur content of 0.2% makes it a very low-sulfur fuel as any fuel with less than 1% sulfur is considered a low-sulfur fuel (Averitt, 1963). The heating value is high as the median heating value of 10,200 Btu/lb (23.7 MJ/kg) is at the upper limit of the reported range of 8,000 to 10,000 Btu/lb of peats (Anon., 1979).

ACKNOWLEDGMENTS

This work was supported by grants from the North Carolina Energy Institute and the United States Department of Energy (DE-AC101-79ET-14693).

LITERATURE CITED

Anonymous, 1979. Peat Prospectus. U.S. Department of Energy, Washington, D.C., 77 pp.

ASTM, 1979. Moisture, ash, and organic matter of peat materials. American Society for Testing and Materials, 1979 Annual Book of Standards, part 19, D2974-71, pp. 451-452.

Averitt, Paul, 1973. Coal, pp. 133-142. In: D. A. Brobst and W. P. Pratt, eds., United States Mineral Resources. U.S. Geological Survey Prof. Paper 820.

Cameron C. C., 1973. Peat, pp. 505-513. In: D. A. Brobst and W. P. Pratt, eds., United States Mineral Resources. U.S. Geological Survey Prof. Paper 820.

Oaks, R. Q., Jr. and D. R. Whitehead, 1979. Geologic setting and origin of the Dismal Swamp, southeastern Virginia and northeastern North Carolina, pp. 1-24. In: P. W. Kirk, Jr., ed., The Great Dismal Swamp. University Press of Virginia, Charlottesville.

Prouty, W. F., 1952. Carolina bays and their origin. Geological Society America Bull., 63:167-224.

Radforth, N. W. and C. O. Brawner, 1977. Muskeg and the Northern Environment of Canada. University of Toronto Press, Toronto, 399 pp.

Pocosins: Ecosystem Processes and the Influence of Man on System Response

Curtis J. Richardson

ABSTRACT

The value of pocosin ecosystems and their internal processes at the global and regional levels are analyzed in terms of the global carbon budget and nutrient outputs into adjacent estuarine ecosystems. It is estimated that the total development of 0.5 million acres (202 x 10^5 ha) of pocosins has resulted in a release of 7 x 10^6 t C yr^{-1}. This C loss rate is close to that of the Okeechobee regions of Florida and the San Joaquin Valley in California. Combined carbon losses from these three areas alone represent 0.5% of the entire world's fossil fuel emission. The loss of wetlands as long-term carbon storage units is also discussed. The drainage of pocosin ecosystems with organic soils and their subsequent use in agricultural and cattle operations has resulted in significant outputs of phosphorus (i.e., over twenty and seventy times that of natural pocosins and crop covered mineral soils in the region, respectively) to canal drainage water. The conversion of pocosins in the Albemarle Sound region to fertilized agriculture lands results in a greater than threefold output of nitrogen and a twenty-eightfold increase of phosphorus. This equals nearly 20% of the total P loadings to the area and since Albemarle Sound appears to be P limited, the increased inputs are most likely to accelerate the eutrophication process; and, in fact, may be partly responsible for the recent Chowan River tributary algae blooms. An integrated approach to pocosin management that takes into account the ecosystem concept of land–water interactions is discussed along with a series of research and management recommendations.

Key Words: ecosystem management, nitrogen, phosphorus, estuaries, carbon flux, peat, N/P ratio

INTRODUCTION

Bormann in his 1976 paper, "An Inseparable Linkage between Conservation of Natural Ecosystems and the Conservation of Fossil Energy," pointed out many of the values that natural ecosystems provide to society and noted that their contributions are rarely included when decisions are made to alter ecosystems. Why is this? Have the ecologists been unable to articulate the importance of natural ecosystems or adequately quantify the consequences of altering ecosystems and their natural processes? Have industry and the public failed to distinguish the difference between the applied ecologists' objective of trying to understand, quantify, and moderate the degree of man's influence on our delicate life support system, the biosphere, and the often quoted environmentalists' view of preservation at any cost? Are we against good resource management?

In general, most of us feel that we are carrying out good resource management. Unfortunately, our perceptions of good or optimum resource management today is much like Kipling's classic story of the description of an elephant given by blindfolded men, each holding onto a different part of the pachyderm. This does not mean that our management is bad. We understand and properly manage, for our objectives, the part on which we have a hold, but we can't see the whole organism nor do we know where it's going or how good its health is.

Thus, I contend that forestry and agriculture understand the intricacies of optimizing stand and crop yields, improving genetic stocks, and growing monocultures on a short-term basis. Extractive industries continue to maximize their output while reducing the per unit cost, and conservationists utilize wilderness areas to attempt to freeze the system in time, thus preserving species gene pools and unique natural landscapes. All of these are done under the title of good resource management. As Eugene Odum (1979) has so often asked, "Where is the ecosystem concept in this type of management?"

The purposes of this paper are to:

1. Demonstrate the importance of including the ecosystem concept in pocosin management;
2. Assess our current knowledge about the value of pocosins ecosystem processes at a global and a regional level;
3. Address the effects that disturbance has on system processes and in turn on pocosin outputs to adjacent ecosystems;
4. Point out that different management strategies for pocosins can produce changes in inputs to downstream estuarine ecosystems; and, finally,
5. Make management recommendations based on ecosystem concepts and ecological values.

Like all ecosystems, pocosins can be viewed in a systems framework (Figure 1) which includes boundaries that can be used to determine biotic, geologic, and meteorologic inputs and outputs. The outputs (yields) are controlled by the rate of processes and interactions among the biotic and abiotic components of the ecosystem. The rates at which exchange, storage and uptake processes occur are continuously changing in response to both predictable and stochastic variations in climatic conditions, the biota, the abiotic milieu, and the effects of *Homo sapiens* as he attempts to utilize and manage these ecosystems. Inputs (e.g., energy, water, and nutrients) vary through time and are considered forcing functions that alter process rates. The forcing functions can vary naturally through time but are often greatly influenced by man's activities. For example, a significant increase in dust particulates in the atmosphere in central Ireland is attributed to the vast acreage of highmoor bog peatlands (>135,000 acres [54,600 ha]) that are

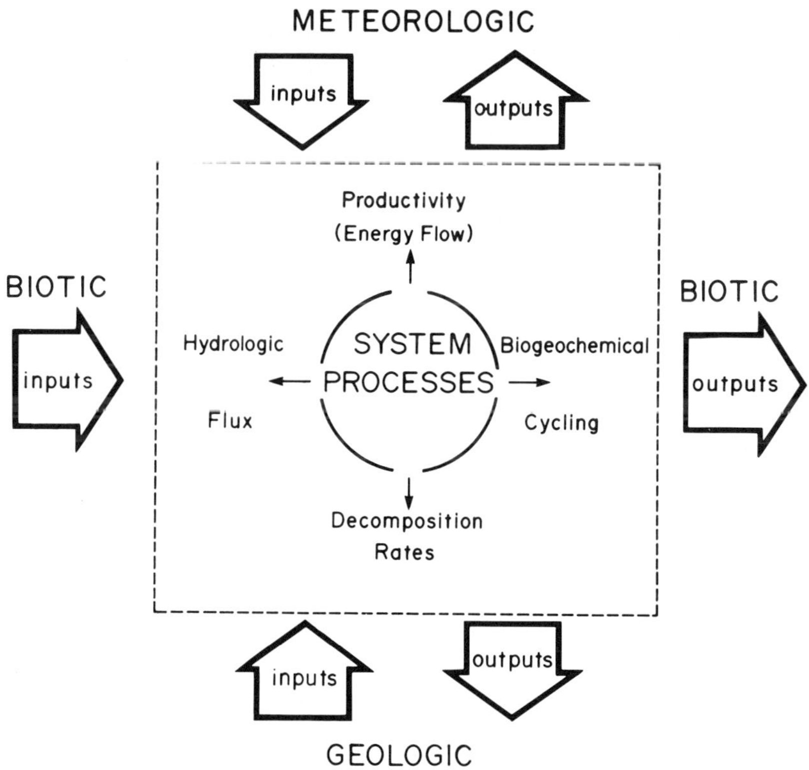

FIGURE 1. *Generalized model of a pocosin ecosystem, the system processes, and the inputs and outputs across the defined wetland boundary. Boundary shown as a dashed line.*

being mined for energy (Cole, 1980, Agricultural Institute, Lullymore, Ireland, personal communication).

Good ecosystem management of pocosins, therefore, requires that we determine not only the effects of inputs and outputs to and from the system but also gain an understanding of disturbance and assess the effects that it has on the processes controlling ecosystem dynamics. Pocosin ecosystem processes must be viewed at global, regional and local scales of value.

POCOSIN ECOSYSTEM PROCESSES AND THEIR VALUES

Global Scale—The Carbon Balance

The value of pocosins to global processes is difficult to quantify. One global scale question of recent concern is the role of organic soils in the world carbon cycle (Armentano, 1979). Atmospheric carbon has been on a continuous rise, 0.9 ± 0.4 ppm/year, for the past two decades (Keeling et al., 1976). The rise has been attributed to the combustion of fossil fuel (Baes et al., 1979; Broecker et al., 1979) and the destruction of forests (Woodwell et al., 1978). The consequences of this dramatic rise in atmospheric carbon are unknown, but the scientific community (Wong, 1978; Bolin et al., 1979) indicates that the greenhouse effect and all the ramifications of increased global temperatures are the central concern.

There are several important aspects to the role of organic soils, which may contain three or four times atmospheric and world biotic storage (Bohn, 1976; Broecker et al., 1979), in the global carbon flux. First, poorly drained organic soils such as our southeastern pocosins have provided a sink for carbon storage over the last few thousand years (see Daniel, this volume). Second, the draining of these organic soils greatly increases biochemical oxidation, subsidence, and the subsequent release of carbon to the atmosphere (Mathur et al., 1979). Finally, the proposed large-scale utilization of peat for energy may alter the capacity of these ecosystems to function as a carbon sink and will surely increase atmospheric CO_2. The consequences of these changes are not well understood. We desperately need data on the rates of carbon accumulation and storage in pocosins and the effects of drainage on decomposition rates, subsidence, and the release of CO_2 into the atmosphere.

It may appear that any increase in organic soil oxidation in pocosins as a result of man's utilization (i.e., agriculture, forestry, mining) is trivial and that this concern is just another example of environmental flag waving. However, sixty-seven years of farming and draining on 3.1×10^5 ha of Histosols in Everglade agricultural areas south of Lake Okeechobee, Florida, have resulted in 3.3 m (10 ft) of subsidence of soils with a current annual rate of loss of 2.5 cm per year (Stephens, 1974). This area alone currently releases 9×10^6 t C

yr^{-1}, about 0.2% of the entire world's fossil fuel emissions (i.e., 5000 x 10^6 t C yr^{-1} due to fossil fuel burning and cement production; Bolin, 1979).

The drainage and complete conversion of approximately 2.02 x 10^5 ha (5.0 x 10^5 acres) of organic soil in North Carolina since 1962, more than 20% of the total pocosin area (estimate for peat-covered bogs only), the current ownership patterns, and the resource management strategies that include ditching and draining indicate a potential for major carbon loss from these wetlands. It will be further increased in the near future if current drainage and ditching rates continue (see Richardson et al., this volume).

A study on organic soils of North Carolina by Dolman and Buol (1967) suggested peat depth changes in the Albemarle region. They found that drainage alone reduced peat thickness by almost 60 cm in fifty years and that compaction, fire, and oxidation could reduce peat by as much as 178 cm (Table 1).

From the data in Table 1, an estimated minimum subsidence rate of 2 cm a year over the last fifty years, as a result of man's activities, was calculated. The bulk density of North Carolina pocosin peats averages 0.45 g/cc (Maki, 1974), the soil organic matter content is 68%, and the carbon content of organic matter averages 56% (0 to 35 cm, six sites in tidewater region, Dolman and Buol, 1967). A 2-cm subsidence rate on 0.5 million acres (202 x 10^5 ha) of developed North Carolina wetlands would release 7 x 10^6 t C yr^{-1}. Thus, we may already be approaching the carbon loss rate of the Okeechobee region of Florida and are near the carbon loss rate (8 x 10^6 t C

TABLE 1. *Estimated Subsidence of Organic Soils in Washington County, North Carolina, as a Result of Drainage, Fires, and Farming (Adapted from Dolman and Buol, 1967)*

Site	Activities	Natural vegetation	Previous thickness of organic soils (cm)	Present thickness of organic soils (cm)	Loss (cm)
Reference	Drainage*(50 yrs)	Mixed hardwood	170	112	58
1	Drainage, fires, farming	Mixed hardwood	178	0	178
3	Drainage, fires	Mixed hardwood	173	53	120
4	Drainage, fires	Grasses, sedges, and scattered trees	170	52	118
5	Drainage, fires	Nyssa-taxodium swamp	253	165	88

*It is assumed that an organic deposit will lose approximately one-third of its thickness upon drainage (Farnham and Finney, 1965).

yr^{-1}) reported for the San Joaquin Valley in California by Mathur et al. (1979). Combined carbon losses from these three areas alone are 0.5% of the entire world fossil fuel emission, and yet these peatlands make up less than 1% of the freshwater wetlands area in the United States.

The draining of Histosols (soils that must contain at least 12 or 18% organic carbon by weight and exceed 30 cm in depth [U.S.D.A., 1975]) which contain 15% of global carbon (Ajtay et al., 1979) and the burning of peat for energy could significantly affect atmospheric carbon levels. The major concern may not only be the direct CO_2 input into the atmosphere but also the loss of wetlands as long-term carbon storage areas. If mankind finally concludes that the increasing levels of atmospheric carbon are adversely affecting our biosphere, we will be hard pressed to find manageable ecosystems to help control CO_2 levels. The ocean appears limited in CO_2 buffering capacity due to the rate of CO_2 transport across the air–sea interface and the vertical mixing of the sea (Broecker et al., 1979; Wong, 1978). Continued cutting of forests and burning of coal and other fossil fuels and the subsequent release of CO_2 is unavoidable in the decades ahead. Where are the carbon sinks of tomorrow to be found?

Wetlands currently accumulating and storing carbon, as well as newly created areas (e.g., partially mined wetlands) with this potential, should be identified and maintained as part of a key controlling system for the global carbon balance. World peatlands with an area of 4.5×10^8 ha (Armentano, 1979) and an accumulation rate of 300 kg ha^{-1} yr^{-1} of carbon (weighted calculation by region and area from Table 10; Richardson and Allen, 1979) could, for example, store 135×10^6 t C yr^{-1} or nearly 3% of the entire annual atmospheric input of CO_2 ($5{,}000 \times 10^6$ t C yr^{-1}; Bolin, 1979).

This does not mean that we should be against the development of some wetlands or the burning of some peat for energy. Good resource and ecosystem management requires that all benefits and costs be examined in terms of both short- and long-term economic values and ecological consequences. For example, most of us would much rather see peat from pocosins burning in a power generating plant than smoldering over thousands of acres of bombing ranges. (Note: Air Force bombing was responsible for burning 30,000 acres and 28,000 acres of pocosin in 1971 and 1980, respectively.) It is also quite possible that the carbon storage in the growth of pine plantations on drained pocosins may exceed the soil oxidation losses caused by drainage. Unfortunately, the data do not exist to make these comparisons, since until recently there did not seem to be any reason to ask these questions. However, it is clear that we cannot afford to overlook the role of natural and managed pocosins in the carbon cycle before we totally alter pocosins and forever remove their natural carbon-accumulating capabilities.

Regional Scale—Pocosin Outputs

On a regional basis the potential outputs from drained wetlands that are of the most concern are fresh water, nutrients, organic matter, bacteria, heavy metals, and pesticides. Daniel (this volume) and Gilliam and Skaggs (this volume) demonstrate that drainage does not significantly increase the total outflow of water from pocosins but rather dramatically increases the peak flows. This means that periodically, and quite possibly at a different season than normal, downstream systems will receive not only increased volumes of fresh water but also dissolved nutrients and suspended materials. The effects of this change on receiving waters such as estuarine ecosystems are unknown although Street and McClees (this volume) present evidence that fresh water may be the most severe pollutant to estuarine systems.

BACKGROUND NUTRIENT OUTPUT DATA FROM NATURAL AND DISTURBED POCOSINS

Barber and his colleagues (1979) recently completed a study on the influence of the Open Grounds agricultural development on water quality. This 48,000-acre (19,392 ha) farm includes the entire watershed of the upper half

TABLE 2. *A Comparison of Mean Annual Concentrations of Constituents in Pocosin Seepage and Farm Ditch Water during the Clearing and Drainage Phase of Wetlands Development in North Carolina (adapted from Barber et al., 1979)*

Constituents	Pocosin seepage water	Ditch water
Dissolved oxygen (mg/l)	2.7	3.2
pH	4.4	6.5
Seston**(μg/g)	6.6	120.0
Turbidity (JTU)	2.3	62.4
Particulate organic carbon (μg/g)	1.7	50.4
Chlorophyll A (μg/kg)	0.7	3.5
Nitrate N (μg/g)	N.D.*	0.01
Ammonia N (μg/g)	0.02	0.05
Phosphate (μg/g)	N.D.	0.015

*N.D. = Not detectable within a limit of 0.02 (μg/g).
**Seston = All suspended particulate matter.
Note: μg/g = ppm, μg/kg = ppb, JTU = Jackson turbidity units.

of the South River, a shallow lateral estuary of the Neuse River–Pamlico Sound system in North Carolina. The clearing, ditching, and conversion of 20,000 acres (8,080 ha) of pocosins to farmland was started in 1974 and completed by 1977. The effects of the clearing and ditching activities resulted in increased levels of nitrate, ammonia, phosphate, and dissolved oxygen concentrations and pH in farm ditch water versus natural pocosin outflow (Table 2).

Particulate organic carbon, turbidity, and seston levels were an order of magnitude higher in the canal outflows compared to the pocosin seepage yields. Some of these effects, although dramatic, are expected only during the development phase. Barber et al. (1979) also compared estuary water quality at a point where a major drainage canal from the farm emptied into the estuary with a point where farm outflow water had first percolated through a *Juncus* marsh before entering the estuary. Salinity patterns and nitrogen concentrations were analyzed from the two outflow areas since they are known to have significant effects on shrimp survival and phytoplankton growth rate, (Barber et al., 1979). They found that the salinity pattern stayed near 10 to 12 ppt at the marsh outflow site compared to 0 to 2 ppt where farm output (Figure 2A) was placed directly into the estuary. The marsh border thus reduced freshwater intrusion by fourfold. Freshwater flushing and strong salt intrusions have also become more common the longer the farm has been in operation (Figure 2B) and nitrogen concentrations have been elevated more often in the vicinity of the canal outflow (Figure 2C).

A later analysis (Figure 2D) shows that highest nitrogen concentrations occurred most frequently during farm activities. Barber et al. (1979) suggest that modified pocosins cannot buffer the estuary against freshwater influx or saltwater intrusion and they conclude that "large-scale drainage of wetlands for agriculture has serious long-term detrimental effects on the receiving estuaries, but that changes in the estuary can be somewhat ameliorated if the salt marsh borders are used as the receiving body rather than the estuary."

Gilliam and Skaggs (this volume) and Skaggs et al. (1979) have analyzed the effects of large-scale agricultural development at First Colony Farms on drainage water in the Albemarle–Pamlico region.

Fertilization of cropland on mineral soils resulted in little or no increase in nitrate nitrogen (NO_3-N) and total phosphorus (TP) outputs, a threefold increase (0.4 vs. 1.4 kg/ha) in ammonium nitrogen (NH_4-N) yields, and a 2.3 kg/ha increased output (2.7 vs. 5.0 kg/ha) of total Kjeldahl nitrogen (TKN) over a sixteen-month period. Pocosin and pasture land outflow on deep peat when compared to a mineral soil system revealed several interesting differences. Total phosphorus output from the organic soils on pasture land was 14.1 kg/ha for a sixteen-month period, over twenty and seventy times that of pine pocosins and crop covered mineral soils, respectively. Total nitrogen output over a 1.3-year time period from pasture land was 8.4 kg/ha,

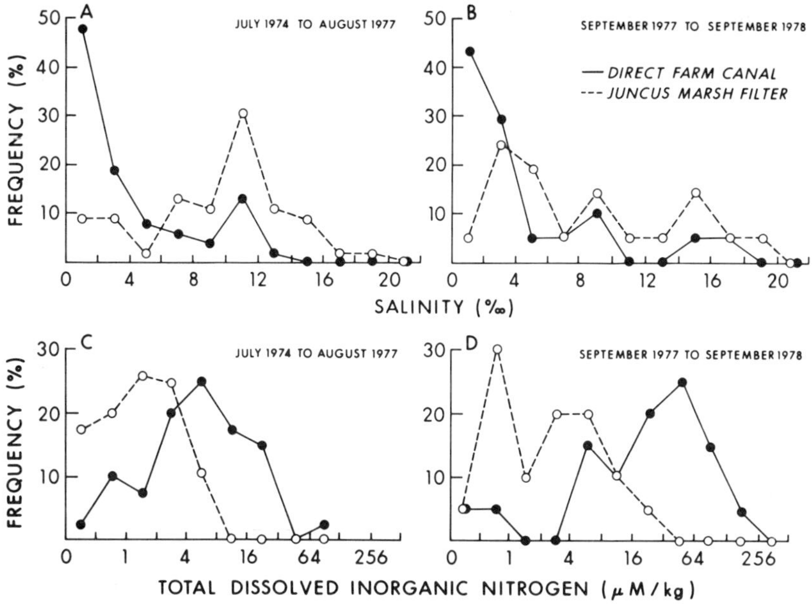

FIGURE 2. *Salinity and total dissolved inorganic nitrogen values in the South River estuary, North Carolina (adapted from Barber et al., 1979).*

1.5 times pocosin and corn–soybean output and three times the pine outputs on mineral soil.

It is apparent that both deep and shallow organic soils cannot retain phosphorus as well as mineral soils and that P fertilization results in a significant output of phosphorus to drainage waters from organic versus mineral soils. Skaggs et al. (1979) also reported that more total coliform bacteria were lost from a cultivated field on organic soil than an undeveloped site. They also found that pasture land had the highest concentration of coliform bacteria and that grazing land had significant levels of fecal coliform outputs as compared to about zero output from cultivated lands.

A Comparison of Ecosystem Outputs

When compared to other ecosystems, natural pocosin (i.e., drained but vegetation not significantly altered from pond pine/bayberry) outputs for NO_3-N and NH_4-N are well below those measured for bogs and forest ecosystems on mineral soils (Table 3). Total Kjeldahl nitrogen yield for a natural pocosin on organic soils was six times less than that reported for an eroding blanket bog in England but it more than tripled when measured on pocosins converted to cropland. Annual total phosphorus yields from pocosins on organic soils are above outputs from a forested perched bog in Minnesota and a northern hardwood ecosystem in New Hampshire but are below outputs from the eroding bog in England and the altered pocosins (agriculture) yields. The significant increase of TP from fertilized agricultural land on organic soils is an order of magnitude higher than any other ecosystem output and should be viewed as a point of concern (Table 3).

Some insight into the long-term capabilities of bogs to assimilate and/or absorb phosphorus can be gained from a fertilization study on drained and undrained blanket bogs in Ireland. During the first year of fertilization, only a slight increase of phosphorus outputs over background levels was noted (Burke, 1975). However, by the second and third year of fertilization, outflow of P had increased significantly. By the third year of fertilization, only 42% and 16% of the added P were retained by the undrained and drained bog. From this continued study, Burke (1975) concluded that the capacity of acid peatlands to store P on a long-term basis was limited. From the Skaggs et al. (1979) study (also see Gilliam and Skaggs, this volume), the ability for altered pocosin ecosystems on organic soils to retain P also appears limited.

In summary, the output differences noted for natural ecosystems and altered pocosin ecosystems can be attributed to three causes: (1) the inputs of fertilizer or animal wastes to cropland and pastures; (2) the effects of monoculture establishment on system processes such as productivity, mineral cycling, and decomposition; and (3) a differential sorption and exchange capacity of mineral versus organic soils. The ecological concern from the data at hand appears to be centered on increased P and bacterial output from altered wetlands. The latter is of special concern because of bacterial contamination in downstream estuarine oyster and clam harvesting areas (Street and McClees, this volume).

Important questions that must be addressed are: What are the amounts of these constituents (primarily P and bacteria) that leave the drainage ditches and flow into downstream ecosystems?; second, What are the effects of the outputs to receiving ecosystems such as an estuary?; and finally, If the output levels are considered detrimental to the receiving ecosystems, then what alternative management strategies can be realistically employed to reduce outputs?

Land/Water Interactions

The Albemarle Sound and the Pamlico River will be used as a case study to answer the above questions and determine the relationship between increased nutrient additions and eutrophication problems in the estuary.

Jaworski (1979) classified the Albemarle Sound as noneutrophic, with turnover approximately twice a year and an external loading of 8.0 kg $ha^{-1}\ yr^{-1}$ of phosphorus and 71 kg $ha^{-1}\ yr^{-1}$ of nitrogen. The ratio of atomic N to P loadings was 20, which indicates that phosphorus is the limiting

TABLE 3. *A Comparison of Nutrient Yields for Blanket Bogs, Perched Bogs, Pocosins, Developed Pocosins, and Forested Watersheds*

Research site, ecosystem type dominant vegetation and soil	Yield of nutrients Kg Ha^{-1} Yr^{-1}						
	NO_3-N	NH_4-N	TN	DP*	TP**	K	Ca
Pennine, England (blanket bog)[A] (Sphagnum-Calluna, organic)	2.9***		17.7	0.4	0.9	9.0	54.0
Glenamoy, Ireland (blanket bog)[B] (Carex-shrub, organic)	4.5	6.7	N.D.†	0.2	N.D.	4.7	22.0
Albemarle-Pamlico, N.C. (pocosin)[C] (pond pine-bayberry, organic)	0.1	0.3	3.0	N.D.	0.3	N.D.	N.D.
Albemarle-Pamlico, N.C. (agriculture)[C] (corn-soybeans, organic)	0.5	0.6	10.0	N.D.	8.4	14.4	69.0
Albemarle-Pamlico, N.C. (pasture)[C] (fescue, organic)	1.0	1.0	5.0	N.D.	6.1	N.D.	N.D.
Minnesota, U.S.A. (perched bog)[D] (black spruce-aspen, mineral-organic)	0.3	0.6	1.9	N.D.	0.08	1.3	3.5
New Hampshire, U.S.A. (northern hardwood)[E] (beech-maple, mineral)	3.6	0.3	4.0	0.007	0.02	1.9	13.7
Albemarle-Pamlico, N.C. (pine)[C] (pine, mineral)	0.7	0.3	1.7	N.D.	0.2	N.D.	N.D.

A. Crisp (1966).
B. Burke (1975) filtered samples.
C. Skaggs et al. (1979, annual yields were estimated from August 1976 to August 1977).
D. Verry (1975).
E. Likens et al. (1977).
†N.D. = No data.

*Dissolved only.
**Total includes particulate.
***Total N in solution.

nutrient, since an N/P ratio above 16 has been found to be P limited, and a ratio below 16 indicates nitrogen as the limiting factor (Redfield, 1958; Jaworski, 1979). Bowden and Hobbie (1977) also suggested phosphorus to be the limiting nutrient for this estuary.

The Pamlico River estuary was classified as eutrophic (Jaworski, 1979) and had an N/P ratio of 7, which indicates that nitrogen is limiting. Kuenzler et al. (1979) showed higher levels of nitrogen and phosphorus loadings as compared to Jaworski's 1976 data and also found higher proportional levels of phosphorus as compared to nitrogen (i.e., N/P ratio 3 for most of the year) especially in the vicinity of Texasgulf phosphate mine outputs into the Pamlico River. Their study suggests that the Pamlico is nitrogen limited and that care should be taken to restrict inputs of nitrogenous materials.

With the previously given information, the magnitude and potential effects that nitrogen and phosphorus outputs from converted pocosins may have on these two estuaries can be estimated. Outputs into field ditches from agricultural ecosystems on organic soils are 10 kg ha^{-1} yr^{-1} (N) and 8.4 kg ha^{-1} yr^{-1} (P) (calculated from Skaggs et al., 1979). This level may not initially flow into an estuary due to sorption by canal sediments, uptake by organisms along and in the channel, and denitrification. However, it is important to recognize that agricultural fertilization is an annual event. Thus, channel outputs of nutrients will increase through time as soil sorption capacity is reached, uptake by organisms plateaus, and if hydrologic flow is accelerated to a point where retention time in the ditches and canals is dramatically reduced (i.e., peak flow for short time periods is a typical result of channelization) (Daniel, Gilliam and Skaggs, this volume).

The nitrogen and phosphorus outputs from agricultural wetlands when multiplied by a minimum estimate of 25,000 hectares for the area of converted pocosin in the watershed (Richardson et al., this volume) results in a 250 and 210 metric tons yr^{-1} input of nitrogen and phosphorous, respectively, to drainage ditches in the Albemarle region. If left as natural pocosins and not fertilized, the N and P output estimates would be 75 and 7.5 metric tons yr^{-1}, respectively. Thus, the conversion of pocosins to fertilized agricultural lands results in a greater than threefold output of nitrogen and a twenty-eightfold increase for phosphorus. If all the phosphorus reached the estuary, this would equal 20% of the entire 1974 estimates of loadings for the Albemarle Sound. The N/P loading ratio from pocosin versus agricultural land would also be changed from 22 to 3, respectively. Since the Albemarle Sound appears to be phosphorus limited, the results of the shift in the loading ratio would most likely greatly accelerate the eutrophication process. The recent severe algae blooms in the Chowan River tributary to Albemarle Sound may be partly attributable to such increased phosphorus loadings.

The Pamlico River estuary is a different problem because management strategies must include controlling nitrogen influenced eutrophication problems. It has a smaller volume of water than the Albemarle Sound (980 x 10^6

m^3 versus 6,500 x 10^6 m^3, respectively,) an external loading of 39.3 kg ha^{-1} of P and 123 kg ha^{-1} yr^{-1} of N and a much lower N/P ratio (Jaworski, 1979). A minimum estimate of pocosin wetlands that have been converted to agricultural lands in this watershed is 32,000 hectares (Richardson et al., this volume). The agricultural land outputs of nitrogen and phosphorus in m.t. yr^{-1} is estimated to be 320 and 268, respectively. Thus, potential agricultural outputs represent 11% and 30% of the total nitrogen and phosphorus loadings (1976 estimate; Jaworski, 1979) for the Pamlico. The atomic N/P loading rate of 3 from agricultural lands on organic soils is about half of the 7 reported by Jaworski (1979). It would appear that the conversion of pocosins to agricultural land in this area would not significantly alter the ratio but could increase the total inputs of N and P over natural pocosin systems of the same area by 224 and 258 m.t. yr^{-1}. The effects of these increased inputs are unknown.

To put the loadings of phosphorus from agricultural wetlands into a regional perspective, the estimates of inputs from several studies were compared (Table 4). Converted pocosins could contribute approximately 30% of Jaworski's estimated total P loadings and 16% of Kuenzler's total P estimate for the Pamlico (Table 4), the difference being due mostly to the large input from the Texasgulf mine into the Pamlico River, which was accounted for only in Kuenzler's estimate. The potential magnitude of phosphorus output (16 to 30% of present total loadings) from fertilized agricultural land on former organic pocosins could have a significant effect on receiving waters.

TABLE 4. *A Comparison of Nitrogen and Phosphorus Loading Estimates for the Pamlico*

Metric tons year N	P	References and sources
		Richardson (1979)*
		Agricultural or converted pocosins
320	286	totalling 32,000 ha
		Kuenzler et al. (1979)
522	331	Watershed (river)
143	17	Rainfall
829	479	Advection from Pamlico Sound
	1670	Total
		Jaworski (1979)
		Pamlico River
	905	estuary (1976 data)

*This is a potential level of input since it is based on outputs to drainage ditches (Skaggs et al., 1979) and needs to be verified in terms of actual yields into the estuary.

Accelerated eutrophication rates can be expected for those estuaries with an atomic N/P ratio above 16, unless steps to mitigate P output are taken.

RESEARCH AND MANAGEMENT RECOMMENDATIONS

It seems clear that problems may arise if consideration is not given to an integrated approach to pocosin management that takes into account the ecosystem concept of land–water interactions. Enough data exist to suggest that converted pocosin ecosystems and their altered system processes can have a significant effect on adjacent rivers and estuaries. The magnitude of the effects and the rate of change are unknown. What is clear is that the managers of altered pocosin systems now need to recognize the link between their landscape and the adjacent estuarine system. Both systems can be productive and profitable if a set of best management practices is established that takes into account the linkages between these ecosystems.

Unfortunately, we have little or no data on productivity, mineral cycling, and decomposition/accumulation rates in pocosins, and thus current management guidelines can only be based on a "black box" concept because we do not understand the most important internal processes of pocosin ecosystems. If, for example, we knew that nutrient uptake rates of pocosin vegetation were high, then we might be able to set aside buffer areas near streams and estuaries as filtering systems to adjacent farmland runoff. Is this feasible? How much area would be needed?

It has been suggested (Charles Gresham, Clemson University, personal communication) that some pocosin species like *Gordonia*, which have high productivity rates, might be grown for biomass and then be used for fuel to produce energy. Are we not better off cropping the vegetation as a renewable biomass resource rather than mining and burning and thereby exacerbating the organic C losses referred to earlier? Or should we totally change the system and produce food crops? How much pocosin land should be left in its natural state to act as a buffering system? All of these questions indicate that we know very little about pocosin ecosystems. We are also ignorant of the long-term consequences in water quality, regional hydrology, peat oxidation and subsidence, and the CO_2 flux rates that will result from altering these wetlands. Society may currently place a higher value on pocosins in an altered state, but the consequences of total conversion of these wetlands would apparently result in significant changes in adjacent ecosystems. Doucette and Phillips, in a 1978 conference on agricultural and forest land drainage in North Carolina, pointed out the real issue: "the need to wisely balance the continuing development of agriculture and forestry with the protection of wetlands, estuaries, nursery areas, and water quality in general." The wise use and proper management of pocosin wetlands will, however, require us to implement many of the following recommendations.

Recommendations

1. Include the ecosystem concept in future management plans.
2. Improve our knowledge base about ecosystem outputs (yields of nutrients, bacteria, chemicals, and fresh water) from:
   A. Pocosins (drained and undrained),
   B. Agriculture on wetlands,
   C. Forestry on wetlands,
   D. Peat mining on wetlands.
3. Determine the effects that drainage has on such system processes as:
   A. Productivity,
   B. Mineral cycling,
   C. Hydrologic flux,
   D. Peat accumulation and oxidation rates.
4. Develop a land use map that includes:
   A. Land use patterns (through time),
   B. Drainage (output locations),
   C. Undrained pocosins,
   D. Ownership trends.
5. Develop management guidelines for the coastal area that include:
   A. Analysis of canal outflow rates and regulation of point source outputs of fresh water into estuaries with key nursery areas;
   B. Suggested minimum fertilization levels needed to maximize growth by soil type;
   C. Maintenance of high water tables during nongrowing seasons to decrease oxidation rates, dust problems, and increase denitrification;
   D. Evaluation of use of marshes, swamps, or artificial buffers as filters for runoff from agriculture;
   E. Improve crop management practices to reduce nutrient (P, Cu, etc.), pesticide, and bacterial outputs to minimal levels.
6. Determine if there is a cause and effect relationship among altered wetlands, their outputs to estuaries and rivers, algal blooms in Chowan River and a regional decline in the fishing industry.

LITERATURE CITED

Ajtay, G. L., P. Ketner and P. Duvigneaud, 1979. Terrestrial primary production and phytomass. In: B. Bolin, E. T. Degens, S. Kemps, and P. Ketner, eds., Scope 13. The Global Carbon Cycle. J. Wiley and Sons, 491 pp.

Armentano, T. V., ed., 1979. The role of organic soils in the world carbon cycle: Problem definition and research needs. U.S. Dept. of Energy Report, No. DOE/ET/10040-2, from a workshop at The Institute of Ecology, Indianapolis, Indiana.

Baes, E. F., Jr., H. E. Goeller, J. S. Olson and R. M. Rohy, 1977. Carbon dioxide and climate: The uncontrolled experiment. Amer. Sci., 65:310-320.

Barber, R. T., W. W. Kirby-Smith and P. E. Parsley, 1979. Wetland alterations for agriculture, pp. 642-651. In: P. E. Greeson, J. R. Clark and J. E. Clark, eds., Wetlands Functions and Values: The State of Our Understanding. American Water Resources Association (TPS 79-2), 674 pp.

Bohn, H., 1976. Estimate of organic carbon in world soils. Soil Sci. Soc. Am. Proc., 40:468-70.

Bolin, B., E. T. Degens, S. Kemps and P. Ketner, eds., 1979. The global carbon cycle. John Wiley and Sons, New York, 491 pp.

Borman, F. H., 1976. An inseparable linkage: Conservation of natural ecosystems and the conservation of fossil energy. Bioscience, 26:754-759.

Bowden, W. B. and J. E. Hobbie, 1977. Nutrients in Albemarle Sound, North Carolina. Univ. of N.C., Sea Grant Pub.: UNC-SG-75-25.

Broecker, W. S., T. Takahashi, H. J. Simpson and T. H. Peng, 1979. Fate of fossil fuel carbon dioxide and the global carbon budget. Science, 206: 409-418.

Burke, W., 1975. Fertilizer and other chemical losses in drainage water from blanket bog. Ir. J. Agric. Res., 14:163-178.

Crisp, D. T., 1966. Input and output of minerals for an area of Pennine Moorland: The importance of precipitation, drainage, peat erosion, and animals. J. Appl. Ecol., 3:327-348.

Dolman, J. D. and S. W. Buol., 1967. A study of organic soils (Histosols) in the tidewater region of North Carolina. Tech. Bul. No. 181, North Carolina Agricultural Exp. Station, Raleigh, N.C., 52 pp.

Doucette, W. H. and J. A. Phillips, 1978. Overview: Agricultural and forestland drainage in North Carolina's coastal zone. Center for Rural Resource Development, Report No. 8, North Carolina State University, Raleigh, N.C.

Farnham, R. S. and H. R. Finney, 1965. Classification and properties of organic soils. Advances in Argon., 17:115-162.

Jaworski, N. A., 1979. Sources of nutrients and the scale of eutrophication problems in estuaries. In: An International Symposium on the Effects of Nutrient Enrichment in Estuaries, May 1979. Williamsburg, Virginia.

Keeling, C. D., R. B. Bacastow, A. E. Bainbridge, C. A. Ekdahl, Jr., P. R. Guenther, and L. S. Waterman, 1976. Atmospheric carbon dioxide variations at Mauna Loa Observatory, Hawaii. Tellus, 28:538-551.

Kuenzler, E. J., D. W. Stanley, and J. P. Koenings, 1979. Nutrient kinetics of phytoplankton in the Pamlico River, North Carolina. Water Resources Research Institute of the University of North Carolina, Report No. 139.

Likens, G. E., F. H. Bormann, R. S. Pierce, J. S. Eaton, N. M. Johnson, 1977. Biogeochemistry of a forested ecosystem. Springer-Verlag, New York, 146 pp.

Maki, T. E., 1974. Factors affecting forest production on organic soils. In: Aandahl, ed., Histosols: Their characteristics, classification, and use. Soil Sci. Soc. of America, Special Pub. No. 6.

Mathur, S. P., L. H. Allen, and J. Duxburg, 1979, pp. 13-17. In: Armentano, T.V., ed., The role of organic soils in the world carbon cycle: Problem definition and research needs. TIE Report to DOE, No: DOE/ET/10040-2.

Odum, E. P., 1979. The emergence of ecology as a new integrative discipline. Science, 195:1289-1293.

Redfield, A. C., 1958. The biological control of chemical factors in the environment. Amer. Sci., 46:205-221.

Richardson, C. J. and L. H. Allen., 1979. Estimates of carbon accumulation rates for some natural peatlands, pp. 20-21. In: Armentano, T.V., ed., The role of organic soils in the world carbon cycle: Problem definition and research needs. TIE Report to DOE, No: DOE/ET/10040-2.

Skaggs, R. W., J. W. Gilliam, and T. J. Sheets., 1979. Effects of large scale agricultural land development on drainage waters. Progress report to EPA.

Stephens, J. C., 1974. Subsidence of organic soils in the Florida Everglades region of Florida. Contribution from the Division of Drainage and Water Control, U.S.D.A. Soil Conservation Service.

United States Department of Agriculture, 1975. Soil taxonomy: A basis system of soil classification for making and interpreting soil surveys. U.S.D.A. Handbook No. 436, 754 pp.

Verry, E. W., 1975. Streamflows chemistry and nutrient yields from upland-peatland watersheds in Minnesota. Ecology, 56:1149-1157

Wong, C. S., 1978. Carbon dioxide—A global environmental problem into the future. Marine Pollution Bulletin, 9:257-264.

Woodwell, G. M., R. H. Whittaker, W. A. Reiners, G. E. Likens, C. C. Delwiche, and D. B. Botkin., 1978. The biota and the world carbon budget. Science, 199:141-146.

Section II. Nonindustrial Values

Values of Pocosins to Game and Fish Species in North Carolina

Tom D. Monschein

ABSTRACT

Pocosins are extremely valuable as habitat for a variety of game birds and mammals, furbearers and fish in the coastal plain of North Carolina. Pocosins provide the last stronghold for the black bear in coastal North Carolina. Pocosins receive the greatest use by bears and contribute a greater value of food to their annual diet than other habitat types. The total black bear population in eastern North Carolina is estimated to be between 750 and 1,000. Pocosins offer good hunting and trapping along with some limited fishing opportunities. Although pocosins have escaped development in the past, they are receiving increased attention today. Developers are scrutinizing these areas more seriously due to advances in technology which now make exploitation not only possible but economically feasible. The effects of utilization of these lands, whether it be for agriculture, forestry management, mining, recreation or human occupation, will have overall detrimental impacts on animal populations if not approached with multiple use planning in mind. Habitat destruction forces dispersal of wildlife, increases the vulnerability of animals due to lack of escape cover, and reduces the available food supply. Irreversible habitat loss in the past has eliminated animal species in many areas. Therefore, wildlife management practices must be an integral part of land use activities for wild animals to persist in pocosins. Ultimately, the future of wildlife in pocosins rests with those who own the land and how they choose to manage it.

Key Words: game mammals, game birds, game fish, furbearers, hunting, fishing, trapping, reproduction, habitat requirements, management techniques

INTRODUCTION

Pocosins provide an abundance of wildlife habitat in coastal North Carolina. As is true with any habitat type, the usefulness of pocosin habitat varies for different species of wildlife; therefore, each species will be reviewed separately. Although a wide variety of nongame species utilize these habitats (see Wilbur, this volume), this paper will discuss the values that pocosins provide to native game species and summarize results of recent research on game species in pocosins. Also evaluated are opportunities available for hunting, trapping, and fishing; current methods of habitat management for wildlife; and effects of current land use trends on game populations in pocosins.

A game species is defined as a wild mammal, bird or fish which possesses qualities of wariness and escape that challenge the skill of the hunter or fisherman and which are proclaimed by law to be a game species. Game management is defined as the art of producing sustained crops of game for recreational use. Fish and game are renewable resources produced and supported by land and water; therefore, it would seem appropriate to begin with a brief description of pocosin habitat characteristics.

Extending from Virginia to northern Florida, along the lower Atlantic coastal plain, is a series of wet upland bogs known as pocosins. Approximately 2.3 million acres or 68% of the nation's pocosins (Shaw and Fredine, 1956), which the United States Soil Conservation Service classifies as Type 8 Wetlands, were located along the coastal plain of North Carolina in the early 1960s. (Richardson et al., this volume, gives an analysis of present pocosin acreage and development patterns.) For a complete description of pocosin vegetation and communities, pocosin soils geology and hydrology, see Christensen et al. and Daniel, this volume.

GAME SPECIES IN POCOSINS

Big Game Mammals

The black bear (*Ursus americanus*) and white-tailed deer (*Odocoileus virginianus*) are the only big game species found in pocosins.

Black Bear

Historically, the black bear was found throughout North Carolina. Bartram (1792) and Lawson (1967) indicate that bears were numerous statewide and used to a great extent by both Indians and early settlers for food and clothing.

Since the turn of the century, however, the piedmont region has been closely settled, farmed and industrialized. Consequently, the bear has been largely eliminated from that region. In more recent years, the bear has been rapidly driven to the more remote and rugged sections of the mountain and coastal regions. The nucleus of the mountain population is the Great Smoky Mountains National Park, while pocosins provide the last stronghold of highly desirable habitat for the coastal bear population. Ultimately, the degree of development has an adverse effect upon black bear populations. That is, as development activities increase, bear populations will decrease due to habitat loss and increased vulnerability to hunting. The black bear thus requires a wilderness refuge.

Reproductive studies have shown that female breeding ages in coastal bears ranged from 2.5 to 17.5 and corpora lutea (a mass of yellow tissue formed in the ovary by a graafian follicle that has discharged its ovum; if the ovum is fertilized, this tissue secretes a necessary hormone) counts average 2.09 per pregnant female (Collins, 1974). Normally, breeding begins when females are 3.5 years old (Erickson and Nellor, 1964). Collins (1974) found active corpora lutea in 80% of the 3.75-year-old females harvested in North Carolina. When breeding begins, cubs are produced only every other year. Breeding occurs in June and July and cubs are born in late January or early February. Reproductive success is closely related to the quality and quantity of available food. Thus, it can be seen that population recruitment occurs at a slow pace, making it necessary to maintain a sufficient proportion of healthy breeding age females in the population.

Studies concerning habitat needs of coastal bears have revealed that a complex of habitat types is required to meet food needs at different seasons, to provide alternate foods during years when major food producing species have low yields and to provide protection. Hamilton (1978) indicated that foraging habitat, denning habitat and escape habitat were the three habitat components recognized. From telemetry studies, pocosins were found to receive the greatest use by bears and to contribute the greatest volume of food to the annual diet. Hamilton (1978) found that males occupied much larger annual home ranges (average 23,000 acres; 9,300 ha) than did females (average 2,000 acres; 800 ha). Principal natural foods of coastal bear are: (spring) greenbriar berries, vegetative material, ants (*Formicidae*); (summer) blueberries, huckleberries, blackberries, switch cane, ants; (fall) sweet gallberry fruits, sweet bay, black gum berries, oak mast; (winter) greenbriar berries, gallberries (Hardy, 1974; Landers et al., 1979) (see Christensen, this volume, for scientific names). Relatively large, nearly impenetrable pocosins and swamps are important in providing seclusion and protection from disturbance during denning. Hamilton (1978) indicated that all of the bears he observed denning had bedded in shallow depressions on the ground surface in dense pocosin thickets of fetterbush and laurel greenbriar. Escape cover, perhaps the most critical component of black bear habitat, is also provided by the extensive pocosins and swamps in the coastal region.

In the late 1960s, bears were being killed faster than they could reproduce and approximately one-third of all bears harvested were being taken outside the established hunting season (Collins, personal communication, 1979). At that time, several problems and reasons for the black bear decline were identified. The major problem was that bear habitat was being destroyed at an alarming rate. Beekeepers trying to protect their beehives and crops from depredation were taking a great toll, and previously inaccessible areas were being opened by private developers with roads which made bear more accessible (Collins, 1977). In the past, road construction probably would not have had serious detrimental effects on black bear populations. Today's technology, however, has given the hunter a much greater edge on his quarry. Methods of hunting have changed drastically with the advent of four-wheel drive vehicles, citizen's band radios and large organized bear hunting clubs.

Wildlife biologists have been collecting black bear kill information since 1969. Information gathered has enabled biologists to evaluate the relationship of black bear kills to vehicle roads in eastern North Carolina. Between 1969 and 1977, approximately 61% of hunter-harvested black bears were killed within one-half mile of a road, and approximately 77% were killed within one mile of a road (Table 1). Age structures and population modeling indicate that known mortality of coastal bear represents 20% of the hunted population each year (Collins, personal communication, 1979).

To reduce the hunting pressure on bear populations, changes were put into effect by the North Carolina Wildlife Resources Commission starting in 1967 that provided that no hunting of bears be allowed except during the regulated season. The bag limit was reduced in eastern North Carolina from two per day with no season limit to one per day and two per season. In 1971

TABLE 1. *Relationship of Black Bear Kills to Vehicle Roads[1] in Eastern North Carolina between 1969 and 1977[2]*

Distance from kill to nearest vehicle road	No. of kills	Accumulative no. of kills[3]	Accumulative % of kills
Killed in a road	13	13	14.8
Killed within 50 yds. of road	8	21	23.9
Killed within 100 yds. of road	3	24	27.3
Killed within 200 yds. of road	2	26	29.5
Killed within 300 yds. of road	4	30	34.1
Killed within 1/4 mile of road	12	42	47.7
Killed within 1/2 mile of road	12	54	61.4
Killed within 3/4 mile of road	2	56	63.6
Killed within 1.0 mile of road	12	68	77.3
Killed within 1.5 miles of road	8	76	86.4
Killed within 2.0 miles of road	3	79	89.8
Killed within 3.0 miles of road	7	86	97.7
Killed within 4.0 miles of road	2	88	100.0

1. A vehicle road is one that can be traversed with a four-wheel vehicle.
2. Data compiled by John M. Collins, Principle Investigator, Black Bear Research, North Carolina Wildlife Resources Commission, Morganton, N.C. 28655.
3. Data collected from 88 hunter-harvested black bears during the period 1976 to 1977.

the bag limit was reduced again to one per day and one per season. Also in 1971, a bear sanctuary system was established. Seventeen sanctuaries consisting mostly of pocosin habitat and totaling approximately 461,000 acres (186,500 ha) are scattered from Currituck County southward to Brunswick County in eastern North Carolina. Of this acreage, one-third consists of state owned land, one-third is federally owned, and one-third is privately owned.

Sanctuaries were set up to serve two purposes. The first objective was to deter illegal activities and to protect bear populations from harassment. The second goal was to establish areas of surplus bears to help maintain populations in nonsanctuary areas. It is impossible to determine the exact number of bears in an area, but activity indices have indicated that, thus far, the sanctuary program is helping to protect bears (Benton and Sanders, 1979).

In 1975, black bear populations in North Carolina were given the status of "special concern" (Collins, 1977). Also in 1975, a mandatory tagging and kill reporting system was initiated to gain valuable information on numbers of bear killed.

Bear populations have declined over the years, but are now fairly stable due to inaccessibility of remaining habitat and more restrictive seasons and bag limits (Collins, personal communication, 1979). Presently occupied bear habitat on the coast overlaps very closely with remaining pocosins (see Richardson et al., Figure 2, for indications of remaining pocosin). Population densities have been estimated at one bear per 4.4 mi^2 in Bladen County (Hamilton, 1978) and one bear per 6.3 mi^2 in Dare County (Hardy, 1974). The total black bear population in eastern North Carolina, including those on sanctuaries and in closed counties, is estimated to be between 750 and 1,000.

The future of the black bear population in eastern North Carolina depends on the degree to which this valuable resource can be used wisely and, most importantly, on the amount of suitable habitat preserved. The last remaining habitat will probably be large tracts of public and commercial timber company lands. Pocosins, hopefully, will play a major role in providing the last source of highly desirable habitat.

White-tailed Deer

The history of white-tailed deer in North Carolina can be separated into four periods: precolonial, exploitation, recovery, and present.

In the precolonial period, deer populations and their habitat remained relatively stable over long periods of time even though deer were widely used for food, clothing and tools by the Indians (Newsom, 1969). The Indians were practicing habitat management of a somewhat crude form by maintaining rather large openings in the forest with the use of fire (Pruntz, 1965). Therefore, deer habitat in this stage was influenced only by the effects of natural (lightning) fires, those set by Indians, and other natural phenomena. In general, deer were widespread and fairly abundant in pocosins during this period.

During the exploitation period, the writings of early travelers through the South include numerous accounts of the abundance of deer (Bartram, 1792). The dependence of early settlers on deer for food and clothing is well known. Settlement and clearing of land, market hunting for meat and hides and hunting without restrictions throughout the year reduced deer populations to an all-time low in the South by 1920 (Barick, 1951). Deer had been reduced to scattered remnant herds that were confined largely to the most remote and inaccessible habitat types such as that provided by pocosins.

The recovery was initiated by the establishment of National Forest Preserves in the early 1900s. The passage of the Pittman-Robertson Act in 1936 provided the key to the restoration of wildlife throughout the United States, with some southern states initiating deer restocking programs in the late 1930s. The establishment and enforcement of hunting regulations and the reversion of 10 million acres of farmland to forest in the southeastern United States following World War II gave deer the needed protection and habitat for a tremendous increase in population. By 1951, every state in the South had an active program of deer restoration (Barick, 1951). In the late 1950s, most states started working toward either-sex deer seasons (i.e., hunting of either male or female deer) to control the expanding deer populations.

In the South today, the white-tailed deer is hunted on approximately 90% of the total land area; forty years ago, only 30% of the land area was open to deer hunting, and some of this land supported no deer (Newsom, 1969). Today, North Carolina has a deer population estimated to be greater than the entire population of the United States in 1895. The legal annual harvest of deer in North Carolina has climbed from 15,000 in 1950 to an estimated 40,000 annually during the years 1973 through 1978.

Generally speaking, the deer herds in eastern North Carolina are at or fast approaching the carrying capacity of the habitat. Carrying capacities vary considerably with different habitats on the coastal plain. Although pocosins are not the most productive habitat for deer, they do support moderate populations. Extensive tract-count surveys have been conducted by the North Carolina Wildlife Resources Commission in 1977 and 1978 to determine population densities in pocosins and pocosin borders. Results of these surveys have shown that pocosins support approximately six deer per square mile as compared to about eighteen deer per square mile along pocosin borders, where more plant species are available for food (Osborne, 1978). The best coastal habitat for deer is bottomland hardwoods which may support up to thirty-five to forty deer per square mile. The marked difference in population densities is a result of the quantity and quality of available food. Because hard mast is generally not available and soft mast is limited as a source of food in pocosins, deer are largely dependent on browse (Hazel et al., 1978). Pocosins in their natural climax stage support a low deer browse resource, and deer do not find all forage plants palatable. Undisturbed pocosin vegetation contains low amounts of crude protein, phosphorus, boron and calcium for body maintenance of deer (Sossaman and Weber, 1974). Thus, carrying capacities are limited unless management techniques are applied. (Methods of improving deer browse in pocosins will be discussed separately under management techniques.)

Preferred foods utilized by deer in pocosins and along pocosin borders have been identified by recent studies. Sossaman and Weber (1974) found that important spring food items are red maple, blackberry, raspberry, mushrooms, pepperbush, grasses and other tender leafy parts; the summer diet consists of red maple, greenbriars, swamp cyrilla and mushrooms; fall food items include swamp cyrilla, red maple, large gallberry, sweet bay, red bay and American holly; and principle winter foods are swamp cyrilla, greenbriars, large gallberry and American holly (see Christensen, this volume, for scientific names).

Problems facing game managers today and in the future are to maintain healthy populations within carrying capacities of the habitat. Parasite counts can be used to indicate whether deer numbers are below, at or above land carrying capacities (*Abomasum* parasite count, Eve and Kellogg, 1977). By studying the health of deer, population densities and habitat conditions, biologists are able to make recommendations annually for needed harvests. Deer are very prolific and can overpopulate an area without either-sex hunting. This aspect of deer management, however, has not as yet been accepted by the public to the degree that allows the latitude necessary to manage the deer herds properly.

Future research needs for the management of deer in eastern North Carolina will involve monitoring the status of deer populations and existing habitat conditions and using that knowledge to set hunting seasons and bag limits to keep herds at healthy population levels. Development of quick, economical and reliable methods with which to evaluate deer population levels and habitat conditions would be very helpful.

Small Game Mammals

Small game mammals found in pocosins include the marsh rabbit (*Sylvilagus palustris*), cottontail rabbit (*Sylvilagus floridanus*) and gray squirrel (*Sciurus carolinensis*).

The marsh rabbit is considered common throughout pocosins while the cottontail rabbit is present to a somewhat lesser degree and is most abundant along pocosin borders. The gray squirrel population is considered light and is found mostly along the narrow hardwood drains in pocosins.

Historically, both species of rabbits were present in pocosins and served as a source of food for Indians, early settlers and predator species such as the bobcat and gray fox (Bartram, 1792). Agriculture has created favorable "edge" habitat which has benefitted some populations, but the overall effect of habitat loss has been a decline in total numbers. Gray squirrels have also decreased in total numbers due to loss of habitat in mature mast producing hardwood trees and shrubs (Hall and Kelgon, 1959).

Rabbits may produce three or four litters per year and the gray squirrel produces two litters per year (Palmer, 1954). Both rabbit and gray squirrel populations are subject to drastic population fluctuations due to available food and reproductive success.

In summer, rabbits subsist largely on tender herbaceous plants, but in winter they frequently resort to twigs and bark of young trees. There is a lack of research on food habits of rabbits in pocosin habitat, but plant species present in pocosins that are known foods in other habitats include red maple, blueberry, blackberry, greenbriar and various grasses (Martin et al., 1951). Gray squirrels utilize young buds of woody plants in spring; mushrooms, blackberry and some insects such as caterpillars, beetles and ants in summer; hard mast and fleshy mast fruits in fall; and bark, twigs and stored mast in winter (Martin et al., 1951).

Most of the hunting for these species in pocosins occurs in the easily accessible border areas and hunting pressure is considered light.

The future of these small game species in pocosins will depend on the amount of remaining habitat and how it is managed. Future research needs on these species should include the identification of preferred foods and determination of population status.

Furbearers

A furbearer is defined as a wild animal which is so classified under the laws of North Carolina, the pelt of which is authorized to be sold under regulations of the Wildlife Resources Commission. Furbearers found in pocosins include the bobcat (*Lynx rufus*), river otter (*Lutra canadensis*), mink (*Mustela vison*), gray fox (*Urocyon cinereoargneteus*), raccoon (*Procyon lotor*), muskrat, (*Ondatra zibethicus*) and opossum (*Didelphis marsupialis*).

The bobcat, gray fox, raccoon and opossum are considered common throughout North Carolina pocosins. The river otter and mink are commonly found along canals and streams running through pocosins. The muskrat is common in streams and canals from the Virginia line south to the Neuse River but is found to a much lesser degree from the Neuse River to the South Carolina line. Specific data on the abundance and total harvest of these animals are not currently available.

The Wildlife Resources Commission has a furbearer study under way to obtain more detailed information on the population status of the fox, raccoon, bobcat, and otter. These four animals are difficult to assess compared to other wildlife species; new and different techniques have had to be developed. The first segment of the study will involve mailing questionnaires to all fur dealers. From this survey, biologists will be able to determine the extent of the fur market in North Carolina and the total harvest of furbearers in the state.

A cooperative venture between the Wildlife Resources Commission and North Carolina State University is evaluating the status of bobcat and river otter populations. The objective of this study is to determine population status and harvest figures for both species. The results of these studies should give biologists valuable information which can be used to manage these species more effectively in the future.

Upland Game Birds

Upland game birds that utilize pocosins include the bobwhite quail (*Colinus virginianus*), American woodcock (*Philohela minor*) and mourning dove (*Zenaidura macroura*).

Most native game birds were common in colonial times, but not nearly as abundant as some species have become today. The transformation of wilderness into agricultural lands has actually created an increase in the supply of choice plant foods utilized by upland game birds. This change has favored wildlife species that thrive in or near border zones. This is especially true with the bobwhite quail and the mourning dove. Corn, soybeans, wheat, and millets are preferred crop foods of quail and doves. Increased acreage of these crops is currently found on converted pocosin lands in North Carolina (see Barnes, this volume).

Studies in the Atlantic coastal plain have demonstrated that legumes are the most important quail foods (Weber, 1976). Legumes, however, are lacking in natural pocosins due to the acidic, wet and poorly drained soils. Therefore, the variety of foods available for quail is extremely restricted in natural pocosins. Robinson and Barkalow (1979) found that red maple samaras and red bay fruits were the most important food items in pocosin habitat converted to pine. Insects are utilized mostly in the summer when brood rearing occurs.

Mourning doves are, for all practical purposes, totally seed eaters and take advantage of agriculture whenever possible. Therefore, natural pocosins provide very little as a food source. The main value pocosins provide to doves is cover for nesting and roosting. Considerable breeding occurs in the coastal plain, but since the species is migratory, greatest populations occur when northern flocks arrive in the fall and winter.

Unlike quail and doves, the woodcock has suffered from man's activities. Wet bottomlands are the preferred habitat but, unfortunately, are also desirable agricultural lands after drainage. The woodcock's diet consists of 90% animal matter. About two-thirds of its animal diet consists of earthworms. The remainder is made up of insects (mostly flies, beetles and caterpillars) and crustaceans, millipeds, centipedes and spiders (Martin et al., 1951). The small quantity of plant food includes a vareity of seeds, of which blackberry is the only known plant utilized in pocosins.

Previously, it was thought that virtually all rearing was accomplished in Canada and the northern United States, but recent studies have shown that a significant number of woodcock are breeding in the coastal area of North Carolina. The greatest number of woodcock is found in North Carolina during the winter following migrations from Canada and New England. Studies have shown that populations peak in pocosins during February (Betsill, 1978). Migrations take place mostly at night for reasons not fully understood. Woodcock normally use open fields for roosting at night and return to thick cover, such as that which pocosins provide, during the day (Betsill, 1978).

The future for mourning doves and quail looks bright because of their compatibility with agriculture. The fate of the woodcock, however, will depend largely on the availability of breeding grounds and wetland areas for food sources and cover. Future research on these species should include the monitoring of population levels and available habitat.

Game Fish

Little information is available on the early history of the fishery resource that occurred in pocosins. It is assumed, however, that at one time saltwater fish species inhabited areas where pocosins occur today. When the seas receded and pocosins began development, the fish species that evolved had adapted to highly acidic water resulting from organic peat soils. Man's influence on pocosins since that time by digging canals and ditches to increase water runoff has had the effect of lowering the acidity and increasing the fertility of the water, thereby eliminating some fish species and at the same time creating more favorable conditions for other freshwater species.

Game fish species that occur today in canals, lakes and streams in pocosins include the redfin pickerel (*Esox americanus*), chain pickerel (*Esox niger*), yellow perch (*Perca falvescens*), warmouth (*Lepomis gulosus*), flier (*Centrarchus macropterus*), black crappie (*Promoxis nigromaculatus*), bluegill (*Lepomis macrochirus*) and largemouth bass (*Micropterus salmoides*). Pocosins in the southeastern coastal plain of North Carolina are characterized by faster flowing streams that often support red-breast sunfish (*Lepomis auritus*) in addition to those species listed above.

The future of the fisheries resource in pocosins will depend on man's activities and the effects that those activities will have on the quantity and quality of available water.

HUNTING, TRAPPING AND FISHING OPPORTUNITIES IN POCOSINS

In the past, hunters, trappers, and fishermen had little trouble in finding areas in which to enjoy their sports. Today, however, land ownership patterns have made it increasingly difficult for the average person to gain access to private lands. The trend in eastern North Carolina has been toward club hunting. Hunters have banded together in groups, collected membership dues, and leased large tracts of land owned by private timber companies and corporate farms. The hunter or trapper who does not belong to a club has three other choices for obtaining a place to enjoy his or her sport. First, he may be able to hunt or trap as a guest of a club member; second, he might obtain permission from a landowner who has not leased his land; or third, he could choose to pursue his chosen sport on public lands.

The demands on public lands that have been set aside for public recreation are steadily increasing each year. The Wildlife Resources Commission recognized the need for public lands many years ago. Currently, in the coastal area, the commission provides twenty-five tracts of land totaling 729,896 acres (295,378 ha), approximately one-third of which is pocosin, for public use. Of this acreage, six tracts totaling 105,564 acres (427,202 ha) are owned by the commission and nineteen tracts totaling 624,332 acres (252,658 ha) are leased from private landowners. In addition, several years ago, the commission initiated a Public Hunting Grounds Program. Cooperative agreements are signed with private landowners to allow public use with written permission of the landowner. The commission, in return, provides the landowner with permit books, signs to mark his property lines, technical assistance, and planting materials to improve wildlife habitat. This program has been quite successful and is providing ten additional areas totaling approximately 1,500 acres (600 ha) for public utilization in the coastal region.

Fishing opportunities are available in pocosins but are rather limited because of poor access. Most fishing occurs on stream bridges, in road canals and in the larger streams where small boats can be used. The few pocosin lakes generally provide poor fishing because of the extremely acidic water which supports few fish.

The future will bring yet greater demands on available lands for hunting, trapping and fishing. Pocosins will continue to play an important role in providing recreational opportunities for these popular sports. (For an economic analysis of these activities, see Postel, this volume.)

MANAGEMENT TECHNIQUES ON NATURAL AND ALTERED POCOSIN LAND

Until recently, very little has been done to manage pocosins for game species. In most cases, nature was left to take its own course as fires, floods and other natural catastrophic events exerted their influence. Today, however, several habitat manipulation techniques are being utilized to shape and improve pocosins for wildlife.

Controlled burning is a proven method which creates favorable conditions for a large number of species of wildlife. Fire initiates new, rapid and tender growth from existing plants which makes them more palatable to wildlife. Prescribed burning reduces ground litter, thus lessening the risk of wildfire outbreaks in the summer months. Fire has the effect of opening up pocosins which facilitates movement of game and also serves to increase plant species diversity. Studies have shown that fire increases the dominance of desirable plant species utilized by deer such as bog broomsedge, swamp cyrilla, and greenbriar (Wells, 1946).

The prolonged absence of fire leads to dense and highly repressed vegetation, low in stature and few in species number. Improper timing between burns may, however, result in this same condition (Wells, 1946). Burning too frequently can cause removal of peat faster than it forms and deep burning leaves newly exposed peat, which does not favor seedling development. The proper timing of burns during the year and between years is, therefore, very important. Piece by piece burning of 50 acres (20 ha) or less is desirable in maintaining habitat diversity and is much safer than burning larger tracts. January and February are usually the best months to burn because fires will burn cooler, damage to trees is minimal, wildlife nests will not be destroyed, and fires are more controllable at this time.

A fundamental condition which should exist at the time of burning is a sufficiently shallow water table to protect the peat from deep destruction. To keep the necessary ground fire going, only a few inches of duff should be dry. Best results are obtained when burns are made just prior to an oncoming rain in order to make sure the peat is extinguished. Burning at intervals of every four to six years is usually sufficient to maintain suitable habitat for wildlife in pocosins. (For further information on fire effects, see Christensen, this volume.)

Roll-chopping involves the use of a bulldozer and a heavy drum chopper to cut down vegetation and disturb the soil. Chopping is done in the summer months during dry periods. Chopping small blocks of 50 acres or less creates habitat diversity. Knocking down the vegetation exposes the ground surface to sunlight which stimulates the growth of young, tender shoots of perennial shrubs and annual plants that are desirable to deer, quail, rabbits and other wildlife. After chopping, the vegetation is controlled in later years by burning. Both chopping and burning will, in effect, refurbish pocosin habitat and increase carrying capacities for many game species.

Studies have shown that the use of fertilizer results in a significant increase in forage production in disturbed pocosin habitat. Hazel et al. (1978) studied pocosins converted to loblolly pine and found that regenerated stands with similar site treatment practices and fertilized with triple superphosphate (0-46-0) at the rate of 45 to 46 kilograms (kg) per hectare (ha) produced 300% more forage for deer than unfertilized stands during the first growing season. The same study found that forage production peaked during the fourth year following site treatment (728 kg/ha) and was approximately seven times as great as the production in natural pond pine stands (100 kg/ha). It should be noted, however, that while young loblolly pine plantations may be temporarily productive to wildlife for the first four to five years, they rapidly deteriorate in value thereafter. Fertilization in natural pocosin habitat has the effect of increasing mast production of fruit bearing plants.

Present forestry management practices are creating some adverse effects on wildlife populations in swamps and pocosins. The conversion of hardwood forests to softwoods, for short rotation timber production, is most harmful to black bear populations which depend heavily upon mast from oak and blackgum to build up winter fat. Prior planting on pocosin sites converted to pine can, however, provide some wildlife species with a supplemental food supply beyond the four-to five-year point. The practice of third row thinning provides a pulpwood cutting and at the same time improves the stand for growth. The vacant row is then replaced with a legume wildlife food strip which provides food and cover for wildlife plus better access. Another practice that will enhance wildlife in pine plantations is to prescribe burn on a three- to five-year rotation. Burning will encourage herbaceous growth and help to maintain openings. When stands are regenerated or converted, at least two den trees per five acres should be retained for cavity nesting birds and mammals. Mast producing trees, old house sites, water areas and thickets should be left whenever possible.

Clearcutting adds a new dimension to the natural habitat by increasing edge and creating open areas and, more importantly, it stimulates growth of additional wildlife food plants for a few years. Clearcut areas should be kept under 50 acres and be irregularly shaped to benefit wildlife the most.

The best program for integrating wildlife management and commercial forestry practices is long-range planning for good age-class distribution in the regenerated forest to ensure that areas of young and older plantations are constantly available.

Effective wildlife conservation practices can be applied on pocosin that has been converted to agricultural land. Leaving strips and odd corners of grain crops, rotating crops to allow natural food growth, strip cropping to form edges, leaving hedgerows and windrows for cover, planting annual and perennial food strips and leaving desirable mast producing trees along field edges are a few practices that will allow a compatible relationship between agriculture and many wildlife species.

Pocosins in their natural state have perhaps the lowest value to waterfowl of any wetland habitat type. A management practice that produces quality waterfowl habitat in pocosins, however, involves the construction of impoundments. Canals are dug and dikes with gates are created. The dikes are seeded, and a pump is installed at the water source (a creek or canal).

The impoundment is managed by manipulating water levels to stimulate aquatic growth and to create good conditions for waterfowl. Initially the vegetation is burned off and the area flooded immediately. This eliminates most of the undesirable vegetation and encourages the growth of aquatic plants. In succeeding years, the water may be drawn down to allow various emergents such as smartweeds (*Polyganum* spp.), millets (*Echinochloa* and *Panicum* spp.), and annual weeds to become established. Eventually, permanent waterfowl food plants such as waterlilly (*Nymphaea odorata*), water shield (*Brasenia schreberi*) and various duckweeds (*Lemna*, *Spirodela*, *Wolffia*, *Wolffiella* spp.) may be established.

Thus, a habitat once impenetrable to waterfowl can be developed into an area of high natural resource yield for puddle ducks such as the wood duck (*Aix sponsa*), black duck (*Anas rubripes*), and mallard (*Anas platyrhynchos*). While impoundments are primarily for the benefit of waterfowl, they also provide excellent habitat for various furbearers and fish species.

CONCLUSIONS AND MANAGEMENT IMPLICATIONS

The management of any population of wild animals is indeed extremely difficult, and it becomes even more complicated when it must be accomplished coincidentally with that of other resources of the land. The denser the human population, the more intense the system of management that is needed to supply the same number of persons with recreational opportunities, food, timber products and energy. In the future, pocosins will have to be managed to ensure the perpetuation of the wildlife resources and yet to provide hunting, trapping and fishing opportunities.

The fate of pocosins rests with those who own the land. Landowners naturally would like to realize a return from their investments. One way to accomplish this would be to include management for wildlife in their land use plans and lease or charge for hunting, trapping, and fishing privileges. Forestry and agricultural practices which best complement wildlife management practices should be used to facilitate fuller utilization of the land resources. We are living in a time when the decisions we make regarding land use are vital to the survival and general well-being of wildlife. Ultimately, the quantity and diversity of wildlife is directly proportional to the quantity, quality, and diversity of available habitat.

LITERATURE CITED

Barick, F. B., 1951. Deer restoration in the southeastern United States. Proc. Southeast. Assoc. Game and Fish Comm. Fifth Ann. Meeting, 18 pp.

Bartram, William, 1792. Travels through North and South Carolina, Georgia, east and west Florida. Dover Publications, New York, 414 pp.

———, 1940. The travels of William Bartram. Facsimile Library, New York, 361 pp.

Benton, R., and T. Sanders, 1979. An analysis and evaluation of the black bear sanctuary program in North Carolina. P-R progress reports, W-57.

Betsill, C. W., 1978. Status of woodcock populations in North Carolina. P-R progress reports, W-57.

Collins, J. M., 1974. Some aspects of reproduction and age structures in the black bear in North Carolina. Proc. Southeast Assoc. Game and Fish Comm., 27:163-170.

Collins, J. M., 1977. A brief summary of the black bear in North Carolina. Boone and Crockett Club Workshop, Kalispell, Mont., 9 pp.

Erickson, A. W., and J. E. Nellor, 1964. Breeding biology of the black bear. Mich. St. Univ. Res. Bull. 4, pp. 5-45.

Eve, H., and F. Kellogg, 1977. J. Wild. Manag., 41(2):169-177.

Hall, E. R., and K. R. Kelsor, 1959. The mammals of North America. The Ronald Press Co., New York, 2 volumes, 1083 pp.

Hamilton, R. J., 1978. Ecology of the black bear in southeastern North Carolina. M.S. Thesis, University of Georgia, Athens, Ga., 214 pp.

Hardy, D. M., 1974. Habitat requirements of the black bear in Dare County, North Carolina. M. S. Thesis, Va. Poly. Tech. Inst., Blacksburg, Va., 121 pp.

Hazel, D. W., A. J. Weber, and S. T. Cherry, 1978. Deer browse production associated with the practice of site conversion in a North Carolina pocosin. Proc. Southeast Assoc. Game and Fish Comm., 30:513-524.

Landers, J. L., R. J. Hamilton, A. S. Johnson, and R. L. Marchinton, 1979. Foods and habitat of black bears in southeastern North Carolina. J. Wild. Manag., 43(1):143-153.

Lawson, J., 1967. A new voyage to Carolina. The University of North Carolina Press, Chapel Hill, 305 pp.

Martin, A. C., H. S. Zim, and A. L. Nelson, 1951. American wildlife and plants: A guide to wildlife food habits. Dover Publications, Inc., New York, 500 pp.

Newsom, J. D., 1969. History of deer and their habitat in the South, pp. 1-4. In: White-tailed deer in the southern forest habitat: A symposium. South. For. Exp. Sta., Southeast. Section of the Wildlife Society, and Stephen F. Austin University, Nacogdoches, Tex., 130 pp.

Osborne, J. S., 1978. Population densities of white-tailed deer in Northeastern North Carolina. P-R progress reports, W-57.

Palmer, R. S., 1954. The mammal guide. Doubleday and Company, Inc.,

Garden City, N.Y., 384 pp.

Pruntz, M. C., 1965. Some geographic views of the role of fire in settlement processes in the South. Proc. Ann. Tall Timbers Fire Ecol. Conf., 4:161-167.

Robinson, I. R., Jr., and F. S. Barkalow, Jr., 1979. Bobwhite quail foods in pocosin habitat converted to pine. J. Wild. Manag., 43(2):516-521.

Sossaman, E. C., and A. J. Weber, 1974. Seasonal food habits of white-tailed deer (*Odocoileus virginianus*) in a treated North Carolina pocosin. Proc. Ann. Conf. Southeast. Assoc. Game and Fish Comm., 27:125-142.

Shaw, S. P., and C. G. Fredine, 1956. Wetlands of the United States: Their extent and their value to waterfowl and other wildlife. Fish and Wildlife Serv., U.S. Dept. of the Interior, Circ. 39.

Weber, A. J., 1976. Fall and winter food habits of the bobwhite quail in the sandhills of North Carolina. Proc. Southeast. Assoc. Game and Fish Comm., 29:687-694.

Wells, B. W., 1946. Vegetation of Holly Shelter Wildlife Management Area. N.C. Dept. of Cons. and Development, Bull. No. 2, 40 pp.

Pocosin Natural Areas in North Carolina

John B. Taggart

ABSTRACT

Originally dominating hundreds of thousands of acres on the North Carolina coastal plain, pocosins are rapidly being consumed by a variety of land uses. Preservation of these ecosystems will depend largely on their becoming publicly owned lands set aside as state parks, national forests, game lands, wildlife refuges, etc. A survey of pocosin lands in state and federal ownership is made by dividing the coastal plain into four sections of geographic diversity: northern, central, southern, and sandhills. Location, administration, pocosin extent, and management practices are discussed for each tract. Based on substantial scientific documentation as to the interrelation of fire and pocosin vegetation, it is recommended that experimental prescribed burn plots be established in representative areas to assess the best fire management policy. The need for thorough pocosin inventories and preserve designations is also discussed.

Key Words: natural area, low pocosin, high pocosin, succession, fire, diversity, management.

INTRODUCTION

From the time the first European settlers began to occupy portions of the North Carolina coastal plain, pocosins have typically been regarded as impenetrable wetlands of pine and/or evergreen shrubs. One of the earliest pocosin descriptions is given by John Brickell in 1737: " . . . being very wet and low lands so full of canes and underwood, that there is no passing thru them, many of which are several miles in length" (Wells, 1932). The desolate and forbidding appearance of pocosins causes many people to consider them as "swamp wastelands" with little or no thought given to preservation.

Dr. B. W. Wells (1928, 1932, 1942, 1946) was one of the first scientists to describe pocosins. He classifies them as a seral stage within a coastal plain successional sequence. He attributes pocosin occurrence to a combination of topographic, geologic, and pedologic factors with fire and hydrology being important controlling parameters. Typical pocosin sites include broad shallow stream basins, drainage basin heads, and broad flat uplands which are waterlogged for long periods when rains are frequent, but these lands generally dry out at the surface during drought periods. Wells (1932) summarizes the pocosin habitat by saying: "Thus the shrub bog site is one that is poorly drained but never carries water of measurable depth on the surface." Pocosin plant composition, according to Wells, is determined largely by hydroperiod and frequency of fire. A similar relationship of soil, hydroperiod, and fire was described for the Green Swamp by Kologiski (1977; see Christensen, Table 1, this volume). Christensen (this volume) points out that in some areas (e.g., low pocosin of Croatan National Forest) the pocosin vegetation may persist as a topoedaphic climax, although community structure and species composition will gradually change.

In attempting to segregate similar pocosin types, the North Carolina coastal plain can be divided roughly into four geographic areas based on

FIGURE 1. *Location of North Carolina pocosin natural areas.*

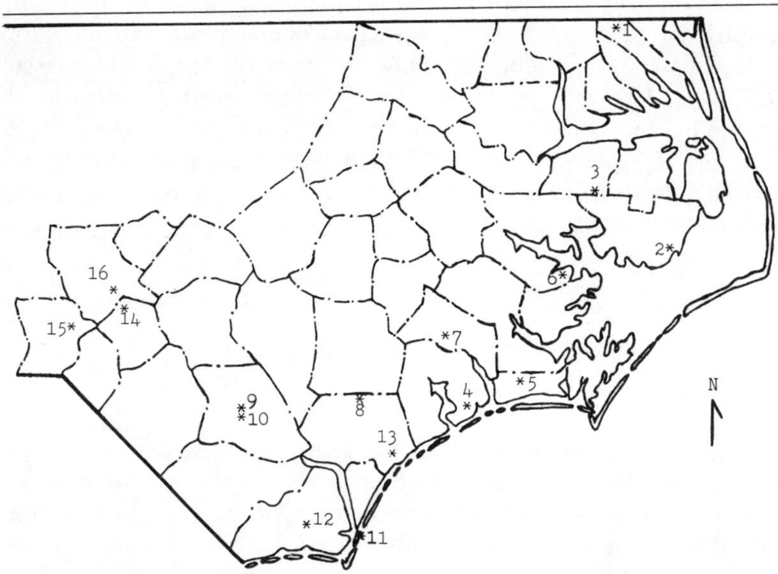

1. Dismal Swamp State Park
2. Gull Rock Game Land
3. Pungo National Wildlife Refuge
4. Camp Lejeune Marine Base
5. Croatan National Forest
6. Goose Creek Game Land
7. Hofmann Forest
8. Angola Bay Game Land
9. Bladen Lakes State Forest
10. State Lakes
11. Carolina Beach State Park
12. Green Swamp
13. Holly Shelter Game Land
14. Fort Bragg Military Reservation
15. Sandhills Game Land
16. Weymouth Woods Sandhills Nature Preserve

similarity of flora, fauna, topography, soils, and geology. Section I extends from the Virginia state line to the Pamlico River. The vegetation of this area is considered part of the Dismal Swamp flora (Kearney, 1901; Braun, 1950). Section II consists of the central coastal plain region from the Pamlico River to the New River at Jacksonville. Section III comprises the southeastern counties of Pender, New Hanover, Columbus, Brunswick, and Bladen. This

TABLE 1. *North Carolina Pocosin Natural Areas*

Section of state	Name of site (managing agency)	Estimated pocosin size acres	hectares
I (northern)	Dismal Swamp State Park (N.C. Division of Parks and Recreation)	1,500	600
	Gull Rock Game Land (N.C. Wildlife Resources Commission)	3,000	1,200
	Pungo National Wildlife Refuge (U.S. Fish and Wildlife Service)	1,000	400
II (central)	Camp Lejeune Marine Base (U.S. Marine Corps)	5,330	2,232
	Croatan National Forest (U.S. Forest Service)	25,854	10,342
	Goose Creek Game Land (N.C. Wildlife Resources Commission)	3,500	1,400
	Hofmann Forest (Champion International Corporation)	15,025	6,010
III (southern)	Angola Bay Game Land (N.C. Wildlife Resources Commission)	20,000	8,000
	Bladen Lakes State Forest (N.C. Division of Forest Resources)	not available	
	Carolina Beach State Park (N.C. Division of Parks and Recreation)	5	0.2
	Green Swamp (The Nature Conservancy)	13,850	5,605
	Holly Shelter Game Land (N.C. Wildlife Resources Commission)	30,000	12,000
	State Lakes (N.C. Division of Parks and Recreation)	not available	
IV (Sandhills)	Fort Bragg Military Reservation (U.S. Army)	not available	
	Sandhills Game Land (N.C. Wildlife Resource Commission)	not available	
	Weymouth Woods Sandhills Nature Preserve (N.C. Division of Parks and Recreation)	12	4.8

is a region of maximum plant diversity because a number of pocosin and savannah species reach their northern limit in this area (Radford et al., 1968). Portions of Robeson, Scotland, Lee, Moore, Harnett, Cumberland, Hoke, and Richmond counties, commonly known as the sandhills, comprise Section IV. Pocosins in this region are small in size and have developed over different topographic and geologic conditions than the other areas (Wells and Shunk, 1931; Wells, 1932). A general map showing the distribution of natural areas in North Carolina is shown in Figure 1.

Within each section there are a number of public and private land holdings which represent examples of regional diversity. Because of the current trend toward pocosin development, future preservation may ultimately be confined to the state and federal properties such as national forests, wildlife refuges, state parks, and game lands. The following assessment of present pocosin natural areas details primarily the public ownerships, although it must be remembered that other large undisturbed pocosin acreages do exist (e.g., private farms, timber company lands, etc.), but these areas are not protected from future development.

The term natural area as used in this paper refers to either designated pocosin preserves or public lands containing pocosin tracts which are unaltered. See Table 1 for the estimated size of natural areas and managing agencies.

DISTRIBUTION OF POCOSIN NATURAL AREAS

Pocosins in the Northern Section of Coastal North Carolina

This portion of the coastal plain contains a considerable amount of interstream pocosin acreage, the largest tracts being on the Albemarle–Pamlico peninsula centered in Washington, Tyrrell, Dare and Hyde counties. The best examples are located in mainland Dare County. First Colony Farms owns a major portion of this four-county pocosin area. The eastern portion of the Dare County peninsula was burned in the early 1970s by the Stumpy Point fire which covered approximately 30,000 acres. Pocosin community diversity is locally highest in the burned areas with various pond pine/shrub and pond pine/cane communities as well as small isolated openings containing bog herbs such as pitcher plants and sundews.

A Hyde County tract owned and managed by the North Carolina Wildlife Resources Commission contains a good example of local pocosin vegetation. Gull Rock Game Land has been timbered to some extent, but a pocosin block of approximately 3,000 acres remains unaltered (1 acre = 0.4047 hectares; for natural area ac/ha conversions, see Table 1). Proposed management of the site includes clearing 1,315 acres of pocosin for waterfowl impoundments and clearing and burning of 100 acres for big and small game management. There are no plans for prescribed burning of the pocosin vegetation (Division of Game, 1980).

The Pungo National Wildlife Refuge (U. S. Fish and Wildlife Sevice) contains a 1,000-acre Pocosin Research Natural Area located east of Pungo Lake in Washington and Hyde counties. The natural area will receive no specific management; however, if a fire starts, there will be no attempt to extinguish it (Mr. John Fields, Superintendent, Pungo National Wildlife Refuge, 4 October 1979, personal communication).

Approximately 1,500 acres of pocosin in Camden County are contained within the Dismal Swamp State Park, managed by the North Carolina Division of Parks and Recreation. The division has no plans for specific management of this northernmost pocosin natural area (Master Planning Unit, 1976).

Pocosins in the Central Section of Coastal North Carolina

The primary public pocosin holdings in this section include Hofmann Forest, Croatan National Forest, Goose Creek Game Land, and Camp Lejeune Marine Base. Hofmann Forest, situated in Jones and Onslow counties, is owned by the North Carolina Forestry Foundation and the School of Forestry at North Carolina State University. The land is leased to Champion International Corporation, which manages the timber production. The 25-acre Nere Elexus Day Pond Pine Natural Area within the property has been exempted from cutting or burning. *Pinus serotina* specimens in this stand are estimated to be 160 years old, making it one of the oldest stands of pond pine remaining (Whetstone, 1977). The successional stage of this pocosin is advanced, judging from the closed subcanopy of *Acer rubrum* and *Gordonia lasianthus*. Much of Hofmann Forest has been converted to pine plantation, but approximately 15,000 acres of pocosin remain undisturbed. However, this land probably will be converted to timber in the future (Mr. Wally Wicks, Manager, Hofmann and Southern Forest, 14 January 1980, personal communication).

Croatan National Forest (U. S. Forest Service) covers portions of Jones, Craven, and Carteret counties and contains a total of 25,854 acres proposed as a pocosin wilderness area. This area contains some of the best examples of high pocosin (pond pine–mixed hardwood) and low pocosin (pond pine/shrub and shrub bog) in the state. The present Forest Service policy is no pocosin burning except for a belt of vegetation across the property which, when burned, will act as a firebreak (Mr. Lynn Young, District Ranger, Croatan National Forest, 14 October 1979, personal communication). Dr. Norman Christensen of Duke University has been studying the fire ecology of the Croatan pocosins (including prescribed burn areas) and will make recommendations based on his findings to the Forest Service regarding management requirements for maintaining pocosin integrity (7 November 1979, personal communication).

Goose Creek Game Land (N.C. Wildlife Resources Commission) contains about 3,500 acres of pocosin in Beaufort and Pamlico counties. The Division of Game (1980) has proposed new road construction, cutting 10 acres of pocosin, and burning 1,000 acres of marsh and dikes (no pocosin acreage mentioned).

Camp Lejeune Marine Base, situated between Swansboro and Jacksonville in Onslow County, contains approximately 5,330 acres of pocosin scattered throughout the 58,000 acres of forest. The management policy at Camp Lejeune is oriented primarily toward timber production with no mention of natural areas in the natural resource management plan (Marine Corps Base et al., 1975).

Pocosins in the Southern Section of Coastal North Carolina

This section, although smaller than the previous sections, contains the largest amount of public pocosin acreage. This is encompassed by the following state owned properties: Angola Bay, Holly Shelter, Bladen Lakes State Forest, State Lakes, and Carolina Beach State Park. A portion of the Green Swamp in Brunswick County is owned by The Nature Conservancy, a private nonprofit conservation organization.

Of the two local North Carolina Wildlife Resources Commission Game Lands, Angola Bay (Pender and Duplin counties) and Holly Shelter (Pender County), only Holly Shelter will receive any measure of pocosin fire management. Approximately 5,120 acres of pocosin will be burned over a five-year period by contract with the North Carolina Forest Service. A total of eight blocks of pocosin will be laid out initially to be control burned in the program. Each block will be approximately 640 acres. Permanent firebreaks will be established where natural breaks are lacking to avoid the probability of wildfire (Division of Game, 1980). Detailed studies of Holly Shelter have been done by Wells (1946) and Smith and Deyle (1976). From a comparison of these two papers, it is clear that the approximate pocosin acreage in 1946 (38,500 acres) has decreased due to fire exclusion and hardwood invasion.

The North Carolina Division of Forest Resources administers the Bladen Lakes State Forest near Elizabethtown in Bladen County. The area is particularly significant because it contains a number of Carolina bays (see Christensen et al., this volume). These bays fill gradually by peat accumulation, giving rise to numerous wetland communities including high and low pocosin. Approximately 13,000 acres of the state forest is too wet to be utilized for timber production. These bays will be left in their natural condition with no prescribed burning (Mr. Claude Hood, Superintendent, Bladen

Lakes State Forest, 16 October 1979, personal communication). Just how much of the area is pocosin cannot be determined; however, a study of the bays of the state forest by Ashton and Ashton (1979) documents the plant communities as well as significant flora and fauna.

Near the state forest are several lakes (Salters, Jones, Singletary, White, Bay Tree, and Bushy) administered by the North Carolina Division of Parks and Recreation. Bushy Lake in Cumberland County is an example of highly diverse natural bay vegetation. The lake will be maintained as a natural area, but no special plans for management exist, one problem being that the state does not own the entire bay. A 133-acre portion of the Singletary Lake shoreline has been designated as Turkey Oak Natural Area (Master Planning Unit, 1977) and contains a pocosin–bay forest area of 43 acres which was burned several years ago. Plans are to repeat this procedure in the near future. Salters Lake is a largely undisturbed open-water bay surrounded by evergreen bay forest, pocosin, and sand ridge communities. There are no plans for either development or prescribed burning. Nearby Jones Lake has a park area on the east side of the water and, to the northeast, communities identical to Salters Lake. White and Bay Tree lakes already have a significant amount of development precluding pocosin preservation.

Farther to the south, in New Hanover County, the North Carolina Division of Parks and Recreation maintains a small 5-acre pocosin tract at Carolina Beach State Park. The pond pine/evergreen shrub communities occupy two adjacent circular depressions which are probably lime sinks resulting from slumping due to cracks in an underlying detrital limestone, the Cape Fear Coquina formation (Taggart, 1980). This pocosin was partially burned in February 1978, and future plans include burning the entire area during the winter of 1980-81. Monitoring systems will be set up with help from Dr. Norman Christensen (Duke University) to determine vegetational changes and to modify future burning plans.

Situated in central Brunswick County, the Green Swamp is a large area of swamp forest, pocosin, and savannah, punctuated by sand ridges or "islands," as they are known locally. Approximately 26,000 acres have been recognized by the National Park Service (1979) as "the most unspoiled and unique portion of the Green Swamp." Kologiski (1977) studied this tract and found that approximately one-half of the area was covered by pine–hardwood (high) or pine–ericalean (low) pocosin. Savannahs have been burned frequently in past years for wildfire prevention. At this time, there is no plan by either of the major landholders of the 26,000 acres, The Nature Conservancy (13,850 acres) and Federal Paper Board Company (12,150 acres), intentionally to burn any of the pocosin vegetation. Land use alternatives are being considered for The Nature Conservancy property (National Park Service, 1979), while the Federal Paper land ultimately may be converted to pine plantation.

Pocosins in the Sandhills Section of Coastal North Carolina

The sandhills represent a distinct geologic area in North Carolina characterized by fluvial sand ridges and swales originally vegetated by extensive longleaf pine communities (Wells and Shunk, 1931; Dr. Albert Radford, Professor of Botany, UNC-Chapel Hill, 5 September 1979, personal communication). Pocosins in the sandhills are confined to depressions between hills or seepage slopes created by waters issuing from clay layers situated beneath the porous sands. Fire was common in presettlement days and played a vital role in maintaining the plant and animal diversity (Goodwin and Carter, 1977). With the suppression of fire and rapid development throughout this economically desirable area, few tracts of extensive natural vegetation remain. Public property encompassing pocosin habitat in the sandhills is confined to three tracts: Weymouth Woods Sandhills Nature Preserve, Fort Bragg Military Reservation, and the Sandhills Game Land. Weymouth Woods Sandhills Nature Preserve, near Southern Pines in Moore County, contains a 12-acre pocosin which is burned as a part of the overall management plan. The Division of Parks and Recreation also plans to develop a monitoring system similar to that described for Carolina Beach State Park.

Fort Bragg Military Reservation is administered by the United States Army and covers portions of Moore, Hoke, and Cumberland counties. Fire lines have been cleared in a grid pattern every tenth mile and wetlands (pocosins, swamp forests) have fire lines plowed around them as well. Fires are set on a seasonal basis but are confined to the upland longleaf pine/wire grass communities. The reservation is primarily used for military training and timber production (Mr. Lance Peacock, Inventory Specialist, N.C. Natural Heritage Program, 4 December 1979, personal communication).

The Sandhills Game Land, located in Scotland, Moore, and Richmond counties, is maintained by the Wildlife Resources Commission (WRC) which pursues an active winter and summer burning program. Fires set in the pine grasslands are now allowed to burn into the pocosin areas until they self-extinguish. Mr. Terry Sharpe, wildlife biologist for the WRC, has noted (24 October 1979, personal communication) a marked increase in pocosin plant diversity since the recent decision to let the pocosins burn. The area is on a 100-year timber rotation.

FUTURE CONSIDERATIONS

In summarizing the preceding survey of pocosin natural areas in North Carolina, a few points are clear: (1) Pocosins vary in their natural features throughout the coast plain; (2) There are very few large undisturbed pocosin natural areas; and (3) The majority of public pocosin lands do not contain prescribed burn plots.

In considering what the future needs for pocosin preservation should be, we must know more about this ecosystem and its components. As mentioned above, pocosin composition varies as exemplified by the presence of Venus' fly traps and pine barrens tree frogs in certain Brunswick County pocosins (Wilbur, this volume) and the absence of these species in Dare County. Pocosins may occur in broad interstream areas, Carolina bays, lime sinks, etc., with mineral or organic soils. Therefore, we need a more thorough understanding of the various pocosin types in order to select representative areas for possible protection by acquisition.

A comprehensive system for basic inventory of natural areas has been developed by Dr. Albert E. Radford et al. at the University of North Carolina at Chapel Hill. In the analysis of a given natural area, not only biology but also climate, soils, geology, topography, hydrology, and physiography are considered. The combination of these basic components will yield a more complete picture than just a plant and animal inventory. Information from such studies is being kept on file and computer by the North Carolina Heritage Program housed within the Division of Parks and Recreation.

Beyond descriptive qualities, detailed quantitative studies will be required for determining the nutrient cycling, hydrology, and other important facets of this ecosystem. Such information may be invaluable for justifying pocosin preservation in order to maintain adjacent estuaries, groundwater regimes, and other vital conditions (see Richardson, this volume).

The state and federal agencies that have not formally designated specific pocosin preserves within the public lands cited, should do so. This will help to focus attention on the need for pocosin preservation and protect these natural areas from future changes in land use.

What should be done to manage present and future pocosin natural areas is important because of the pyric nature of the vegetation. Past pocosin studies all include reference to fire (Wells, 1928, 1932, 1942, 1946; Garren, 1943; Penfound, 1952; Woodwell, 1956; Wells and Whitford, 1976; and Kologiski, 1977). Just how often or at what time of the year a burn should occur to adequately maintain a specific pocosin seral stage is not certain. The optimal fire regime undoubtedly varies with the particular site in question.

If succession from pocosin or bay to hardwood forest does occur, certain plants and animals may be affected. Rare plants such as white wicky (*Kalmia cuneata*), rough-leaf loosestrife (*Lysimachia asperulaefolia*), Venus' fly trap (*Dionaea muscipula*), sweet pitcher plant (*Sarracenia rubra*), and dwarf fothergilla (*Fothergilla gardenii*) will gradually be shaded out by the increased overstory (Dr. Albert Radford, Professor of Botany, UNC-Chapel Hill, 12 November 1979, personal communication). Populations of the pine barrens tree frog (*Hyla andersoni*) will be adversely affected because their prime breeding habitat is the acid waters of open pocosin pools (Dr. Henry Wilbur, Associate Professor of Zoology, Duke University, 6 November 1979, personal communication and this volume). Red-cockaded woodpeckers

(*Picoides borealis*) occasionally inhabit mature pond pines, and proper habitat for these birds would also be lost by allowing hardwood succession. Pocosins are also one of the last refuges for large mammals such as black bear (*Ursus americanus*) and posssibly panther (*Felis concolor*) (Ashton and Ashton, 1979; Monschein, this volume). Whether these mammals would be affected by increased vegetative cover is not certain.

It is therefore recommended that at least one prescribed burn plot be established and monitored within a natural area in each of the four coastal plain sections previously described. In Section I, a tract possibly could be isolated at the Gull Rock Game Land and/or Dismal Swamp State Park. The Croatan National Forest would serve as an adequate representative of Section II. In addition to Carolina Beach State Park, Section III plots would also be desirable at Holly Shelter, Bladen Lakes, and The Nature Conservancy property in the Green Swamp. Monitoring changes at the managed pocosins of the Sandhills Game Land and Weymouth Woods would document burning in Section IV. The knowledge gained from studies of various burned and nonburned pocosin regimes would be invaluable for developing a comprehensive management policy for pocosin preserves and the rare plants and animals within them.

In delimiting a prescribed burn area, it must be remembered that ditching has a tendency to "dry out" pocosins over organic soils. As the water table is lowered, a thicker layer of peat will be exposed to the air (Heath, 1975). Thus, ditching can create the possibility for a more intense peat burn than would occur under natural hydrologic conditions. Hardwood invasion will also increase in pocosin soils that have been drained (Dr. Albert Radford, Professor of Botany, UNC-Chapel Hill, 6 November 1979, personal communication), thus accelerating the successional sequence depicted by Kologiski (1977). It is therefore recommended that the extent of ditching (length, depth, and width) around pocosin natural areas be kept to a minimum to avoid these undesirable effects.

Because of the rapid development of pocosins and the many unanswered questions concerning their ecology, more research is needed to understand and preserve these wetlands. A number of publicly owned pocosin areas exist, but do these encompass the full diversity of biology, geology, pedology, and hydrology? Only further study utilizing qualitative and quantitative inventories will tell. Acquisition can then be focused on the most desirable tracts (see Roe, this volume, for methods of pocosin acquisition). Proper management of pocosin natural areas is just as important as their acquisition. Programs need to be developed to maintain examples of all pocosin seral stages. Prescribed burn plots will be necessary for maintaining some stages, while other sites should be allowed to proceed through succession naturally.

LITERATURE CITED

Ashton, R., and P. Ashton, 1979. Contract report on the Bladen Lakes area. Unpublished report prepared for the N.C. Natural Heritage Program, Ralcigh, 90 pp.

Braun, E. L., 1950. Deciduous Forests of Eastern North America. Blakiston Co., Philadelphia, Pa., 590 pp.

Division of Game, 1980. Wildlife management in North Carolina. Application for federal aid in wildlife restoration by the N. C. Wildlife Resources Commission, Raleigh.

Garren, K. H., 1943. Effects of fire on vegetation of the southeastern United States. Bot. Rev., 9:617-654.

Goodwin, L. M., and J. H. Carter III, 1979. Draft management plan, Weymouth Woods Sandhills Nature Preserve. Division of Parks and Recreation, Raleigh, N.C., 52 pp.

Heath, R. C., 1975. Hydrology of the Albemarle–Pamlico region, North Carolina. U.S. Geological Survey, Raleigh, N.C., 98 pp.

Kearney, T. H., 1901. Report on a botanical survey of the Dismal Swamp region. Contr. U.S. Nat. Her., 5:321-585.

Kologiski, R. L., 1977. Phytosociology of the Green Swamp, North Carolina. Ph.D. Dissertation, North Carolina State University, Raleigh, 169 pp.

Marine Corps Base et al., 1975. Natural resource management plan. Camp Lejeune, N.C., 344 pp.

Master Planning Unit, 1976. Dismal Swamp State Park master plan. Division of Parks and Recreation, Raleigh, N.C., 63 pp.

______, 1977. State Lakes master plan. Division of Parks and Recreation, Raleigh, N.C., 70 pp.

National Park Service, 1979. Green Swamp-Study of Alternatives-Executive Summary. U.S. Dcpartmcnt of thc Intcrior, 12 pp.

Penfound, W. T., 1952. Southern swamps and marshes. Bot. Rev., 18:413-446

Radford, A. E., H. E. Ahles, and C. R. Bell, 1968. Manual of the Vascular Flora of the Carolinas. University of North Carolina Press, Chapel Hill, 1183 pp.

Radford, A. E., et al., 1980. Natural Heritage: Classification Inventory and Information. University of North Carolina Press, Chapel Hill, 674 pp.

Smith, E. L., and R. Deyle, 1976. Holly Shelter Game Land—Preliminary study. Unpublished report prepared for the Division of Parks and Recreation, Raleigh, N.C., 8 pp.

Taggart, J. B., 1980. Carolina Beach State Park Natural Area. Unpublished report prepared for the Division of Parks and Recreation, Raleigh,

N.C., 41 pp.

Wells, B. W., 1928. The major plant communities of the coastal plain of North Carolina and their successional relations. Ecology, 9:230-242.

______, 1932. The Natural Gardens of North Carolina. University of North Carolina Press, Chapel Hill, 458 pp.

______, 1942. Ecological problems of the southeastern United States coastal plain. Bot. Rev., 8:533-562.

______, 1946. Vegetation of Holly Shelter Wildlife Management Area. N.C. Department of Conservation, State Bull. 2, 39 pp.

______, and I. V. Shunk, 1931. The vegetation and habitat factors of the coarser sands of the North Carolina coastal plain: An ecological study. Ecol. Mono., 1:234-254.

______, and L. A. Whitford, 1976. History of stream-head forests, pocosins, and savannahs in the Southeast. Jour. Elis. Mit. Sci. Soc., 92(4):148-150.

Whetstone, R. D., 1977. Nere Elexus Day Pond Pine Natural Area. Unpublished report prepared for the National Landmark Study. University of North Carolina, Chapel Hill, 8 pp. and 4 maps.

Woodwell, G. M., 1956. Phytosociology of coastal plain wetlands of the Carolinas. M.A. Thesis, Duke University, Durham, N.C., 49 pp.

Interpretation of Pocosins in North Carolina: The State of the Art

Ray E. Ashton, Jr.

ABSTRACT

Very little interpretive information on the natural history or management of pocosins in North Carolina is available to planners and the public. Only two state facilities—Carolina Beach State Park and Weymouth Woods Nature Preserve—provide some interpretive services on pocosins. Reasons given for the relative lack of such services include the low priority given to this ecosystem, the relative scarcity of scientific information and shortage of funds for environmental education in the inner coastal plain due to the comparatively sparse human population and the consequently low financial base. Cooperative efforts between state and federal agencies and the private sector to develop a plan and funding for three regional interpretive centers are recommended.

Key Words: interpretation, environmental education, coastal plain, regional centers, interagency cooperative plan, boardwalks, driving tours, community involvement

INTRODUCTION

Knowledge of an ecosystem—its natural history, its importance to the overall ecology of an area, and its potential value to mankind—must precede actions to protect that ecosystem. Such knowledge leads to appreciation of the ecosystem and ultimately should lead to a reasonable management plan that permits the ecosystem to continue to exist and also allows for a representative example of the ecosystem to be set aside in its "natural state" for interpretation.

As a case in point, for many years most of us misunderstood and virtually treated with contempt the vast tidal marshes of the eastern United

States. For several hundred years these wetlands were abused and altered. Today, through scientific research and through interpretation of this research for the public and for planners, many if not most people acknowledge the value of these habitats. We consequently have made significant strides in our efforts to protect them.

Our knowledge of pocosins, and especially our attempts to interpret their nature and value, today stand where our efforts on salt marshes stood fifty years ago. We do not yet have a complete catalog of what lives in those unique areas nor an understanding of the ecological, hydrological, or other relationships that pocosins have with the surrounding coastal environments (Ashton and Ashton, 1979; Richardson, this volume).

Because we know so comparatively little about their natural history, we do not interpret pocosins adequately to the general public. The public thus remains ignorant of their nature and value and continues to view pocosins as vast wastelands of importance only if drained and reclaimed for farmland or housing developments.

One might ask how pocosins, as unique habitats supporting rare, endangered or threatened plants and animals (see Christensen et al., Wilbur, and Monschein, this volume) were ignored during the period of intensive environmental concern and education in the late 1960s and early 1970s. There are several reasons for this neglect, but the paramount reason is that pocosins are inhospitable places. People enjoy roaming along the coast and through the mountains, but hiking through a wild pocosin is difficult if not impossible. In addition, the demography and economy of the coastal plain, with low populations and a dearth of industry, provide little financial support or incentive for environmental education. Historically, pocosins have been viewed as a hindrance to progress, whether this progress be farming, community building, or industrialization.

INTERPRETATION TODAY

Interpretive programs on pocosins in North Carolina lack the sophistication, planning, and funds seen in marine and coastal education. Considerable state and federal monies have gone into such facilities as the Hampton Mariners Museum of the North Carolina State Museum, Marine Resource Centers, state parks, and national seashores. The inner coastal plain has been generally ignored, with the following exceptions:

1. Carolina Beach State Park (Taylor, 1979). This has the only real nature trail, a boardwalk, through a pocosin area. Some attempt has been made to manage the pocosin area through prescribed burning and to provide some interpretive materials. Currently, this area has suffered heavily from vandalism. Signs have been destroyed, plants

removed, and undesirable side trails developed by visitors. Comprehensive interpretive materials are lacking, and no year-round interpretive program has been developed. Insufficient staff and lack of a comprehensive operations and educational plan appear to be factors hindering programs at this facility.

2. Croatan National Forest. No attempt at interpreting pocosins or other coastal plain habitats has yet been made. The booklet, "Insect Eating Plants on the Croatan National Forest, North Carolina," is well written and could be used as a model for developing similar but more general materials on coastal plains environments. The Neusiok Hiking Trail was recently completed. It crosses thirteen miles of forest and private lands including some pocosins.
3. Jones Lake State Park. Outstanding examples of pocosins occur in this area (Master Planning Unit, 1977). The only interpretive efforts occur during the summer months when a staff naturalist is present. The naturalist leads trips on nature trails that in part go through pocosins. Some guided tours are conducted in other seasons by the park superintendent and other staff members. Some minor interpretive programs are included in the master plan for this area.
4. Weymouth Woods, Sandhills Nature Preserve. A twelve-acre area of sandhills pocosin exists on the preserve property (Goodwin and Carter, 1979). An interpretive trail runs 0.3 mile through the area and is used as part of the nature walk program. The museum and its interpretive materials on sandhills communities are well done, and the staff is available and well trained to conduct programs.

Other Interpretive Efforts on Pocosins

Field trips and programs on coastal plain environments are conducted periodically by the North Carolina State Museum of Natural History (particularly by its Beaufort branch, the Hampton Mariners Museum), the North Carolina Marine Resource Centers, and the Lake Waccamaw Depot Museum. The state museum's publication, "Endangered and Threatened Plants and Animals of North Carolina" (Cooper et al., 1977), describes coastal habitats, including pocosins, and the floral and faunal elements of these habitats which are considered endangered, threatened or of special concern.

Current Problems

No major plans by any state or federal agency provide interpretation of pocosins in North Carolina. Agencies that are or could be involved in coastal plain interpretation and management consider these areas to be of low priority.

No substantial funding from state, federal or local agencies has been made available for pocosin interpretation. Without a plan, no real funding is likely.

There are no full-time, trained interpretive biologists on the staff in any of the pocosin areas. Only part-time summer naturalists are hired in state parks. Occasionally, park personnel with other major responsibilities may be called upon to function in this capacity. Without a long-range interpretive plan and permanent staff, little can be done to establish a solid educational effort at any facility.

Several agencies are now developing minor plans for their facilities, either to expand or renovate existing facilities or to develop new ones. Current plans at Bladen Lakes State Forest call for a drive-through trail with emphasis on the history of forestry in the area. A boardwalk into Carolina bay pocosin and interpretive signs will be part of the plans (Joe Hogue, personal communication). At Carolina Beach State Park, some renovation of the pocosin trail is planned and will include a self-guiding sign system. Plans to continue management of the pocosin are under way (John Taggart, personal communication).

INTERPRETATION IN THE FUTURE—A PROPOSAL

The main objective of a comprehensive interpretive plan is to provide regional centers for inner coastal plain environments, including pocosins. One in Croatan National Forest would serve Carteret, Craven, Pamlico, Jones, Onslow (Jacksonville), Lenoir (Kinston), Greene, Pitt, and Duplin counties. Other areas that should be considered in such a plan are Carolina Beach State Park and the Green Swamp, depending on its ultimate ownership.

The regional centers would provide educational services to school districts and residents and to tourists from the coastal and piedmont areas of North Carolina. Printed materials, audiovisual programs, and other services could be provided for a much larger region.

Developing the Plan

The plan could be developed through interagency cooperation. Participants might include the divisions of State Parks and Recreation, and Forest Resources; the Department of Natural Resources and Community Development; the State Museum of Natural History and Hampton Mariners Museum, Department of Agriculture; the Division of Archives and History, the Department of Cultural Resources; the Office of Marine Affairs, Department of Administration; the United States Forest Service; the United States Fish and Wildlife Service; county and city school districts within the region; representatives from the state university system; timber companies; and other industrial representatives that may express interest. The primary organizations in such a plan would be the Division of State Parks and the United States Forest Service since recommended sites fall under their jurisdiction. Thus, any facilities developed probably would be funded through these two agencies, which would assume reponsibility for them. The consortium of interested agencies could produce a plan for each facility, not unlike the original plans for the North Carolina Marine Resources Centers.

Facilities

Within each of the interpretive centers there should be facilities for museum exhibits that would illustrate the natural history of all habitats within the coastal plain, as well as the geologic history, geology, hydrology, soils, archaeology, and plant and animal communities of the coastal plain. Resource management on the coastal plain should also be portrayed. Within these centers, classrooms and laboratory facilities should be provided in order to further the proposed natural history education programs.

Interpretive nature trails should be established at each center. Boardwalks should be placed over wet areas, including pocosins, and other areas that may be subject to destruction should be protected from public overuse.

The boardwalks at Carolina Beach State Park have no railings. This has led to habitat destruction by visitors walking off the boardwalk to observe and illegally collect plants. This could be remedied in part by adding a railing barrier, which is fenced at the bottom. The rail would also provide a surface for interpretive signs, including signs in braille for the blind. Boardwalks should be wide enough to comfortably accommodate large classes and other groups and barrier-free for the physically impaired. In open low areas, such as pocosins in Carolina bays, photography and observation towers could be constructed to allow visitors an opportunity to see the community patterns of the coastal plain. Examples of these recommended facilities exist in Everglades National Park, Okefenokee National Wildlife Refuge, and the Francis Beidler Forest in Four Holes Swamp.

Where appropriate, as at Bladen Lakes State Forest, auto tours originating at the centers could be developed. A numbered sign system along roadways would coincide with a map and interpretive materials which could be used by visitors to get an overview of coastal plain habitats. At each numbered site, various natural features, explained in the booklet, would be evident from the vehicle. A similar plan could be adopted for hiking trails such as the one mentioned in the Croatan National Forest and those planned for Bladen Lakes State Forest.

The interpretive centers could develop audiovisual materials for use by schools, scout groups and other organizations. These materials should be arranged in education units that would meet the needs of classroom teachers. Basic biological and ecological concepts would be discussed with coastal plain environments and biota used as examples. Various "hands on" materials and objects could also be developed to accompany slides, videotapes or films.

Special events, classes and other activities could be developed at these centers. Such activities not only provide a maximum use of the facilities but also involve the community in the centers and thus generate subsequent support for their programs. Volunteer programs and citizen support groups would increase the ability of the centers to meet program demands and provide another avenue of community support.

CONCLUSION

Current attempts to interpret pocosins in North Carolina are restricted and poorly developed because of the low priority given interpretation of these unique coastal plain habitats and the consequent lack of skilled staff. Other contributing factors are the relative inaccessibility of pocosins and the lack of sufficient scientific data on which to build an educational base.

To solve these problems, I have recommended a coordinated effort on the part of the state, federal and local agencies to create a plan and provide funding to develop three regional interpretive centers. The development of these centers would not only provide much needed educational enrichment for inner coastal plain areas but also would lead to a greater understanding of pocosins and other unique coastal environments. The ultimate result can only be a deepened appreciation of the areas and management to ensure their continued existence.

LITERATURE CITED

Anonymous, 1975. Insect eating plants on the Croatan National Forest, North Carolina. U.S. Forest Service, New Bern, N.C., 14 pp.

Ashton, P. S. and R. E. Ashton, Jr., 1979. Biological survey of the Carolina bays of Bladen Lakes State Forest and Suggs Mill Pond, Bladen County, North Carolina. North Carolina Heritage Program, North Carolina Parks and Recreation, unpublished.

Cooper, J. E., S. S. Robinson, and J. B. Funderburg, eds., 1977, Endangered and threatened plants and animals of North Carolina. State Museum of Natural History, Raleigh, N.C., 444 pp.

Goodwin, M. and J. Carter, 1979. Weymouth Woods management plan. North Carolina Parks and Recreation, unpublished.

Master Planning Unit, 1977. State lakes master plan. North Carolina Parks and Recreation, Raleigh, N.C., 70 pp.

Taylor, B., 1979. Carolina Beach State Park—Venus' fly trap management procedure. North Carolina Parks and Recreation, unpublished.

The Preservation of Pocosins: An Overview

Charles E. Roe

ABSTRACT

The preservation and conservation of pocosin ecosystems, as well as other wetlands, is a high priority for the maintenance of North Carolina's natural diversity. Perhaps 100,000 acres of pocosin are held in public ownership. However, these habitats are too often considered wastelands by their managers. Realization of the ecological importance of specific pocosins is the necessary first step to preserve these elements of our natural diversity. Application of formal protection safeguards is necessary to ensure the continued existence of pocosins. A variety of protection methods, described in this paper, may be applied for pocosin protection. This range of conventional and innovative protection techniques may enable preservation of critical pocosin areas identified through comprehensive inventory. The means to conserve and preserve pocosin ecosystems exist if we determine to do so.

Key Words: natural diversity, natural heritage, preservation.

INTRODUCTION

Christensen, Monschein, and Wilbur (this volume) have underscored the fact that pocosin ecosystems serve as critical habitats for many native plant and animal species. Although generally "unloved" and unappreciated by human society, pocosins are at least as important to the maintenance of natural diversity as are more aesthetically appealing natural communities. For those of us concerned with the preservation of North Carolina's natural diversity, the conservation of pocosin ecosystems, as well as other wetland habitats, is a high priority.

The inaccessibility and inhospitable conditions of pocosins no longer can be expected to ensure their continued existence. Technological sophistication, added to economic incentives, permits massive conversion of pocosins to industrial and agribusiness uses (see Campbell and Hughes, Campbell, Barnes, and Harwood and McMullan, this volume).

Several tracts of pocosin are in public ownership (Richardson et al., this volume). Yet, we must be acutely aware that public ownership of any natural area is not synonymous with protection. Government ownership of pocosin wetlands will contribute little to their survival unless adequate management is maintained. Management objectives and practices are the crucial determinants (see Taggart, this volume). In fire dependent ecosystems, like the pocosins, it is essential that prescribed burning be regularly employed. Also, drainage and manipulation of water tables in the vicinity of pocosins may adversely affect their natural qualities.

The principal and highly fragmented pocosins in public ownership or designated as nature preserves by private owners include (for a complete list and acreage, see Taggart, this volume):

1. Green Swamp (The Nature Conservancy),
2. Bladen Lakes (N.C. Division of Forest Resources),
3. Bushy Lake Natural Area (N.C. Division of Parks and Recreation),
4. Holly Shelter Gameland (N.C. Wildlife Resources Commission),
5. Angola Bay Gameland (N.C. Wildlife Resources Commission),
6. Croatan National Forest pocosins (U.S. Forest Service),
7. Pungo National Wildlife Refuge (U.S. Fish and Wildlife Service),
8. Gull Rock Gameland (N.C. Wildlife Resources Commission),
9. Goose Creek Gameland (N.C. Wildlife Resources Commission).

Most of these public lands were considered wastelands and as such were reclaimed into the public domain in the 1930s and 1940s. The one exception is the Green Swamp Sanctuary.

The protection status and management policies for these areas vary dramatically. In some cases, the pocosins are treated by their administrators at best as *de facto* wilderness and at worst as wastelands with little or no management attention. Even where a site has been officially designated as a research natural area or national wilderness, very little management planning has been done. Most of the potentials for environmental education and interpretation in pocosins are lost because public land administrators have not invested the interest or expenditures for creating visitor centers, boardwalks, trails, information stations, and the like (Ashton, this volume).The failure to treat the publicly owned pocosins as important resources for environmental education, scientific research, or ecological reserves creates the popular impression that pocosins are wastelands awaiting some practical economic or industrial use. Unfortunately, government land managers too often share that erroneous perspective. The state Wildlife Resources Commission 1981 to 1986 gamelands development plan, for instance, proposes to drain and timber hundreds of acres and to construct major road and canal networks in its publicly owned pocosins. Before the public can be expected to understand the ecological significance of pocosins, the public servants—that is, the public land managers—must understand the uniqueness and importance of pocosins as wildlife reserves and natural reservoirs.

POCOSINS OF SPECIAL INTEREST FOR PRESERVATION

Pocosins are among the ecosystems of special interest to the Natural Heritage Program. The North Carolina Natural Heritage Program, a unit of the state's Department of Natural Resources and Community Development, is responsible for identifying the state's most significant natural areas and subsequently planning for their protection. The goal of the Natural Heritage Program is the preservation of natural diversity in North Carolina. This is the first comprehensive attempt to determine, through an intensive statewide inventory, the state's most important natural areas. Through the inventory, areas of prime ecological significance can be identified and recommendations for protection of these areas can be made.

Several pocosin areas are among the sites of greatest priority in the Natural Heritage Program's protection recommendations. Whereas good representations of pocosin ecosystems exist in public ownership in the southern portions of the coastal plain, few pocosins are protected either in the interior sandhills–Carolina bay region or in the northern sector (tidewater or Pamlico region). The ecological associations of these northern and interior pocosins are not adequately protected, and the extent of the pocosins is being rapidly reduced. We recommend preservation of pocosin tracts in Dare County (along highway 264, southwest of Stumpy Point and near Manns Harbor) and other tracts in Dare, Hyde, and Tyrrell counties in association with the Alligator River. These and other pocosins in that region are currently being inventoried by the Natural Heritage Program. Also, we recommend protection of a pocosin that is part of a large Carolina bay complex in Bladen County, as well as a series of Carolina bay ecosystems in Robeson, Hoke, and Scotland counties. We believe these tracts possess ecological resources of state or national significance. They should be set aside as nature preserves or wildlife refuges.

While we rank these areas of pocosin and several others already in public ownership as among the highest preservation priorities in the state, there are other pocosin sites that possess natural features or rare species of special merit. A variety of conservation techniques might be applied for their protection (Heritage Conservation and Recreation Service, 1979; Roe, 1976). I will briefly describe these methods.

CONSERVATION TECHNIQUES FOR WETLANDS

The North Carolina Registry of Natural Heritage Areas is one means to encourage conservation of outstanding natural areas in private or public ownership (Natural Heritage Program, 1979). The registry honors the owners and administrators of recognized natural areas for their intent to conserve the natural qualities of the land. This nonbinding, nonregulatory program recognizes landowners for being good conservationists and awards framed certificates in appreciation of their stewardship. This approach is primarily educational. An eligible natural area is entered on the registry only after the owner voluntarily agrees to its recognition. The state Department of Natural Resources and Community Development has registered pocosin areas in the Green Swamp, Bushy Lake, and Pungo Refuge and is prepared to nominate pocosins in Croatan National Forest, Bladen State Forest, and elsewhere.

Environmental impact assessment is now required on many proposed federal and state projects. Inventory information, such as that collected by the Natural Heritage Program, is providing data necessary for informed decisions about land areas suitable or unsuitable for the state's continued development. Many valuable natural areas have been destroyed from a lack of awareness and understanding of their biological significance. Environmental impact assessment and use of natural resources inventory data should help eliminate the inadvertent destruction of prime natural areas and prevent unnecessary conflicts.

Attempts to use "police power" regulations to control land uses in rural areas typically have been restricted to zoning, subdivision ordinances, and building permits. Generally, these regulations have been ineffective in preserving environmentally important land. In North Carolina the agricultural and industrial timber operations that have been most responsible for converting pocosins incur comparatively little regulation by state agencies (see Heath, this volume). The principal regulatory program affecting development within pocosin areas is the Department of the Army's Corps of Engineers permit requirements for structures and work in or affecting navigable waters. The Corps may reject an application on the occasional finding that the project will have an adverse impact on the public interest.

Compensable regulations, while seldom used in this nation, are advocated by some as a method of exercising strict public control over land use by providing compensation for property value losses due to regulation. The compensable regulation approach may possibly be effective in preserving open spaces in urban fringes, but its utility and feasibility for other areas is highly questionable.

A more traditional effort to influence land use is through property tax incentives. North Carolina, like the majority of the states, provides preferential tax assessment for farmland and timberland. The intent is to maintain rural land uses in urbanizing counties. The method has not been extended to encourage preservation of natural lands. However, the state programs of preferential tax assessment are now generally in disrepute because of their failure to provide more than a weak holding action until speculative desires are satisfied or until stronger restrictions are imposed. Some effectiveness might be gained if preferential taxes were linked strictly to lands specifically identified as important to the public interest for their agricultural or natural values.

Land acquisition may be advisable to assure protection of highly critical natural areas and may be achieved by several means. Public agencies and conservation organizations may occasionally be able to purchase land at full market value for a park, refuge, or preserve. More often, gifts of land or bargain sales are sought (Sussman and Roe, 1979). National and state tax laws encourage individuals and corporations to donate property to government agencies or charitable conservation groups. Outright land donation will result in the greatest tax benefits to the donor. A "bargain sale" of property to a qualifying organization or agency at a price that is less than its fair market value is a partial donation and a partial sale. The donor may deduct as a charitable contribution for income tax purposes the difference between the fair market value of the property and the actual sale price. Federal Paper Board Company's donation of 13,850 acres of Green Swamp pocosin, savannah, and pineland to The Nature Conservancy and Union Camp's donation of its Dismal Swamp and Chowan Swamp properties to The Nature Conservancy are prime examples of how the tax laws work to encourage preservation of outstanding natural areas.

Landowners derive considerable advantages from donations (or bargain sales) to conservation organizations like The Nature Conservancy or to public agencies. Four of these advantages follow.

1. Frequently, donation of land nets the owner's estate greater solvency. Income and inheritance tax laws encourage preservation of natural lands through tax deductible gifts. Under prevailing laws, gifts of land for conservation can represent from 30% to 50% deducted from the donor's adjusted gross income.
2. Land is so flexible as a direct philanthropic device that its simple conversion to cash can destroy not only the landscape but also lose the owner a unique opportunity in estate planning.
3. There are compelling arguments why certain landowners should consider donations of their property for public-interest natural lands. It should come as no surprise that almost all the arguments revolve around one thing—taxes. Proper application of existing tax laws makes conservation both practical and efficient.
4. Even among speculators, both professional and amateur, there are many with vision who would like to see the land used properly as well as profitably.

It is our hope that the corporate owners of the pocosin areas considered of highest preservation priority may consider donating tracts for preserves.

North Carolina's property and easement laws make conservation easements a viable preservation technique (Peacock and Roe, 1979). By entering into an agreement which creates a conservation easement, a landowner can retain private ownership while still preserving the natural integrity of the resource. Certain property rights are acquired from the landowner. An agreement between the owner of the land and a qualified conservation organization creates the easement under which the owner conveys to the holder of the easement the right to prevent certain uses of the land or to use it for specific purposes. The easement ensures that the owner will keep the land substantially free from future development or detrimental activities. The owner may use, sell, lease, or convey the land subject to the explicit terms and conditions of the easement because neither title nor right to possession of the land is conveyed by the easement agreement.

Conservation easements may be temporary or permanent. Those granted in perpetuity will more fully guarantee permanent protection of the land and provide maximum tax benefits to the owner. In addition, an easement in perpetuity binds subsequent purchasers or heirs of the property.

The fair market value of an easement in perpetuity that is given to a qualified recipient is a deductible item according to federal and state tax laws. Gifts of easements are thus deductible in the same manner as other gifts of land. The difference between the appraised fair market value of the property *before* and *after* granting the easement determines the value of the easement. Not only does an easement reduce a landowner's property tax burden by restricting the future uses of the land, but it also decreases its full cash value to the owner and, consequently, its assessment value for tax purposes.

Conservation easements are an attractive alternative for the protection of natural lands in private ownership. Easements provide the landowner an opportunity to preserve valuable natural lands while maintaining private ownership and gaining considerable tax benefits. Having endorsed the utility of easements for preserving natural lands in general, I must point out a problem in their applicability for pocosin protection. The property values derived from private ownership of pocosins lie principally in the potential timber and mining values. These are the same development uses that would be denied by a conservation easement. While a conservation minded private individual or hunting club might find an easement desirable to ensure protection of a pocosin habitat and to win tax benefits, an industrial owner would likely see little advantage in an easement. In this case, acquisition of fee-simple title is probably the only realistic means to prevent destruction of a pocosin environment.

Private conservation foundations provide alternatives to government acquisition (Roe and Sussman, 1979). A conservation foundation—in some states called a land trust—is a private, nonprofit, charitable (and tax exempt) corporation created to acquire and manage lands in the public interest. The Nature Conservancy and National Wildlife Federation are examples of national conservation foundations, but a foundation may also focus on a particular town, watershed, county, or region. A citizen's organization has the flexibility and interest that government agencies may lack. A foundation can act quickly and apply a number of acquisition techniques available only to nonprofit organizations. It is conceivable that a conservation foundation established for the protection of natural areas in the North Carolina coastal region or for the preservation of wetlands in North Carolina could become an important instrument for the conservation of some pocosins.

A range of conventional and innovative protection techniques exists and could be applied for the preservation of critical pocosin habitats. Realization of the ecological importance of specific pocosin areas is the necessary first step to preserve these elements of our natural diversity. If we hope to see a fraction of the pocosins set aside and managed as ecological reserves, education and value recognition of land managers and the public is of critical importance. There may be some parallels here to the public awakening in the past two decades to the significance of coastal marshlands. The means to conserve and preserve representative pocosin ecosystems exist if we determine to do so.

LITERATURE CITED

Heritage Conservation and Recreation Service, U.S. Department of the Interior, 1979. Land conservation and preservation techniques. Government Printing Office, 75 pp.

North Carolina Natural Heritage Program, 1979. North Carolina Natural Heritage Program report. N.C. Dept. of Natural Resources and Community Development, Raleigh, pp. 37-40.

Peacock, L., and C. E. Roe, 1979. Conservation and historic preservation easements, to preserve North Carolina's heritage. N.C. Dept. of Cultural Resources and Dept. of Natural Resources and Community Development, Raleigh, 36 pp.

Roe, C. E., 1976. Innovative techniques to preserve rural land resources. Environmental Affairs, Vol. V, No. 3, Boston College Law School, 419-446.

Roe, C. E., and R. Sussman, 1979. Forming a conservation foundation in North Carolina. Heritage Conservation and Recreation Service and N.C. Dept. of Natural Resources and Community Development, Raleigh, 30 pp.

Sussman, R., and Roe, C. E., 1979. Protecting North Carolina's heritage . . . gifts of land for conservation. Heritage Conservation and Recreation Service and N.C. Dept. of Natural Resources and Community Development, Raleigh, 16 pp.

Section III. Industrial Values

Forest Management Systems in North Carolina Pocosins: Weyerhaeuser

R. G. Campbell and J. H. Hughes

ABSTRACT

Physical and economic factors continue to make North Carolina pocosins very attractive for intensive forest management. The high water tables, heavy brush, and nutrient deficient soils demand intensive drainage, roading, site preparation, and fertilization to produce acceptable plantation growth. Research programs have developed combinations of treatments that increase plantation productivity two or three times over natural stands. An example illustrating the increase in productivity from a natural stand site index 45 ft in 25 years to 80 ft in 25 years for an intensively managed plantation is presented. This represents an increase from 40 to 225 cu ft of growth per year over a 25-year rotation. Development of stand cultural practices including fertilization, thinning, weed control, and perhaps pruning will increase production of large diameter, high quality logs for solid wood products.

Key Words: loblolly pine, drainage, fertilization, site preparation, productivity, coastal plain, plantations

INTRODUCTION

The importance of southern pine in domestic and international trade is usually not realized by the general public. Two recent statements by Zoebel (1979) emphasize the present importance and future uncertainty of adequate timber supply to meet demand. "The South will remain the major wood basket for this nation and foreign markets for at least a quarter century" and; "There is real doubt, however, whether the South can fulfill the demands that will be placed on it for conifer wood in the future." Although the recent controversy over United States Forest Service supply and demand projections (USDA, 1974) has been somewhat resolved (LeMaster, 1978), the supply shortfall could be even larger as timber is substituted for nonrenewable resources and developed as an energy source. Without substantial new technology and investment, forest industry will grow only 25 to 50% of our needs.

In North Carolina, industry owns 12% of the commercial forest land, the government owns 9%, and small landowners control 79% (Knight, 1977). The current regeneration levels provide explicit reasons for the projected shortfall. Only 34% of harvested areas in North Carolina are being regenerated. For each acre harvested, national forests are regenerating one acre; forest industry is planting 1.1 acres; and private nonindustrial owners are regenerating only 0.1 acres, or less than 10% of harvested acres (Forest Industries Council, 1979).

This paper will describe Weyerhaeuser's High Yield Forest program in North Carolina pocosins. The basic concept of this program is to maximize economic forest growth by applying optimum management practices to specific soil types and landforms.

COASTAL PLAIN LANDFORMS

The coastal plain of North Carolina is composed of depositional terraces produced by the intermittent rising and lowering of sea level during the glacial and interglacial sequences of the Pleistocene period (see Daniel, this volume). Erosional and depositional landforms have developed on these surfaces. Soils on lower coastal plain surfaces range from sands and clays to organics including slowly permeable clays and deep organics. Poorly drained forest soils can be discussed as landform groups of shorelands, flats, bays, and pocosins. River swamps and brackish marshes are not considered suitable sites for intensive forestry and are omitted from this discussion. The potential for forest growth on the various coastal plain landforms varies greatly. For the purposes of this discussion, emphasis is placed on pocosins although the other landforms can have somewhat similar management practices and growth responses. Pocosins are major landforms characterized by lack of a definite slope gradient, a blocked drainage pattern, and the highest elevation in a localized area—a raised bog. The major management advantages of utilizing pocosins are good growth potential after drainage, few erosion problems, and relatively large uniform areas with adequate soil moisture.

LAND ACQUISITION AND FOREST MANAGEMENT

Weyerhaeuser Company's ownership is concentrated on the pocosins and upland flat landforms with some ownership of shorelands, bays, and lowland flats. The majority of present company land lies in a dozen or so major pocosins in the middle and upper parts of the lower coastal plain at elevations of 20 to 40 ft. Acquisition was concentrated in this zone because the natural stands contained high pine timber volumes and were located close to the original mill at Plymouth and newer mills at New Bern and Jacksonville, North Carolina. These sites have shallow organic and wet mineral soils that grow mixed pine—loblolly, pond, and longleaf—in the natural forest. Hardwoods and cypress are confined to small ponds, natural drains, and breaks in the pocosin rims.

The historical impetus for timberland management has been to assure a present and future supply and continuous flow of pine timber to the mills. In the 1930s, 40s and early 50s the strategy was to buy high volume timberland, block adjacent tracts into large area composites, and build road systems for fire protection and harvesting. The primary raw materials supply was purchased from landowners and independent loggers who delivered roundwood to railroad sidings, barge landings, or directly to the mill. Company timber was harvested only in emergencies. Very few pine seedlings were planted during this period. At most, in all of eastern North Carolina, only a few thousand acres of abandoned agricultural fields were planted to trees. However, significant natural regeneration began during the late 1940s when the forest industries and the North Carolina Forest Service banded together to control the menace of wildfire that annually blackened the pocosins. Much of the pocosin pine harvest of the 1970s dates back to regeneration that resulted from fire control of the late 1940s. This fire control effort is still necessary as today's plantations and natural stands face the threat of destruction each spring.

Large-scale cutting of company timber, especially in the pocosins, began in the late 1950s and early 1960 as a first step toward more intensive forest management. These early clearcuts became the first artificial regeneration blocks in the pocosins. Site preparation consisted of drum chopping, burning and disking. Some blocks were planted by hand although the majority were aerially seeded. By the late 1960s it was apparent that planted tree growth rate was at best "fair" when compared to similar plantations on upper coastal plain and piedmont sites. Many of the aerially seeded blocks were also failures. Excessive water and severe phosphate deficiency reduced survival and growth. Specific research was needed to permit economic plantation development in pocosins.

THE IMPACT OF FORESTRY RESEARCH

Weyerhaeuser began a research program in North Carolina in 1969 to learn how to increase growth of plantations in pocosins. Since then over 120 man-years of research effort have been invested in the pocosin challenge. Between 1972 and 1977, the New Bern Forestry Research Field Station concentrated over half of its research effort on the development of an understanding of the benefits and impacts of pocosin water management. The first five years, until about 1974, were considered the "learning curve." Recent research studies on drainage, site preparation, and fertilization have produced definitive results that increase plantation growth with improved practices.

Drainage

Drainage is the removal of water from a landform with subsequent lowering of a groundwater table. An immediate concern is the impact on water use in the surrounding area. Understanding of aquifer recharge and water movement in geologic strata has required development of modern drilling technology to generate a data base. Daniels et al. (1978) have recently refuted one popular theory of pocosin water relationships. The authors give substantial evidence that the large interstream divides—the pocosin areas—are *not* recharge basins for the deep water aquifers that lie below them. For example, the Big Pocosin, which lies between the Neuse and Pamlico rivers is *not* the recharge for the underlying Castle Hayne aquifer. This aquifer is recharged much further to the west, in the middle and upper coastal plain. Rain falling on the Big Pocosin either becomes surface runoff or recharges the surface water table. There is no connection between the surface water table and the deep water aquifer. Improved surface water movement does not impact the deep aquifer which supplies domestic water for residents in the surrounding areas. (For a more complete discussion of the regional geology and hydrology see Daniel, this volume.)

Successful plantation management of pocosins requires an understanding of soil water as it affects tree growth. Soil/water relationships in undrained pocosins exhibit seasonal extremes. The water table depth may range from 1 ft above the soil surface to perhaps 4 ft below, varying by soil type, timber volume, and distance to natural drainage. High temperature, wind, evaporation, transpiration, and low rainfall contribute to rapid drops in the surface water table during the spring wildfire season. Late spring and early summer rains usually return the water table to the soil surface. Maximum drawdown of the water table in early fall may be delayed by summer thunderstorms and hurricanes. Continuously high water tables occur throughout the winter months due to low rates of evaporation and transpiration. Seasonal water table fluctuations vary dramatically on an annual basis depending on rainfall patterns. In a drained pocosin, seasonal fluctuations of water table depth are considerably less (see Gilliam and Skaggs, figures 3 and 4, this volume). Ditching lowers the surface water table by an average of 1 or 2 ft throughout the year. Standing surface water is minimized, although complete soil saturation will occur during the winter months. Water management reduces the lengths of periods of soil saturation during the growth season by one-half to two-thirds (Campbell, 1976).

Relationships between drainage and forest productivity have been developed by many researchers (Klawitter and Young, 1965; Maki, 1971; Maki, 1974; Miller and Maki, 1957; and Terry and Hughes, 1978). Soil type, topography, distance to and effectiveness of natural and artificial drainage systems, rainfall, time of year, site damage, subsequent ameliorative treatments, and their respective interactions are important factors in these relationships. Soil/site work has shown that the best growth for natural stands of loblolly pine occurs on somewhat poorly drained to moderately well drained soils (Campbell, 1978). Control of groundwater levels in poorly drained pocosins alters natural site conditions enough to allow intensive plantation management of loblolly pine.

Two basic approaches to water management research were used concurrently. First, water table levels and fluctuations were correlated with tree growth on a series of monitoring plots established on transects across old ditch systems over a range of pocosin soils supporting loblolly plantations. Next, water table levels were determined on ditch spacing studies established during harvest and regeneration. Water table levels and tree growth could then be expressed as a function of ditch spacing by soil type. Combinations of these biological data within the framework of environmental constraints and economic considerations resulted in development of procedures that served as guidelines for an operational drainage program.

Benefits from the water management program include additional plantation growth and increased equipment operability. Miller and Maki (1957) and Maki (1974) have also documented the tremendous growth response to North Carolina pocosin drainage. The literature review of supporting studies in Table 1 by Terry and Hughes (1975) discusses growth response ranging from 80% to 1300%. Weyerhaeuser studies have further documented growth differences for loblolly plantations in pocosins with as much as ten times the wood production on drained plots as on undrained plots. This convincing biological evidence mandates that adequate drainage be a characteristic of intensively managed forests.

Operability considerations also have a strong influence on the management decision to control water. Excessive rainfall, complicated by the hurricanes in August and September of 1971, severely impeded harvesting and regeneration activities. Without adequate drainage systems, the high subsurface water levels and the exceptionally large amounts of surface water prevented equipment operation on some soil types. Other sites could be logged only by accepting extreme levels of soil disturbance. The loss of as much as one-third of the potential productivity of these sites, even with ameliorative treatments, was not a desirable option. The need to have a continuous wood supply during wet weather further motivated both research and operational programs for pocosin drainage.

TABLE 1. *A Summary of Studies that Have Shown Southern Pine Growth Response Resulting from Drainage (from Terry and Hughes, 1975)*

Study	Soils	Species	Ages[A]	Unit[B] basis	Distance to canal (drained)	Mean annual growth drained	Mean annual growth undrained	Percent increase over undrained
Miller and Maki (1957)	Portsmouth fine sandy loam	Planted loblolly	0-17	m^3/ha (OB)	60.9 m	17.9	1.28	1,298
Graham and Rebuck (1958)		Natural pond	0-22	m^2/ha	121.9 m	0.74	0.41	80
Klawitter and Young (1965)	Plummer, Rains loamy fine sand	Natural slash	19-22	m^3/ha	76.2 m	9.0[D]	4.9[D]	84
White and Pritchett (1970)	Leon fine sand	Planted slash	0-5	m^3/ha (OB?)	46 cm[C]	14.6	5.7	156
					92 cm[C]	13.3	5.7	133
		Planted loblolly	0-5	m^3/ha	46 cm[C]	7.6	1.3	585
					92 cm[C]	4.9	1.3	277
Brightwell (1973)	Bayboro-Bladen-Coxville	Planted slash	8-16	m^3/ha (IB)	10 m	0.006	0.0014	329
Weyerhaeuser	Bayboro-Bladen	Planted loblolly	0-13	m^3/ha	10 m	4.3	0.54	696

A. Ages used for calculations, from beginning of drainage to time of final measurement.
B. BA = basal area at 1.3 m; IB = inside bark; OB = outside bark.
C. Water table constantly maintained at this depth.
D. 50-year site index of 16.8 m (55 ft) prior to drainage, apparent site index after drainage 22.8 m (75 ft).

Water management on a tract begins with the accumulation of topographic, soils, and engineering data. A complete engineering plan of road locations, natural drainage patterns, and potential outlets is developed. Most pocosin tracts can be effectively drained with a pattern system rather than a prescription system. Prescription systems are directed toward increasing the rate of surface water removal by cleaning and deepening natural drains. Natural gradients and topography located from aerial photography and ground surveys are used in engineering this type of system. Pattern systems use rectangular grids of ditches to remove surface water and to lower the subsurface water table on landforms with little relief and poorly defined natural drains (pocosins, bays, and flats). Careful engineering is required to delineate elevation changes of less than 2 ft per mile. Both systems utilize a primary outlet located at the lowest elevation on the tract to carry water to its natural outflow in a drain, swamp, or creek. Road canals or secondary ditches collect water from the field ditches or third stage ditches and carry it to the outlet. The need for sound engineering and soils data to orient and space ditches in an effective system rather than just digging ditches cannot be overemphasized.

Site Preparation

The primary objective of site preparation is the creation of plantable microsites suitable for survival and growth. The use of bedding or ridging on most pocosin land achieves the desirable tillage effects of disking while creating an elevated microsite. On poorly drained soil types, beds provide rooting depth in soil that is not completely saturated. Work by McKee and Shoulders (1970) in Louisiana has shown that 73% of the variation in height growth of six-year-old slash pine was associated with average depth to the water table during the winter months. On soil types with summer droughts, the short-term growth advantages of bedding over disking may not be maintained. Fine textured, wet soils in the Atlantic coastal plain rarely experience drought stress, and growth advantages are fairly stable. Volume responses reported by Malac and Brightwell (1973) and Terry and Hughes (1975) were still exceeding 100% at ages 8 to 13. The oldest study on company land is eighteen years old with a stable 8 ft of height advantage for bedding over flat planting. Competition control, nutrient concentration, and tillage are additional benefits of bedding. Terry (1978) documents the increase in organic matter, P, Ca, and macropore space associated with bedding. Extensive operational data have shown the relationship between good plantation growth and well-shaped beds formed under dry conditions. Good bedding requires disposal of logging slash from the previous stand as well as adequate drainage. Current regeneration practices include bedding on all poorly drained soils.

Fertilization

Extensive areas of soils deficient in phosphorus have been identified in the southeastern coastal plain (Ralston and Richter, 1980). Wet, acid soils have P in chemical combinations with Fe, Al, Ca, and organic matter adsorbed on clay particles. Research has shown that soils with low P levels and high P retention do not provide sufficient nutrients for optimum tree growth (Wells et al., 1973). Early research by the Cooperative Research in Forest Fertilization (CRIFF) program at the University of Florida demonstrated the tremendous pine growth response to P at planting on some soil types (Pritchett and Smith, 1970). Weyerhaeuser began preplant P fertilization research at New Bern in 1969 with the installation of several operational trials. Experimentation progressed from comparison strips to replicated plot studies as early results showed dramatic responses. Tree height response at age 3 was 54% to 168% greater than flat-planted seedlings for 60 lb of P per acre incorporated in beds across a range of soils (Terry and Hughes, 1975). Various rates, materials, and methods of application have been examined over a range of soil types in replicated plot studies. Diammonium phosphate (18-46-0) and rock phosphate (0-30-0) have shown good early response on some soil types. Long-term (seven-year) tree height response for phosphate incorporated in beds continues to be 99 to 158% greater than for unfertilized, flat planted trees (Terry, 1978). Operational prescriptions of 200 lb per acre of triple superphosphate (0-46-0) or diammonium phosphate (according to soil type) banded and incorporated into a bed are currently being used.

Operational guidelines based on research findings are applied in a sequential procedure to develop each pocosin tract and to regenerate each clearcut block. Previous reports document this work (Terry and Hughes, 1975; Campbell, 1976; Terry and Hughes, 1978; Campbell, 1978). By 1974, it was apparent that well-managed pocosin plantations were some of the most productive forests in the South. Intensive management includes site specific prescriptions for drainage, slash disposal and site preparation techniques, preplant fertilization, and assigning appropriate genetic sources by major soil types. Stand cultural activities include aerial fertilization, weed control, insect control, cultivation, and thinning. Intensive management of Weyerhaeuser's small percentage of deep organic soils is also under way. Three-year-old plantations on these organic soils are attaining phenomenal growth rates. This success is a result of applying principles learned on wet mineral sites in the early 1970s to the more difficult organic areas.

IMPACT OF INTENSIVE FOREST MANAGEMENT: AN EXAMPLE

The impact of intensive forest management can be illustrated with a time sequence of aerial photographs of a given pocosin area. Figures 1 and 2 are such a sequence for a few thousand acres of Weyerhaeuser's Big Pocosin tract in Craven and Beaufort counties. Figure 1 was photographed March 10, 1948; Figure 2 was photographed January 30, 1978, thirty growing seasons after Figure 1. Interpretation of these figures demonstrates trends that are representative of Weyerhaeuser's intensive forest management of pocosins.

By 1948, the Big Pocosin had "felt" the intrusions of man. The most obvious features in Figure 1 are canals of the Little Swift Creek drainage district—the remains of a bankrupt cooperative farming effort of the late 1920s. Limited drainage was established but no farming was ever begun. In Figure 1 the three parallel canals are about a mile apart and flow from northwest to southeast (from upper left to lower right in the photo). These three artificial drains empty into the channelized head waters of Little Swift Creek in the lower right of the photo. The white line in the right (eastern) one-third of the photo is Flat Swamp Road, a dirt state road that centers on the

FIGURE 1. *Weyerhaeuser ownership in the Big Pocosin near the Craven-Beaufort county line in 1948.*

broad clay rim of the pocosin. This clay rim separates Little Swift Creek basin (east and south in the photo) from the shallow organic and wet loam soils of the Big Pocosin (west and north in the photo). Other man-made features include a few small active or abandoned agricultural fields adjacent to Flat Swamp Road. The truly dominant feature of Figure 1 is the openness of the land. In fact, much of this pocosin has historically been called savanna land, defined on the basis of vegetation as grassland with scattered clumps of timber. The old growth timber in these clumps was harvested by railroad logging forty years prior to Figure 1 (early 1900s). The second growth forest, like the old growth, was maintained in savanna by periodic wild or man-caused fire. For Figure 1, forest occupies no more than 30% of the land area. About 90% of this appears to be pine, with pure clumps and mixed stands of loblolly, pond, and longleaf pines. In this slightly-altered-by-man pocosin, stand volume was about 500 to 1,000 cu ft per acre. Height growth at 25 years (site index, base age 25) was about 45 ft.

FIGURE 2. *Weyerhaeuser ownership in the Big Pocosin near the Craven-Beaufort county line in 1978.*

Figure 2 illustrates the tremendous changes during the thirty-year period, 1948 to 1978. Fire control was the first forest management practice to impact the pocosin/savanna. This control was accomplished by the combined forces of the forest industries and the North Carolina Forest Service in the early 1950s. As a result of fire control, pine seedlings were allowed to grow and to develop into continuous, dense stands across the savanna land. The savanna vegetative community, which had been maintained by fire, no longer exists. From Figure 2 we can see that many of these stands have already been harvested and replanted. The typical harvest block has two stand ages, about 25 to 30 years for the postfire regeneration and 50 to 60 years for the second growth clumps. Site index is 45 to 50 ft at 25 years. Harvest volumes range from 1,500 to 3,000 cu ft per acre. In this example, fire control alone increased wood volume production by about 200%.

The next practice to impact the pocosin was road construction. In the 1950s and 1960s roads were established at the rate of about 2 linear miles per 1 sq mi of land area. These roads, built on the original drainage district canal spoil piles, gave access for forest fire control as well as for other forestry activities. Roading density was more than doubled in the 1970s to facilitate natural stand harvesting. Major roads are now one-half mile apart and many crossing roads have been constructed. Major roads have been graveled to permit continuous, all-weather hauling of heavy equipment, timber, and fertilizer.

Artificial drainage has been a factor in pocosins for over fifty years (figures 1 and 2). As previously described, about 2 linear miles of drainage was dug for each square mile of land area; however, intensive, engineered drainage systems were dug in the 1970s. Drainage density for Figure 2 ranges from 8 to 16 mi of ditching per 1 sq mi of land area, depending upon soil type. Drainage is designed to remove surface water to permit harvest and site preparation activities and to improve tree growth. However, water tables remain relatively high even during the dry season, from 2 to 7 ft below the ground level. The phenomenal forest growth gains that result from precision drainage are described by Campbell (1976) and Terry and Hughes (1978). The oldest plantation in Figure 2 was planted in 1960. Site preparation included piling and burning the logging slash, flat disking, followed by planting with unimproved one-year-old loblolly pine seedlings. Standing volume at age 21 from seed is more than 2,000 cu ft per acre. Site index is about 50 ft in 25 years.

Most of Figure 2 has been harvested and regenerated since 1970. Perhaps 30% remains in natural stands. Site preparation activities have intensified steadily during the last ten years. Regeneration activities include logging, slash disposal, extra ditching, bedding, preplant phosphorus fertilization, and planting with genetically improved seedlings. Growth response to each of these treatments has been significant. For Figure 2, plantations in the 4-to-10-year-old range are growing at rates which place them in the site index range of

60 to 80 ft in 25 years. This is 15 to 35 ft better than the natural stands. Yields are five to seven times greater than those prior to 1948 and are two to three times greater than yields resulting from fire control in the early 1950s. These plantations are the High Yield Forest.

Silvicultural treatments promise additional volume and value gains at harvest time. Experimental blocks in Figure 2 have received chemical weed control, which will increase volume by about 500 cu ft per acre. Supplemental fertilizer has been aerially applied to one of the older plantations. This single application will yield about 200 to 300 cu ft per acre of additional growth over a five-year response period. Repeat fertilizations will produce 25 to 35% more total volume in the final harvest. Thinning and pruning have been applied to experimental blocks in Figure 2 to increase the quality and the value of the final crop trees. A greater volume of high-value plylogs and sawlogs will be produced by these treatments.

FOREST INDUSTRY AND POCOSINS—THE FUTURE

Weyerhaeuser and other industrial forest owners will continue to increase the intensity of pocosin management in the future. The general trend for private forest industry worldwide is toward more intensive management and higher investment on company lands. This increase in intensive management and investment is especially appropriate for North Carolina. Consider the aspects that make North Carolina and the pocosins unique among United States forest regions. North Carolina is situated near the largest markets in the United States and Europe, the largest markets in the world. This strategic location gives a transportation advantage which will be increasingly important in the future. Flat topography has allowed intensive site preparation and stand culture that is impractical in piedmont or mountain areas. The high level of pine productivity in intensively managed pocosins should support a continuation of these trends into the future.

Physical and economic factors also have made pocosins highly attractive for forestry. Most pocosins remain in large, uniform, easy to manage tracts. Historically, many tracts developed timber stands as wildfire was brought under control, but they remained underutilized because high water tables prevented access for logging. Timber companies supplied the required capital for roading and drainage of these tracts. The adverse conditions for pine growth of high water table, heavy brush, and nutrient deficient soils were removed with intensive drainage, roading, site preparation and fertilization. Lower levels of management often do not produce acceptable results.

Desirable stand cultural systems for pocosin plantations are beginning to emerge. Rotations of twenty-five to thirty-five years will be relatively long by southern pine plantation standards for two reasons. The first is unique to wet soil profiles. Pocosin soils, with drainage, continue to produce good height, volume, and value growth at advanced ages. Subsoil drought conditions often develop on upland sites, but this rarely occurs in pocosins. The second factor contributing to a longer rotation is related to the desirable end product. The highest values are obtained from plylogs and sawlogs. Longer rotations are required to develop the large diameters and high stem qualities that are necessary for these products. Plantations to be harvested in the year 2000 are already five to ten years old. Stand treatments between now and then will include two or three fertilizer applications, one or two heavy thinnings, and perhaps pruning for clearwood production on the most productive land. Fire, chemical, and/or mechanical methods will be employed to control (but not eliminate) competing vegetation.

As the price of timber, land, labor, equipment and energy increases, harvest utilization from each acre will increase. This has occurred in the past and will continue to occur in the future. Limbs, tops, and stumps as well as stems will be harvested to provide energy and chemicals as well as pulp chips and solid wood products. This nearly complete harvest will reduce site preparation costs and increase the number of productive acres in the subsequent plantation by eliminating slash piles. Because of these factors, and because of technology advances in tree improvement and regeneration, the subsequent plantations on altered pocosins will be much more productive than those of today.

LITERATURE CITED

Brightwell, C. S., 1973. Slash pine plantations respond to water control. Union Camp Corp., Woodland Res. Note No. 26, 3 pp.

Campbell, R. G., 1976. Drainage of lower coastal plain soils, pp. 17-27. In: W. E. Balmer, ed., Proc. Sixth Southern Forest Soils Workshop, Southern Forest Soils Council, Charleston, S.C.

Campbell, Robert G., 1978. The Weyerhaeuser land classification system, pp. 74-81. In: W. E. Balmer, ed., Proc. Soil Moisture . . . Site Productivity Symposium, U.S.D.A. Forest Service, State and Private Forestry.

Daniels, R. G., E. E. Gamble, W. H. Wheeler, J. W. Gilliam, E. H. Wiser, and C. W. Welby, 1978. Water movement in surficial coastal plain sediments, inferred from sediment morphology. N.C. Ag. Expt. Sta. Tech. Bull. No. 243, 31 pp.

Forest Industries Council, 1979. North Carolina forest productivity report. Forest Farmer, 39(2):9, 32-33.

Graham, B. F., Jr., and A. L. Rebuck, 1958. The effect of drainage on the establishment and growth of pond pine (*Pinus serotina*). Ecology, 39:33-36.

Klawitter, R. A., and C. E. Young, Jr., 1965. Forest drainage research in the coastal plain. J. Irrig. Drain. Div., Proc. Amer. Soc. Civ. Eng. Vol. 91;

No. IR3, Proc. Pap. 4456.

Knight, H. A., 1977. Stand-age profile of North Carolina's timberland. U.S.D.A. For. Ser. Resource Bull. SE-38. Southeast. For. Expt. Sta., Asheville, N.C., 15 pp.

LeMaster, D. C., 1978. Timber supply, nonindustrial private forest land and the conventional view. J. For., 76:365-367.

Malac, B. F., and C. S. Brightwell, 1973. Effect of site preparation on growth of planted southern pines. Union Camp Corp., Woodland Res. Note No. 29, 9 pp.

Maki, T. E., 1971. Drainage: Effect on productivity. For. Management Tech. Sess., Proc. 50th Anniv. Meeting, Appalachian Sec., Soc. Amer. For., 15 pp.

Maki, T. E., 1974. Factors affecting forest production on organic soils. In: Aandahl, ed., Histosols: Their characteristics, classification and use. Soil Sci. Soc. America.

McKee, W. H., Jr., and E. Shoulders, 1970. Depth of water table and redox potential of soil affect slash pine growth. For. Sci., 16:399-402.

Miller, W. D., and T. E. Maki, 1957. Planting pines in pocosins. J. For., 55:659-663.

Pritchett, W. L., and W. H. Smith, 1970. Fertilizing slash pine on sandy soils of the lower coastal plain, pp. 19-41. In: C. T. Youngberg and C. B. Davey, eds., Tree growth and forest soils. Oregon State Univ. Press, Corvallis.

Ralston, C. W., and D. D. Richter, 1980. Identification of lower coastal plain sites of low soil fertility. So. Jour. Applied Forestry, 4:84-88.

Terry, T. A., 1978. Factors related to the growth of intensively managed loblolly pine (*Pinus taeda* L.) on selected soils in the North Carolina lower coastal plain. Ph. D. Dissertation, N.C. State University, Raleigh, N.C., 163 pp.

Terry, T. A., and J. H. Hughes, 1975. The effects of intensive management on planted loblolly pine (*Pinus taeda* L.) growth on poorly drained soils of the Atlantic coastal plain, pp. 351-377. In: B. Bernier and C. H. Winget, eds., Forest soils and forest land management. Proc. 4th N. Am. For. Soils Conf. Les Presses de L'Université Laval, Quebec.

Terry, T. A., and J. H. Hughes, 1978. Drainage of excess water—why and how?, pp. 148-166. In: W. E. Balmer, ed., Proc. Soil Moisture . . . Site Productivity Symposium. U.S.D.A. Forest Service, State and Private Forestry, Atlanta, Ga.

U.S.D.A. Forest Service, 1974. The outlook for timber in the United States. U.S.D.A. For. Resource Rep. 20, 374 pp.

Wells, C. G., D. M. Crutchfield, N. M. Berenyi, and C. B. Davey, 1973. Soil and foliar guidelines for phosphorus fertilization of loblolly pine. Southeast For. Expt. Sta., U.S.D.A. For. Serv. Res. Pap. SE-110, 15 pp.

White, E. H., and W. L. Pritchett, 1970. Water table control and fertilization for pine production in the flatwoods. Univ. of Fla. Agric. Expt. Sta. Tech. Bull. 743, 41 pp.

Zoebel, B. J., 1979. Tropical imports no long-term threat to southern timber growers. Forest Farmer, 39(2):6-7, 35-38.

Peat for Energy Program: First Colony Farms, Inc.

R. N. Campbell, Jr.

ABSTRACT

The feasibility of utilizing peat for energy has increased significantly since the oil shortage of the mid-1970s. With a Btu value of 10,189 per moisture free pound and a sulfur content of only 0.26%, peat compares very favorably with eastern coal in terms of energy output but is much lower in sulphur content. An experimental peat harvesting program utilizing both milled and sod production techniques is outlined. It suggests great potential for the future utilization of peat for energy generation in eastern North Carolina.

Key Words: peat fuel, energy, harvesting, electricity, milled peat, sod peat

INTRODUCTION

A study done by Research Triangle Institute (McMullan, 1975) projects that First Colony Farms has over 145,000 acres (58,679 ha) of peat deposits which can be harvested without undue adverse ecological impact (Editor's note: A water quality and hydrology study is under way at North Carolina State University to analyze peat mining effects), and that these deposits contain about 203,000,000 moisture free tons. This is equivalent to about 164,000,000 tons of good grade eastern coal, or 676,000,000 barrels of number 6 fuel oil.

A chart published in October 1977 by the Institute of Gas Technology shows the total peat resource in the United States to be 1,443 quads, slightly less than half of which is in the contiguous forty-eight states. If this is correct, the peat resource is greater, and by a substantial margin, than the combined proven reserves of petroleum, natural gas and uranium (see Table 2, Harwood and McMullan, this volume.)

With the abundance of peat in the United States, and with all its significant advantages over coal, why has nothing serious been done to develop peat as a major energy resource? The most obvious answer is another question—before the oil embargo in 1973, with oil at less than $3 per barrel and coal at comparable cost, who needed peat? Those days of cheap oil and coal are gone, and it seems unlikely that government or industry can long continue to ignore this tremendously valuable national asset.

WHAT IS PEAT?

Peat is a fuel formed through decomposition of organic matter over several thousand years in a water saturated, oxygen starved environment (see Daniel, this volume). It can be thought of as young coal, and its physical and chemical characteristics vary widely, depending primarily on the material from which it was formed, the water regimen and the degree of decomposition (age).

The degree of decomposition of First Colony's peat was analyzed by the Peat Institute in Leningrad, U.S.S.R., at from 45 to 60%. This is considered to be ideal since peat in this range combines high heating value with low ash. More highly decomposed peats have high heating value but usually also have much higher ash content. First Colony's peat has decomposed beyond the fibrous state—in the raw state, it has the appearance and feel of a heavy, reddish brown grease.

This raw peat, upon being exposed to sunlight and wind, undergoes an irreversible drying process. It loses considerable volume, becomes granular and will not return to its original greasy state when rewet. If it did not have this characteristic, milled or sod peat harvesting might not be economically feasible.

THE NATURE OF FIRST COLONY PEAT LANDS

Most of the farm's harvestable peat occurs on untimbered, poorly drained lands covered with waxy leafed shrubs, such as gallberry and bayberry, and, in some cases, scattered pond pine (see Christensen, this volume, for vegetation analysis of pocosins). The land is too poorly drained for efficient timber production. First Colony attempted to develop some of its peat acreage into permanent pasture for cattle but soon found that the problem of wood removal and high acidity made this a prohibitively expensive endeavor.

Many eastern North Carolina farmers have attempted over the years to develop peat lands for agricultural purposes (see Barnes, this volume). Some of those who started with very low land costs and a lot of patience have succeeded in varying degrees. At today's land prices, with the inflated costs of all facets of land development for agriculture and with the current levels of farm prices, it is not as economically attractive to develop these peat lands for agricultural purposes.

PEAT VS. COAL

The only disadvantage of peat compared with good grade eastern coal is that it takes more tonnage and more cubic yards of it to produce the same amount of heat.

In 1976 the U.S. Bureau of Mines ran proximate and ultimate analyses on nineteen samples of the farm's peat (Table 1). The average of these samples showed a Btu value of 10,189 per moisture free pound. Most of the peat will be produced as extruded cylinders that weigh about 15 lb/cu ft at 30% moisture content (MC). To produce a million Btu of usable heat (allowing for evaporation of the moisture) will require about 5.85 cu ft of sods weighing about 146 lb.

Eastern coals with which peat will compete will range from about 11,500 to 13,000 Btu/lb as received (6 to 8% MC), and will weigh about 60 to 70 lb/cu ft in the pile. On the average, production of a million Btu of usable heat will require about 1.35 cu ft of coal weighing about 87.8 lb. Figures show that it takes a little over four times the volume and a little less than twice the weight of 30% MC peat to equal coal.

First Colony peat is considerably cleaner burning than coal. The Bureau of Mines tests show the peat to have an average of 0.26% sulphur (Table 1) compared with an average of 1.0 to 7 or 8% for eastern coal. Peat ash averages 4.75% and coal ranges from about 6 to 15%.

TABLE 1. *Average Values of Proximate and Ultimate Analysis of Nineteen Samples of First Colony Peat*

Proximate analysis	Peat (moisture free)	Ultimate analysis	Peat (moisture free)
Volatile matter	62.9	Hydrogen	5.46
Fixed carbon	32.4	Carbon	59.05
Ash	4.7	Nitrogen	1.39
	100.0	Oxygen	29.08
		Sulphur	0.26
		Ash	4.72
			100.00
British thermal units			10,189

Peat is highly reactive and gasifies quite readily. The Bureau of Mines samples averaged 62.9% volatiles and 32.4% fixed carbon (Table 1). Extensive proximate and ultimate analyses performed in 1978 and 1979 by Commercial Engineering and Testing Company have tended to confirm the Bureau of Mines test results.

Peat lies exposed on the surface which eliminates the costly overburden removal and reclamation problem faced by coal strip miners. Peat lands that are very unproductive (from an economic standpoint) in their natural state can become highly productive row crop land once the peat has been removed (see Barnes, this volume).

FOREIGN USAGE OF PEAT AS AN ENERGY RESOURCE

Peat has long been used in Ireland and the U.S.S.R. for generating electric power, and its use is being rapidly developed in other countries such as Finland and Sweden (Harwood and McMullan, this volume). The Irish generate about one-third of their electrical energy from peat-fired plants, and in 1975 (the last year statistics were available) the U.S.S.R. harvested about 200,000,000 metric tons (50% MC), one-third of which was used to fuel electric generating plants (Campbell, 1979).

In September 1977, representatives of First Colony Farms and Bechtel Power Corporation (who were doing a feasibility study for First Colony) visited a 630 megawatt, peat-fired generating plant in Shatura, U.S.S.R. This plant was built originally in 1920 with small, grate type, peat-fired boilers. Over the years, these were replaced with larger units, and in 1971 to 1972, the Soviets installed three 210 megawatt generating units, each served by two 105 megawatt peat-fired (suspension) boilers. The technicians at the plant claim these units maintain 95% availability burning peat at 50 to 55% MC, which is much wetter than the 30% First Colony hopes to harvest.

The peat-fired Irish plants are 25 and 40 megawatt and the Finns are in the 140 megawatt range. The Finns generate around 65 megawatts of electricity at these plants, the rest of the production being steam for community heating.

So, whereas peat for power is new in the United States, it is far from new abroad. The technology and hardware are fully developed, and there is quite a long history of successful operations.

PEAT HARVESTING TECHNOLOGY: CURRENT PRACTICE

Prior to 1930, peat harvesting in the United Kingdom, Europe and the U.S.S.R. could best be described as a cottage industry using primitive, labor intensive methods.

Starting around 1930, the Soviets systematically began developing technology and equipment for harvesting peat by the milled and sod peat methods. With either method, the first step is bog preparation which will normally take about two years prior to the beginning of actual harvesting.

Bog preparation begins with the installation of a complete system of drainage ditches and canals designed to remove surface and subsurface water, and to provide harvest strips which vary in width from 20 to 40 meters and which are normally 500 meters long.

The next phase of bog preparation begins from one to two years after the drainage system is completed and consists of removing surface vegetation and then subsurface wood to a depth of about 40 cm with a continuous stump pulling machine. This step is followed by creating a uniform 1 to 1.5% slope from the side ditches to the center of the strip to provide good surface drainage. This is accomplished with an auger-planer.

After the harvest strip surface has been sloped accurately and dressed smooth, the remaining pieces of small wood are removed by a simple, tractor drawn machine which consists of large drums outfitted with many rows of sharp spikes. As these roll across the surface, the wood is impaled on the spikes and is combed off into hydraulically dumped trays. When this operation is completed, the harvest strip is ready for either milled or sod peat production.

Milled peat is produced by working a thin top layer of the bog surface to provide maximum exposure to sunlight and wind in order to expedite drying. Today, the Soviets have a complete line of special milled peat harvesting machinery, each piece of which is designed to accomplish one particular part of the whole process.

The Finns started intensive development of their peat resource much later than the Soviets, and although they have developed their own machinery, it closely follows the concepts developed in the U.S.S.R. The first step in milled peat production in Finland is accomplished by a tractor-drawn milling machine which consists of a series of drums, each equipped with many rows of truncated conical spikes 2 or 3 cm long. These drums rotate rapidly as the machine moves across the surface, and they thoroughly scarify a layer of peat perhaps 2 cm deep.

The milling operation is followed by turning this top layer of peat with a very simple, tractor-drawn spoon harrow. The turning operation may be repeated several times depending upon drying conditions. When the peat reaches 50% MC or less, it is ready for harvesting.

Most harvesting is accomplished with a vacuum harvester which is nothing more than a giant vacuum cleaner. It makes successive passes over the entire harvest strip, and it sucks the dried granulated peat through narrow nozzles several meters wide and several centimeters high. The peat is separated from the air in a cyclone and falls into a 20 cubic meter bin which is dumped onto the storage pile after being filled.

Peat is normally stockpiled at both ends of the harvest strips in continuous windrows which may be 10 or more meters high. The stack is built and kept uniform by an inclined bucket stacker. Milled peat characteristically will maintain the moisture content at which it was stored—rain affects only the top several centimeters; the interior of the pile remains dry.

Both the Soviet Union and Finland produce some peat in "sod" form. This method involves digging peat from a depth of 40 cm and extruding this relatively wet material through 80-mm dies so that it comes out as a continuous cylinder of a diameter that breaks into individual pieces averaging perhaps 30 cm in length. These sods fall back onto the bog surface where they are left until they reach about 35% MC, at which time they are mechanically harvested.

Both the Soviets and the Finns harvest most of their fuel peat by the milled peat method, which, they say, is less expensive for them than the sod peat method.

Our experience with both methods had led us to conclude that this difference must be because of their extremely short harvest seasons (two and one-half months for Finland, three and one-half for the U.S.S.R.), coupled with the longer drying time required for sods (three and one-half to four weeks to get to 35% MC). By contrast, North Carolina has an eight- to nine-month harvest season, and we have gotten under 20% MC in mid-summer and under 35% in early spring and late fall in less than half that time.

In the early days of peat production in the U.S.S.R., the Soviets experimented with hydraulic peat mining, but they abandoned this method because it was more expensive than the milled peat method.

KEY EVENTS LEADING TO FIRST COLONY'S EXPERIMENTAL PEAT HARVESTING PROGRAM

First Colony's interest in developing its peat as an energy resource began in mid-1975 when Hercules Corporation began looking into the feasibility of harvesting peat and using it as a feedstock for the production of methanol. Hercules did extensive testing, both field and laboratory, and concluded that the peat would make an excellent feedstock. For reasons unknown to us, Hercules did not proceed with a commercial venture.

This venture, despite not going forward to a commercial operation, whetted our interest and the following year we invited a delegation from the Soviet Union's industrial equipment exporting arm, Machinoexport, to visit the farm. Their apparent reaction to the peat deposits was enthusiastic.

In 1976 and 1977, various First Colony personnel, together with engineers from two consulting firms that were studying economic feasibility of power generation using peat as fuel, visited the Soviet Union and Finland to observe power plants and peat harvesting operations.

In March 1977, two of the Soviet Union's top peat harvesting experts visited the farm to examine our peat deposits and to advise us on implementation of a harvesting program. Their reaction to the quality and uniformity of our deposits was highly enthusiastic, and they expressed confidence that their equipment and methods would work on our peat despite the large quantity of large buried wood in our bogs.

Following the visit of the Soviet experts, First Colony ordered a complete set of their bog preparation and milled peat harvesting equipment, and in October of 1977, we made arrangements with a Finnish company to rent a complete set of bog preparation and milled peat harvesting equipment, as well as a small, single head sod machine. Both the Soviet and Finnish equipment arrived in late 1977 and, with the help of two technicians from each country, it was assembled and partially debugged by the end of the year.

THE 1978 EXPERIMENTAL HARVESTING PROGRAM

The need for an experimental harvesting program arises from two major differences between the farm's deposits and those in the U.S.S.R. and Finland. These differences pose potential problems which could be evaluated only by actually experimenting with foreign methods and equipment. First, the farm's deposits contain large quantities of large, sound, Atlantic white cedar and cypress logs and stumps which may extend from top to bottom of the deposit (see Daniel, this volume, for more information on peat deposit charactersitics). By contrast, most of the foreign bogs observed have relatively small amounts of wood of recent origin which occurs, for the most part, in the upper layer of the bog. The second difference is that our peat, being more highly decomposed than the foreign peats, poses greater equipment flotation problems.

With the coming of good weather in early spring 1978, the experimental milled peat harvesting program began with the help of three Finnish technicians. A delegation of Soviet technicians arrived in April and proceeded with the final steps of bog preparation on two harvest strips, each 40 m wide by 0.5 km long.

It quickly became apparent that neither the Finnish nor Soviet ditching, augering or wood removal equipment could economically cope with the large buried wood. As the milled peat experiment continued, we began considering the possibility of leaving the wood in place and modifying the harvesting method so that it would be shredded and mixed with the peat to form a composite fuel. The heat value of such a composite fuel is reduced on the order of 1% below pure peat, which is insignificant compared with the potential saving in harvesting costs. The one question was whether or not such a composite fuel could be satisfactorily and economically pulverized for suspension burning (i.e., firing).

Samples of the composite fuel were sent to Combustion Engineering and to the Babcock and Wilcox Company, and they, in turn, sent samples to their West German affiliates. The reports were favorable—no significant problem in pulverizing, particularly at lower moisture contents.

With these favorable reports, the decision was made to postpone temporarily the experimental milled peat harvesting and to concentrate on sod peat production, since it seemed to offer a more economical method of harvesting wood and peat together.

The "digging" member on the sod machine is a circular plate which has around its periphery 45 mm diameter cutters oriented like the paddles on a paddle wheel. The plate is canted 15° off the vertical so that when the machine is operating, it is cutting a slot in the ground that is the width of the cutter, 15° off vertical and 40 cm deep. The rotation of the cutting plate is against the direction of motion of the prime mover so that the first material encountered by a cutter is raw peat 40 cm below the surface which will be at 82% MC. As this cutter moves on around, it picks up a certain amount of relatively dry peat near the surface, producing a mixture which, ideally, will be in the range of 66% to 69% MC. This range produces a well-formed sod which dries quickly. As the cutter emerges from the surface, this material is slung off by centrifugal force into the bottom of a cylinder. In the cylinder is an auger which forces the material through a die (or dies) where, upon emergence, it breaks up into individual cylinders which average about 30 cm in length. These are deposited on the surface where they remain until air dried to the desired moisture content.

The cutters are extremely effective in cutting through buried wood which, particularly when saturated, is quite soft and easily worked.

Starting around July 1978, we concentrated on sod production with the small Finnish machine, accumulating useful data on drying rates and productivity. We all agreed that leaving the wood in place and producing peat in sod form offered the best solution, so in December we ordered six Finnish machines for bog preparation and sod peat harvesting. Three of these machines were designed specifically for First Colony. These are a quadruple head sod machine, the 450 HP base unit which pulls and powers it, and a production miller which mills a 5 meter wide strip of peat and buried wood to depths up to 10 cm. This latter machine is used to pre-mill harvest strip surfaces as the first step in bog preparation and will be used to develop our own method of harvesting milled peat. The other three machines are an auger-planer for shaping the bog surface after milling; a windrower which picks up dried sods from a 5 meter wide strip and deposits them back on the bog surface in a continuous windrow; and a loader which picks up the windrowed sods, elevates them on an inclined conveyor and dumps them into a tractor-drawn cart moving alongside.

THE 1979 EXPERIMENTAL HARVESTING PROGRAM

All of the initial order of equipment was in operation by early June. Early in the year, we ordered a stacker and a second base unit capable of operating not only the stacker but any of the other equipment except the quadruple head sod machine. We also ordered a ditcher designed to cut 400 linear meters to a depth of 1.5 meters per hour. It will shred all the buried wood and disperse the excavated peat and wood over the surrounding surface.

We spent 1979 accumulating information on sod production, the various aspects of bog preparation, and drying rates on various sizes and types of sods, and on developing methods for bog preparation and milled peat production. We also worked on in-field transportation using rubber-tired, tractor-drawn carts which we borrowed from United States Sugar Corporation.

Our goal in bog preparation is to leave all of the wood in the ground and to produce a 50 meter wide harvest strip which is sloped 1 to 1.5% from ditches to center and which is so perfectly graded that ponding does not occur. This grading is of the utmost importance to rapid, uniform drying and to increasing the productivity of the windrowing and loading operations.

The procedure starts with pre-milling the outside quarters of the 50 m strip to full depth (10 cm). The peat and shredded wood produced by this operation are then augered toward the center of the strip. We then pre-mill to full depth a 10 meter wide strip down both ditches and repeat the augering operation. At this point, the bog is roughly shaped, and no appreciable quantity of buried wood has been dislodged. The final step is accomplished with an ordinary motor grader on Terra tires. A skilled operator can quickly have the bog surface looking like a superhighway subgrade.

The auger extruders operate successfully within a narrow range of moisture content. If the extruded materials fall under 60% MC, high loads are imposed on extruder parts and on the base unit hydraulic pump drives. This condition results when the top layer of dry material is too thick. We are exploring the feasibility of avoiding this condition by taking off enough of the layer as milled peat to raise the moisture content of the material going into the extruder to the mid-60% range.

If the moisture content of the extruded material gets much above 68% to 70%, the product is a ropey material, rather than a well-formed cylinder, which has very poor drying rates. This condition can be remedied by milling and turning a 10 cm layer of peat to produce enough dry materials to reduce the moisture content of the extruded material to the mid-60% range.

Production with a sod machine will have to stop when we reach the bottom 40 cm or so layer of fuel peat—otherwise the cutters will be getting into underlying mineral soil which will ruin the fuel. At this point, we will have to switch to milled peat production.

Our work during 1979 has shown that milled peat can be stored without cover the year-round without appreciable change in moisture content and with no danger of spontaneous ignition. The Soviets have many occasions of spontaneous ignition, but we have detected temperatures no higher than 43°C (110°F) in our stockpiles. The possible explanation for the difference in ignition problems is that our peat has such a high percentage of very fine material that oxygen intrusion of the pile is much less than that of the Soviets.

PEAT HARVEST PROGRAMS FOR 1980 AND THE FUTURE

The Finnish Suokone miller will be the primary tool in developing milled peat technology, and the entire 50 meter wide harvest strip will first be milled to a depth of 10 cm. During mid-summer, we may be able to harvest milled peat in layers of perhaps 5 cm. During the spring and fall, however, we will probably mill 10 cm, then roll the surface and harvest in somewhat thinner layers. This may involve using the Soviet miller described earlier.

After the milled peat is dry enough (25% MC or less), harvesting will be done with a flail type harvester that we have developed on the farm. This machine will elevate the harvested peat and deliver it to a tractor-drawn cart moving alongside.

Further projects will require the continued evaluation of productivity information on all items of equipment and working out the correlation of drying times to meteorological data that we have accumulated over the last several years of the program at the on-site recording station. We will also attempt to analyze the cost of the in-field transportation system and will study the best means of transportation from field stockpiles to an on-site electric generating plant.

CURRENT PROSPECTS FOR COMMERCIAL UTILIZATION OF PEAT

It appears quite likely that the North Carolina Electric Membership Corporation and/or Tideland Electric Membership Corporation will get Rural Electrification Administration support and financing for the construction of a 150 megawatt peat-fired generating plant on First Colony Farms.

A short test was run at Georgia Power Company plant in Albany, Georgia, using peat blended 50% by weight with coal. The blend pulverized satisfactorily, and the test was highly successful. This opens up the possibility of meeting the Environmental Protection Agency's emission standards without scrubbers by blending peat, which has about 0.25% sulfur, with high sulfur eastern coal for use in existing plants that were designed originally for coal but have been switched to oil. Many of these plants have been directed to stop using oil within a short time because of short supplies of crude.

Texasgulf has successfully blended pulverized peat with number 6 fuel oil for use at their Aurora, North Carolina, phosphate plant. This process opens up still another area in which use of petroleum might at least be decreased. A successful test was run recently by the Fuller Company using peat as fuel for brick production.

CONCLUSION

In summary, the number of potential user groups of peat for energy in North Carolina is rapidly growing. The future of this valuable resource is promising. (For an economic analysis of the use of peat for energy, see Harwood and McMullan, this volume.)

LITERATURE CITED

Campbell, R. N., Jr., 1979. Peat for energy program: History, current status and future plans. First Colony Farms, Inc., Creswell, N.C., 25 pp.

McMullan, P. S., 1975. Evaluation of resources, environmental constraints, and economic options available in First Colony Farms. Final report prepared for U.S. Sugar Corporation, Research Triangle Institute, Research Triangle Park, N.C., RTI project 26T-1122.

Agricultural Adaptability of Wet Soils of the North Carolina Coastal Plain

J. S. Barnes

ABSTRACT

Many of the very poorly drained mineral soil types and Histosols (organic soils) of eastern North Carolina have been successfully developed for agricultural production over the past two decades. These soils vary in amount, kind and depth of organic matter on the surface and texture of mineral subsoil, but they are commonly characterized as having a shallow water table much of the year and higher than normal levels of organic matter in the surface layer. They have a low natural pH requiring initial applications of lime at rates of 9.1 to 18.2 metric tons per hectare and are generally low in available phosphorus and copper.

Excess water is removed by a network of canals and field ditches. The saturated hydraulic conductivity of these soils is very low as most of the excess water drains from the land to the field ditches by surface flow.

Once developed, these wet soil types have become some of the most productive soils in North Carolina. Certain costs such as drainage, herbicide and lime may be higher than for the well-drained mineral soils of the coastal plain, but the difference is more than compensated for by high average yields and production efficiency.

Key Words: Histosols, land development, drainage, crop production, agriculture

INTRODUCTION

In recent decades, tens of thousands of hectares of very poorly drained mineral soils and certain Histosols have been and continue to be developed successfully for agricultural production in eastern North Carolina (see Richardson et al., this volume). Such development is a result of increasing demand for cropland, the advent of the bulldozer, dragline and other key machines, and advances in agricultural technology applicable to such soil types.

These soils are commonly referred to as "Blackland soils" because of the accumulation of large amounts of organic matter in the surface layer. They are found along the entire North Carolina coastal plain (Lee, 1955). The best known region of Blackland soils is the Albemarle–Pamlico peninsula. It possesses the largest area of high organic matter soils and is currently the most intensively developed for agriculture and forestry.

A review of successful operations on wetland soils will show that good management skills are required with regard to soil resource evaluation, land development procedures, soil and crop requirements and financial management. This paper will discuss some of the soil resource properties, development requirements, crop responses and economic returns from agricultural dvelopment on wet soils in eastern North Carolina.

COASTAL PLAINS WET SOIL TYPES AND THEIR PROPERTIES CONTROLLING DEVELOPMENT

There is some confusion and/or difference of opinion over the terms "wetlands" and "wet soils." Wet soils are those classed as having seasonal or permanent water tables shallow enough to inhibit cultivation. With artificial drainage, "wet soils" represent some of the most productive cropland in the state (Soil Conservation Service, USDA, 1977). According to the Soil Conservation Service, there are about 2,470,800 hectares (ha) of wet soils in North Carolina. The SCS identifies about 800,000 ha of "wetland" soils in North Carolina. These areas are typified by providing basic food elements for the state's commercial fisheries (marshes), serving to reduce flood peaks, increasing spring stream flow and improving water quality by trapping sediment and nutrients (flood plain soils areas) and providing productive wildlife habitat (SCS, USDA, 1977). Properties all such soils or soil areas have in common are:

1. A shallow water table much of the year with water standing at or above the surface part of the year;
2. A higher than normal level of organic matter in the surface layer.

The mineral subsoil of these wet coastal plain soils consists of stratified or layered marine sediments varying in texture from heavy clays to sands (see Daniel, this volume, for geological history of area). Except for the organic accumulation on the surface, development of conventional soil profile layers (A, B, C horizons) has been impaired by the shallow water table. Therefore, mineral layers are mostly depositional alluvial layers and not those layers normally formed by factors of time, weathering, and leaching and deposition

TABLE 1. *Wet Soil Groups Utilized in Agricultural Development in Eastern North Carolina*

Subgroups	Description
Typic Umbraquults	Very poorly drained mineral soils, acidic, with a weak illuvial horizon and a dark surface layer
Typic Humaquepts	Very poorly drained mineral soils, acidic, dark surface layer and no illuvial horizon
Histic Humaquepts	Very poorly drained mineral soils, acidic, and a histic (organic) surface layer 20-40 cm (8-16 in) thick
Terric Medisaprists	Well decomposed Histosols (organic soil) with an organic depth greater than 40 cm (16 in) but less than 130 cm (51 in).
Typic Medisaprists	Well decomposed Histosols with an organic depth greater than 130 cm (51 in).

of clays within the profile (Lee, 1955). For classification purposes, the basic criteria differentiating these soil types or series are the amount, kind, and depth of organic matter, texture of underlying mineral horizons, and depth of textural changes through the defining soil profile (control section).

Most of the wet soil resources utilized in agricultural development in eastern North Carolina are classed in subgroups of soil taxonomy (Table 1) (Soil Survey Staff, 1975; MacKinzie, 1974).

The natural pH of organic horizons is acidic and most commonly found to be in the range of 3.5 to 4.1. The dark surface layer of mineral soils averages 0.3 to 0.4 pH units higher than the pH of organic soils or layers. Mineral subsoil horizons are acidic also with a common pH in the range of 4.1 to 4.7. These pH patterns can be observed in the data presented by Dolman and Buol (1967) describing chemical and physical properties of organic soils in the tidewater region of North Carolina. Infrequent exceptions to the acid conditions occur when mineral layers in the subsoil contain shellfish fragments, and some of the highly reduced blue and blue-green gley layers have a high pH.

These soils are acidic because they are formed from mineral materials with a low base saturation and the geographic area has a warm, humid climate with rainfall exceeding the evapotranspiration rate by approximately 38 cm (15 in) which has been conducive to leaching of the basic elements from the soil strata. Comparing organic soils in North Carolina with the systems of organic soil formations in the northern lakes states, North Carolina organics would compare to the "bog" soils which formed under waterlogged conditions resulting from low relief and excess precipitation which was low in dissolved bases (ombrotrophic or ion poor). This is in contrast with high pH "fen" soils in the northern lakes states which formed in low areas fed by calcium rich (minerotrophic) surface waters and ground waters forced to the surface by underlying bedrock ridges or sandy outwash areas with a high water table (Boelter and Verry, 1977).

The wet soil types of eastern North Carolina contain high amounts of total nitrogen in the surface layer. Work conducted by Tonapa (1974) showed that over 70% of the total nitrogen (N) in nineteen high organic coastal plain soil types (9.2 to 95.6% organic matter [OM]) was in the form of fulvic and humic acids. For soil N to be available to plants, it has to be in nitrate or ammonia forms (mineralized from the organic forms). The study of Tonapa also showed all these soils responded to N fertilization. He could not show a positive relationship between N availability and OM content, total soil N, or C/N ratios. This indicates that other soil chemistry and environmental (aeration and biological) factors are controlling the net release of plant available N.

In a study by Daughtrey et al. (1972), phosphorus (P) was characterized on sixteen high organic matter coastal plain soils (11.1 to 85.8% OM). Over 70% of the total P in these soils was in the organic form. The soils were placed into three categories based on their desorption pattern and amount of P released during desorption. The poorly drained (dark surface) mineral soils of the group were relatively infertile and would respond strongly to P fertility. The Histosols and histic mineral soils were divided between those that mineralized significant quantities of P, but would respond to P fertility, and those that released significant quantities of P and would not respond to P fertility. Contributing factors to release of available soil P were the total amount of soil organic P, percent of total soil P contained in the organic fraction, past fertility and soil type. Experience in the field has shown that the preferred dark mineral soils and histic mineral soils are very responsive to P.

Plant available copper is generally low in most wet soil types of the coastal plain (Younts, 1964). As the organic matter of these soils increases, the amount of copper in soil solution decreases while complexing of applied copper increases. Copper retention, even on mineral soils, is great (Schauble, 1969). Being deficient in copper, most soils need supplemental copper fertilization (Barnes and Cox, 1973; Younts, 1964).

DRAINAGE REQUIREMENTS FOR AGRICULTURAL USE

In order for wet soils to be cultivated successfully, artificial drainage is required for removal of the excess gravitational or free water. This is accomplished by installing a network of canals and field ditches which allows the water to move from the land rapidly enough so as not to restrict aeration of the root zone.

Canals are frequently spaced 0.8 km (0.5 mi) apart with field ditches dug perpendicular to the canals at a common spacing of 90 to 100 m (300 to 330 ft). This creates rectangular fields 7.2 to 8.0 ha (18 to 20 ac) in size which are adapted to efficient use of large farm equipment. The catcher canals flow into transport or outfall canals leading to a local drainage outlet (creek, river, or estuary).

Ditches and canals carry the flow of drainage waters, but most of the water actually drains from the land by surface or sheet flow. The saturated hydraulic conductivity of these soils is very low. It may be as low as 0.01 cm/hr (Badr and Skaggs, 1978). Therefore, field surfaces are shaped and leveled to facilitate surface flow to ditches. In winter months, the water table is close to the surface because of these very low internal conductivity rates. During warmer months, the water table in cultivated fields is lower as a result of drawdown by increasing rates of evaporation and transpiration (Skaggs and Barnes, 1976; Badr and Skaggs, 1978; Skaggs et al., 1980; and Daniel, this volume). In a study by Skaggs et al. (1980) which investigated the effects of agricultural development on drainage waters of three key wet soil types, drainage and development activities resulted in an average annual water table drop of approximately 30 cm (12 in) when compared to the water tables of undeveloped sites of the same soil type. Hence, drainage in most wet soils of eastern North Carolina can provide minimum root zone aeration requirements for many aerable crops, but the impact of drainage on the soil water table is not considered as having a significant effect on average annual water table and groundwater recharge (Skaggs et al., 1980; Maki, 1974).

The drainage of most wet soils areas utilized for agriculture is accomplished by gravity flow through the ditch and canal network. In some locations, however, the effective elevation of the land, in comparison to the elevation of the drainage outlet, does not provide sufficient gradient for adequate drainage by gravity flow. In such areas, drainage pumps are required. Drainage by pumps does impose an additional operating expense, but when the pumps are placed so that the discharge is released in wooded swamp or marsh areas, there are fewer environmental effects. Suspended and dissolved substances and debris have extensive opportunity for removal or filtration before reaching streams or estuaries. The main influence agricultural drainage has on the hydrology is to speed up the flow rate of excess water draining from the land (Skaggs et al., 1980). When this water is released into a wooded swamp or marsh area, there is also a slowing down of the drainage flux or rate entering the receiving stream or estuary, more closely simulating the drainage rate from undeveloped lands (Barber et al., 1978; Richardson, this volume).

LAND CLEARING AND DEVELOPMENT PRACTICES

Clearing the land of trees, brush and buried wood is performed by bulldozers using blades and rootrakes. Any commercial timber is harvested and remaining vegetation is pushed into windrows in the center of rectangular shaped fields. Over a period of years, this debris is disposed of by periodic burning and repiling remaining debris until all has been eliminated.

Development practices start with land sloping and leveling which are performed soon after clearing. Sloping is accomplished by bulldozers using blades pushing soil material from the outer edges to the center of the field. Leveling is accomplished by use of landplanes filling in holes and depression areas.

Newly cleared land has substantial quantities of small wood remaining in the plow layer. For three to five years, this wood is worked out of the soil and removed by using a host of different plows, rakes and loaders, many of which have been developed, designed or adapted specifically for the soil types of the area.

These wet soil types require certain chemical and fertility adjustments to be readied for cultivation. As mentioned before, all of the soils are very acid, most are very low in available P and most have low available levels of copper.

To overcome acid soil reactions, heavy lime applications are required, the actual rate depending on soil type and organic matter content. Lime requirements are generally in the range of 9.1 to 18.2 metric tons/ha (4 to 8 tons/ac), as compared to 4.5 to 9.1 metric tons/ha (2 to 4 tons/ac) on coarser textured mineral coastal plain soils. Once the initial lime requirements are met, maintenance lime is required at the rate of approximately 2.3 metric tons/ha (1 ton/ac) every two to four years. This is approximately the same as for other coastal plain soils. An exception to this maintenance requirement is on the very high organic matter soils which consistently need 2.3 metric tons/ha (1 ton/ac) every two years for several years.

With available P being low in most newly developed wet soils, initial building applications are required. These applications are in the range of 57 to 114 kg/ha (50 to 100 lb/ac) P (P_2O_5) in addition to the normal crop requirement. Once the available P level has been adjusted, subsequent P applications are in line with those for most other coastal plain soils, which is approximately 57 kg/ha (50 lbs/ac) P_2O_5 per crop.

Copper adjustments are also made when wet soils are first developed. An application of 2.8 to 5.6 kg/ha (2.5 to 5.0 lb/ac) elemental copper is made, with only moderate and infrequent applications required thereafter.

KEY PRACTICES FOR CROP PRODUCTION

Histosols and high organic matter mineral soils are traditionally cold-natured soils (MacFarlane and Williams, 1974). With slow soil warming during the spring, corn has shown significant growth responses to low rates of banded N and P. Also, planting on bedded (raised) rows provides more surface area for drying and heat absorption, proving beneficial to early seedling growth. Added benefits to bedding are also realized in improved aeration for seedlings during periods of excessive rainfall and in wind erosion control.

Significant N losses are experienced during periods of heavy rainfall and wet (saturated) soil conditions. These losses are not a result of nitrate leaching, however, but occur through efficient denitrification processes (Gambrell et al., 1974). In order to cope with denitrification potentials and provide adequate N to crops, N is applied close to the time of crop utilization. This generally involves split applications of N between planting time and the period of heavy use during the growth cycle.

As crops are produced, certain weed, disease, and insect pressures may build up. Chemicals and resistant crop varieties are expensive and are not effective in themselves, so crop rotations are essential. The most common rotations are corn-soybeans or corn-wheat-soybeans in a two-year cycle.

CURRENT COSTS AND POTENTIAL REVENUES OF AGRICULTURAL DEVELOPMENT

Current cost estimates for land, drainage, clearing and development of wet soils are shown in Table 2.

Costs differ by location and operation. Variations come primarily from initial land price, timber inventory, soil types being developed and time frame for conducting clearing and development operations. An important point, however, is that almost all the soil types can be developed into good agricultural soils given sufficient time, money, and management. At present, the

TABLE 2. *Current Costs and Potential Revenues of Agricultural Development in Eastern North Carolina Wet Soils*

Categories	Costs (1980)
Land (undeveloped, without timber)	\$1,000-\$1,250/ha (\$400-\$500/ac)
Drainage (canals \$6,000 and ditches \$540/km)	\$200-\$250/ha (\$80-\$100/ac)
Clearing (clearing, raking, sloping)	\$800/ha (\$320/ac)
Development (windrow removal, raking, sloping, liming)	\$800/ha (\$320/ac)
Total	\$2,800-\$3,100/ha (\$1,120-\$1,290/ac)

TABLE 3. *Yield Potentials of Certain Wet Soils in Eastern North Carolina*[1]

Representative soil series[2]	Corn hl/ha (bu/ac)[3]	Soybeans hl/ha (bu/ac)	Wheat hl/ha (bu/ac)	Improved pastures	Adapted vegetables
Typic Umbraquults					
Portsmouth	122 (140)	35 (40)	44 (50)	Good	Fair-Good
Hyde	131 (150)	39 (45)	48 (55)	Good	Fair-Good
Cape Fear	122 (140)	39 (45)	44 (50)	Good	Fair-Good
Typic Humaquepts					
Rutledge	91 (105)	26 (30)	39 (45)	Fair	Fair-Good
Arapahoe	122 (140)	39 (45)	44 (50)	Good	Fair-Good
Weeksville	122 (140)	39 (45)	44 (50)	Good	Fair-Good
Histic Humaquepts					
Conaby	109 (125)	35 (40)	44 (50)	Good	Fair-Good
Wasda	131 (150)	39 (45)	48 (55)	Good	Fair-Good
Roper	131 (150)	39 (45)	48 (55)	Good	Fair-Good
Pettigrew	131 (150)	39 (45)	48 (55)	Good	Fair-Good
Terric Medisaprists					
Pamlico	109 (125)	30 (35)	39 (45)	Fair-Good	Good
Ponzer	117 (135)	35 (40)	44 (50)	Good	Fair-Good
Mattamuskeet	N 61 (70)	17 (20)	26 (30)	Fair	Poor
(Woody)	R109 (130)	35 (40)	39 (45)	Fair-Good	Poor-Fair
Belhaven (Woody)	N 61 (70)	17 (20)	26 (30)	Fair	Poor
	R113 (130)	35 (40)	44 (50)	Fair-Good	Poor-Fair
Typic Medisaprists					
Dare (Woody)	N 61 (70)	17 (20)	26 (30)	Fair	Poor
	R100 (115)	26 (30)	35 (40)	Fair	Poor
Pungo (Woody)	N 61 (70)	17 (20)	26 (30)	Fair	Poor
	R100 (115)	26 (30)	35 (40)	Fair	Poor

1. Yield estimates are for well-developed soil condition, good management and climate (data compiled from USDA Soil Conservation Service official description sheets and file data of the author).
2. N = New, first 5 to 10 years cultivation; R = Ripened, greater than 10 years cultivation.
3. Hl = Hectoliter; ha = hectare.

shallow (terric) and deep (typic) Histosols which have large quantities of residual ground wood (logs and stumps) buried throughout the organic profile are notorious for being difficult and expensive to develop. These soils are generally avoided for agricultural purposes.

Crop yield comparisons by soil type are given in Table 3. Such yields represent production capabilities of soils when utilizing good management techniques under favorable weather. Actual average farm yields may vary due to management, weather, location and degree of land improvement

TABLE 4. *Anticipated Revenue Value per Acre from Corn and Soybeans on Wet Soils in Eastern North Carolina*

Agricultural crop	Price/Bu	Gross revenue/Ac
Corn at 115 bu/ac	$2.50	$287.50
Corn at 115 bu/ac	3.00	345.00
Corn at 115 bu/ac	3.50	402.50
Soybeans at 35 bu/ac	6.50	227.50
Soybeans at 35 bu/ac	7.25	253.75
Soybeans at 35 bu/ac	8.00	280.00

practices imposed on the land. Five-year average yields for corn and soybeans on well-developed soils will be 105 to 130 and 32 to 40 bushels per acre, respectively, for most of these soils. These yields are considerably higher than the state averages of 70 to 80 bu/ac for corn and 22 to 24 bu/ac for soybeans. Certain vegetable crops have also been produced successfully: Irish potatoes, cabbage, broccoli, sweet corn, greens, processing tomatoes, snap beans, peppers (banana, hot and Bell), beets, cucumbers, squash, lima beans, carrots, radishes, lettuce, and even celery. A lack of access to existing processing plants and a lack of sufficient growth in demand for processed vegetables has limited significant expansion with most of these crops at this time.

Table 4 provides an anticipated revenue value per acre for corn and soybeans at various prices per bushel.

From year to year, gross revenue can fluctuate significantly because of yield and price variations. For example, one good farm in Tyrrell County averaged 138 bu/ac in 1977, 87 bu/ac in 1978 and 108 bu/ac in 1979. Prices

TABLE 5. *Production Costs for Corn and Soybeans on Wet Soils in Eastern North Carolina*

Item	Corn ($/Ac)	Soybeans ($/Ac)
Lime	8	8
Seed	16	8
Fertilizer	45	20
Insecticide	7	7
Herbicide	18	16
Equipment	45	40
Labor	40	35
Drainage	6	6
Overhead	6	6
Total	$191	$146

are just as volatile. In a seven-month period in 1979, local corn prices fluctuated from $2.52 to $3.23 per bushel, and soybeans fluctuated from $5.96 to $7.90 per bushel. These market trends also emphasize the requirements for experienced commodity marketing.

Total production costs for crops produced on wet soil types are similar to those for mineral soils. Production costs do not fluctuate as do yields and crop prices, but they do rise steadily. An example of production costs for corn and soybeans produced on wet soils during 1979 is given in Table 5.

Land costs are assessed at an additional $40 to $70 per acre depending on the type of farm, size, ownership versus rental land, time and price of land purchase, etc. After land development is completed, the major differences in production costs between the wet soil types and more well-drained mineral soils will be that the wet soils have approximately 40% higher herbicide costs, 60% higher drainage costs, and the deep organic soils will have a 30% higher lime cost. Where pump drainage is required, there is an additional $17 to $25/ha ($7 to $10/ac) drainage cost. Taking into account these basic differences, wet soil types may have production costs ranging from $20 to $50/ha ($8 to $20/ac) higher than the well-drained mineral soils. The additional cost is more than compensated for by the difference in yield potential. Inversely, well-drained mineral soils of the North Carolina coastal plain do not have the efficiency of labor and machinery that the wet soils areas have once they are properly prepared.

When corn production costs for wet soils are $477/ha ($191/ac) and $150/ha ($60/ac) is charged for land, corn will show a net return to management of $235/ha ($94/ac) if the yield is 101 hectoliters (hl)/ha (115 bu/ac) and the price is $8.50/hl ($3/bu). Soybeans will show a net return to management of $119.40/ha ($47.95/ac) if the yield is 30 hl/ha (35 bu/ac) and the price is $20.58/hl ($7.25/bu) and production costs are $365/ha ($146/ac).

LAND DEVELOPMENT SITUATION IN EASTERN NORTH CAROLINA

When significant acreages in an area are developed for agriculture, there is a major economic stimulus to satellite businesses in that same area. Large amounts of materials, equipment, supplies, and commercial services are utilized where little were used before. Development of these valuable land resources has been a major contributing factor in helping such rural North Carolina counties as Washington, Tyrrell and Hyde start leveling off in population after decades of population decline by providing local jobs to people in these areas. Land values also increase dramatically and the tax structure of the land is upgraded four- to ten-fold. An example of the change in tax structure associated with land development is provided (Table 6) by the tax schedule utilized by Hyde County.

TABLE 6. *Tax Structure for Land in Hyde County, North Carolina (1980)*

Land classes	Valuation ($/Ac)
Good to excellent clear land	750 - 1,000
Woodland	
Excellent	300 - 400
Fair	200 - 300
Very poor	100 - 200
Scrub (low & swamp with small growth)	80 - 120

Development of wet soils can be a sensitive issue in some circles. Certain obvious considerations should be observed by both large and small developers. For example, wetland marshes (fresh and salt water) should be left in their natural state, setbacks should be practiced near streams and estuaries, limited use should be made in floodplain areas, and soil types known to be agriculturally unproductive should be left undeveloped. In addition to their conversion to agriculture, hundreds of thousands of hectares of these soils are owned by large timber companies and are upgraded by drainage, fertilization and improved forestry practices for timber production. Many of these soils areas are considered as having very low value as natural habitat for waterfowl and wildlife (Shaw and Fredine, 1956). Improved forestry practices and fringe effects of agricultural development have improved the habitat for numbers of wildlife species.

On a broader scale, the contributions of "wise" agricultural development on these soil types are significant. The United States is still the most well-fed nation on earth while Americans spend the lowest percentage of their disposable income for food (information from the Agricultural Council of America, Post Office Box 23421, Washington, D.C. 20024). In addition to providing an abundance of economical food for domestic needs, the United States had a positive agricultural trade balance of greater than $15 billion in 1978, and this positive balance continues to increase significantly each year.

The capability of the United States to maintain this productivity is a matter that can no longer be taken for granted. Our quantity of productive farmland is diminishing. The number of acres in farms in the United States dropped 113,000,000 from 1958 to 1978, a drop of 5.6 million acres per year. During the same period, North Carolina farm acres dropped 5,000,000 or 250,000 acres per year (NCDA, 1979). Not all of these acres were in crops. Part of the loss was from shut-downs of small, inefficient field and farm sizes. Some lands were unproductive, erodable land areas. Much of this acreage, estimated to be 400,000 ha/yr, was prime farmland lost to urbanization, road and highway construction, reservoirs, etc. (information from the National Agricultural Lands Study, a multiagency federal team set up in 1979 to assess the problem of loss of agricultural land).

CONCLUSIONS

Once developed, the wet soils utilized for agriculture in eastern North Carolina become highly productive agricultural lands. While their agricultural use for food production currently is not "essential," it is very important. We cannot develop these nor other lands over night just as we cannot find and develop alternative energy sources over night. Once developed, these wet soils become important as productive farmland and will become more important as a matter of national interest with each passing year.

LITERATURE CITED

Badr, A. W., and R. W. Skaggs, 1978. The effect of land development on the physical properties of some North Carolina organic soils. Paper No. 78-2537. 1978 Winter Meeting, Am. Soc. Ag. Engs., St. Joseph, Mich.

Barber, R. T., W. W. Kirby-Smith, and P. E. Parsley, 1978. Wetland alterations for agriculture. Amer. Water Resources Assoc. Proceedings National Symposium on Wetlands, Minneapolis, Minn.

Barnes, J. S., and F. R. Cox, 1973. Effects of copper sources on wheat and soybeans grown on organic soils. Agron. Jour., 65:705-708.

Boelter, D. H., and E. S. Verry, 1977. Peatland and water in the northern lakes states. USDA Forest Service, General Technical Report NC-31, St. Paul, Minn.

Daughtrey, Z. W., J. W. Gilliam, and E. J. Kamprath, 1972. Phosphorus supply characteristcs of acid organic soils as measured by desorption and mineralization. Soil Sci., 115:18-24.

Dolman, J. D., and S. W. Buol, 1967. A study of organic soils in the tidewater region of North Carolina. N.C. Agr. Exp. Sta. Tech. Bull. No. 181.

Gambrell, J. W., J. W. Gilliam, and S. B. Weed, 1975. Nitrogen losses from soil of the North Carolina coastal plain. J. Environ. Qual., 4:311-316.

Lee, W. D., 1955. The soils of North Carolina, their formation, identification and use. N.C. Agri. Exp. Sta. Tech. Bull. No. 115, 187 pp.

MacFarlane, I. C., and G. P. Williams, 1974. Some engineering aspects of peat soils. p. 79-93. In: Aandahl, A. R., et al., eds., Histosols: Their characteristics, classifications, and use. SSSA Spec. Pub. No. 6, Madison, Wisc.

Maki, T. E., 1974. Factors affecting forest production on organic soils, p. 119-136. In: Aandahl, A. R., et al., eds., Histosols: Their characteristics, classification, and use. SSSA Spec. Pub. No. 6, Soil Sci. Soc. Amer., Madison, Wisc.

MacKinzie, W. E., 1974. Criteria used in soil taxonomy to classify organic soils, pp. 1-10. In: Aandahl, A. R., et al., eds., Histosols: Their characteristics, classification and use. SSSA Spec. Pub. No. 6, Soil Sci. Soc. Amer., Madison, Wisc.

N.C. Department of Agriculture, Federal-State Crop and Livestock Reporting Service, 1979. North Carolina Agricultural Statistics, Annual 1978-79.

Schauble, C. E., 1969. Factors influencing copper availability in selected North Carolina coastal plain soils. Ph. D. Thesis, North Carolina State University, Raleigh, N.C.

Shaw, S. P., and C. G. Fredine, 1956. Wetlands of the United States. Circular 39, Fish and Wildlife Service, U.S. Department of Interior, U.S. Government Printing Office, Washington, D.C.

Skaggs, R. W., J. W. Gilliam, T. J. Sheets, and J. S. Barnes, 1980. Effect of agricultural land development on drainage waters in the North Carolina tidewater region. Report No. 159, Water Resouces Research Institute of the University of North Carolina, Chapel Hill.

Skaggs, R. W., and J. S. Barnes, 1976. Drainage and water table control on colloidal muck soils. Paper No. 76-2041, 1976 Annual Meeting, Amer. Soc. Ag. Engr., St. Joseph, Mich.

Soil Conservation Service, 1977. Phase I National Resource Inventory, North Carolina. USDA Bul., Soil Conservation Service, Raleigh, N.C.

Soil Survey Staff, 1975. Soil Taxonomy: A basic system of soil classification for making and interpreting soil surveys. USDA Handb. 436, U.S. Government Printing Office, Washington, D.C.

Tonapa, S., 1974. Nitrogen studies with Histosols. Ph. D. Thesis, Department of Soil Science, N.C. State Univ., Raleigh, N.C.

Younts, S. E., 1964. Response of wheat to rates, dates of application and sources of copper and other micronutrients. Agron. Jour., 56:266-269.

North Carolina's Coastal Fishing Industry and the Influence of Coastal Alterations

Michael W. Street and Joseph D. McClees

ABSTRACT

A survey conducted by the North Carolina Division of Marine Fisheries indicates that the commercial and recreational fishing industry contributed more than $325 million to the coastal economy in 1978. Total employment exceeded 23,000 persons. North Carolina's fishermen take a wide range of species, with most fishermen changing fisheries seasonally. Commercial landings have increased during recent years. Estuarine-dependent species, such as Atlantic croaker, menhaden, penaeid shrimp, blue crab and oysters accounted for more than 90% of the commercial landings during 1974 to 1978. Three species of penaeid shrimp contribute to the North Carolina shrimp fishery: brown (60 to 70%), pink (20 to 25%) and white (9%). Shrimp and most other important commercial species in North Carolina depend on maintenance of a healthy estuarine system. Increased drainage of fresh water into primary estuarine nursery areas appears to lower the production of shrimp and other species in such areas. Future development of coastal pocosins and other wetlands may add to the problem of excessive freshwater inflow to the estuaries. Construction of the fishing port at Wanchese, North Carolina, indicates that coastal development is possible without excess degradation of the surrounding estuarine system.

Key Words: commercial fishing, recreational fishing, commercial landings, shrimp, menhaden, Atlantic croaker, sea trout, oysters, salinity, freshwater drainage, environmental factors, estuary

INTRODUCTION

The coastal fishing industry is defined to include all persons and businesses engaged in commercial and recreational fishing, support of such fishing and utilization of the products of such fishing. Fishing is big business in coastal North Carolina, with an estimated gross product of $325.6 million in 1978. This figure includes all revenues generated by and spent on commercial and recreational fishing; vessel and boat construction, operation and maintenance; shore facilities including fish houses, processing facilities, piers, marinas; and seafood restaurant operations in coastal North Carolina. Replacement value of plants, vessels, equipment, etc., is estimated to exceed $400 million (Table 1).

In order to gather data for this report, the Division of Marine Fisheries conducted a survey of North Carolina's coastal fishing industry during fall 1979, including commercial and recreational fishing, supporting facilities and services, and local seafood restaurants. In all, more than 160 detailed interviews were conducted with industry members to describe North Carolina's coastal fishing industry as it existed in 1978.

Commercial landings in North Carolina in 1978 totaled 299.5 million pounds (134.8 million kg) worth $40.6 million to the fishermen (National Marine Fisheries Service, 1979). Handling, processing, and marketing added another $73.6 million to the value of North Carolina's marine products, with menhaden, blue crabs, and scallops making the greatest contributions to processed value, according to the Division of Marine Fisheries survey.

TABLE 1. *Estimate of Economic Activity and Value of the North Carolina Coastal Fishing Industry, 1978*[1]

Business type	No. units	Employment	Total sales	Replacement value
Commercial fishing dealers, processors, vessels, and boats	668 dealers and processors 11,425 boats and vessels	14,600	$114,200,000	$297,050,000
Head boats, party boats, and fishing piers	189 vessels 73 piers	387	18,400,000	76,418,000
Boat building, repair and supply	43	867	59,900,000	26,825,000
Restaurants[2] and marinas	1,265	7,257	133,100,000	no estimate
Totals		23,111	$325,600,000	

1. From a North Carolina Division of Marine Fisheries survey conducted during October and November 1979.
2. Nonchain restaurants in coastal counties only.

The survey found that a total of 11,409 full-time and part-time commercial fishing boats were licensed in North Carolina. Another 10,280 boats were used by recreational fishermen with nets, crab pots, and other commercial gear, according to information supplied by licensees. The total number of full-time and part-time commercial fishermen was estimated at 12,250, with an additional 2,350 persons employed in fish houses, processing plants, and other activities (Table 1).

Commercial and recreational boat building and services including shipyards, suppliers, net makers, fuel and ice dealers, and marinas employed about 1,200 persons with a gross product of about $83 million (Table 1).

The survey revealed that saltwater recreational fishermen utilized 34 ocean piers, 39 sound and river piers, 189 head boats and charter boats, 171 marinas, and hundreds of miles of accessible shoreline. Approximately 800 persons were employed to serve these fishermen. Of the 189,000 private boats registered by the North Carolina Wildlife Resources Commission in 1978, an estimated 47,000 were used in coastal sport fishing.

This paper describes in more detail North Carolina's coastal fishing industry and discusses some current and potential problems, including the influence that some of man's developmental activities may have on the fisheries.

DESCRIPTION OF NORTH CAROLINA'S FISHING INDUSTRY

Commercial

In general, North Carolina's commercial fisheries are characterized by a large number of small fishing units working principally in estuarine areas. They take a wide range of species which vary considerably in seasonal abundance, with virtually all commercial fishermen utilizing a variety of equipment throughout the year in pursuit of several different species. Principal target species are shrimp, blue crabs, oysters, clams, croaker, and sea trout. The major fishing areas are in Albemarle, Pamlico, and Core sounds and their tributaries, New River, Cape Fear River, and the rivers and creeks of Brunswick County west of Cape Fear River (Figure 1). The recent addition of larger vessels (75 to 95 ft in length) has provided additional catches from beyond the estuarine waters. Most seafood landed in North Carolina ports is shipped elsewhere for processing.

Recreational

Sport fishermen generally fish for the same species and in the same areas as commercial fishermen. Frequently, in fact, they use similar fishing gear. Of the commercial vessel licenses sold in 1978, approximately 47% were sold to boats using commercial gear to catch various species for personal consumption (N.C. Div. of Marine Fisheries, unpublished data). The fall 1979 survey indicated that nine head boats and 180 charter boats took approximately 202,000 fishermen as far as 100 mi (160 km) offshore in search of dolphin, king mackerel, snapper, marlin, sea bass, and other offshore species. Other sport fishermen fished from small boats, piers, jetties, and the beaches seeking coastal species such as flounder, croaker, striped bass, white perch, bluefish, Spanish mackerel, sea trout, and red drum.

NORTH CAROLINA'S COASTAL FISHERY RESOURCES

Two types of resources provide the basis for North Carolina's coastal fisheries: stocks of finfish, crustaceans and shellfish, and the habitat producing and supporting those stocks.

The Habitat

North Carolina's ocean shoreline extends for approximately 315 mi (504 km) from the South Carolina line at Little River Inlet to the Virginia border near False Cape (Figure 1). Within the coastal zone are five general estuarine areas:

1. The southern area, from the North Carolina–South Carolina border to the White Oak River, is characterized by narrow estuaries dominated by saltmarsh cordgrass marshes, muddy bottoms, and diurnal tides of 3 to 5 ft (0.9 to 1.5 m). Salinities are generally above 20 parts per thousand (ppt), except in the rivers where they are somewhat lower. This area contains fifteen ocean inlets and the estuary is generally less than a mile (1.6 km) wide.
2. The central area from the White Oak River to northern Core Sound, including two large bodies of water (Core and Bogue sounds), has diurnal tides generally less than 3 ft (0.9 m). Sandy bottoms predominate, often covered with eel grass and shoal grass. Salinities are generally above 25 ppt. Four ocean inlets are present in this area.
3. Pamlico Sound, its tributaries and bordering black needlerush marshes, cover over a million acres, extending from Core Sound to Oregon Inlet. Bottom type varies from mud to sand, and salinities range from near zero in the upper tributaries, to about 25 ppt near the inlets. Lunar tides are negligible, while wind tides in excess of 2 ft (0.6 m) are common. Only three inlets are located in this area.
4. The Albemarle Sound area, extending north and west from Pamlico Sound, occupies almost 625,000 acres (252,928 ha) of open brackish water, freshwater marsh, and wooded swamps. Wind tides are far

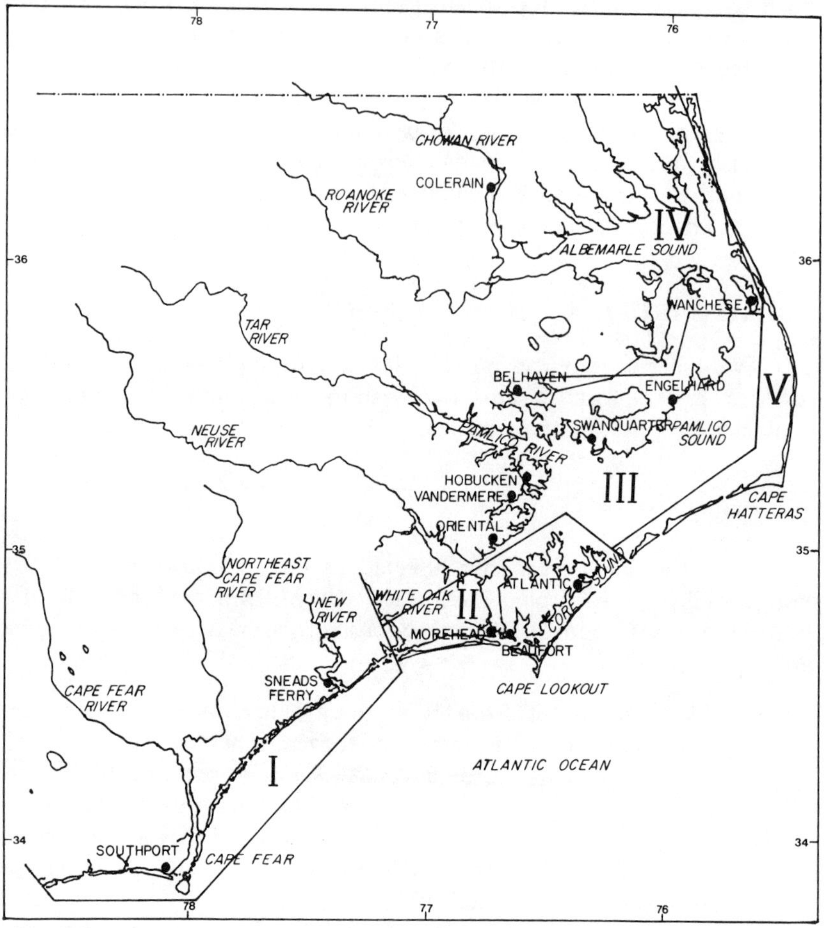

FIGURE 1. *Coastal North Carolina showing major water bodies and ports. The five principal areas are designated by numerals I to V.*

more important than lunar tides. Salinities are generally less than 5 ppt, and the bottom is generally sandy. There are no inlets, and exchange with the ocean occurs through northern Pamlico Sound and Oregon Inlet.

5. The Outer Banks technically include all of North Carolina's barrier islands and beaches, but commonly include only the barrier islands and beaches from Cape Lookout north to the Virginia border. The islands are narrow strips of sand surrounded by shallow, high salinity water. Much more affected by the ocean than Pamlico and Albemarle sounds, these waters experience diurnal lunar tides of 2 to 4 ft (0.6 to 1.2 m), and the bottom type is generally sand.

This vast estuarine system, the largest in any single Atlantic Coast state, occupies more than 2.3 million acres (930,000 ha). Over 90% of this area is covered by water—sounds, bays, rivers, and creeks. The remaining 197,000 acres (79,722 ha) of coastal marshes provide the principal basis of productivity for the entire system. Especially in the Pamlico Sound region, these marshes adjoin many of North Carolina's coastal pocosins. Activities affecting these pocosins can directly affect the downstream estuaries and their productivity.

The Fishery Resources

About 600 species of finfish have been identified from North Carolina's estuarine and ocean waters (Stephen W. Ross, personal communication). About sixty species currently have direct economic value; many other species may have future potential for human use. About 200 species of decapod crustaceans are known from North Carolina waters (Williams, 1965). Only four species of crustaceans are currently exploited, but several others have commercial potential. Approximately 1,300 species of mollusks are reported to occur in North Carolina waters (Porter, 1974); about ten species have been harvested commercially in recent years. Information currently available suggests that thirty to forty additional species may have economic value in the future.

TABLE 2. *Annual Landings and Dockside Value for North Carolina's Commercial Fisheries, 1965 to 1978, Thousands of Pounds and Dollars*[1]

	Finfish		Crustaceans		Shellfish		Total	
Year	Landings	Value	Landings	Value	Landings	Value	Landings	Value
1965	203,410	$ 5,061	27,987	$ 3,067	2,564	$ 1,343	233,961	$ 9,241
1966	222,882	5,014	24,737	3,490	3,313	1,067	250,932	9,571
1967	203,166	4,800	19,281	2,553	2,641	975	225,088	8,328
1968	206,879	4,601	23,899	4,235	1,397	870	232,175	9,706
1969	187,577	5,056	30,126	6,658	1,330	812	219,033	12,526
1970	144,976	4,570	25,999	3,759	2,466	1,036	173,440	9,365
1971	119,236	4,442	22,139	5,918	2,100	930	143,475	11,290
1972	146,847	5,761	19,092	4,923	1,963	1,115	167,902	11,799
1973	111,867	8,516	17,013	6,305	1,573	1,134	130,453	15,955
1974	183,882	10,507	21,636	6,002	1,173	976	206,691	17,484
1975	220,693	12,382	16,256	6,526	1,352	1,092	238,301	20,000
1976	205,616	14,669	18,395	10,604	2,051	2,191	226,069	27,465
1977[2]	231,375	16,353	17,837	9,404	2,048	2,891	251,261	28,648
1978[2]	269,229	24,389	26,567	8,300	3,745	7,920	299,541	40,609

1. Figures may not add exactly due to rounding off. Calculated from National Marine Fisheries Service and Division of Marine Fisheries published and unpublished data.
2. Preliminary estimate.

Table 2 shows North Carolina commercial landings and value from 1965 to 1978. Landings declined during the early 1970s but have recovered to levels exceeding those of the mid-1960s. In fact, 1978 landings were the third highest on record. Most of the increase may be attributed to an increase in finfish catches, particularly edible species such as flounder, croaker, and sea trout, as well as to recovery of the menhaden fishery.

Data for 1974 to 1978 (Table 3) clearly demonstrate that North Carolina's commercial fisheries are based almost entirely on estuarine-dependent species. At some time in their life cycle, these species must utilize estuarine areas which serve as spawning and nursery areas, feeding grounds, wintering areas and migration routes (Reintjes and Pacheco, 1966; Wallace, 1966; Kutkuhn, 1966; Clark, 1967; Weinstein, 1979). Without the various life-supporting conditions (chemical composition, food, cover, temperature, substrate and others) supplied by the estuaries, these species would not be available to our fishing industry.

Even North Carolina's winter trawl fishery, which occurs entirely in the ocean, is based on estuarine-dependent species. In the 1978-79 fishery, croaker, summer flounder, grey trout, spot, and other estuarine-dependent species accounted for almost 87% of the 43.5 million pounds landed (N.C. Div. of Marine Fisheries, unpublished data).

Following is a brief description of North Carolina's shrimp fishery, which depends on maintenance of the estuarine system with its bordering marshes and pocosins for continued production. Three species support the fishery: brown shrimp (*Penaeus aztecus*) account for 60 to 70% of annual landings (2.4 million pounds, heads off); pink shrimp (*P. duorarum*) yield about 20 to 25% of the yearly harvest (0.9 million pounds); white shrimp (*P. setiferus*) comprise the remaining 9% (0.3 million pounds) (N.C. Div. of Marine Fisheries, 1979). All three species are essentially annual crops with the survivors of each year's class producing the next year's fishable stock. There is no apparent relationship between stock size in any one year and stock size in any preceding or succeeding year. Spawning occurs in the ocean, and post-larvae enter the estuaries and move into marsh creeks and bays which serve as nursery areas (Figure 2). Division of Marine Fisheries sampling shows that white shrimp move furthest upstream, tolerating lower salinities than brown shrimp, which appear to prefer salinities of 10 to 20 ppt. Pink shrimp generally utilize the more saline waters of the sounds as nursery areas. As the shrimp grow, they move downstream into the open estuarine waters and the ocean, where fishing takes place.

Principal fishing areas are Pamlico and Core sounds, New River, lower Cape Fear River, and the nearshore ocean from Cape Lookout to South Carolina. The shrimp harvest begins in late winter and extends into the late fall when cold weather apparently triggers an offshore southward migration of brown and white shrimp.

TABLE 3. *Landings in North Carolina's Estuarine Dependent Commercial Fisheries, 1974 to 1978, in Thousands of Pounds*[1]

Species	1974	1975	1976	1977	1978
FINFISH					
River herring	6,210	5,952	6,401	8,524	6,607
Atlantic croaker	6,082	10,252	15,038	18,995	19,945
Flounder	11,812	11,510	11,452	11,137	12,311
Menhaden	121,198	158,805	134,902	158,119	192,324
Mullet	2,138	1,953	2,072	1,835	1,752
Sea trout	6,726	7,356	9,351	8,995	10,947
Spot	5,607	8,300	2,674	3,805	4,878
Striped bass	1,016	1,303	1,038	572	698
Others	14,376	4,406	3,073	9,509	11,743
Subtotal	175,165	209,838	186,001	221,491	261,205
CRUSTACEANS					
Blue crab	13,196	11,092	11,752	12,237	23,606
Shrimp (heads on)	8,440	5,164	6,643	5,600	2,961
Subtotal	21,636	16,256	18,395	17,837	26,567
SHELLFISH (meats)					
Clams	288	285	306	739	892
Oysters	559	425	333	366	450
Bay scallops	220	135	248	257	219
Others	24	23	7	8	77
Subtotal	1,091	868	894	1,370	1,638
Total	197,893	226,962	205,290	240,698	289,409
Total landings	206,691	238,301	226,069	251,261	299,541
Percent estuarine dependent	95.7	95.2	90.8	95.8	96.6

1. Calculated from National Marine Fisheries Service and Division of Marine Fisheries published and unpublished data.

A very small segment of the white shrimp population may overwinter in estuaries along the southern North Carolina coast, particularly the lower Cape Fear River. Water temperatures depressed below 8°C (46°F) for extended periods result in high mortality of overwintering white shrimp (Farmer et al., 1978). Overwintering survivors and some back-migrants from the previous fall support a small spring fishery in the Cape Fear area.

Pink shrimp also remain in North Carolina during the winter. When water temperatures fall to 10° to 12°C (50°F to 54°F), pink shrimp burrow into the substrate and do not emerge until water temperatures of 10°C (37°F)

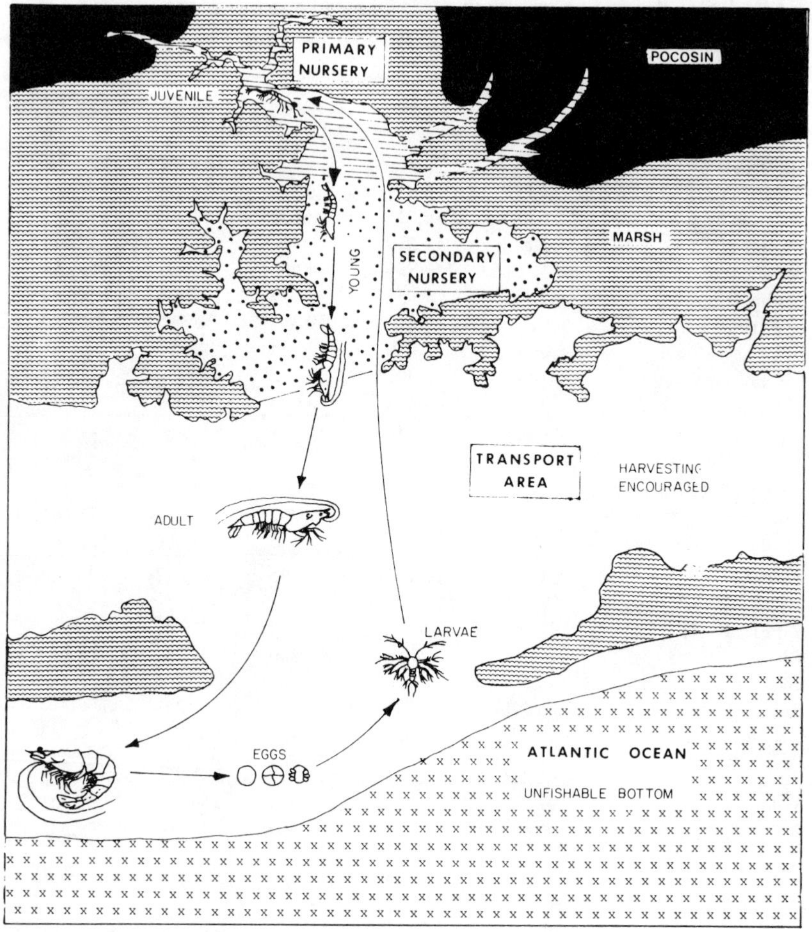

FIGURE 2. *Life cycle of commercial shrimp in North Carolina.*

are reached the following spring (Purvis and McCoy, 1972). Recent information from the Division of Marine Fisheries (unpublished) suggests that water temperatures below 3° C for several consecutive days are lethal to overwintering pink shrimp. Survivors support an important spring fishery, principally in Pamlico and Core sounds and in the ocean near Beaufort Inlet. The North Carolina population of pink shrimp may be endemic to this area. This species does not occur along the coast in commercial quantities between North Carolina and the Tortugas Grounds off Key West, Florida.

Considerable research on the effects of environmental conditions on shrimp has been conducted, particularly concerning salinity (Barber et al., 1979; Barrett and Gillespie, 1973). A prediction model has been developed for brown shrimp abundance in Pamlico Sound, based on salinity and temperature (Hunt et al., 1980).

The migratory fish stocks supporting several important commercial and recreational fisheries are rather poorly understood by biologists. Landings of fishes such as Atlantic croaker, summer flounder, and grey trout (weakfish) have increased steadily in recent years (Table 3). However, we are unsure of the origin of these and other stocks. We do not know the relationship between production (nursery) areas and harvest areas. The vast, highly productive salt marshes extending from the Cape Fear area of North Carolina to northern Florida contain large numbers of juvenile croaker, grey trout, and spot, yet landings of adults of these species in that area are very slight compared to the major North Carolina fisheries: 441,000 pounds from Brunswick County, North Carolina, through Georgia in 1978, while 35.63 million pounds were landed in North Carolina (excluding Brunwick County) during the same period (N.C. Div. of Marine Fisheries, unpublished data; National Marine Fisheries Service, unpublished data). Sampling conducted in South Carolina (Keiser, 1976) and Georgia (Mahood et al., 1974) indicates the relative paucity of adult finfish compared to populations in the central and northern coastal areas of North Carolina.

Considerable work is needed to understand the relationships among production areas and harvest areas for species such as croaker, spot, grey trout, and summer flounder.

RELATIONSHIP OF FISHING TO OTHER COASTAL ACTIVITIES

Fishing is only one of many important activities providing employment in the coastal zone. Other important industries include agriculture, forestry, mining, and tourism (see Barnes, Campbell and Hughes, Campbell, this volume). The interrelationships among these industries and their effects on pocosin resources and in turn on estuarine ecosystems is the subject of much discussion.

Our estuaries are the depository for virtually everything dumped onto the land, into sewers, and into creeks and rivers. All of this material flows in one direction, from the piedmont toward the coast. Whether the substance is domestic sewage, chemical waste, food processing waste, pulpmill effluent, farm drainage, or rainwater, it all affects the estuarine system. Most of us are familiar with the real and potential problems from identified pollutants such as inorganic chemicals, sewage, and fertilizers as pointed out by Gilliam and Skaggs and Richardson (this volume). There is, however, another problem-causing substance, one which is not normally thought of as a pollutant—excessive fresh water.

Brown shrimp, North Carolina's most valuable shrimp species, are particularly susceptible to salinity changes. In 1978, heavy rains during April and May, the principal nursery period for brown shrimp, reduced salinities in known nursery areas to the range of 2 to 4 ppt compared with the normal range of 10 to 15 ppt. Landings during 1978 were about 40% below normal. A similar situation occurred in 1979, although to a lesser degree. Landings of brown shrimp, particularly in Pamlico Sound, were about 20% below average for the year. Heavy rainfall is a natural phenomenon, and the result was expected. However, ever-increasing drainage of coastal pocosins and marshes speeds the flow of fresh water directly to the estuary (Daniel, this volume), reducing the opportunity for this water to be evaporated or absorbed into the peatland.

This problem is particularly severe in the areas bordering Pamlico Sound. Large-scale agricultural and silvicultural development of this area is accelerating. Heath (1975) estimated that 25.7% of the entire Albemarle–Pamlico peninsula had been cleared and was under cultivation in 1973. He predicted that the cleared area of the peninsula, mostly pocosin, would "doubtless increase . . . to at least 1,000 mi^2 by 1980 or to more than 60 percent of the area" (Heath, 1975). Clearing and utilization of such low-lying areas requires drainage on a massive scale, with all fresh water being channeled into the estuarine system.

To investigate the possible effects of freshwater intrusion, the Division of Marine Fisheries monitors relative abundance of juvenile finfish, shrimp and crabs in several tributaries of Rose Bay and Swan Quarter Bay, tributaries of northern Pamlico Sound. Salinity and temperature are recorded during three weekly replicate samples at each of nine sites during the spring and summer. Abundance of juvenile finfish, crabs, and shrimp is recorded for each sample. Weather conditions are monitored at Swan Quarter National Wildlife Refuge nearby. During June and July 1979, salinities were recorded constantly for about six weeks, at one site in a natural creek and at two sites in nearby creeks that had been ditched. During several periods of heavy rainfall, the natural creek maintained a stable salinity regime, while the salinity in the altered creek varied by more than 100% over short periods. During one twelve-hour period, the salinity at one altered site fluctuated from 0.8 to 5.2 ppt about every two hours. Such extreme variations may have severe effects on inhabitants of such an area. Sampling indicates that the altered sites produced lower numbers of shrimp than the natural sites (Pate and Jones, 1981).

Rose Bay, Swan Quarter Bay, the lower Pamlico River and the Pungo River were well known for their oysters prior to the 1960s. Production from these areas is negligible today. The Division of Marine Fisheries has planted thousands of bushels of oyster cultch in Swan Quarter Bay in recent years, attempting to rehabilitate the oyster resources. Success as indicated by the set of larvae has not been very high, particularly when compared to more saline areas.

The Division of Marine Fisheries has begun assembling historic salinity data for the Pamlico Sound area to determine if there is any long-term trend in salinity patterns. A consistent reduction in salinity during certain seasons may account for reduced oyster production and other fisheries problems. One factor in such a trend could be drainage of pocosins and other wetlands.

Tourism is extremely important in the coastal area, largely because the abundant natural resources attract people to the coast. However, the development necessary to serve tourists can often have a negative impact on tourism. Dredging finger canals, improper installation of septic tanks, and channel and marina construction in coastal marshes have all degraded the estuarine values which originally attracted visitors to the coast. Inadequate sewage systems have resulted in closure of public waters to the harvest of clams and oysters, denying these resources to commercial and recreational fishermen. At the end of 1978, almost 450,000 acres (182,100 ha) of estuarine bottoms were closed to shellfish harvesting in coastal North Carolina.

Navigation and waterways are very important to coastal North Carolina. Many of the problems associated with channel and port development in the past have been greatly reduced by adopting engineering techniques which contain spoil materials and scheduling work for periods of relatively low biological activity. Development of the state fishing port at Wanchese is a good illustration. A total of 125 acres (51 ha) of marsh is being sacrificed by dredging and filling. Spoils are contained behind dikes, maintaining the productivity of adjoining areas. Plans are under way to mitigate at least part of the damage through enhancement of nearby estuarine areas. State, federal and private investment at the port will aproach $19 million within the next two or three years. This project will have a beneficial effect on North Carolina's fishing industry, demonstrating that commercial development and natural resources can coexist.

Energy facility development may also influence coastal fisheries in the near future through construction, habitat alteration and socioeconomic influences. Two coastal refineries have been proposed, pipeline corridors have been suggested, and some of the major oil companies are looking at several large areas on the continental shelf for future petroleum development. Morehead City and Wilmington have been suggested as potential support bases for offshore exploration. Peat mining activities may well affect the fisheries through drainage and port development (Richardson et al., this volume).

SOME COASTAL PROBLEMS—AND OPPORTUNITIES

Several problem areas have been discussed. A problem once identified, however, can be viewed as an opportunity to find a solution. Chief among the problems is the influx of excess fresh water from surface runoff, often magnified by man's developmental activities. Mitigation measures need to be developed, such as border plantings, improved siltation control, and ponding of runoff where sufficient land is available. A research project currently under way at North Carolina State University is examining home sewage disposal systems that reduce pollution of estuarine waters. Research is needed to examine fishery management problems associated with a lack of sufficient information on which to base management decisions concerning migratory stocks. Regional cooperation among production and harvesting states is just beginning and must be encouraged.

In development projects, a dollar value can be placed upon buildings, parking lots and roads; usage and income can be reasonably estimated. Similar estimates cannot yet be made for estuaries by assigning values for seafood production, inland storm damage mitigation, waste disposal, and other functions of a dynamic estuary. A bioeconomic study is needed to address this problem by developing methods to assign economic and social values for the whole gamut of estuarine production from carbon fixation to pounds of fish utilized by commercial and recreational fishermen.

All of our fisheries depend, ultimately, on maintenance and enhancement of a productive habitat that can support a wide variety of fish stocks. Maintenance of this habitat is of primary importance, and the Division of Marine Fisheries will continue to work actively wth other state and federal agencies, fishermen, and other interested parties to maintain our estuarine system and to manage the fish stocks derived from that system for the optimal benefit of the citizens of North Carolina.

LITERATURE CITED

Barber, R. T., W. W. Kirby-Smith, and P. E. Parsley, 1979. Wetland alterations for agriculture, pp. 643-651. In: Greeson, P. E., J. R. Clark, and J. E. Clark, eds., Wetland functions and values: The state of our understanding. Amer. Water Res. Assoc, Minneapolis, Minn.

Barrett, B. B., and M. C. Gillespie, 1973. Primary factors which influence commercial shrimp production in coastal Louisiana. Louisiana Wildlife and Fishery Commission, Tech. Bull. No. 9, 28 pp.

Clark, J., 1967. Fish and man. Amer. Littoral Soc., Special Pub. No. 5, 78 pp.

Farmer, C. H. III, J. D. Whitaker, and N. L. Chipley, 1978. Pilot study to determine the overwintering patterns of white shrimp. S.C. Wildlife and Marine Resources Department, Division of Marine Resources, Final report, Contract No. 03-6-042-35105, 93 pp.

Heath, R. C., 1975. Hydrology of the Albemarle-Pamlico region, North Carolina. U.S. Geological Survey, Raleigh, N.C., Water Resources Investigations 9-75, 98 pp.

Hunt, J. H., R. J. Carroll, V. Chinchilli, and D. Frankenberg, 1980. Relationship between environmental factors and brown shrimp production in Pamlico Sound, North Carolina. N.C. Division of Marine Fisheries, Special Scientific Report No. 33, 29 pp.

Keiser, R. K., Jr., 1976. Species composition, magnitude, and utilization of the incidental catch of the South Carolina shrimp fishery. S.C. Marine Resources Center, Tech. Rept. No. 16, 55 pp.

Kutkuhn, J. H., 1966. The role of estuaries in development and perpetuation of commercial shrimp resources, pp. 16-36. In: Smith, R. F., A. H. Swartz, and W. H. Massmann, eds., A symposium on estuarine fisheries. Amer. Fish. Soc., Special Pub. No. 3.

Mahood, R. K., C. D. Harris, J. L. Music, Jr., and B. A. Palmer, 1974. Survey of the fisheries resources in Georgia's estuarine and inshore ocean waters, Part IV, Coastal Georgia—southern, central and northern sections. Georgia Department of Natural Resources, Game and Fish Division, Coastal Fisheries Office, Contribution Series No. 25, 201 pp.

National Marine Fisheries Service, 1979. North Carolina landings, annual summary, 1978. U.S. Department of Commerce, National Oceanic and Atmospheric Administration, National Marine Fisheries Service, CFS No. 7816, 9 pp.

North Carolina Division of Marine Fisheries, 1979. North Carolina shrimp prediction for 1979. North Carolina Department of Natural Resources and Community Development, Division of Marine Fisheries, 5 pp.

Pate, P. P., Jr., and R. Jones, 1981. Effects of upland drainage on estuarine nursery areas of Pamlico Sound, North Carolina. Proceedings of the symposium on freshwater inflow to estuaries, San Antonio, Texas, 1980.

Porter, H. J., 1974. The North Carolina marine and estuarine mollusca—an atlas of occurrence. University of North Carolina, Institute of Marine Science, Morehead City, N.C., 351 pp.

Purvis, C. E., and E. G. McCoy, 1972. Overwintering pink shrimp (*Penaeus duorarum*) in Core and Pamlico sounds. North Carolina Division of Commercial and Sports Fisheries, Special Scientific Report No. 22, 29 pp.

Reintjes, J. W., and A. L. Pacheco, 1966. The relation of menhaden to estuaries, pp. 50-58. In: Smith, R. F., A. H. Swartz, and W. H. Massman, eds., A symposium on estuarine fisheries. Amer. Fish. Soc., Special Pub. No. 3.

Wallace, D. H., 1966. Oysters in the estuarine environment, pp. 68-73. In: Smith, R. F., A. H. Swartz, and W. H. Massman, eds., A symposium on estuarine fisheries. Amer. Fish. Soc., Special Pub. No. 3.

Weinstein, M. P., 1979. Shallow marsh habitats as primary nurseries for fishes and shellfish, Cape Fear River, North Carolina. Fish. Bull., 77(2): 339-356.

Williams, A. B., 1976. Marine decapod crustaceans of the Carolinas. Fish. Bull., 65(1):1-298.

Section IV.
Resource Economics

Peat Energy for North Carolina: An Economic Analysis

Henrick J. Harwood and Philip S. McMullan, Jr.

ABSTRACT

Peat fuel is an untapped source of energy in North Carolina. Current estimates are that North Carolina has 12 quads of thermal energy in its peat fields. If this were all efficiently utilized, it could meet the state's thermal energy needs for eight years at current (1980) consumption levels. This paper examines the economic feasibility of using peat fuel for energy in North Carolina. Estimates are presented of the cost of using peat as a fuel in industrial scale steam boilers and to generate electricity. These costs are compared to those for similar plants fueled by coal. The paper concludes that peat fuel may be profitably harvested and used in the applications studied, given the assumptions used and experience in using peat fuel in other parts of the world.

Key Words: peat, peat fuel, electrical generation, economic feasibility

INTRODUCTION

In the coastal plains region of the southeastern United States, there are thousands of acres of deep organic muck soil in the many pocosins, bogs, and former lagoons that comprise much of the land area of the region (see Ingram and Otte, this volume). This organic soil is plant matter that has decomposed in a water-saturated environment and thereby maintained most of its carbon content. When it has decomposed to a sufficient extent, this organic muck becomes fuel grade peat. North Carolina is believed to have reserves of peat equal to 12 quadrillion (quads) British thermal units (Btu) of energy value (Ingram and Otte, 1980), or about 3% of total United States peat energy reserves (U.S. Department of Energy, 1979). Because North Carolina has few other indigenous energy reserves, these peat reserves could become the state's most important native energy resource for commercial fuel use.

This paper examines the economic feasibility of using peat as fuel for industrial steam and electric power generation in North Carolina. The information for this paper was obtained for a study of wood-fired or peat-fired electrical generation potential in the coastal plains of the state (McMullan and Harwood, 1980). The study was performed by the Research Triangle Institute under contract to the Division of Forest Resources, North Carolina Department of Natural Resources and Community Development.

PEAT CHARACTERISTICS AND END USES

Peat Fuel Characteristics

Although the Atlantic coastal zones of the Carolinas, Georgia, and Florida contain no known coal or petroleum reserves, they have an abundance of peat and wood that could be used as fuel reserves. In many respects, coal, peat and wood are similar fuels. Wood is the least mature of these three organic, plant based fuels. Peat is plant matter that has decayed under water for hundreds of years, and it is sometimes called young coal. Peat becomes coal after it has aged under pressure for millions of years. When artificially dried to remove all moisture, wood contains 8,000 to 9,000 Btu of energy per pound (lb) when burned. Oven dried peat provides from 8,000 to 10,000 Btu/lb and oven dried coal contains about 13,000 to 15,000 Btu/lb. North Carolina peat has been tested at above average Btu/lb values because it is more highly decomposed than most other tested peat deposits (Campbell, 1979, and this volume).

The three fuels are not available in nature in oven dried condition. Green wood contains 45 to 50% moisture after it is chipped for fuel, and extended drying will reduce this to no less than 35% moisture content (MC). Peat is found at 85 to 90% MC in undrained peat bogs, and it is common in northern Europe to harvest after drying to 50% MC. In North Carolina the peat dries naturally to 30% MC in a short period of time, but most experience with peat as a major fuel for steam and electrical generation is based on peat at 50% MC. Coal is mined at 6 to 8% MC. Table 1 shows the heat values of the three fuels at the moisture levels at which they would be fired. Eastern Kentucky

TABLE 1. *Moisture Content and Heat Value of Wood, Peat, and Coal*

Fuel	Moisture content	As-fired heat value
Coal (E. Kentucky)	3.5%	13,750 Btu/lb
Coal (W. Kentucky)	7.5%	12,100 Btu/lb
Peat (Southeastern U.S.)	30.0%	7,000 Btu/lb
Peat (E. Europe)	50.0%	5,000 Btu/lb
Wood	45.0%	4,500 Btu/lb

Sources: Babcock & Wilcox and First Colony Farms, Inc.

coal at 13,000 Btu/lb and North Carolina peat at 7,000 Btu/lb will be used in the economic analyses.

The as-fired heat values in the table are gross heat values. That is, these values represent the Btu/lb in the fuel as delivered to the plant for combustion. Their productive use in a steam generating plant or other combustion use would be limited to the Btu remaining after the moisture and other noncombustibles in the fuel had been removed in the stack gases and vapor. Peat at 50% MC loses 16 to 18% of its gross heat value in combustion, peat at 30% loses 6 to 8%, and coal loses only 1 to 3%. Because of low moisture and higher density, coal can be transported for a lower cost per Btu of gross heat value than peat and more of coal's gross heat value can be converted into steam in the generating plant.

If it is to be competitive with coal, peat must compensate for coal's higher Btu/lb with a lower price per ton at the field. The cost of transportation can be reduced by placing the energy facility closer to the source of the fuel. Peat may never be competitive with coal in a region where both fuels are indigenous, but this rarely occurs. Peat is found in regions of northern Europe that are at great distances from coal reserves. North Carolina is not extremely far from the coal fields of Virginia and West Virginia, but the coastal zone is at a sufficient distance that coal prices increase from $27/ton at the mine to $40/ton at the plant (January 1980 prices).

Peat Reserves

Worldwide peat reserves are estimated at 409 million acres (165.5 million ha), or about 1% of the earth's land area. More than half of this reserve is within the Soviet Union, which is also the largest consumer of peat for energy in the world. About 13%, or 53 million acres (21.4 million ha), of this reserve is within the United States; but, the United States does not currently use peat for its energy properties. Young peat is used to enrich croplands or gardens, but highly decomposed peat is often burned off by farmers to uncover highly productive mixed organic-mineral soil for cultivation. Fuel grade peat is wasted in this process.

The relative importance of peat in the total energy reserves of the United States is seen in Table 2. The United States has 7,300 quads of proven and recoverable energy reserves in its 1977 inventory. Peat reserves were 25% of the total and second only to coal in quantity of reserves. However, the quantity of peat is for estimated total reserves rather than proven and recoverable reserves. Alaskan reserves are about 50% of the total, but parts of Alaska are inaccessible for peat harvesting.

North Carolina's peat reserves cover nearly 650,000 acres (259,000 ha) and may contain as much as 12 quads of energy in 600 million tons of moisture-free peat (Ingram and Otte, this volume). North Carolina consumes

TABLE 2. *United States Fossil Fuel Energy Reserves*

	Energy Equivalent 10^{15} Btu
Coal*	4,800
Peat**	1,500
Shale oil*	450
Natural gas*	350
Petroleum*	200
Total	7,300

*Proven and currently recoverable.
**Estimated total volume.
Source: U.S. Department of Energy, Peat Prospectus, 1979.

about 1.5 quads of thermal or heat energy per year; thus, peat could provide the equivalent of eight years of thermal energy for the state. Peat could replace coal use in North Carolina for thirty years at the 1972 rate of use. The quantity of peat is sufficiently large to supply numerous energy installations over their useful lifetimes even if some large fraction of the reserves is not recoverable.

Worldwide Peat Uses

Almost all peat consumed worldwide for energy is used in combustion to produce industrial steam, residential/commercial heating, and electricity. Like coal, peat can be converted to liquid and gaseous fuels, and this may be its most economical use in the long run. The volatility of peat is much greater than that of coal; thus it converts to gas more efficiently. The technology developed for coal gasification will work as well for peat, and the Institute for Gas Technology in Chicago in cooperation with the Minnesota Gas Company has begun pilot scale experiments. North Carolina and Minnesota peat may be used during the pilot gasification experiment. Other experimenters have used North Carolina peat in brick production (Gay, 1979) and in steam generation using a mixture of peat and coal. Although these experiments are demonstrating practical use of peat fuel, peat energy development is not yet at the commercial stage.

Although interest in peat energy is new in the United States, peat has been used as a fuel in Europe for centuries. The Soviet Union currently produces about 2% (4,000 megawatts) of their total electricity from peat in plants averaging 50 megawatts (MW). They currently are operating a 600 MW plant and expect to add 2,500 MW of peat-fired capacity in the next ten years (Campbell, 1979). Finland produces 3% of its energy needs from peat and is planning to expand this capacity as rapidly as conditions will permit.

Ireland is more dependent upon peat than any other country. Historically, peat has been used in place of scarce firewood in the homes of Ireland, and the domestic use of pelletized peat in homes is still common.

Ireland and the other large European users have demonstrated that peat can be harvested and is competitive as a fuel compared with current world petroleum prices. Conditions similar to those in northern Europe prevail around the Great Lakes and in Alaska. The southeastern Atlantic states may have competitive conditions that are even more favorable to peat use than the Great Lakes region.

Conditions favoring utilization of North Carolina peat include: (1) a more highly decomposed grade of peat than that normally harvested and used in Europe and available in North America; and, (2) a much warmer climate where drying occurs faster and there are many more frost-free days for harvesting. Because of these factors, peat harvesting and utilization should be more economical. Harvested peat will have a much lower average moisture than in other areas, and the higher Btu potential should add to the value.

First Colony Farms of Creswell, North Carolina, has demonstrated in a multiyear experiment that harvesting is feasible with available technology (Campbell, this volume). Commercial operations await only the development of facilities to use this ready supply.

ECONOMIC ANALYSES

Introduction

The primary reason for the increased utilization of peat in Europe and the increased attention to peat in the United States is the recent dramatic increase in prices of the primary fuels. Despite price increases for all commonly used fuels, a wide range of effective prices still exists for different types of energy. Peat will not replace any of the alternative fuels entirely, but it may sell at a price that makes it an effective competitor for many industrial, institutional, and commercial energy users. The purpose of this economic examination is to explore the potential of peat for steam generation and electric power generation in or near the coastal zone of North Carolina. Gasification and liquification are not included in this study, but they should be considered in any long range examination of the use of peat reserves.

Alternative Energy Prices

The prices of alternative fuels in North Carolina are shown in Table 3. Prices are given for fuels in their normal market units and in dollars per one million Btu of gross heat value ($\$/\text{Btu} \times 10^6$).

TABLE 3. *Prices of Alternative Heat Energy Sources*

Heat Source	Price	$/Btu x 10^6
Gasoline	$1/gal	$8.00
Fuel oil	82¢/gal	5.83
Residual	54¢/gal	3.58
Eastern coal at mine	$27/ton	1.08
Eastern coal		
Delivered (utility)	$35-40/ton	1.50
Natural gas	$3/mcf	3.00
Electricity	3¢/kwh	8.80

Source: Research Triangle Institute, telephone survey of fuel suppliers, January 1980.

On the basis of cost per unit of gross heat value, coal is the lowest cost industrial fuel for North Carolina even after delivery from the coal mines of eastern Appalachia. The next lowest cost fuel is natural gas, followed by residual fuel oil. However, the economic advantage of one fuel over another cannot be determined by market prices alone. It is necessary to consider:

1. Initial costs and annual fixed costs of industrial plants using different fuels;
2. Annual operating and maintenance cost differences; and,
3. Differences in the efficiencies with which each plant converts fuel heat value into useful energy.

The factors in this list may vary greatly with the size of the installation and the nature of the equipment used. For example, natural gas technology for home heating is much more advanced than coal technology, and natural gas conversion efficiencies of 75% are common. Home heating with coal has a 55% conversion efficiency. However, coal-fired steam generating plants in industrial use may have conversion efficiencies nearly equal to those of natural gas. In the examples that follow, calculations will be made of the cost of producing industrial steam and electricity using coal. It will be assumed that peat must compete favorably with coal in these applications, and a market price for peat will be derived at which peat should be competitive. It will be shown that the derived price is reasonable when compared to prices at which peat is marketed for such uses in Europe.

Industrial Steam Boiler Comparison

Industrial steam boilers have used fuel oil, residual oil, natural gas, waste wood, and coal to produce steam. Studies by the Research Triangle Institute (McMullan and Harwood, 1980) and others (Enko, 1977) have shown that peat must be an effective competitor with coal if it is to be economically viable as a fuel in the United States. Although there are special situations in which wood, gas, or oil may be most efficient, in this initial economic analysis only coal and peat will be compared.

A rough comparison has been made of the costs of using peat or coal to produce industrial steam. The assumed plant for the comparison has a capacity of 300,000 lb of steam per hour and operates for 80% of the year. Table 4 summarizes the estimates. Using 1978 prices, the coal plant would be constructed for $40/lb of steam capacity, or $12 million. An equal size peat-fired plant would cost 20% more ($14.4 million) because of factors such as a larger furnace and higher materials handling costs. A peat-fired plant may have lower environmental control costs because peat usually has a lower sulfur and ash content than coal (Campbell, this volume), but this illustration does not include that difference. Using an annual fixed charge rate of 30% of investment, the annual fixed charge cost would be $3.6 million for the coal plant and $4.32 million for the peat plant.

Operating and maintenance costs are estimated at 2.5% of total construction costs. This equals $300,000 per year for coal and $360,000 per year for peat plant operations and maintenance. Total costs per year other than fuel are thus estimated at $3.9 million per year for coal and $4.68 million per year for peat.

To be equal with coal in total costs, peat must provide steam at a fuel cost that is below that for coal. A computation will be made of the prices per ton of peat and coal that will produce equal fuel costs per million Btu of generated steam. It will be assumed that there are no differences in steam generating

TABLE 4. *Industrial Steam Boiler Comparison*

	Coal	Peat
Capacity steam	300,000 lb/hr	300,000 lb/hr
Annual utilization	80%	80%
Hours of utilization	7,008	7,008
Fixed Costs:		
Per pound	$40/lb of capacity	$48/lb of capacity
Total construction cost	$12,000,000	$14,400,000
Annual charge rate	30%/yr	30%/yr
Annual fixed charge	$3,600,000	$4,320,000
Operations and maintenance:		
Charge rate	2.5% construction	2.5% construction
Annual cost	$300,000	$360,000
Fuel charge:		
Price/ton	$40/ton	$17.46/ton (derived)
Tons	$123,691 ton/yr	244,019 ton/yr
Total cost fuel	$4,948,000	$4,168,000
Total plant	$8,848,000	$8,848,000

plant efficiencies other than differences inherent in the characteristics of the two fuels. The primary difference in the fuel characteristics is the moisture content. As explained above, peat and coal must use some of their contained heat energies to evaporate moisture and other noncombustibles. Peat has more water per pound and less solid fuel per pound than coal. The energy cost of reducing peat's moisture to that of coal will first be subtracted from peat's gross heat value. The boiler efficiency for the gross heat value of coal will then be assumed to apply to this net heat value of peat.

A realistic conversion efficiency for a larger and higher technology coal-fired steam generating plant might be 85% based on gross or higher heating value of eastern coal. A comparable steam plant for peat would have a lower efficiency because of higher moisture. It will be assumed for this example that coal at 13,000 Btu/lb, 3.5% MC, and 4.5% hydrogen was used in determining the 85% efficiency. Thus, 13,000 Btu of gross heat value provide 13,000 x .85 = 11,050 Btu of steam heat.

A pound of peat at 30% MC would have 7,000 Btu/lb gross heating value. It will be assumed to have 4.5% hydrogen so that it is equal to coal in this respect. The differences in conversion efficiency can then be based only on differences in moisture content. The example peat will have 0.255 lb more water per pound of fuel than will a pound of coal (30% peat moisture less 4.5% moisture). Each pound of water requires 1,040 Btu for evaporation, thus 1,040 x 0.255 = 265.2 Btu out of each 7,000 Btu will be required for removing excess water for each pound of peat. Thus, the heat value of each pound of North Carolina peat will be reduced to a net 6,735 Btu before the 85% conversion efficiency is applied.

1. Because 300,000 lb of steam per hour will be the heat equivalent of 390 million Btu/hr of output, the gross coal heat value would be

$$\frac{390 \times 10^6 \text{ Btu/hr output}}{.85 \text{ (efficiency)}} = 459 \times 10^6 \text{ Btu/hr input,}$$

2. And tonnage required at 13,000 Btu/lb of coal would be

$$\frac{459 \times 10^6 \text{ Btu/hr}}{26 \times 10^6 \text{ Btu/ton of coal}} = 17.65 \text{ tons/hr}$$

3. An 80% or 7,008 hour operating year would require

$$7{,}008 \text{ hours} \times 17.65 \text{ ton/hr} = 123{,}691 \text{ tons}$$

4. Coal at \$40/ton would lead to annual fuel costs of

$$123{,}691 \text{ tons/yr} \times \$40/\text{ton} = \$4{,}948{,}000/\text{yr}$$

5. At this rate, coal could provide gross heat input at

$$\frac{\$4{,}948{,}000/\text{yr}}{123{,}691 \text{ tons/yr} \times 26 \times 10^6 \text{ Btu/ton}} = \$1.54 \text{ per } 10^6 \text{ Btu}$$

and for steam output

$$\frac{\$1.54/10^6 \text{ Btu}}{.85 \text{ (efficiency)}} = \$1.81/\text{per } 10^6 \text{ Btu steam}$$

To be competitive with coal, peat must have a fuel cost of \$4,948,000 less the \$780,000 difference in fixed and operating costs, or \$4,168,000 per year. The calculation of a peat price to make total costs equal to those for coal follows.

1. Since the equivalent peat plant must produce the energy equivalent of 300,000 lb/hr of steam over 7,008 hours of operation each year, the output in Btu of steam is

$$390 \times 10^6 \text{ Btu/hr} \times 7{,}008 \text{ hr/yr} = 2{,}733{,}120 \times 10^6 \text{ Btu/yr}$$

2. And at 85% efficiency, input must be

$$\frac{2{,}733{,}120}{(.85 \text{ efficiency})} \times 10^6 \text{ Btu/yr} - 3{,}215{,}435 \times 10^6 \text{ Btu/yr}$$

3. Peat with an equivalent gross input of 6,735 Btu/lb or 13.47 x 10^6 Btu/ton would require an input of

$$\frac{3{,}215{,}435 \times 10^6 \text{ Btu/yr}}{13.47 \times 10^6 \text{ Btu/ton}} = 238{,}711 \text{ tons/yr}$$

4. In order not to exceed the total cost of coal in production of steam, the price of peat must not exceed

$$\frac{\$4{,}168{,}000/\text{yr}}{238{,}711 \text{ ton/yr}} = \$17.46/\text{ton}$$

5. This is equivalent to an input heat value cost of

$$\frac{\$17.46/\text{ton}}{6{,}735 \text{ Btu/lb} \times 2{,}000 \text{ lb/ton} \times .85} = \$1.52/10^6 \text{ Btu steam}$$

From the above calculations, it is concluded that North Carolina's peat can provide steam at a cost equal to coal when coal sells at $40 per ton and peat sells at $17.46 per ton. This would be the equivalent of coal at $1.54 per million Btu as-fired and peat at $1.25 per million Btu, as-fired (before correction for moisture removal).

Electrical Generation in a Peat-Fired Power Plant

Introduction

Although there are no peat-fired power plants in the United States, the technology is virtually the same as that used in coal, wood, or lignite plants. Some cost data are published on peat-fired plants operated in European countries. European cost data cannot be applied directly to operations of a peat plant in eastern North Carolina, but reasonable assumptions can be made using European cost experience with peat and United States experiences with other fuels.

A peat- or coal-fired electrical generating plant begins with the combustion of the fuel to heat water. The industrial steam boiler used in the example of the previous section could supply almost a third of the high temperature and high pressure steam needed for a 100 MW power plant. The North Carolina Electric Membership Corporation (NCEMC) has considered constructing a 100 MW to 150 MW peat-fired power plant on the peat lands owned by First Colony Farms, Inc., of Creswell, North Carolina. A 100 MW plant was selected for this example because of NCEMC interest, but plants of up to 600 MW size are operating in the Soviet Union. Such large plants are typically complexes with two to four boilers and two condensing turbines per boiler. Boiler and turbine efficiencies are not greatly increased in the larger plants over the 100 MW plant, but there are construction and fuel handling efficiencies in the larger sizes that the example 100 MW plant must forego.

Fixed Costs

Peat plants are more expensive to construct per unit of output than oil-fired or coal-fired plants. Experiences in Finland suggest that peat-fired boilers can cost roughly two times as much as oil-fired boilers and 20% more than coal-fired boilers. Fuel handling and storage account for much of the difference in initial capital costs. Steam turbines and electrical power equipment are identical to that used in a coal-fired plant of similar size.

This study uses an estimate of $700 per kilowatt of capacity as the cost in 1978 dollars of constructing a peat-fired power plant (McMullan and Harwood, 1980). By contrast, large-scale (over 1,000 MW) coal plants using low sulfur coal were constructed for as little as $370 per kilowatt in 1978 (Public

Staff, 1979). The coal-fired plant boiler achieves economies of scale in comparison to the 100 MW peat-fired plant. Such economies were considered by two privately commissioned studies that derived estimates of approximately $700 per kilowatt as the cost of constructing a 100 to 150 MW peat-fired plant.

The peat-fired plant would operate at 80% of capacity on an annual basis, or about 7,000 hours per year. Annual fixed charges would be 14% of construction costs for a cooperative such as NCEMC or 18% for a taxpaying public utility. The $70,000,000 cost of construction would be recovered at 14% per year spread over 7,000 hours of output for a fixed cost estimate of 1.4¢/kwh. At the privately owned utility rate of 18%, the fixed costs would be 1.8¢/kwh. The equivalent annual fixed charges for a high-sulfur, coal-fired power plant are 1.07¢/kwh and 1.38¢/kwh for cooperatives and privately owned plants, respectively, based on a 1,000 MW plant operating for 6,000 hours per year.

Operations and Maintenance

Annual operating and maintenance (O&M) costs for the peat plant are estimated to be 2.5% of the total cost of plant construction. This method of estimating operating and maintenance costs is based on empirical data for coal fired plants compiled by several engineering companies (for example, Resource Planning Associates, Inc., 1977). The O&M costs are thus estimated at 2.5% of $700/kwh or $17.50 per year per kilowatt of capacity, or 0.25¢/kwh for 7,000 hours of annual operation. This compares with 0.15¢/kwh for low sulfur coal and 0.35¢/kwh for high sulfur coal plants where environmental controls add significantly to the costs of operations and maintenance. Coal costs are based on actual operations of 1,000 MW and larger plants, as reported by the North Carolina Public Utilities Commission (Public Staff, 1979).

Fuel Costs

The fuel cost of a peat-fired plant cannot be based on present market prices because there is no market for fuel grade peat in the United States. Prices in Finland in 1977 were $12 to $14 per ton delivered to nearby utilities. However, conditions of harvesting are quite different in Finland than in North Carolina. Peat is harvested at 50% MC rather than 30% and, of equal or greater importance in pricing, peat in Finland is lower in heat value in oven dried comparisons. Because of these factors, North Carolina peat prices may be higher per ton than Finnish prices to account for low moisture/high Btu per pound; but they must compete with abundant native coal reserves that are lower in price per Btu than any alternative fuel available in Finland.

In order to determine a price for peat that would be commercially viable, a price is derived by which a peat-fired power plant can provide electricity at the same cost per kilowatt hour as that of a coal-fired plant. The comparison is based on a 1,000 MW plant for coal because this is the size of incremental coal generating capacity that is typically added. The comparison will be made with a plant fired with high-sulfur coal rather than low-sulfur coal because of the increasing cost and decreasing availability of the latter. The price will be made essentially equal to that of a privately owned utility. Thus, it would be even less expensive than coal in a utility owned and operated by a municipality or cooperative.

Computations by the North Carolina Utility Commission's Public Staff in 1978 dollars are used as the basis for costing the elements of coal-fired plant expenses. Their data show that a new high sulfur coal power plant could produce electricity for 3.08¢/kwh using assumptions relevant to a privately owned utility. On a similar ownership basis, calculations above show peat plant fixed costs of 1.80¢/kwh compared to the Public Staff estimate of 1.38¢/kwh for coal. Estimated operations and maintenance cost for peat would be lower at 0.25¢/kwh compared to Public Satff estimates of 0.35¢/kwh for high-sulfur coal plants. The estimated difference in fixed and O&M costs between coal and peat is 0.32¢/kwh. This difference must be made up by lower peat fuel prices if peat is to provide electricity at 3.08¢/kwh. With high-sulfur coal selling at $33 per delivered ton in 1978, fuel costs of coal-fired plants were 1.35¢/kwh. Peat could have provided electricity at a total cost equal to that of coal if peat fuel costs had been 1.03¢/kwh (1978 dollars). Assumptions must be made about the efficiency of the peat-fueled plant in order to determine a price per ton that is equivalent to 1.03¢/kwh.

The heat rate of a power plant is the number of Btu of input that must be provided to produce a kilowatt hour of output. A kilowatt hour of output is equivalent to 3,413 Btu. If the overall efficiency of a coal-fired power plant were 34%, about 10,000 Btu of input would be required to produce 3,400 Btu or about 1 kwh of output. This input heat value is called the plant's heat rate. Similarly, steam heat input into the turbine to produce 1 kwh of electricity is the turbine heat rate. An estimated plant heat rate is made for a peat-fired plant by assuming a turbine heat rate of 8,000 Btu/kwh, a plant electrical efficiency of 0.95, and a boiler efficiency of 0.85. The final factor needed is the ratio of peat heat value after excess moisture removal (6,735 Btu/lb) to peat heat value as-fired (7,000 Btu/lb), which is 0.962. With these factors, the plant heat rate is estimated to be:

$$\text{PHR} = \frac{\text{THR}}{\text{PEE x BE x HVR}} = \frac{8{,}000 \text{ Btu/kwh}}{(.05)\text{x}(.85)\text{x}(.962)} = 10{,}298 \text{ Btu/kwh}$$

where:

PHR = Plant heat rate,
THR = Turbine heat rate,
PEE = Plant electrical efficiency,
BE = Boiler efficiency,
HVR = Ratio of peat heat values.

With each pound of peat providing approximately 7,000 Btu/lb, it would take one and one-half pounds of peat to produce 1 kwh of electricity. About three-fourths of a pound of coal can produce an equal amount of electricity. If a peat-fired power plant is to have a fuel cost of 1.03¢/kwh, it must sell for 1.03¢/1.5 lb = 0.69¢/lb or $13.73/ton delivered. European peat was harvested and sold for about that price in 1978, but it is higher in moisture and lower in heat content than North Carolina peat.

It has not yet been determined that peat in North America's colder climates can be harvested by traditional methods and compete with coal from eastern or western coal fields. However, the First Colony Farms experiment has demonstrated that European methods work in North Carolina and that even more efficient equipment is feasible in the short run. If peat can be competitive in Finland and Ireland despite higher harvesting costs and lower as-fired heat values, peat in North Carolina may also be competitive. A fuel cost of $13.73 per ton (1978 dollars) should be feasible.

CONCLUSION

Table 5 summarizes the cost factors in power generation for five different fuel types. The coal and nuclear estimates are based on 1,000 MW plants and the cost factors were developed by the North Carolina Utilities Commission using 1978 cost estimates (Public Staff, 1979). The wood and peat estimates were derived by the Research Triangle Institute (McMullan and Harwood, 1980) for a 25 MW and a 100 MW plant, respectively. Fixed and total costs are given for a municipality/cooperative and also for a privately owned utility.

It can be seen from the table that nuclear power was least expensive in 1978 under the assumptions of the Utilities Commission. There have been complaints by the opponents of nuclear power that these costs underestimate the fuel cost by minimizing or not including the cost of disposal, by ignoring the cost of accidents, and by equating the cost of shutdown for coal to that for nuclear. Because of such objections by numerous public groups, it is assumed

TABLE 5. *Cost to Generate Power in New Plants (1978 Dollars)*[1] *(Cost in ¢/kwh)*

Type plant	Fixed cost	Fuel cost	O&M cost	Total cost
High sulphur coal[2]	1.07[3] 1.38[3]	1.35	0.35	2.77 3.08
Low sulphur coal[2]	0.96 1.22	1.70	0.15	2.81 3.07
Nuclear[2]	1.40 1.80	0.60	0.25	2.25 2.65
Wood	2.60 3.34	2.00	0.40	5.00 5.74
Peat	1.40 1.80	1.03	0.25	2.68 3.08

1. Plants completed and beginning operation in 1978.
2. Coal and nuclear plants operating 6,000 hours per year.
3. Fixed and total costs presented for ownership by a municipality or electrical membership corporation (upper figure) or by a privately owned public utility (lower figure). The annual fixed charge rates for these two types of ownership are 14% and 18%, respectively.

Source: Research Triangle Institute.

that peat's competitive price should match that for coal rather than for nuclear. Under the assumptions of this paper, peat is equal to privately owned coal plants at a fuel price of 1.03¢/kwh, which equates to $13.73 per ton or just under $1 per million Btu of higher heat value. At this price, it would provide electricity at a lower total cost per kilowatt hour than wood and equivalent to that for coal-fired alternatives.

Because peat is located in the environmentally sensitive coastal zone, it is appropriate to question the wisdom of removing peat in this region. The Research Triangle Institute study from which this paper was drawn has examined the available evidence on possible detrimental effects of peat mining or harvesting on the region. The study concluded that there are no apparent environmental problems that cannot be avoided by proper drainage. Although there are many acres of peat where mechanical drainage will be required after peat harvesting, much more of the peat reserves are at higher elevations where natural drainage is possible even after fuel-grade peat is removed.

It is concluded that peat is an economically competitive fuel for use in power plants and industrial steam plants in North Carolina. Its uses as a fuel will transform land with limited economic productivity into land productive for energy, agriculture, and wildlife. These benefits would accrue in a coastal plains region that has traditionally lagged behind the rest of the state in personal income per capita.

LITERATURE CITED

Campbell, R. N., Jr., 1979. Peat for energy program: History, current status and future plans. First Colony Farms, Inc., Creswell, N.C., 25 pp.

Enko, Inc., 1977. Utilizing peat as a fuel. Enko, Inc., Bellevue, Wash., 40 pp.

Gay, B. M., 1979. Feasibility of using North Carolina peat for firing bricks. North Carolina State University Extension Service, Raleigh, N.C., 20 pp.

Ingram, R. and L. Otte, 1980. 1980 annual report on peat resources of North Carolina. Annual report to the N.C. Energy Institute and U.S. Department of Energy. Department of Geology, University of North Carolina, Chapel Hill.

McMullan, P. S., and H. J. Harwood, 1980. Impact and feasibility of wood- or peat-fired electric generating plants in the coastal zone of North Carolina. Research Triangle Institute, Research Triangle Park, N.C., 200 pp.

Public Staff, 1979. Analysis of long range needs for electric generating facilities in North Carolina. N.C. Public Utilities Commission, Raleigh.

Resource Planning Associates, Inc., 1977. The potential for cogeneration in six major industries by 1985. Report prepared for the Department of Energy, Office of Conservation and Solar Applications, Washington, D.C., 188 pp.

U.S. Department of Energy, 1979. Peat Prospectus. U.S. Government Printing Office, Washington, D.C., 120 pp.

An Economic Analysis of Intensive Timber Management of Pocosins

William D. Lindenmuth and J. Michael Vasievich

ABSTRACT

A financial analysis of intensive plantations of loblolly pine on drained pocosins on the coastal plain of North Carolina is presented and compared with less intensive forestry on the same sites. Financial returns were calculated for pessimistic, median, and optimistic market conditions. Intensive plantations for pulpwood in 25 years showed rates of return as high as 5.9% above inflation for site index 40 lands and 7.6% on site 60 areas for optimistic market conditions. These returns could be as low as 0.9% (site index 40) and 2.7% (site index 60) for pessimistic markets. Holding these intensive plantations for an additional five years to age 30 greatly increased returns due to some sawtimber recovery. Rate of return increased from 7.6% for pulpwood at 25 years to 12.6% for the same plantations at 30 years on high index sites and the most favorable costs and stumpage prices. Without intensive site preparation and field drainage, timber yields and returns were substantially lower in all cases. The study showed that intensive loblolly pine plantations on drained pocosins could be very profitable, especially on better sites and when held to 30 years for sawtimber production.

Key Words: intensive timber management, loblolly pine, pocosins, eonomcics, pulpwood, sawtimber.

INTRODUCTION

Pocosins traditionally have been viewed as marginal lands for any type of commercial development, primarily due to the high costs of draining them. *Pinus serotina* (pond pine) has been harvested from the pocosins for many generations, but not until recently have pocosins been extensively drained for intensive management of timber (see Richardson et al., this volume). As land values have increased, timber companies have seen pocosins as less expensive land where they could greatly increase productivity with drainage and intensive site preparation. Timber companies argue that much higher initial costs for drainage and stand establishment on pocosins are justified by rising timber prices and increased productivity.

Published literature contains very little data on costs or yields of plantations on pocosins. Research has been more extensive in countries such as Ireland, Finland, and Great Britain where peat bogs are important as agricultural and forest lands as well as a source of fuel. Schlandt (1955) discussed the profitability of applying drainage to growing trees and concluded that it was profitable at that time. However, no published economic analyses have been aimed at intensive timber production on pocosins.

This paper addresses the question of just how profitable is the intensive timber management of pocosins and discusses some of the reasons why forest products companies are following this course. The effects of variations in costs and timber prices on profits are also examined.

Three methods of timber production on pocosins are evaluated in this study. The first option is pulpwood production on a 25-year rotation without field drainage or intensive site preparation. The second option adds field drainage and site preparation to produce pulpwood on a 25-year rotation. The third management option includes drainage and intensive site preparation for a 30-year rotation to yield some sawtimber. This sawtimber management regime is applied only to site index 60 land or better. All plantations are loblolly pine (*Pinus taeda*). Site indexes are based on the height of trees 25 years old.

These models do not attempt to determine the best management scheme for pocosins. Rather, characteristic management levels have been chosen to represent a range of likely alternatives. The evaluations provide information on returns generated by industrial timber management of pocosins and do not apply to other lands or classes of owners.

METHODS AND DATA

Financial analyses of timber projects require information on costs of production, yield projections, expected stumpage prices, and the production schedules involved. Most of these data used in this analysis were obtained from a combined mail and telephone survey of timber companies that own large areas of pocosins in eastern North Carolina. Five large companies are undertaking the majority of forestry investments on these lands. Their responses provided data on: (1) ownership, (2) drainage and site preparation methods, (3) stand establishment practices, (4) costs of timber management practices, (5) species planted, (6) stocking levels of plantations, (7) range of site indexes, and (8) expected sawtimber and pulpwood yields. Additional data were obtained from forest inventories provided by the USDA Forest Service and the North Carolina Forest Service.

One problem in this analysis was that agencies and corporations have varying definitions of pocosins (see Richardson et al., this volume). Some viewed pocosins as Carolina bays; others used a more extensive definition which included savannas. A broad definition to incorporate these views of pocosins was used in this analysis so that the data were applicable to the region in general. Also, ranges of costs and yields were incorporated into the economic analysis to cover the wide variety of site conditions found on these lands.

Stand Management

The first management regime (Option 1) assumes minimal site preparation, a rotation length of 25 years and the harvesting of all timber as pulpwood. Site preparation includes only the building of roads with parallel roadside drainage ditches, and planting. Extensive field drains are not constructed. Usual planting densities range from 500 to 800 trees per acre.

The second management schedule (Option 2) introduces extensive site preparation and field drainage. All yields harvested at the rotation age of 25 years are assumed to be pulpwood. Planting densities of 500 to 900 trees per acre are customary. Site preparation includes clearing, piling and burning of all slash, bedding and fertilization.

The third management schedule (Option 3) is the same as intensive pulpwood production except that the rotation age is lengthened to 30 years. All initial costs are the same for both options. The longer rotation age results in higher yields and also produces some sawtimber as well as pulpwood. Yields are assumed to be 30% sawtimber and 70% pulpwood. Only the best land (site index 60 or better on a 25-year basis) is included for this option. Yield estimates for lower quality sites were not available for 30-year rotations with intensive site preparation. Trees planted at densities of 500 to 700 per acre are assumed.

No thinnings are considered for any of the management options.

Costs

Table 1 is a summary of costs reported by the surveyed companies for drainage, site preparation, planting, and other management activities. A range of costs was determined for each practice. The high and low costs represent the range of all costs reported for each practice. The average figure is the mean values given by all corporations.

All companies surveyed are building grids of drainage ditches on their land. Two types of ditches are used. Field ditches, spaced 10 to 25 chains

TABLE 1. *Establishment and Maintenance Costs for Intensive Management of Pocosins*

Practices	Low	1979 Costs ($/acre)[1] Medium	High
Roads and drainage	50	75	110
Field drainage	17	27	38
K-G blade	35	42	45
Pile and burn	45	78	110
Drum chop and burn	32	41	60
Bedding	17	23	35
Disking	—	—	18
Planting	27	37	50
Fertilizing	—	—	20
Road/ditch maintenance (per year)	2	3	5

Note: 1 acre = 0.4047 hectares.

apart, drain water into secondary ditches which usually run parallel to roads. The secondary ditches carry water from the field to a river, canal, or waterway. Because roads and secondary ditches are built simultaneously, cost figures are combined. Costs for roads with secondary ditches and field ditches were reported by the companies as a cost per mile. Therefore, to obtain consistency with other costs, these values were converted to a cost per acre.

Not all practices listed in Table 1 were used by all timber managers on all sites. Practices used depended on the condition of each site following harvest and the intended timber management schedule. The lowest site preparation cost estimates for each production option were determined by listing the minimum practices used by each surveyed company. The low cost figures for these practices were then added. High costs for site preparation were calculated by listing the practices used in the most comprehensive management scheme of any of the companies surveyed. The high cost figures were applied to these practices and tallied. The average cost for site preparation is the sum of the average cost values for practices used by a majority of the companies surveyed. These figures are summarized for each management scheme in Table 2.

Stocking and Yields

Yields were derived from Coile and Schumacher (1964) and Smith (1978). Coile and Schumacher's yield tables for loblolly pine were used for less intensively managed stands (Option 1). Coile and Schumacher's yield tables are widely used for sites that have not been drained. However, these tables may overestimate productivity because they contain data for areas that

TABLE 2. *Timber Production Costs on Pocosins*

	1979 Costs ($/acre)		
	Low	Medium	High
Low-intensity management			
Road construction	50	75	110
Planting	27	37	50
Total initial cost	77	112	160
Intensive management			
Road construction	50	75	110
Field ditch construction	17	27	38
Site preparation	118	153	200
Planting	27	37	50
Fertilization	—	—	20
Total initial cost	212	292	418

Coile and Schumacher called savannas. The authors defined these sites as land that "... tends to be flat and is often higher than the surrounding areas, hence surface drainage is poor during wet seasons . . ." (p. 69). Smith's estimates were used for yields of loblolly stands after drainage and site preparation (options 2 and 3). Smith's data were limited in that few plantations have completed an entire 25-year rotation. Some of the estimates for yields at the rotation ages used here fall outside the range of plot data reported by Smith (1978).

TABLE 3. *Yields for Loblolly Pine Plantations With Minimum Site Preparation and No Field Drainage (Option 1)*

	Yields (ft^3/acre)		
	Low	Medium	High
Site Index 40			
Total pulpwood yield	649	738	777
Mean annual growth	26	30	31
Site Index 50			
Total pulpwood yield	1,132	1,290	1,359
Mean annual growth	45	52	54
Site Index 60			
Total pulpwood yield	1,785	2,035	2,143
Mean annual growth	71	81	86

Source: Coile and Schumacher (1964, p. 69-81).
Note: 1 ft^3/acre = 0.0699 m^3/ha.

TABLE 4. *Yields For Loblolly Pine Plantations With Intensive Site Preparation and Field Drainage (Options 2 and 3)*

	Yields (ft^3/acre)		
	Low	Medium	High
25-year Rotation			
Site Index 40			
Total pulpwood yield	3,860	4,437	4,745
Mean annual growth	154	177	190
Site Index 50			
Total pulwood yield	4,754	5,466	5,845
Mean annual growth	190	219	238
Site Index 60			
Total pulpwood yield	5,639	6,483	6,933
Mean annual growth	226	259	277
30-year Rotation			
Site Index 60			
Pulpwood	4,948	5,650	6,284
Sawtimber	2,121	2,412	2,693
Total yield	7,069	8,062	8,977
Mean annual growth	236	269	299

Source: Smith (1978, p. 35-38).
Note: 1 ft^3/acre = 0.0699 m^3/ha.

All companies surveyed regenerated loblolly pine by planting. Stocking classes ranged from 500 to 900 stems per acre with 700 reported most often. Companies reported site indexes of 40 to 60 on a 25-year base depending on site preparation and drainage.

Estimates of yields for drained and undrained sites are similar to projections given by the timber corporations. A range of high, medium, and low yields is used. Yield expectations for pulpwood production without drainage are shown in Table 3. Pulpwood and sawtimber yields on intensively managed and drained sites are shown in Table 4. It was assumed that the product mix was 70% pulpwood and 30% sawtimber for intensive management on a 30-year rotation on drained sites.

Prices

Prices for southern pine stumpage in the coastal plain region of North Carolina were obtained from *Timber Mart South* (Norris, 1979). Data were averaged for April 1979 to September 1979 to provide high, medium, and low base prices. Six-month average prices for pulpwood and sawtimber are given in Table 5. Future timber prices were projected to increase above the current base prices. An average price increase of about 2.5% per year is most likely for

TABLE 5. *Average 1979 Stumpage Prices in the Coastal Plain of North Carolina*

Product	Prices		
	Low	Medium	High
Pulpwood ($/cord)	6.00	8.33	9.42
Sawtimber ($/Mbf)[1]	108.00	158.00	187.00

1. Sawtimber prices per thousand board feet, Scribner log rule.

softwood timber in the South according to the most recent projections by the USDA Forest Service (1980). Real increases in stumpage values have been evident for the past several decades. Projected deficits in softwood timber supplies in the South promise to sustain a real increase over the next twenty to thirty years. A somewhat more conservative rate of 2% real increase in stumpage prices per year was used in this study.

The economic analyses were done in réal terms with costs and prices treated as constant dollars. Each analysis assumed that costs will increase at the same rate as inflation. The real rate of increase in costs is zero. Since almost all costs occur at the present as initial establishment costs, this assumption has little effect on the analyses. A real discount rate of 4% was used to calculate present net worth. This rate reflects the average long-term return expected on capital invested in timber production. Nominal discount rates also include inflation. However, by discounting all costs and revenues in real terms, the effect of inflation is eliminated. Hence, a real discount rate of 4% is lower than a corresponding nominal rate.

RESULTS

The financial analysis calculated the present net worth and rate of return for each management option. Many possible combinations of assumptions were evaluated. Each calculation consisted of a different set of costs, timber prices, and yield estimates for each management option on several site indexes. Results presented here show three combinations of costs and prices to reflect a range of market conditions. An optimistic projection reflecting favorable market conditions was based on low costs and high timber prices. The pessimistic conditions were based on high costs and low prices. The median financial projections used medium costs and prices. These input values are summarized in Table 6.

Present net worth was calculated for the first rotation of each option with a real discount rate of 4% and is shown in Table 7. Internal rate of return for the first rotation is displayed in Table 8 for each option.

TABLE 6. *Financial Assumptions Used For Optimistic, Median, and Pessimistic Market Conditions*

Management option	Market conditions Optimistic	Median	Pessimistic
1. Pulpwood production, low intensity management			
Initial cost ($/acre)	77	112	160
Pulpwood price ($/cord)	9.42	8.33	6.00
Rate of price increase (%/year)	2.0	2.0	2.0
Rotation age (years)	25	25	25
2. Pulpwood production, intensive management			
Initial cost ($/acre)	212	292	418
Pulpwood price ($/cord)	9.42	8.33	6.00
Rate of price increase (%/year)	2.0	2.0	2.0
Rotation age (years)	25	25	25
3. Sawtimber/pulpwood production, intensive management			
Initial cost ($/acre)	212	292	418
Pulpwood price ($/cord)	9.42	8.33	6.00
Sawtimber price ($/Mbf)	187	158	108
Rate of price increase (%/year)	2.0	2.0	2.0
Rotation age (years)	30	30	30

DISCUSSION

The forest manager is faced with several initial choices. He must decide whether to install field drainage and practice intensive forestry or to plant trees without additional drainage and intensive site preparation. He also may choose not to practice forestry at all and use the pocosins for some other purpose or to sell the property. Once committed to forestry, he must determine the most suitable number of trees to plant per acre. A decision to hold a plantation to a longer 30-year sawtimber rotation can be postponed until quite late in the rotation, depending on stand and market conditions.

Present net worths shown in Table 7 indicate that financial performance is quite sensitive to site quality and yields. This suggests that managers can achieve much higher returns by careful selection of sites and application of management practices that increase yields. Although thinning was not included in the management schedules, this practice may by required to achieve projected sawtimber volumes on a 30-year rotation. A detailed investigation of thinning intensity and timing was not within the scope of this study.

A comparison of present net worths for Option 1 (low intensity pulpwood) and Option 2 (intensive pulpwood) shows that neither option is profitable for pessimistic market conditions. Under these financial assumptions, Option 2 would likely lose more than Option 1 which requires a much

TABLE 7. *Present Net Worth of the First Rotation by Site Index, Management Option, and Number of Trees Planted (Calculated with a 4% Real Discount Rate)*

Site index	Management option[1]	Yields	Present net worth ($)/ Market condition Optimistic	Median	Pessimistic
40	1	Low	-28	-67	-126
	1	Medium	-21	-61	-122
	1	High	-19	-58	-120
	2	Low	55	-58	-265
	2	Medium	98	-19	-237
	2	High	121	2	-221
50	1	Low	7	-34	-102
	1	Medium	19	-23	-95
	1	High	24	-19	-91
	2	Low	121	2	-221
	2	Medium	174	50	-186
	2	High	202	76	-167
60	1	Low	56	10	-70
	1	Medium	74	27	-58
	1	High	82	34	-53
	2	Low	187	62	-177
	2	Medium	249	119	-136
	2	High	282	150	-114
	3	Low	1,532	1,199	588
	3	Medium	1,775	1,410	733
	3	High	2,008	1,610	871

1. Management options: 1 = Pulpwood production, low intensity management,
2 = Pulpwood production, intensive management,
3 = Sawtimber/pulpwood production, intensive management.

smaller initial cash outlay. Option 2 is preferred if the market conditions are median with average costs and prices for site index 50 or better land. For optimistic market conditions with low costs and high stumpage prices, present net worths for Option 2 are more than double those for Option 1 and range from $121 to $282 per acre. For land with site index 40, plantations without intensive site preparation will not pay off under any market condition considered in this analysis. Option 2 will only be able to show a profit on site 40 land under optimistic market conditions.

The financial analysis indicates substantial additional returns from holding intensive plantations for several more years to increase sawtimber

TABLE 8. *Rate of Return on the First Rotation by Site Index, Management Option, and Number of Trees Planted*

Site index	Management option[1]	Yields	Rate of return (%)/Market condition Optimistic	Median	Pessimistic
40	1	Low	2.1	0.2	*
	1	Medium	2.6	0.7	*
	1	High	2.8	0.9	*
	2	Low	5.0	3.1	*
	2	Medium	5.6	3.7	0.6
	2	High	5.9	4.0	0.9
50	1	Low	4.4	2.5	*
	1	Medium	5.0	3.0	0.2
	1	High	5.2	3.2	0.4
	2	Low	5.9	4.0	0.9
	2	Medium	6.6	4.7	1.6
	2	High	6.9	5.0	1.9
60	1	Low	6.4	4.4	1.6
	1	Medium	6.9	4.9	2.1
	1	High	7.1	5.2	2.3
	2	Low	6.7	4.8	1.7
	2	Medium	7.3	5.4	2.4
	2	High	7.6	5.7	2.7
	3	Low	11.7	9.9	7.2
	3	Medium	12.2	10.4	7.7
	3	High	12.6	10.8	8.1

* = Negative rate of return.
1. Management options: 1 = Pulpwood production, low intensity management,
2 = Pulpwood production, intensive management,
3 = Sawtimber/pulpwood production, intensive management.

yields. For site 60 land, present net worth for a sawtimber rotation (Option 3) can exceed $2,000 per acre with optimistic markets. Even with high costs and low prices, holding an intensive pulpwood plantation (Option 2) for an additional five years to produce some sawtimber (Option 3) can mean the difference between a loss and a profit. The analysis shows that sawtimber rotations are highly profitable on better pocosin sites, even if poor markets are expected.

Annual rate of return provides one measure for comparing investments. Although this criterion can be misleading at times, it does reflect the accumulation of returns to the initial investment capital. These timber investments can have a rate of return as high as 12.6% above inflation under the best circumstances for intensive sawtimber rotation. The low intensity pulpwood rotation can yield only 7.1% at best on site 60 land.

Financial returns calculated for this analysis show that intensive management of pocosins for timber can have very high returns for a forest products company. These firms find such investments attractive for several other reasons as well. First, large homogeneous tracts of even-aged forest created from converted pocosins offer operational economies of scale. After conversion, these pocosin stands are well suited to the use of mechanization and large-scale operations. Another feature of these timber investments is that some or all of the initial costs of site preparation and roading can be recovered quickly through the use of whole-tree chipping to remove the original forest. Often, these tracts are near mills. Companies may prefer to trade higher than normal stand establishment costs on nearby converted pocosins for the costs of producing timber on more fragmented and distant tracts. Another plus is that large blocks of pocosins can be purchased as single units. This results in substantial savings in the costs associated with finding, appraising, and purchasing many smaller parcels. All factors considered, pocosins appear to be outstanding opportunities for expansion of a company's timberland base and future wood supply.

RESEARCH NEEDS

Several factors have not been included in this analysis. First, income tax effects are not shown. Tax treatment for roading and site preparation activities done in conjunction with harvest and removal of the original pocosin forest varies among companies. Also, accounting practices in the transfer of timber from woodland to mill can affect taxes and investment performance. The overall effect of income taxes is to reduce net revenue and, hence, returns on these timber investments. Second, this analysis is based on only the first timber rotation on converted pocosin land. All costs for roading and drainage are included in initial plantation costs, even though these capital investments may outlast the first planting. Future rotations have the effect of increasing returns to these high initial costs. However, the effect on rate of return or present net worth is not usually large because additional costs and revenues occur in the distant future. Taxes and the effects of multiple rotations were not included in the industrial survey or the analysis but should be investigated further before commitment of capital to these long range ventures.

The greatest source of error in this analysis is the yield assumptions. Most pocosins have not been intensively managed for even one complete rotation. The data presented by Smith (1978) and used in estimating yields on intensively managed sites is untested. Most data were taken from young stands and yields were extrapolated to older stands. Although yield projections used here may appear high, they are within the range of expected yields for intensively managed and drained pocosins reported by the companies surveyed.

Another potential problem stems from timber price assumptions. Historical trends are assumed to continue, but there is no guarantee that they will. This is especially true if longer rotation lengths are assumed. Ranges were used in costs and prices to compensate for these uncertainties. These ranges provide the timber manager with an idea of the risks involved in a given management option.

All financial analyses use a set of "realistic" assumptions. They are usually simplified and do not take into account all variables considered by an investor. Circumstances which are unique to one situation are not usually included in a general model. For example, this analysis shows that the most profitable industrial forest use of pocosins is sawtimber production. However, this may not be the case if a company already has a pulp mill in the area. The cost of shutting down the mill might be high and consume the additional profit that could be obtained from sawtimber. Likewise, circumstances which are not unique to a given situation but vary so much from one situation to another normally are not incorporated into a model. In this study, a range of stumpage values was used because transportation costs can vary greatly. A timber company may opt to purchase land that has a site index of 40 rather than more productive land simply because it is closer to the mill.

Land values are not considered in this analysis because, once the land has been purchased, it can be regarded as a sunk cost. If land values increase (as is probably the case) and the property is sold, the total rate of return will increase. Additional comparisons are needed to determine whether or not buying inexpensive land, such as pocosins, and increasing its yield with intensive management is more profitable than purchasing more expensive land with a higher productivity that would require lower expenditures for site preparation to accomplish the same yields.

More research also needs to be done to determine what method of site preparation has the greatest rate of return. In this analysis the major difference among the options was the amount of site preparation and drainage. However, no attempt was made to determine which method of site preparation would yield the highest rate of return (see Campbell and Hughes, this volume). For example, would piling and burning be more economical than drum chopping and burning? Does fertilization increase yields enough to justify the added expense? Would it be more profitable to increase the stocking at planting and then thin the stand to produce sawtimber?

SUMMARY

A financial analysis of intensive plantations of loblolly pine on drained pocosins is presented and compared with less intensive forestry on the same sites. Costs per acre for roading, drainage, and intensive site preparation ranged from \$212 to \$418. Roading and planting without field drainage cost from \$77 to \$160 per acre. Economic projections were made for pessimistic, median, and optimistic market conditions. Yields per acre ranged widely, but were as high as 299 ft^3/acre/yr for the best sites (site index 60) on a 30-year rotation.

Intensive plantations for pulpwood in 25 years showed rates of return as high as 5.9% above inflation for site 40 land and 7.6% on site 60 areas for optimistic market conditions. These returns could be as low as 0.9% (site index 40) and 2.7% (site index 60) for pessimistic markets. Holding these intensive plantations for an additional five years to age 30 greatly increased returns due to some sawtimber recovery. Rate of return increased from 7.6% for pulpwood at 25 years to 12.6% for the same plantations at 30 years on high sites and the most favorable costs and stumpage prices. Without intensive site preparation and field drainage, timber yields and returns were substantially lower in all cases.

The study shows that intensive loblolly plantations on drained pocosins can be very profitable, especially on better sites and when held to 30 years for sawtimber production.

LITERATURE CITED

Coile, T. S. and F. Schumacher, 1964. Soil-site relations, stand structure, and yields of slash and loblolly pine plantations in the southern United States. T. S. Coile, Inc., Durham, N. C.

Norris, F. W., 1979. Timber Mart-South. Timber Mart-South, Inc., Highlands, N. C., Vol. 4, Nos. 4-9.

Schlandt, E. A., 1955. Drainage in forest management in the South, pp. 564-568. In: The Yearbook of Agriculture. U. S. Dept. Agric., Washington, D. C.

Smith, J. L., 1978. Volume yields of site prepared loblolly pine plantations in the lower coastal plain of the Carolinas, Georgia, and north Florida. Unpublished M. S. Thesis, University of Georgia, Athens.

U.S. Department of Agriculture, Forest Service, 1980. An analysis of the timber situation in the United States 1952-2030. Review draft, unnumbered report, Washington, D.C.

The Economic Benefits of Pocosin Preservation

Sandra L. Postel

ABSTRACT

Pocosin wetlands in their natural state provide multiple benefits to society. Measurable benefits accrue from hunting, the maintenance of estuarine water quality, flood control and, potentially, water supply. Assuming moderate value appreciation and interest rates, hunting benefits would yield a present worth of $125 per acre over a fifty-year period. Should the average annual value of the shrimp catch from Pamlico Sound decline permanently from the average over the period 1959 to 1978 to the 1978 level, an annual loss in revenue to the local economy of approximately $2.2 to $2.5 million would result. Significant nonquantifiable benefits include the maintenance of critical habitats for black bear and other threatened species, ecosystem preservation and option value. Because the market fails to attribute to these preservation benefits a price commensurate with their true social value, the clearing and draining of pocosins will tend to proceed beyond the socially optimum point. At present, the extent to which preservation benefits would be foregone as a result of development is largely uncertain, although clearly related to the type of development and management practices undertaken. Documentation of the effects of drainage and development on the preservation values is necessary before analyses of the economic costs and benefits can be performed and determinations made as to the acreage and location of pocosins which should be preserved to maximize societal welfare. At present, given the uncertainty and irreversibility of development consequences and the likelihood that increasing environmental opportunity costs will be realized as more and more acres of pocosin are removed from their natural state, a conservative policy toward pocosin drainage and development is warranted.

Key Words: collective goods, cost-benefit analysis, intertemporal inefficiency, local economic impact, market failure, opportunity costs, option demand, recreation benefits.

INTRODUCTION

Pocosins in their natural state provide multiple benefits to society (see Monschein, Daniel, Richardson, this volume). While some benefits accrue from direct, on-site uses of the land, others are diffuse and are manifest only in downstream activities and uses. Because many of these benefits are in the form of collective goods which have prohibitively high transaction costs associated with them, an owner of wetlands does not receive monetary compensation for the benefits society derives from retaining this land in its natural state. It is not possible, for example, to provide flood control only to those who pay a fee. Flood control benefits derived from natural pocosins are available to everyone in the protected area regardless of whether payment is made. Moreover, even if the beneficiaries were willing to pay the owner, the costs of carrying out this type of transaction would make it infeasible.

A problem of resource misallocation thus arises as a result of the market's failure to attribute to these wetland benefits a price commensurate with their true social value. When evaluating alternatives to develop pocosin wetlands, the private owner does not include in his costs the value of the foregone preservation benefits. They are external costs, born by society. It follows, therefore, that more than the socially optimum amount of wetlands will be removed from their preserved state and placed into development uses. With development pressure increasing, it is essential to identify these preservation benefits and to determine as accurately as possible their true social value. Only then can a complete assessment of the benefits and costs be made for any given development project.

Benefits derived from natural pocosins are of three basic types: (1) direct, on-site benefits in the form of recreational activities such as hunting, (2) "downstream" benefits related to the role of pocosins in estuarine water quality maintenance, water purification, water retention and flood control, and (3) nonquantifiable benefits including critical habitat maintenance, ecosystem preservation and option value. At present, not enough is known about the ecological functions of pocosins to quantify each of these benefits. Much of the discussion which follows is therefore qualitative and conceptual in nature. A framework is provided, however, for incorporating these preservation benefits into analyses of site-specific development and preservation proposals.

DIRECT PRESERVATION BENEFITS: HUNTING VALUES

A substantial body of literature has developed in recent years dealing with the economics of outdoor recreation. Because public recreation resources are made available on a free or nominal charge basis, the true value of these resources to public users is not discernable from the usual types of market demand analysis. The price paid by users of recreation resources rarely reflects the full value derived from that use; thus some estimate of the beneficiaries' "willingness to pay" must be made to ascertain that total value. Economists have developed and applied several techniques toward this end (e.g., Clawson and Knetsch, 1966).

Recreation Areas Selected

Since hunting is the primary recreational activity on pocosins, the values thus derived were taken as the measure of recreation benefits. A mixture of small and large game species inhabit pocosins, including deer, black bear, marsh rabbit, cottontail rabbit, bobcat, otter, mink, muskrat, raccoon and gray fox (Monschein, this volume). Deer and bear are the species most hunted. Hunting data were available for the North Carolina Game Lands; several of these game lands (composed primarily of pocosins) were chosen for the analysis. All are located in the east-southeast portion of the state and, with one minor exception (Pender County), are within the twelve-county region designated by the North Carolina Wildlife Resources Commission as District 2 (Table 1).

Estimates of the number of hunting trips made to these game lands during the 1977-78 hunting season were taken from the results of a survey mailed to game land hunters by the Wildlife Resources Commission. Questionnaires were mailed to 6,275 holders of game land use permits and sportsman's licences. The response rate was 58.8%.

For purposes of this analysis, these District 2 game lands were treated as a single recreational unit. Although combining the acreages and hunting trips

TABLE 1. *Hunting Trips to Primarily Pocosin Game Lands in North Carolina*[1]

Game land	Acreage	No. of trips (1977-78)
Holly Shelter	48,795	6,680 (37.3)[2]
Angola Bay	21,134	
Croatan[3]	167,569	61,733 (18.1)
Misc. District 2 Group		24,924 (18.0)
Big Pocosin	24,115	
Hofmann Forest	29,654	
Lukens Island[4]	6,000	
Penderlea	11,000	
Tuscarora	1,362	
Total	310,585	93,337

1. Taken from 1979-80 Hunting and Fishing Maps for North Carolina Game Lands.
2. Numbers in parentheses are proportional standard errors [(Std error/mean) x 100)].
3. Includes combined acreage of three Croatan game lands.
4. Acreage is approximate.

Note: 1 acre = 0.4047 hectares.

masks the hunting value of any one game land, it does provide a way of partially accounting for substitution among them. It is not possible in this paper to provide a complete characterization of the individual game lands used in the analysis; but it should be recognized that qualitative differences do exist among them (e.g., fewer roads at Holly Shelter versus Croatan Game Lands discourages vehicle use and heavy hunting pressure).

Benefit Estimation: Description and Application of the Model

By providing habitat capable of sustaining populations of wildlife species desirable for hunting, pocosins in their natural state offer direct recreation benefits to the public. These benefits can reasonably be expected to continue indefinitely, provided hunting pressures are checked before wildlife species are eliminated and assuming no drastic change in societal preferences eliminates hunting as a recreational pursuit.

An allocation model developed by Fisher et al. (1972) was adapted and applied to estimate the value of pocosins for hunting. The procedure is to calculate the present worth of a future stream of benefits based on a determined initial-year benefit, according to the following formula:

$$\sum_{t=0}^{T} b_o^h \frac{(1 + \alpha_h)^t}{(1 + i)^t} \qquad \text{where:}$$

b_o^h = the initial year's hunting benefits,
α_h = the annual rate of increase in the hunting benefits,
i = the interest rate,
T = the terminal year; for this analysis, year 50.

Determining hunting benefits in the initial year involved multiplying the dollar value representative of the benefit derived from a hunting trip by the total number of hunting trips made that season. As determined by the survey of game land hunters, 93,337 hunting trips were made to the selected game lands during the 1977-78 hunting season, the initial year chosen for the analysis.

To estimate the value of a hunting trip, I used the results of a questionnaire developed as part of a study to derive a multiple-use management model for the Great Santee Swamp in South Carolina (York et al., 1975). I applied a simplified version of the Delphi interview ("willingness to pay") valuation method. Two rounds of questionnaires were sent to experts in recreation analysis, economics and natural resource management asking them to indicate what they believed would be a "reasonable value for an average participant," expressed in dollars per user day, for certain specified recreation activities. The approach used does not conform to the best interview method for deriving willingness to pay (see Clawson and Knetsch, 1966); the unit value results should therefore be treated as illustrative rather than definitive willingness to pay estimates.

The mean unit benefit value for deer hunting under "average" conditions was $6.60 per user day, and for small game, $3.60 per user day. Based on the average of these values, a benefit value of $5.00 per hunting trip was used as a starting point in the pocosin analysis. This value lies within the range of unit benefit values for specialized recreation suggested by the Water Resources Council. Sensitivity tests were performed using $3.00 and $7.00 as the value per user day. Multiplying the number of trips by the value per trip and dividing by the total number of acres on the game lands yielded initial year benefit values (b_o^h) of $1.50 per acre for the $5.00 per user day estimate, $.90 per acre for the $3.00 estimate, and $2.10 per acre for the $7.00 estimate; i.e., the per acre value ranged from $.90 to $2.10.

Trends in factors affecting recreation demand—primarily increasing population and income—are the basis for use of an annual per unit appreciation rate for hunting benefits (α_h). Based on reported populations of the twelve counties in WRC District 2 in 1960 (N.C. Statistical Abstract, 1976) and projected populations in the same counties for 1990 (N.C. Department of Administration, 1976), the trend in population for the total region is approximately a 1% increase per year. (This trend varied significantly among individual counties with several indicating population decreases.) Per capita income for the region (excluding New Hanover County because of unavailability of data) indicated an average increase, after adjustment for inflation, of 5.2% per year as determined over the period 1959 to 1974.

Assuming constant prices, tastes and preferences, a given percentage increase in income will cause an equal percentage increase in the amount a person devotes to each item in his or her budget. Yet, as income levels increase, a greater proportion of income becomes discretionary and is spent on recreational activities (Boyet and Tolley, 1966). Moreover, long-term trends indicate that the percentage of disposable income spent on outdoor recreation is increasing at a rate faster than for general recreation (Clawson and Knetsch, 1966).

These findings suggest the need to apply an income elasticity greater than one when dealing with recreation demand (i.e., the percent change in the quantity of recreation demanded will be greater than the percent change in income). The proper elasticity for hunting on the pocosins of eastern North Carolina is unknown. Based on the range of income elasticities for parks and recreation areas determined by Boyet and Tolley (1966) and Bergstrom and Goodman (1973), an elasticity of 1.5 was chosen for the analysis. In this latter study, which derived income elasticities for ten different states, all six of the statistically significant coefficients were greater than or equal to 1.5. Thus, 1.5 would seem to be a fairly conservative elasticity estimate. No corresponding elasticity was applied to population as evidence indicates that, at least for recreation in parks, the quantity of recreation demanded increases in direct proportion with an increase in population (Boyet and Tolley, 1966).

Assuming a linear imputed demand function, total benefits will be increasing at a rate equal to the sum of the individual rates of population and income increases. Thus, combining the population and income trends for the twelve North Carolina counties and applying the appropriate elasticities yield an annual rate of appreciation of hunting benefits equal to approximately 9% [(5.2 x 1.5) + 1 = 8.8]. This estimate was tested for sensitivity using appreciation rates of 0, 5, and 13%. Clearly, at some point in time, congestion of hunters would reduce the value of hunting benefits. However, given the relatively low hunting pressure on most pocosin areas at present and the difficulty of quantifying hunter satisfaction with varying levels of use, this factor was not included in the analysis.

Empirical support for this theoretically justified application of a benefit appreciation factor is found in the results of the game land survey. Between the 1973-74 hunting season and the 1977-78 season, the number of hunting trips increased on the Croatan Game Lands alone by 114.5%—from 28,782 (proportional standard error of 18.2) to 61,733 (proportional standard error of 18.1)—a more than 20% compound annual rate of increase. The survey estimated hunting trips to Holly Shelter and Angola Bay to have increased from 5,982 in the 1973-74 season to 6,680 in 1977-78, but this increase was not statistically significant.

Results

Applying these benefit values and appreciation rates to the model yielded present worth and annual equivalent values for the hunting benefits as presented in Table 2. Discount rates of 5, 7 and 10% were applied to a fifty-year time period. Computed benefits ranged from a present worth of $8.92 per-acre and an annual equivalent of $.90 per acre (assuming a $3.00 user day value, a 10% interest rate and an appreciation rate of 0) to present worth and annual equivalent values of $1,136.25 per acre and $62.27 per acre (assuming a $7.00 user day value, a 5% interest rate and an appreciation rate of 13%). Under the moderate assumptions of a $5.00 per trip hunting value, a 9% benefit appreciation rate and a 7% interest rate, hunting benefits yield a present worth of $125 per acre.

It is important to note that the calculated range of per-acre benefit values applied in the analysis ($.90/acre to $2.10/acre) is close to, although somewhat above, the range of per-acre fees that hunting clubs actually pay to hunt on privately owned pocosin. Timber companies that lease their land to hunting clubs generally charge between $.35 and $1.00 per acre for a year-long lease.

TABLE 2. *Hunting Benefits Derived from Selected North Carolina Game Lands*

Interest rate	Alpha (α)	Present worth ($/acre) B=.90	Present worth ($/acre) B=1.50	Present worth ($/acre) B=2.10	Annual equivalent ($/acre) B=.90	Annual equivalent ($/acre) B=1.50	Annual equivalent ($/acre) B=2.10
.05	.00	16.43	27.38	38.34	.90	1.50	2.10
.05	.05	45.00	75.00	105.00	2.47	4.11	5.75
.05	.09	134.50	224.17	313.84	7.37	12.28	17.20
.05	.13	486.96	811.61	1136.25	26.96	44.48	62.27
.07	.00	12.42	20.70	28.98	.90	1.50	2.10
.07	.05	28.86	48.09	67.33	2.09	3.49	4.88
.07	.09	74.77	124.61	174.45	5.42	9.03	12.65
.07	.13	242.41	404.02	565.62	17.57	29.29	41.01
.10	.00	8.92	14.87	20.82	.90	1.50	2.10
.10	.05	17.05	28.42	39.79	1.72	2.87	4.01
.10	.09	35.96	59.94	83.91	3.63	6.05	8.47
.10	.13	96.26	160.44	224.61	9.71	16.19	22.66

Hunting Benefits as Opportunity Costs of Development

To the extent that these hunting values would be lost or diminished as a consequence of pocosin development for agricultural production, timber management, peat mining or some other alternative use, they represent opportunity costs of development. Difficulty arises in performing a marginal analysis of these opportunity costs because they not only vary with the type of development and the surrounding habitat and environmental conditions, but also with the stages of development. Hunting benefits on pocosins that have been drained and prepared for timber management may be enhanced for approximately the first four years. Clear-cutting and applying lime to the open land may increase forage by about 300 to 400% during this initial stage. As the planted pine trees reach considerable height, they begin to shade out the understory growth upon which the deer and other wildlife feed. The home-range of a deer—the most hunted species on pocosins—is approximately 1 sq mi (2.590 sq km); thus, if not enough food is available within this area the deer will either relocate or starve. Clear-cutting smaller areas, maintaining tree stands of a variety of ages, and burning every four or five years are practices which could be beneficial to wildlife but which are generally not economically desirable to timber companies (Monschein, personal communication, 1979).

With the exception of some migratory species, wildlife also suffers from large agricultural operations which remove all cover and means of protection.

Some species of wildlife have to a large extent disappeared from Open Grounds Farms in Cartaret County where few protected areas remain. The negative effects of farming operations on wildlife can be somewhat mitigated to the extent that islands or corridors of trees are left standing and mechanical cultivation rather than chemical fertilization is practiced (Monschein, personal communication, 1979).

Pointing to the problem of the accessibility of suitable hunting areas, a 1976-77 mail survey of licensed hunters in North Carolina revealed that 16% considered lack of a place to hunt to be the factor most severely limiting the amount of hunting undertaken. Furthermore, of those hunters responding from District 2, 43.5% indicated that they have a "difficult time" obtaining permission to hunt big game on private property (Betsill, 1978).

As more land is converted to agricultural production, pressure will increase on state game lands. At present, the hunting pressure on most pocosin areas is not very great. Should some or even most of the privately owned pocosin areas be altered from their natural state, it is likely that enough public and private areas exist as substitutes to accommodate those hunters currently hunting on pocosins. This of course presupposes a non-diminishing acreage of these substitutes, such as upland mixed hardwood areas, a presupposition which may not necessarily hold true.

Thus, the extent to which hunting benefits represent an opportunity cost of development depends upon the type of development and management practices undertaken and upon the availability of suitable substitutes. Although determining the precise marginal cost of development in terms of foregone hunting values is not feasible, one can state that the opportunity cost is likely to increase in value as more acres are placed into alternative uses.

DOWNSTREAM BENEFITS

In determining the preservation benefits of pocosins, it is essential to consider not only the values afforded by direct, on-site uses such as hunting, but also "downstream" benefits derived from their natural ecological functions. Unlike direct benefits which are explicit and easily recognized, benefits derived from the "free work of nature" performed by wetlands are frequently neglected or at best grossly undervalued (Gosselink et al., 1973). Until the threat arises of either having to allocate scarce resources to ensure that certain benefits continue to be forthcoming, or of possibly losing these benefits altogether, naturally occurring life-support values are taken for granted and hardly viewed as benefits at all.

Estuarine Water Quality Maintenance: Salinity and the Shrimp Fishery

Pocosin wetlands are an integral part of the hydrologic regime of coastal North Carolina and, as such, play an important role in maintaining estuarine water quality (see Daniel, Richardson, Gilliam and Skaggs, this volume). By absorbing and storing water and releasing it gradually, natural pocosins provide a protective buffer for the coastal marshes and estuaries. Draining these wetlands reduces their buffering capacity causing runoff to occur much faster during periods of heavy rainfall than is the case under unaltered conditions (Heath, 1975; Daniel, this volume). Pressure is thus placed on the surrounding marshes and estuaries to absorb the impact of these changed hydrologic conditions (Barber et al., 1979).

The role of pocosins in maintaining the salinity levels of the estuaries may be their most important function relating to water quality. Fresh water flowing into the estuaries is the primary determinant of estuarine salinities (Heath, 1975). Salinity levels are a crucial factor for the survival of many estuarine-dependent species, with shrimp being among the most sensitive as well as the most important commercially. (See Street and McClees, this volume, for discussion of shrimp life cycle and salinity dependence.)

Research by the North Carolina Division of Marine Fisheries (1978) on the shrimp in Pamlico Sound has shown that there is a strong correlation between salinity in the primary nursery areas and the number of juvenile shrimp successfully utilizing these nursery areas. A strong, positive relationship also exists between juvenile abundance in the nursery areas and shrimp harvest for a given year (Hunt et al., 1979).

Although this link between salinity, number of juveniles and shrimp landings is well established, the effect of wetlands drainage on salinity is not yet firmly documented. It has been noted that abnormally heavy freshwater runoff into nursery areas appears to decrease quite substantially the abundance of shrimp as well as other commercially important species (Barber et al., 1979). This may be due directly to the effect of decreased salinities on these species or to their being prematurely forced out of the primary nurseries into areas that do not provide adequate food or protection.

Serious implications regarding the water quality effects of pocosin drainage were raised in a detailed study of the South River, a shallow lateral tributary of the Neuse River/Pamlico Sound system (Barber et al., 1979). Results of this study are discussed by Richardson, this volume. Similar concerns have been raised regarding the Cape Fear River system where it has been suggested that periodic increases in freshwater inflow at the river's mouth are resulting in wider fluctuations in the fresh water–salt water interface, posing potential long-term consequences for the shrimp fishery. It has been stated that "destruction of wetland areas along the Cape Fear River and its tributaries has undoubtedly contributed to this increased flow" (Hawley, 1974, p. 58).

Analyzing Potential Economic Losses from a Harvest Reduction

Among the most important commercial estuarine species in North Carolina are flounder, croaker, sea trout, shad, spot, crabs, shrimp and oysters (Street and McClees, this volume). Of these, shrimp and southern flounder are the species most sensitive to salinity changes in the estuary and would likely be the species most affected by any altered estuarine conditions caused by pocosin drainage (Spitsbergen, Division of Marine Fisheries, Morehead City, N.C., personal communication, 1979). Because a decline in shrimp and flounder populations could reduce the revenue entering coastal economies, it is necessary to consider the value of this fishery resource in determining the benefits provided by pocosin wetlands.

Largely because of the complexity of the physical and biological factors involved, and the masking of local drainage effects by the natural variability operating within the system, it is not possible at this time to determine with any precision the opportunity costs of pocosin drainage and development in terms of reduced fisheries harvests. Some attempts have been made, however, to deal with biological uncertainty in order to determine the economic loss associated with estuary degradation. One such method (Meyer and Dolphin, 1977) converts uncertainty into risk by estimating a probability distribution covering the range of possible impacts. By relating the dollar value of estuarine resources to the proportionate loss, and the proportionate loss to the probability of occurrence, an expected value of economic loss is derived. But lacking any empirical basis upon which to assign probabilities to potential impacts, only a hypothetical analysis of the potential economic losses associated with a reduction in the fisheries is possible. Such an analysis can be supported by the scientific evidence previously presented (Barber et al., 1979; Heath, 1975; Hunt et al., 1979; Street and McClees, this volume), but it generally lacks the specificity needed for a more comprehensive economic impact assessment.

The Pamlico Sound shrimp fishery was chosen for this analysis of potential economic impacts. Although brown shrimp is the variety for which salinity requirements have been most closely documented, the landings and values used in the analysis were for all shrimp species because of the unavailability of disaggregated data. Pink shrimp overwinters and may therefore be affected more by the severity of winter months than by absolute salinity levels (Spitsbergen, personal communication, 1979). However, given that brown shrimp accounts for more than two-thirds of the total shrimp catch from Pamlico Sound and that salinity plays a role in the survival of all shrimp species, the use of aggregated data is justified. Finally, Pamlico Sound was chosen because it is the water body from which the largest shrimp catch is obtained and for which the most detailed studies relating shrimp catch to environmental parameters have been conducted.

At the outset, it is important to distinguish between the local economic effects associated with a reduction in the shrimp fishery and the societal effects. The capital and labor resources serving as inputs into the Pamlico Sound shrimp fishery could, presumably, although perhaps with some difficulty, be allocated elsewhere in the economy with little or no net loss to society. It could justifiably be argued that such a reallocation would result in a net gain to society due to the common property nature of the shrimp fishery resource. It is now well established that exploitation of a common property resource with open access leads to the dissipation of all economic rent derived from that resource (Gordon, 1954; Scott, 1955). The fishery thus adds little in terms of economic value or gain to society. Consequently, a reallocation of resources into other productive sectors which do yield economic rents would be socially beneficial according to economic efficiency criteria.

From the perspective of the local economy, however, an economic loss clearly would be realized from a reduction in the total value of the fishery. Initially, this loss would be equal to the reduction in the value of ex-vessel landings. Over the long term, capital and labor would move out of the fishery and into other more productive economic sectors, thus partially ameliorating the economic loss.

In determining the potential loss in revenues brought about by a decline in the Pamlico Sound shrimp fishery, it is necessary to establish a relationship between the value of the shrimp landings for a given year and total value of the Pamlico Sound commercial fishery for that year. It is conceivable that increases in the landings of other species in a year when shrimp catch is low could partially offset the expected decline in the total value of the fishery. Depending upon the amount of substitution which took place, total value of the Pamlico Sound fishery could perhaps be unrelated to the value of the shrimp catch. If such were found to be the case, one could not argue justifiably that economic benefits are provided by natural pocosins through their role in maintaining the water quality characteristics essential for a viable shrimp population.

Relationship between Values of Shrimp Catch and Total Catch

Linear regression analysis was used to test the null hypothesis that there is no correlation between total shrimp value for a given year and total value of all commercial species from Pamlico Sound for that year. Data were obtained on the total catch, total value, shrimp catch and shrimp value for Pamlico Sound from 1959 to 1978. Because of unavailability of data, four years (1964, 1965, 1967, and 1968) were omitted from the analysis. With shrimp value being composed of two factors—shrimp catch and shrimp price—the regression equation took the following form:

$$TV_t = a + b\,[(PRSH_t)\ (SHLBS_t)] \text{ where:}$$

TV_t = the total value of the commercial catch from Pamlico Sound in year t, adjusted to 1967 dollars,

$PRSH_t$ = the price of shrimp in year t, adjusted to 1967 dollars,

$SHLBS_t$ = the shrimp catch in pounds (heads on) from Pamlico Sound in year t.

Figure 1 portrays the results of the regression. The computed intercept and slope values yielded the equation:

$$TV_t = \$1{,}114{,}615.65 + 1.07\,[(PRSH_t)\,(SHLBS_t)]$$

The T value obtained for the intercept was 5.52 ($PR > |T| = .0001$ for H_O: $B_O = 0$). The T value for the slope was 7.70 ($PR > |T| = .0001$ for H_O: $B_O = 0$). At the 95% confidence interval, the slope of the regression equals $1.07 \pm .298$. The correlation proved statistically significant. An R^2 value of .81 was obtained with an F value of 59.24 ($PR > F = .0001$ for H_O: $R^2 = 0$).

A linear relationship therefore exists between value of the shrimp catch and value of the total commercial catch. This indicates that very little substitution takes place with the result that a $1 decline in shrimp value yields a $1 decline in the value of the total catch. When total value and shrimp value are compared over time (1959 to 1978), one year, 1978, stands out as abnormal in that shrimp value was extremely low while total value was approximately average. Discussions with biologists at the North Carolina Division of Marine Fisheries indicated that in 1978 many fishermen fished for sea scallops and clams rather than shrimp due to the low level of the shrimp population. In addition, the value obtained from crabs in 1978 was approximately 100 to 150% higher than was normally obtained in the years examined, totaling nearly $1 million more than the comparable figure for 1977. This explained why a higher total value than would be expected from the regression was obtained for that year. According to the fisheries biologists, the availability of suitable substitutes in this poor shrimp year was a fortuitous occurrence which cannot be expected to continue. Moreover, with only one year out of nineteen exhibiting marked divergence, the relationship between shrimp value and value of the total catch stands on an accurate predictive model.

Application to a Hypothetical Case

From a policy perspective, it is useful to have some measure of the values at risk when alternative land uses are under consideration. The following hypothetical case is thus constructed in order to provide a measure of these potential values as well as to point out areas of needed research.

It is assumed that the nursery function of the Pamlico Sound tributaries is affected by altered hydrologic conditions brought about by drainage such that the average shrimp catch is reduced in future years to the lowest amount recorded over the period 1959 to 1978. This amount is 707,500 lb (321,205 kg), the landings recorded for 1978. The benefits of preserved pocosins then are measurable by the diminished value of the total Pamlico Sound catch. Specifically, for any given year t, the benefits are measured by:

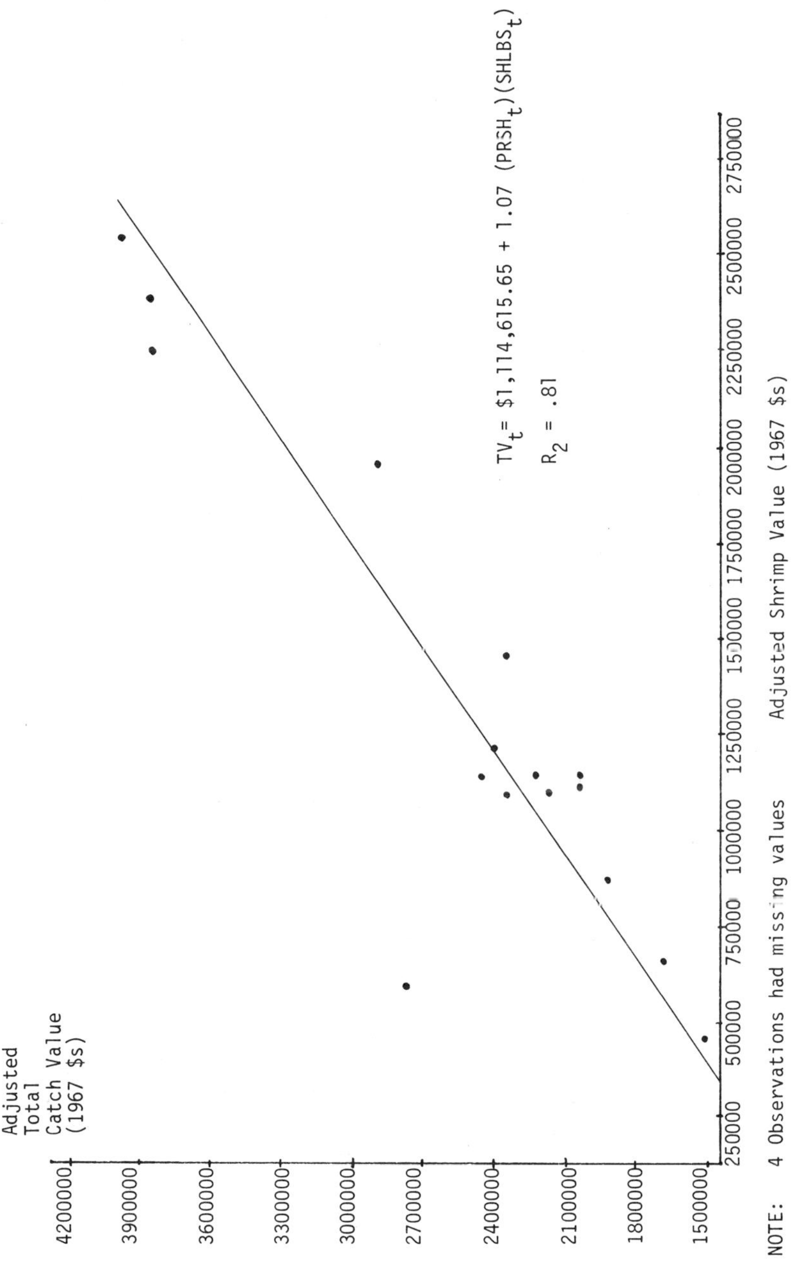

FIGURE 1. *Adjusted shrimp value versus adjusted total catch value.*

$$[(SHLB_a - SHLB_m)\,(PRSH_t)] \text{ where:}$$

$SHLB_a$ = the average shrimp catch in pounds over the period 1959 to 1978,

$SHLB_m$ = the minimum shrimp catch in pounds over the period 1959 to 1978,

$PRSH_t$ = the expected price of shrimp in dollars per pound, year t.

The price of shrimp was taken as the average 1978 price, $1.60 per pound. For future year loss determinations, this would likely be a conservative estimate since the real price of shrimp has increased fairly consistently over time.

Applying these data, the annual loss in value is equal to:

$$[(2{,}536{,}890.9 - 707{,}500)\,(1.60)] = \$2{,}927{,}025$$

Assuming 15 to 25% of this amount does not enter the local economy but is lost to operating and maintenance expenditures outside the local area, the total annual loss to the local economy would range from approximately $2.2 million to $2.5 million. After some period of time, perhaps five years, it would be necessary to account for movement of capital and labor resources out of the shrimp fishery and into other economic sectors. In the short term, however, losses would not be made up elsewhere. In view of the fact that unemployment is generally higher and per capita income is lower in the counties surrounding Pamlico Sound compared to the state as a whole, such a loss could have substantial adverse effects, especially over the short term.

NONQUANTIFIABLE VALUES

Even if it were possible to quantify accurately the value of each of the benefits previously discussed in this volume—hunting (Monschein), estuarine water quality (Richardson), water supply and flood control (Daniel)—a significant portion of the total benefits are nonmonetizable and thus go unrecognized in a traditional cost-benefit analysis. Their exclusion from a decision analysis could thus lead to a socially nonoptimum choice. Qualitative benefits associated with pocosins include critical habitat maintenance, natural ecosystem and wildland preservation, and option value.

Critical Habitat Maintenance

Natural pocosins provide the last remaining desirable habitat for the black bear population in eastern North Carolina (Monschien, this volume).

Hamilton (1978) has described three habitat components important for the black bear: foraging habitat, denning habitat, and escape habitat. The black bear observed by Hamilton utilized pocosin areas for all three of these habitat requirements. Moreover, it was found that undisturbed pocosin was required in large tracts particularly to provide the seclusion and protection needed for denning in winter. A 1972 survey of nine southeastern states indicated that insufficient habitat was one of the factors most limiting bear populations (N.Y. State Department of Environmental Conservation, 1972). As recently as 1972, the status of the black bear in North Carolina was classified as "safe." By 1975, however, the bear population was given the status of "special concern" by a symposium on endangered and threatened plants and animals. Accelerating habitat destruction resulting from human encroachment was viewed as the prime cause of the decline in the number of bear.

It is important to note Hamilton's finding that bear make little or no use of pine plantations and most agricultural fields. Thus, conversion of pocosins to timber or agricultural production apparently destroys vital habitat. Hawley (1974) has concluded from his study of the present and future status of eastern North Carolina wetlands that "disappearance or extensive modification of these remaining wetlands will ensure the disappearance of the black bear from this part of the state."

Pocosins also provide critical habitat for the American alligator and the pine barrens tree frog, with the latter occurring almost exclusively in or near pocosins (Cooper et al., 1977; Wilbur, this volume). The endangered eastern cougar has also been sighted in pocosin areas.

Several plants of threatened and endangered status are also harbored by the pocosin ecosystem (Christensen, this volume). Spring flowering goldenrod, whitewicky Kalmia and rough-leaf loosestrife are endangered endemics, the latter being found only in the lower coastal plain pocosins of the Carolinas. The well-known Venus' fly trap, a threatened endemic, is a savannah species closely associated with pocosin areas. Its habitat has been increasingly threatened by encroaching development (Cooper et al., 1977).

Clearly, the benefits of protecting these species cannot be easily added to the benefit side of an economic analysis. A decision to protect and preserve rarity values is a reflection of ethical and moral judgment. Although it is impossible to compare measurable development benefits with these qualitative values, a policy choice can be clarified by asking the question: For a particular area, what net benefits are sacrificed by foregoing conversion of pocosin to timber or crop production which potentially may lead to the loss of a species?

Ecosystem Preservation

As well as providing critical habitat for threatened and endangered species, pocosins represent a natural ecosystem of intrinsic value for its uniqueness and the potential it offers for basic ecological research. The unique plant community, soil types, and hydrologic relationships characteristic of pocosins have not been thoroughly studied. They are thus being destroyed before it is fully known what is being lost. Natural biota represent a potentially valuable reservoir of genetic information. As Krutilla and Fisher (1975) have pointed out, with particular reference to the potential medicinal value of biological specimens, "preserving the option to examine all species among the natural biota represents a value of some consequence for human welfare."

Finally, value completely nonutilitarian in nature derives from the mere existence of pocosin as a remaining portion of rapidly diminishing wetlands of all types. In 1974, it was estimated that inland and coastal wetlands covered 70 million acres or 3.5% of the United States, excluding Alaska. This is slightly more than half of the original 127 million estimated acres of wetland (Goodwin and Niering, 1974). The natural pocosin wetland area in North Carolina may be only 30% of its original 2 million plus acres (Richardson et al., this volume). With wetlands and, indeed, wildlands of all types becoming increasingly scarce resources, this psychic benefit, which might appropriately be called "existence value," can be expected to increase.

Option Value

Option value, as elucidated by Weisbrod (1964), becomes relevant in public policy decisions when (1) infrequent use or purchase is made of the goods or service in question, (2) there is uncertainty on the part of individuals regarding future demand for the commodity or service, (3) any decision to curtail the supply of the goods or service is irreversible, and (4) it is not feasible to exclude persons from consumption. Because of the irreversibility and uncertainty conditions, additional value should be attributed to an alternative which retains an option for future consumption or use of the goods or service. As Krutilla (1967) has pointed out, no evidence need exist that this option will in fact be exercised at some later time. There is value simply in being able to make a future choice from a greater range of options. Indeed, it is a central postulate of welfare economics that an expansion of choice represents a welfare gain while a reduction of choice constitutes a welfare loss (Fisher and Krutilla, 1974). Clearly, there is value in refraining from making a decision today when it can be better made tomorrow after more information and knowledge are acquired regarding the consequences of various alternatives.

Leaving the pocosins in their natural state for the present does not foreclose the option of converting them into areas suitable for timber or agricultural production or some other use in the future. However, conversion of these lands from their wild state is very likely irreversible. The resulting hydrologic and biotic changes would be permanent and any adverse consequences resulting from these alterations would be felt in perpetuity. Particularly until more is known about the environmental effects of pocosin development, there is value (option demand) in refraining from making a decision with irreversible consequences.

RESEARCH NEEDS

At present, the consequences of alternative actions are not known with any precision. More research and data are needed to yield a stronger empirical base before an optimization model for management of this wetland resource can be derived. Most pressing among these research needs is that of acquiring data identifying the effects of drainage on the water quality of the tributaries and estuaries that receive the runoff from these drained lands. Studies directed toward this end have begun, as evidenced by the freshwater drainage project being carried out by the Division of Marine Fisheries in the Rose Bay drainage system. More data are also needed on the hydrologic role of pocosins, particularly on the effects of draining various acreages in various locations.

Documentation of these scientific cause-effect relationships is necessary before a marginal analysis of the economic costs and benefits can be done to determine the number and location of pocosins which should be preserved to maximize societal welfare. Where preservation is not an option, the results of these studies will be useful in developing management strategies or regulations to mitigate any adverse environmental effects related to development.

CONCLUSIONS

Pocosin wetlands in their preserved state provide multiple benefits to society, all of which may be diminished to some extent by conversion of these lands to alternative uses. Given the uncertainty which exists at present regarding the environmental effects of pocosin drainage and development, combined with the irreversible nature of these development activities, a conservative policy toward pocosin alteration is warranted. As increasing amounts of pocosin wetland are drained and developed for timber or agricultural production, peat harvesting or other uses, less of the natural buffering capacity remains and there is greater chance that adverse environmental effects will occur. Some percentage of pocosin acreage is undoubtedly expendable. That is, there is a relatively low environmental opportunity cost associated with some amount of development. However, it is quite feasible that beyond some point these environmental costs (which equal the preservation benefits) will begin to increase rapidly. Given that greater than expected environmental costs may occur and that, since the preservation services do not enter into markets, the functional work of nature is frequently undervalued, developed systems will tend to grow beyond their optimum size and at the expense of natural systems. As more acres are developed, the marginal benefit derived from those remaining increases.

Finally, economic decisions with implications for the future must take into consideration the moral responsibility of the present generation for the welfare of future generations. Members of upcoming generations may value and be willing to pay more for the benefits provided by natural pocosin wetlands than those in the current generation. A situation of intertemporal inefficiency thus arises, the significance of which is increased by the irreversible nature of the development decision. The addition to agricultural or timber output made possible by pocosin development may be viewed by future generations as inadequate compensation for the loss of a viable shrimp fishery or the loss of the black bear from the region. Thus, combined conditions of uncertainty and irreversibility pose important questions of intergenerational equity and the socially optimum decision over time.

With appropriate data, economics can gelp determine where development can take place with minimum diminution of preservation services. Economic concepts can also guide policy toward the most cost-effective means of compensating for market failure.

ACKNOWLEDGMENTS

Special thanks is extended to Charles Paulsen, fellow graduate student at the School of Forestry and Environmental Studies, Duke University, and now a research assistant with Resources for the Future in Washington, D.C., for his help in developing the modeling aspects of this paper.

LITERATURE CITED

Barber, R. T., W. W. Kirby-Smith, and P. E. Parsley, 1979. Wetlands alterations for agriculture, pp. 642-651. In: P. E. Greerson, J. R. Clark and J. E. Clark, eds., Wetland functions and values: The state of our understanding. ARWA TPS 79-2, 674 pp.

Bergstrom, T. C., and R. P. Goodman, 1973. Private demands for public goods. American Economic Review, 63(3-5):280-296.

Betsill, C., 1978. Results of the mail survey of game land hunters. Wildlife Resources Commission, N.C. Dept. of Natural Resources and Community Development, Raleigh, N.C.

Boyet, W. E., and G. S. Tolley, 1966. Recreation projection based on demand analysis. Journal of Farm Economics, 48(4, Pt. 1):984-1001.

Clawson, M., and J. L. Knetsch, 1966. Economics of Outdoor Recreation. The Johns Hopkins University Press, Baltimore, Md.

Cooper, J. E., S. S. Robinson, and J. B. Funderburg, 1977. Endangered and threatened plants and animals of North Carolina. North Carolina Museum of Natural History, Raleigh, N.C.

Fisher, A. C., and J. V. Krutilla, 1974. Valuing long run ecological consequences and irreversibilities. Reprint No. 117, Resources for the Future, Inc., Washington, D.C.

Fisher, A. C., J. V. Krutilla, and C. J. Cicchetti, 1972. Alternative uses of natural environments: The economics of environmental modification. In: J. V. Krutilla, ed., Natural Environments. The Johns Hopkins University Press, Baltimore, Md.

Goodwin, R. H., and W. A. Niering, 1974. Inland wetlands: Their ecological role and environmental status. Bulletin Ecological Society of America, 55(2)2-6.

Gordon, H. S., 1954. The economic theory of a common property resource: The fishery. Journal of Political Economy, 62:124-142.

Gosselink, J. G., E. P. Odum, and R. M. Pope, 1973. The value of the tidal marsh. Institute of Ecology, University of Georgia, Athens, Ga.

Hamilton, R. J., 1978. Ecology of the black bear in southeastern North Carolina. M. S. Thesis, University of Georgia, Athens, Ga.

Hawley, A. J., 1974. The present and future status of eastern North Carolina wetlands. Water Resources Research Institute of the University of North Carolina, Report No. 87, Raleigh, N.C.

Heath, R. C., 1975. Hydrology of the Albemarle–Pamlico region of North Carolina—A preliminary report on the impact of agricultural developments. U.S. Geological Survey, Water Resources Investigations, Washington, D.C.

Hunt, J. H., R. J. Carroll, and V. Chinchilli, 1979. Relationship between environmental factors and brown shrimp production in Pamlico Sound, N.C. N.C. Dept. of Natural Resources and Community Development, Division of Marine Fisheries, Morehead City, N.C.

Krutilla, J. V., 1967. Conservation reconsidered. Reprint No. 67, Resources for the Future, Inc., Washington, D.C.

Krutilla, J. V., and A. C. Fisher, 1975. The Economics of Natural Environments—Studies in the Valuation of Commodity and Amenity Resources. The Johns Hopkins University Press, Baltimore, Md.

Meyer, P. A., and D. R. Dolphin, 1977. A system for determining economic loss associated with estuary degradation. Coastal Zone Management Journal, 3(4).

New York State Department of Environmental Conservation, 1972. Proceedings of the 1972 black bear conference. Wildlife Research Laboratory, Delmar, N.Y.

North Carolina Department of Administration, 1976. North Carolina population projections. Revised Demographic Research Branch, Division of Research, Office of State Planning, Raleigh, N.C.

North Carolina Statistical Abstract, 1976. Research and Development Section, Division of State Budget and Management, Raleigh, N.C.

North Carolina Wildlife Resources Commission, 1979. 1979-80 hunting and fishing maps for North Carolina game lands. Division of Game, WRC, Raleigh, N.C.

Scott, A., 1955. The fishery: The objectives of sole ownership. Journal of Political Economy, 63:116-124.

Weisbrod, B. A., 1964. Collective-consumption services of individual-consumption goods. Quarterly Journal of Economics, 78(3):471-477.

Wharton, C. H., 1970. The southern river swamp—A multiple-use environment. Bureau of Business and Economic Research, School of Business Administration, Georgia State University, Atlanta, Ga.

York, D. W., B. C. Dysart III, and L. W. Gahan, 1975. Multiobjective water resources planning: Methodology to achieve compatibility between environmental amenities and economic development. Water Resources Research Institute, Clemson University, Clemson, S.C.

Section V.
Law and Policy

Political Economy of Alternative Management Strategies for Pocosins in North Carolina

Milton S. Heath, Jr.

ABSTRACT

This paper examines several alternative strategies for pocosin management and protection, in light of recent legislative actions concerning land use management and environmental protection in North Carolina. It identifies farmers, forestry interests and electric utilities as the most potent lobbying constituencies on these matters.

One promising strategy for pocosin management would utilize existing procedures where they apply, such as the Endangered Plant Act and the Coastal Area Management Act. Working with landowners to develop balanced voluntary approaches to development and preservation of pocosins may also have promise in some areas. The prospects for a third strategy—organizing to prevent unwarranted clearing or drainage of pocosins—are likely to turn on the relative political strengths of local interests in the affected area. The most ambitious strategy, obtaining new framework legislation for pocosin management, would require a large-scale political effort to attract the support of uncommitted constituencies. This strategy would probably fail in today's political environment without the support of farm and forestry interests.

Key Words: Coastal Area Management Act, constituencies, drainage, Endangered Plant Act, legislation, lobbying, (pocosin) management strategies, N.C. Departments: Agriculture, Human Resources, NRCD.

INTRODUCTION

This paper addresses alternative management strategies for pocosin lands in North Carolina from the perspective of law and public policy. It begins by identifying some of the issues of resource law and policy that may be expected to arise in the context of these alternative strategies. Constituencies likely to be concerned about these issues are noted, together with their governmental alignments. Case studies are cited concerning previous constituency interactions on analogous environmental matters. And, finally, the paper offers a prediction of the positions likely to be taken by these constituencies on the issues.

ISSUES

The location of pocosin lands, scattered throughout the coastal plains of eastern North Carolina, means that they lie in the natural path of lumbering and farming activity and of utility expansion. Other developmental activities may take place here and there, but the prevailing developers are likely to be lumbering, farming and utility interests. In either case, clearing and draining of pocosin lands ordinarily will be a necessary first step en route to development (Daniel, this volume).

Without belaboring the issue by multiplying preservation or developmental alternatives, then, I will explore the following illustrative issues in this paper:

1. Clearing and drainage of pocosins for farming;
2. Clearing and drainage of pocosins for timbering;
3. Clearing and drainage of pocosins for power lines, railroads, telephone lines, and other utility facilities;
4. Preservation of pocosins;
5. Preservation of specific pocosin lands;
6. Clearing and mining of pocosins for peat. (Although it may be arguable that all peat lands do not qualify, strictly speaking, as pocosins, I am accepting the working assumption of the conference that they do qualify.)

CONSTITUENCIES

The principal developer constituencies associated with these issues are farmers; pulp and paper firms; lumber and timber companies and other forest managers; and utility and railroad companies. The forest managers generally speak for themselves, politically, or occasionally through trade organizations. Farmers speak for themselves or through their farm organizations, such as the North Carolina Farm Bureau and the North Carolina Grange. Naturally aligned local governmental agencies include drainage districts, mosquito control programs and, more often than not, boards of county commissioners. (The term "mosquito control programs" is used as shorthand for various local governments engaged in mosquito control activities.) State agency allies include the Department of Agriculture and, potentially, the Department of Human Resources (which monitors and promotes mosquito control activities). Some units of the Department of Natural Resources and Community Development (NRCD) might naturally align themselves with developer interests, such as the state Forest Service and the state Soil and Water Conservation Commission, but they would probably be balanced by preservation interests within the department. The complexity of this department's position is increased by its need to represent, in addition, such diverse interests as the commercial fishing industry and the sports fishing and hunting interests. Other state agencies, such as the departments of Commerce and Administration, occasionally might be enlisted on the side of particular farming or timbering projects, but we have no hard evidence to justify assuming regular active alignments of this sort.

The principal preservationist constituencies are environmental and conservation groups (e.g., the Sierra Club, Conservation Council, Wildlife Federation and some local groups such as the Rose Bay Fishermen of Hyde County). Commercial fishing interests probably would align themselves with preservation interests in this context, if they spoke with one voice (which they often do not). University based interests often may be favorably disposed to preservation (although at times they may be counterbalanced by other university based researchers). From time to time preservationists may enlist the active support of a governor, a lieutenant governor, a speaker of the house, a secretary of NRCD or other political leaders, but political realities make these alignments more likely the exception than the rule.

CASE STUDIES

Introduction

In this section, the roles of some of the principal actors on the legislative scene are explored in a series of case studies and other analyses of pertinent recent legislative experience. These analyses—which will serve as a basis for evaluating the legislative implications of alternative pocosin management strategies—will examine:

1. The enactment of the Coastal Area Management Act of 1974;
2. A series of successful actions by farmer organizations involving environmental and land use legislation during the 1977 and 1979 legislatures;
3. Enactment of forest conservation legislation and forestry tax incentives in 1977 and 1979;
4. The long-standing lobbying strength of the utility industry;
5. Passage of an Endangered Plant Act and rejection of a Natural Heritage Bill in 1979.

The Coastal Area Management Act

The Coastal Area Management Act (CAMA) was enacted in 1974 (N.C. Sess. L., 1973, Ch. 1284). It capped an effort that began with a 1969 legislative resolution directing that a long-term study be made "with a view of the preparation of a comprehensive and enforceable plan for the coastal zone of North Carolina" (N.C. Sess. L., 1969, Ch. 1164). Passage of CAMA came after an intensive legislative struggle that preoccupied the 1974 General Assembly from beginning to end (Heath, 1974). Arrayed in favor of the bill were the administration and its allies; the great preponderance of piedmont legislators, reflecting their constituents' interest in coastal protection; modest legislator support from the coast and the mountains; conservation and environmental groups, then at the peak of their political strength; and an assortment of business and governmental leadership who wanted to encourage a balanced approach of quality development combined with protection of fragile areas. Opponents were led by a number of coastal and mountain legislators, reflecting pockets of strong opposition in some coastal localities, apprehension about a similar bill regulating mountain areas, intense hostility to the bill in some developer and banking quarters, and general conservative resistance to a new and untried program. Clustered about the outright proponents and opponents were lobbyists who wanted to get concessions for their clients without staking out a pro or con position on the bill. The lobbying process on the bill was described contemporaneously as follows:

> Proposals for new regulatory laws are routinely scrutinized by lobbyists or special interest groups who, although not wishing to attack the proposals frontally, want "a little exemption" or escape clause for their interest group. CAMA was no exception to this practice. Indeed, its course through the 1974 General Assembly was accompanied by veritable waves of lobbyists tending faithfully to the interests of their employers. First came the League of Municipalities . . . . As the word got around that the coastal bill might be for real, there followed in close succession the utilities (primarily the power companies), trailing in their wake the telephone companies and railroads; the forestry industry (i.e., the large lumber companies); organized agriculture; the resort area developers; and the ever-present petitioners for a grandfather clause to protect pending projects. Hardly needing organized lobbyists was the collection of interests often referred to as "the little man."
>
> In a familiar tactic, most of the lobbying interests waited until the bill was in committee or on the floor in 1974 before letting their wishes be known. Experienced lobbyists rarely waste their efforts on unripened bills. With a complex bill that affects many interests, the result is to clog the legislative works at a crucial point in the bill's consideration. This vastly complicates the task of the bill's sponsors, who must simultaneously keep the bill moving to avoid losing

> momentum, keep the main thrust of the bill before the General Assembly, and tend to a hord of lobbyists who dog their footsteps. In the case of the coastal bill, the waves of special interest lobbyists who descended on the Senate Committee on Natural and Economic Resources and the House Committee on Water and Air Resources were a principal factor in keeping the bill in committee in both houses from January 17 to April 2. During this period, hardly a day passed when Senator Staton and Representative Whichard were not negotiating with at least one interest group, and hardly a committee meeting passed that was not preoccupied by consideration of the latest progress report on amendments about to be generated by these negotiations (Heath, 1974, p. 384).

The net result of this activity was the acceptance of a series of amendments involving some concessions to each of the major lobbying interests. The thrust of these amendments may be capsuled as follows:

1. City and county government interests stimulated changes that considerably strengthened local governments' representation on the Coastal Resources Commission and the role of the commission in planning and enforcement.
2. Farm and forestry interests secured partial exemptions from the application of several enforcement provisions to farming and lumbering.
3. Utility and railroad interests secured amendments ensuring that ordinary upgrading and maintenance would not require permits and that siting of generating and transmission facilities would not be subject to dual regulation.
4. Resort area developers secured a series of minor procedural changes that simplified the application of the act to their activities, and procedures were added to moderate the application of the act to small homeowners and builders.
5. Opponents and critics of the bill lost a number of amendment battles to make major inroads on the bill. They helped secure amendments to increase local involvement in the program; to facilitate access to the courts for the purpose of testing regulatory takings issues; to spell out more specific standards in critical area provisions; to shift the burden of proof in some situations to the government; and to insert a variance procedure and a moderate grandfather clause.

The net result of all of this "constituency interaction" was to leave the main thrust of the coastal bill intact, while increasing its chances of passage by eliminating or reducing a number of grievances of affected interests.

If passage of CAMA was taken in some quarters as a favorable omen for more of the same, in retrospect this confidence would appear to have been misplaced. More realistically it represented an unusual set of circumstances not likely to be duplicated soon or often in North Carolina politics—a set of issues uniquely attractive to the populous piedmont constituency; the incumbency of a Republican governor who strongly supported the coastal bill and who tightly controlled the largest number of Republican Senate and House votes in the General Assembly in modern history; and the peaking of the political influence of the environmental movement. There is little or no carryover of these conditions to contemporary consideration of pocosin land use proposals.

CAMA, as enacted, contains provisions that may be used to protect or preserve some pocosins or their flora. Specifically, the CAMA procedures for control of development in areas of environmental concern in the twenty coastal area counties might serve these objectives. For further analysis on how CAMA might be utilized as a management tool for pocosins see Brower and Noneman, this volume.

Growing Agricultural Influence on Land Use—Environmental Issues, 1975 to 1979

Two decades ago, at a meeting of the Commission on Reorganization of State Government to consider a proposed strengthening of state water resources agencies, a succinct appraisal was made of farmer influence on resource policy issues in North Carolina. "If you can satisfy the farm interest, you can get a bill on this subject," observed the chairman of the commission, Senator Robert Morgan of Cleveland County. The senator was quite accurate at the time, and little has changed since then. The reason is quite simple: farmers cast a lot of votes, and they more than carry their weight in North Carolina politics.

Recent experience with land use and environmental proposals has shown the farm forces to be effective in securing the defeat of measures they oppose as well as in securing the adoption of measures they support.

Two 1977 developments illustrate the defensive strength of politically organized agriculture. That year's principal land use proposal, a product of three years of painstaking study commission work, would have created a Land Resources Commission to coordinate the development of land classification plans for every county outside the coastal area (S565-H980). Objecting, among other things, to the feature of the bill that mandated planning for every county, agricultural spokesmen succeeded in bottling up the bill in committee despite administration support. Another land use bill embodying clarifying amendments to CAMA proposed by the Coastal Resources Commission died in the face of a series of harassing amendments sponsored by farm forces when the bill came up for debate in the House (H1117).

Agriculture's offensive strength is illustrated by two 1979 legislative successes, passage of the farm nuisance law and an exemption from water pollution control enforcement procedures. The farm nuisance law limits nuisance suits against farmers by its provisions that no agricultural operation that has functioned properly for more than one year can be considered a public or a private nuisance because of changed conditions in the locality, if the operation was not a nuisance when it began (N.C. Sess. L., 1979, Ch. 202). This law is responsive to farmers' complaints about being sued by suburbanites who move to the country and then object to the normal farming activities of the area. The pollution exemption bill emerged from the concern of the North Carolina Farm Bureau and other farming interests with pending administrative proceedings addressed to algal blooms on the Chowan River. The bill, as enacted, exempts farm operations from the special order procedure of the state water pollution control act (N.C. Sess. L., 1979, Ch. 889). The speed with which farm interests obtained passage of this extraordinary pollution control exemption was especially impressive. Less than three weeks after its introduction late in the 1979 session, the bill became law.

Forestry Legislative Successes, 1977 to 1979

Legislative effectiveness comes naturally to the timber industry and its governmental allies in North Carolina, a leading forestry state. The large lumber companies have regular lobbyists in the General Assembly, and the North Carolina Forest Service is the largest division in the Department of Natural Resources and Community Development. There are many owners of small forest tracts in North Carolina, and legislators often own forest land or have important constituents who own forest land. This means that forestry legislation will usually fall on sympathetic ears in the General Assembly.

The successes of the North Carolina Forest Service and the industry in obtaining passage of recent forest management bills offer a case in point. In 1977 the General Assembly enacted the first phase of a program that was described contemporaneously as follows:

> An ambitious package of legislation developed by the North Carolina Forest Service in consultation with the forestry industry is designed to spur a long-term program of improved forest management and conservation (N.C. Sess. L., 1977, Chs. 562, 1077 and 573). Its objective is to augment production of forest products while promoting environmentally sound practices through a system of grants to landowners to encourage approved silvicultural management. Its supporters hope that this largely voluntary program for better forest conservation will reduce or eliminate the need for forest practices legislation of a more compulsory nature similar to laws that have been enacted recently in other leading timber producing states. The

details of the program are contained in the three bills described below (Heath and McConnaughey, 1977, p. 202).

Follow-up action concerning tax consequences was adopted in 1979. The Revenue Act of 1979 included provisions adopting state income tax incentives for forest conservation and improvements paralleling recent federal tax breaks on the same subjects (N.C. Sess. L., 1979, Ch. 801). The net effect is to further encourage forest landowners to undertake the programs promoted by the 1977 legislation.

Particularly impressive was the smoothness with which forestry interests surmounted several difficult legislative obstacles. The 1977 legislation was originally conceived as a departmental bill but it got bogged down in the bureaucracy. Lumber industry spokesmen picked up the ball, secured legislative sponsors and obtained passage of a set of rather complex bills that had encountered some objections within the industry, despite the lack of departmental endorsement. In 1979, individual bills that had been unable to move separately were skillfully maneuvered into the general revenue bill that was developed late in the session.

The Utility Companies

Effective lobbying by utility companies and carriers is an established tradition in the North Carolina General Assembly. Each of the electric power companies, railroads, and telephone companies has had one or more resident full-time legislative lobbyists for decades. They are on at least nodding terms with all of the legislators and they are close acquaintances of many powerful members. State government executives know them as forces to be contended with on all measures affecting utility company interests and often as helpful allies on legislative matters.

The special concern of the utility industry with land use legislation lies in the industry's broad and indefinite statewide exposure to the risk of being impacted by such legislation.

Locations of future power and telephone transmission lines, power generating sites or railroad lines often cannot be determined until far along in the planning process, and lead times of five, ten or even fifteen years from initial planning of these facilities until construction are commonplace. Land use or environmental restrictions that are not keyed by law to particular locations thus present continuing risks to these companies. For this reason any legislation looking to the protection of pocosin lands scattered throughout the North Carolina coastal plain is bound to receive close scrutiny from the powerful utility lobbying corps.

The 1979 Legislative Record on Rural Land Use Protection Measures

Rural land use protection legislation received mixed reviews in 1979. Early in the session an NRCD departmental bill to create a statutory structure for a natural heritage program was summarily killed in Senate committee, as a result of effective lobbying by utility interests and other opponents concerned over the potential scope of the bill (S262). Nonetheless, the program itself was funded by appropriations without further substantive legislation (Heath and Postel, 1979, pp. 179-180).

North Carolina's first comprehensive endangered plant act was enacted as Chapter 964 of the 1979 Session Laws. It authorized a variety of protective measures for endangered species as well as threatened plants and plants of special concern. University research interests, led by North Carolina Botanical Garden director, Ritchie Bell, were instrumental in developing and promoting the bill. A key factor in securing passage of the act was the choice to place administration of the program within the Department of Agriculture. This step, taken with the department's approval, significantly increased the bill's chances of passage.

Tentative Conclusions from Case Studies

1. The 1974 CAMA experience was unique to a particular time and place, and is not transferable.
2. In this field, the farm lobby has been a potent force with a strong constituency and is well organized for both offensive and defensive action.
3. In this field, the utility–railroad lobby has been effective defensively.
4. In this field, the timber lobby has been effective offensively.
5. In this field, the North Carolina Department of Agriculture, among the state and local government interests, has the most consistently strong recent record of effectiveness.
6. Promising strategies for the benefit of pocosins include administrative action without further legislation (but this is no panacea: *vide* the 1979 legislation exempting farmers from water pollution enforcement) and legislation supported by the farm sector.

MANAGEMENT STRATEGIES FOR POCOSINS

In light of the case studies, we return now to the issues that were raised earlier. What are the prospects for preservation of pocosin lands, or alternatively, for agricultural or timbering or utility projects that entail the clearing and drainage of pocosin lands?

TABLE 1. *Potential Constituencies and Their Governmental Alignments*

Issue		Pro	Con	Uncertain
1. Clearing and drainage of pocosins for farming	Private	Farm organizations	Environmental and conservation groups	Utility and railroad companies, forestry interests
	Government	N.C. Dept. Agriculture N.C. Dept. Human Resources Drainage districts County commissioners Mosquito control programs		N.C. Dept. of NRCD Governor, Lt. Governor
2. Clearing and drainage of pocosins for timber	Private	Forestry interests	Environmental and conservation groups	Utility and railroad companies, farm organizations
	Government	Drainage districts		N.C. Dept. of NRCD N.C. Dept. Agriculture N.C. Dept. Human Resources Governor, Lt. Governor County commissioners Mosquito control programs
3. Clearing and drainage of pocosins for utility facilities	Private	Utility and railroad companies	Environmental and conservation groups	Forestry interests Farm organizations
	Government			N.C. Dept. of NRCD N.C. Dept. Agriculture N.C. Dept. Human Resources Governor, Lt. Governor Speaker County commissioners Drainage districts Mosquito control programs

4. Preservation of pocosins	Private	Environmental and conservation groups University-based research interests	Utility and railroad companies	Forest interests
	Government			N.C. Dept. of NRCD N.C. Dept. Agriculture N.C. Dept. Human Resources Governor, Lt. Governor Speaker County commissioners Drainage districts Mosquito control districts
5. Preservation of specific endangered species	Private	Environmental and conservation groups University-based research interests		Utility and railroad companies, forest interests Farm organizations
	Government	N.C. Dept. of NRCD N.C. Dept. Agriculture		N.C. Dept. Human Resources Governor, Lt. Governor Speaker County commissioners Drainage districts Mosquito control programs
6. Clearing and mining of pocosins for peat	Private	Mining companies Utility companies	Environmental and conservation groups	Farm organizations Forestry interests
	Government			N.C. Dept. of NRCD N.C. Dept. Agriculture N.C. Dept. Human Resources Governor, Lt. Governor Speaker County commissioners Drainage districts Mosquito control programs

Table 1 reflects my educated guess concerning the probable alignment of the major private constituencies and their governmental allies. In some cases I believe the likely alignments are fairly clear; in others, I am quite uncertain of the results. Most of the uncertainties involve the positions of general political leaders, such as the governor at the state level or county commissioners at the local level. (The secretary of Natural Resources and Community Development often falls in the uncertain category, too, because of the breadth of his responsibilities, covering developmental as well as conservation programs.) In some situations, however, I am also hesitant to predict the positions of the private constituencies.

Potential strategies for management of pocosins include:

Alternative 1—Organizing to prevent unwarranted clearing and drainage of pocosins for various developmental activities;

Alternative 2—Organizing to support legislation that would provide a framework for management, including long-term protection of some pocosins;

Alternative 3—Utilizing existing procedures for protection of some pocosins, such as the Endangered Plant Act and CAMA;

Alternative 4—Working with landowners to develop voluntary systems that will take into account the need for protection as well as developmental activities affecting pocosins (for example, see Roe, this volume).

There is no reason not to pursue several or all of these alternatives, as far as time and resources allow. My attention has been focused mainly on the first three alternatives, and my findings point to alternative 3 as the most likely to succeed. I have hardly explored alternative 4 but it may offer as much promise as any of the other approaches. A model for this approach might be the work of soil conservation agencies with farmers, seeking to encourage voluntary, cooperative land treatment and soil conservation measures.

The attainment of alternative 2 would involve a large political effort to attract the support of the uncommitted constituencies, their normal governmental allies, and the general political leaders. My conclusions would suggest that the agricultural and forestry constituencies would be a key to success or failure.

Alternative 1 is likely to involve a series of localized engagements; success or failure would probably turn more on the position of local interests than of statewide agencies and groups.

LITERATURE CITED

Heath, M. S., Jr., 1974. A legislative history of the Coastal Management Act. 53 N.C.L. Rev., 345-398.

Heath, M. S., Jr., and J. McConnaughey, 1977. Natural resources and the environment. N.C. Legislation 1977, Institute of Government, Chapel Hill, N.C.

Heath, M. S., Jr., and S. Postel, 1979. Natural and economic resources and the environment. N.C. Legislation 1979, Institute of Government, Chapel Hill, N.C.

The Formulation of a Management Plan for Pocosins in Coastal North Carolina

David J. Brower and Nancy Dalton Noneman

ABSTRACT

The appropriate management of a pocosin depends on the formulation of an effective management plan. The resource must be defined and its social, ecological, and economic significance must be determined. The political climate toward the management of the pocosin and the fiscal resources available to implement a plan must be assessed. Management goals must be developed. The existing management plan (the de facto plan) must be evaluated in terms of effectiveness in achieving the goals. Ineffective elements of the de facto plan should be discarded. Additional management techniques needed to achieve the desired goals should be selected.

The final management plan should be formulated to include the appropriate elements of the de facto plan and any additional management techniques needed. Land ownership and acquisition, regulation, and taxation are three techniques that are available for use in a management plan for pocosins.

Key Words: land use planning, law, regulation, planning, taxation, land ownership, resource management plan

INTRODUCTION

This paper presents a process for the formulation of a management plan for pocosins. First, the framework for a formulation process is outlined and then tools and techniques that could be included in a management plan for pocosins are discussed.

FORMULATION PROCESS

To formulate a resource management plan, it is necessary to:

1. Define the resource and its geographic area;

2. Determine the significance of the resource in terms of its ecological, economic, and social contributions;
3. Assess the political climate with regard to managing the resource;
4. Evaluate the fiscal resources available to implement a management plan;
5. Establish resource management goals based on the resource significance, its political climate and the available fiscal resources;
6. Identify and assess the effectiveness of the existing management plan in achieving these goals;
7. Identify other management tools and techniques and evaluate their effectiveness in achieving management goals for the resource;
8. Formulate a management plan by assembling a system of tools and techniques (including the existing management plan) that will achieve management goals for the resource.

An effective management plan depends on a good working definition of the resource and an accurate delineation of the resource area to be managed. The hydrology and geology (Daniel, this volume) and vegetation (Christensen, this volume) are among the characteristics that must be examined to define the parameters of the pocosin resource. Maps of the resource system based on its physical characteristics are needed as a basis for the management plan (see Richardson et al., this volume). In addition to the physical boundaries, ownership patterns are often a necessary component of the maps.

The legitimacy and viability of a management plan for pocosins will depend on the ecological, economic and social significance of the resource. A complete discussion of the value of pocosins is beyond the scope of this paper but is vital to the success of a management plan. (For a preliminary analysis of the ecological, economic, industrial, recreational values of pocosin, see appropriate sections in this volume.) For example, the function of pocosins as a habitat for threatened or endangered species is given by Monschein, Wilbur, this volume. The economic value of pocosins as a source of recreation is covered by Postel, this volume. The value of pocosins to the region as an ecosystem for study and education and their aesthetic contribution to society as natural areas is covered by Taggart, Ashton, this volume. These types of data provide the basic rationale and justification for the proposed management plan.

Before the scope of a management plan can be determined, it is important to determine the political climate with regard to the resource at the local, regional, state and even national levels. The degree of management that is possible depends on the prevailing attitude about the resource. A management plan should be in harmony with the political climate of the area. It is desirable to know the answers to questions such as:

1. How controversial are the competing uses of the resource?
2. Is there a perceived *need* for management?
3. How much support is there for a management plan?

Pocosins are not a high priority issue in coastal North Carolina. Only recently has the drainage of pocosins begun to create any controversy among the residents of the coast. The level of awareness and concern of the public must be considered. Yet, the fact that concern for resource management has not reached a critical level should not imply that management is not necessary. An effort must be made to inform the public about the resource and to get public input in the management process. Anticipation of resource conflicts and the development of a strategy to protect the resource in advance of the conflicts will lead to the most effective management.

Another important step in the planning process is the determination of the fiscal ability to support a resource management program. The money available for management of the resource will influence the tools that are included in the management plan. For example, a management plan that proposes that a great deal of land be acquired would be much more expensive than one that relies solely on regulation. Administrative costs of the plan, however, should not be overlooked. A complex regulatory program depending on triggering thresholds and performance standards can be much more expensive to administer than a simple self-executing permit system. This step will also involve a determination of which units of government are to assume management responsibility. This step may require evaluating the costs and benefits of environmental quality against the costs and benefits of economic growth.

The goals for the management plan are based on the environmental, economic, political and social data gathered in the previous steps. The development of management goals will involve the balancing and choosing among competing goals of different segments of society. One way to achieve a good combination of uses is to determine from the environmental, economic and social data which pocosins are most crucial for particular functions. For example, areas that are vital for habitat preservation or water quality protection could be preserved, while areas of less ecological importance in their natural state could be drained and used for agriculture, timber or mining. The pocosins that are to be drained and converted to other uses under the plan also need to be managed to protect adjacent areas through the use of techniques such as erosion and sedimentation controls.

The next step of the process involves identifying and evaluating management tools and techniques that are (1) currently guiding decisions regarding the development of pocosins (the de facto management plan); (2) currently in effect but would need modification to apply to pocosins; and (3) in the literature but need to be adopted by a legislative body to be a part of the management plan. These tools and techniques fall into four categories: land ownership and acquisition, regulation, taxation, and spending (see Roe, this volume). They may and do exist simultaneously at all levels of government. The important task is to identify them properly, to understand the effect that each has or will have in an effort to achieve the goals of the management plan, and then to blend them into a coherent management plan.

A de facto management plan consists of all the public policy (explicit or implicit), formal policy, patterns of activity, and administrative practice that shape decisions regarding the development of a particular area or resource. For a pocosin the de facto management plan might include such disparate elements as tax incentives or disincentives for certain types of investment, a local zoning ordinance, and the state highway and outdoor recreation plans and budgets. Before the desirability of new elements of a management plan can be considered, the effect of existing plans must be understood. In this context the term plan is used loosely. The elements of de facto management are rarely, if ever, described as a plan. They are more of a "nonplan" moving in contradictory and disharmonious directions. Nevertheless, it is important that these elements be brought into harmony with the goals for the resource. If this is not possible, the disharmony must be recognized and taken into account.

Once the impact of the de facto management plan has been determined, it is possible to ascertain what additional policies must be adopted to achieve the desired goals. These additional policies may be found in policy areas that do not currently apply to pocosins but, because of their nature, might be easily adapted so that they do apply. Adaptation may be accomplished legislatively, by the legislative body that adapted the original policy, by amending the policy to enlarge its purview. In some cases policy can be modified by the administrative agency responsible for the implementation of the policy. This can be done by revising the regulations or by simply changing priorities or administrative practice, depending on the policy. Requisite changes can sometimes be achieved through the judiciary by persuading the court that the present policy is improper and should be altered.

After examining all existing policy, the next area to examine is options that exist but have not yet been adopted by the relevant jurisdiction. These range from traditional to newer concepts: from a traditional zoning ordinance to a transfer of development rights program. In the formulation of a management plan there is a great temptation to simply adopt the plan of another jurisdiction with minimal changes. Frequently, after a plan receives more than the usual publicity, copies of it appear across the country. Thus there are "Petaluma systems" and "Ramapo systems" in any number of places besides Petaluma, California, and Ramapo, New York. The problem is that there are few, if any, places that are sufficiently like Ramapo or Petaluma to use their management systems effectively. Learning from the experience of others has great merit but adopting the experience verbatim is not learning from it.

The remainder of the paper will focus on tools and techniques that are in use or that could be modified or adapted for use in a management plan for pocosins.

LAND OWNERSHIP AND ACQUISITION

To date, land ownership is the only tool that has been consciously focused on pocosin management. Numerous pocosins are currently in public ownership, (see Richardson et al., Taggert, this volume), but the inventory of the size and precise location of these pocosins is only partially completed. If it is determined that more pocosin land needs to be acquired, several types of acquisition could be used. These include negotiated purchase by government or private conservation groups, condemnation by governmental entities, and donation (see Roe, this volume). Purchase of the entire fee interest of a parcel of land, whether by negotiated purchase or by the use of eminent domain, is the most effective method of resource control. It is also the most expensive method. Consequently, only those parcels of pocosin that have the greatest need for preservation or are the most susceptible to development should be purchased in fee. The acquisition of less than fee interests, such as conservation easements, may be less expensive and can accomplish the same management objective if skillfully drawn. Several North Carolina statutes provide authority for the purchase of fee or less than fee interests of pocosins by governmental units. The Coastal Area Management Act (N.C. Gen. Stat., Sections 113A-100 to 128 [1975]) authorizes the use of eminent domain to acquire the fee or less than fee of an environmental concern where it has been determined by a court that the enforcement of regulations issued under CAMA would constitute an unconstitutional taking. This is applicable to a pocosin only if the pocosin is designated as an area of environmental concern (AEC). (See later discussion of AECs under CAMA.)

State statutes other than CAMA authorize the use of eminent domain. North Carolina General Statutes, Section 160A-353 (1976) allows local governments to acquire land by purchase, gift or other actions for parks and recreation. Also, North Carolina General Statutes, Sections 160A-401 to 407 (1976) enable counties or cities to aquire land in fee or less than fee for open space areas and conservation of natural or scenic resources. North Carolina General Statutes, Section 130-162 (1974) authorizes municipalities that operate their own water supply systems and water companies that operate under a charter from the state or a license from a municipality to condemn interests in land to protect their water supply from contamination. Thus, if it is shown that a pocosin is vital to a town's water supply, eminent domain can be used under this statute to acquire the wetlands and to protect them for their ecological value.

On the state level, several statutes authorize state agencies to use eminent domain. For example, the Department of Natural Resources and Community Development has the power to acquire land for state parks and forests (N.C. Gen. Stat., Section 113-34 [1978]), and the Wildlife Resources Commission can acquire land to establish wildlife refuges and management areas (N.C. Gen. Stat., Section 113-306 [1978]). North Carolina General Statutes, Sections 113A-135 to 143 (1978) created the North Carolina Land Conservancy Corporation which has the power to acquire and preserve areas in their natural state, but the statute has never been implemented.

It appears that eminent domain could be used by state and local governments to acquire pocosins and freshwater wetlands to the extent that the preservation of their functions would fulfill the legislative purposes set forth in the statutes. Thus, increased knowledge about wetland functions and values is critical to the protection of wetlands by acquisition, especially by eminent domain.

REGULATION

Regulations affecting pocosins may take place at the federal, state and/or local levels of government. For an analysis of the influence of agriculture, forestry, and utilities lobbies on the formulation and passage of state regulations see Heath, this volume.

Federal Regulation

On the federal level, the two programs most relevant to pocosin management are the Federal Water Pollution Control Act of 1972 (FWPCA) 33 U.S.C. 1251 et seq., P.L. 92-500 (1972) and the Coastal Zone Management Act of 1972 (CZMA), 16 U.S.C., §1451 et seq., P.L. 92-583 (1972). (Because the CZMA provides funds to states to develop and administer coastal management programs, it will be considered later at the state level.) The Federal Water Pollution Control Act (FWPCA) of 1972 was passed by Congress with the express purpose of restoring and maintaining the chemical, physical, and biological integrity of the nation's waters. The goals set up by the legislation include achieving "fishable and swimable" waters by July 1, 1983, and the elimination of discharges of pollutants into navigable waters by 1983 (33 U.S.C. §1251 [Supp. V, 1975]).

The heart of the legislation is Section 301(a) which provides that it is unlawful to discharge any pollutants from any point source into water of the United States unless a permit is obtained under Section 402 or 404. Section 402 establishes the National Pollution Discharge Elimination System (NPDES) under which the administrator of the Environmental Protection Agency is allowed to issue permits for the discharge of pollutants if certain conditions are met.

Section 404 allows the secretary of the Army, acting through the chief of the Corps of Engineers, "to issue permits after notice and opportunity for public hearing, for the discharge of dredged and fill material into navigable waters at specified disposal sites" (33 U.S.C. §1344[a]). This section could have implications for pocosin management. The statutory mandates and the judicial interpretations of the FWPCA have made the Corps of Engineers the only federal agency with the power to regulate wetlands on a large scale (Notre Dame Lawyer, 1977).

The Corps's only control over pocosins arises when drainage ditches from pocosins are connected to navigable waters. This permit requirement is an indirect control that extends only to ditches built after 1979 (Wright, 1979). Although the Corps currently does not exercise direct jurisdiction over pocosins, the expansion of the definitions of "navigable waters" and "dredged and fill" materials under the 1977 amendments to the FWPCA indicates that some regulation of pocosins could be possible under 404.

The Corps's most recent rules for 404 administration were published on July 19, 1977, pursuant to the 1977 amendments to the FWPCA. The rules enumerated four categories of waters that are included within the definition of waters of the United States. These categories are:

1. Coastal and inland waters, lakes, rivers, and streams that are navigable waters of the United States, including adjacent wetlands;
2. Tributaries to navigable waters of the United States, including adjacent wetlands;
3. Interstate waters and their tributaries, including adjacent wetlands;
4. All other waters of the United States, such as isolated lakes and wetlands, intermittent streams, prairie potholes, and other waters that are not part of a tributary system to interstate waters or to navigable waters of the United States, the degradation of which could affect interstate commerce.

The regulations define wetlands as "areas that are inundated or saturated by surface or ground water at a frequency and duration sufficient to support, and that under normal circumstances do support, a prevalence of vegetation typically adapted for life in saturated soil conditions. Wetlands generally include swamps, marshes, bogs, and similar areas (92 Fed. Reg. 37, 127 [1977]). From the definitions set out in the Corps's regulations, it appears that pocosins could fall into the fourth category of waters of the United States if it were shown that disturbance within the pocosin would affect interstate commerce.

The 1977 Amendments to the FWPCA included some exemptions to the requirement of 404 dredge and fill requirements. The permit exemption most relevant to pocosins is for normal farming, silviculture, and ranching activities, such as plowing, seeding, cultivation, minor drainage, or harvesting (33 U.S.C. §1344 [f] [1] [A]). Thus it appears that while pocosins may fall within the Corps's definition of wetlands, many activities for which pocosins are drained would be exempt from Section 404. In addition, under the Corps's definitions of dredged and fill materials, the clearing and burning of wetlands fall outside of the Corps's 404 jurisdiction. A change in elevation through dredge and fill is required to invoke the power of the Corps (Wright, Permitting Division, U.S. Army Corps of Engineers, Wilmington, N.C., personal communication, 1979).

A recent case, *Avoyelles Sportsmen's League, Inc. v. Alexander*, 1979, (Civil Action 78-1428, U.S. District Court for the western district of Louisiana, Alexandria Division) may expand the activities that the Corps regulates to include the clearing of wetland vegetation within pocosins. The land involved in this case is an overflow or backwater area for the Bayou Natchitoches basin in Louisiana. The area is subject to the average annual flood, meaning that it can be expected to flood at least once every year. The district court in the Avoyelles case held that clearing of trees and vegetation which are part of the waters of the United States constitutes the discharge of dredged material and therefore requires a 404 permit. The court reasoned that wetlands include the vegetation on the land and that the land without the vegetation cannot serve the purposes of the FWPCA. The court went on to say that the bulldozing and clearing of wetlands gouged out sloughs which constituted dredged material. Similarly, the leveling effect of clearing and the redepositing of soil constituted fill material for 404 purposes. It concluded that clearing activities were not normal farming operations under the exemption section, and thus were not exempt from the permit requirement.

At this writing, the Avoyelles case is in the United States Court of Appeals. If the district court's ruling is upheld, the case could be a landmark decision relating to wetland protection. Although the case is not a direct treatment of pocosins, it shows the continued tendency of the courts to broaden the jurisdiction of the Corps over a greater number of activities and types of wetlands. Thus, the clearing of pocosins whether for mining, agriculture, or silviculture could come under the scrutiny of the Corps under the Avoyelles decision. Although the Section 404 permitting process is not currently a functional part of the de facto management program for pocosins, the statutory and institutional framework for regulation of pocosin drainage is intact under the FWPCA.

State Regulation

On the state level numerous regulations exist which do not address pocosins directly but which could be modified for use in a strategy for pocosin management. Perhaps the most notable candidate is the North Carolina Coastal Area Management Act (CAMA). North Carolina passed CAMA in 1974 in response to the 1972 Federal Coastal Zone Management Act.

The legislative findings and goals of CAMA include the coordination of resource management in the coastal zone. The specific goals of the legislation include the following:

1. To insure that the development or preservation of the land and water resources of the coastal area proceeds in a manner consistent with the capability of the land and water for development, use, or preservation based on ecological considerations;
2. To insure the orderly and balanced use and preservation of our coastal resources on behalf of the people of North Carolina and the nation;
3. To establish policies, guidelines and standards for "protection, preservation, and conservation of natural resources including but not limited to water use, scenic vistas, and fish and wildlife. . ." (113A-102 [b]).

These enumerated goals indicate that CAMA was designed to develop an integrated system of resource management which is capable of protecting coastal resources, such as pocosins, from irreparable damage and of fostering economic growth in the coastal region. Pocosins currently receive virtually no management or protection under CAMA. However, similar to the FWPCA, CAMA does provide an institutional framework within which a management strategy for pocosins could be developed.

CAMA has a two-tier system for resource management. The first tier is composed of fragile areas in which virtually any development will have a detrimental effect *on the surrounding land* and coastal waters and which have been designated under CAMA as AECs. The second tier is composed of local land use plans prepared by the counties and municipalities in the twenty-county region covered by CAMA.

Within the first tier, the Coastal Resources Commission (CRC) has responsibility for designating AECs, for devising standards for permissible activities within them, and for establishing a permitting process for development within the AECs. Four categories of AECs are included in CAMA: the estuarine system, ocean hazard areas, public water supplies and fragile coastal resource areas. The definitions which the CRC has attached to these categories limit the possibilities of the designation of pocosins as AECs. No pocosins have yet been designated as AECs by the CRC.

It is possible that under the current definitions pocosins could be designated under the fragile coastal resource category. Included within this group are coastal complex natural areas, coastal areas that sustain remnant species, and unique geologic formations. Coastal complex natural areas are defined as those areas which support native plants and animal communities by providing habitat conditions that have remained essentially unchanged by human activities. Coastal areas that sustain remnant species are those areas which support native plants or animals threatened and endangered within the coastal area. Pocosins containing endangered species could be designated under this category. Unique coastal geologic formations are areas which contain geologic formations that are unique or otherwise significant components of coastal systems or are especially notable examples of geologic formations or processes (U.S. Department of Commerce, 1978). This category seems to be most suitable for some pocosins. It is quite possible that pocosins found in conjunction with the Carolina bays could be designated as AECs within this category.

Areas which are to be designated AECs under the fragile coastal natural resource areas must be nominated on a case by case basis by sponsoring groups or individuals and then approved by the CRC. Currently, no AECs have been nominated for this category.

Within the AECs, development is regulated by a permitting process, the administration of which is divided between the CRC and the locality. The CRC issues permits for major development within AECs; the local government issues permits for all other development. Major development is defined by CAMA as any development which requires licensing or other form of approval from a state agency or which "occupies a land or water area in excess of 20 acres; or which occupies on a single parcel a structure or structures in excess of a ground area of 60,000 sq ft (N.C. Gen. Stat., Section 113A-118 [d] [1] [1978]). The definition of "development" in CAMA exempts from the provisions of the law "use of any land for the purpose of planting, growing, or harvesting plants, crops, trees or other agricultural or forestry products . . . except where excavation or filling affecting estuarine waters or navigable waters is involved" (N.C. Gen. Stat., Section 113A-103 [5] [b] [4] [1978]). Thus, it appears that if a pocosin were designated as an AEC, timber and agricultural activities would be exempt from the permitting process unless more information were gathered to show the effects of filling or excavating pocosins on estuaries.

Some degree of control is held by the state within AECs. Local ordinances and regulations within AECs must be consistent with the local land use plans. Although the localities develop their own land use plan subject to the approval of the CRC, once the plan is adopted, the CRC has the power to modify local ordinances that affect AECs to make those regulations consistent with the local plan (N.C. Gen. Stat., Section 113A-111 [1978]).

The second tier of management under CAMA is the local land use plans which must be prepared in conformance with the CRC guidelines by the fifty-two coastal counties and municipalities that are covered by CAMA.

The guidelines require that the plans address five basic areas:

1. Local policies concerning population and economic trends, adequate housing, protection of natural resources, historic resources and environment;
2. Data collection and analysis to review present land use patterns, to

analyze constraints on carrying capacity, and to predict future demands for land;

3. Existing land use;
4. Proposed AECs; and
5. A land classification map of the jurisdiction (U.S. Dept. of Commerce, EIS, 1978).

The land classification has the potential to be a strong tool in the allocation of pocosin resources. The localities are required to divide their land into the following categories: developed, transition, community, rural, and conservation. A locality in its placement of pocosins and other freshwater wetlands within the land classification system can determine whether those wetlands will be protected in their natural state in the conservation category, will be managed as a renewable resource within the rural category, or will be developed and serviced to various degrees in the community or transition categories. But for the plans to affect pocosins at all, they must be implemented.

The CRC's power to review the local land use plans does not include the authority to revise local zoning ordinances or other local regulations to be consistent with the state guidelines or the local plan. The CRC can only recommend such changes to the locality. This inability on the part of the state to require implementation of the local plans outside of the AECs is a serious weakness of CAMA with respect to natural systems protection. Localities desiring to develop policies toward freshwater wetlands can revise or adopt zoning ordinances that are consistent with the local land classification system, but they are not required to do so (Schoenbaum and Rosenberg, 1976).

In terms of an overall management strategy for pocosins, CAMA has several limitations. First, CAMA covers only those twenty coastal counties which are adjacent to or adjoining the Atlantic Ocean or any coastal sound. Thus, pocosins that are not located within CAMA's jurisdiction do not have the institutional framework needed for an integrated management program. Therefore, management of the more inland pocosins must come from existing state and local laws or from new legislation dealing with freshwater wetlands. Second, inclusion of pocosins in the AEC tier is doubtful. Proof of the fragility and importance of the pocosin habitat to coastal waters is necessary to warrant consideration of pocosins as an AEC. If pocosins are approved as an AEC category under the fragile coastal natural resource areas grouping, such designation would most likely cover only small acreages of pocosin and would not constitute a pervasive management strategy. The local land use planning process required under CAMA is probably the strongest possibility for management of pocosins under North Carolina state law. Through this planning mechanism, either the locality (in its individual plan) or the state (in the CRC guidelines) can develop plans regarding pocosin allocation, but under current legislation there is nothing to require that those plans be followed.

Several other state statutes affect or could be modified to affect pocosins. Chapter 156 of the North Carolina General Statutes contains the drainage laws for the state which by and large encourage the drainage of pocosins. Under this chapter, it is possible for an owner of "pocosin, swamp or flatlands" that cannot be drained without cutting a canal or ditch through the lands of others to petition the Superior Court of the county to allow drainage of the swampland through canals in the lands of other owners. Where there are several pieces of land owned by separate owners who would benefit by such drainage canals, these owners may petition the Superior Court to form a drainage corporation. Chapter 156 also provides for the creation of drainage districts declaring that the reclaiming of "wet, swamp or overflowed land . . . is a public use and benefit conducive to the public health, convenience and welfare." This statute was passed in 1909 at a time when swamps and wetlands were considered to be a menace to society. While the statute does provide authority for the conversion of pocosins, it may need revision to become useful in a pocosin management plan.

The Department of Natural Resources and Community Development administers a dredge and fill permit program under the auspices of North Carolina General Statutes, Section 113-229 (1978). This permit system is limited to filling and excavation projects in any estuarine waters, tidelands, marshlands or state owned lakes. Marshlands are defined in the statute as any salt marsh or other marsh subject to regular or occasional flooding by tides, including windtides, and thus pocosins and other freshwater swamps not subject to tidal action are excluded. North Carolina General Statutes, Section 113-230 (1978) gives the secretary of the Department of Natural Resources, with the approval of the Marine Fisheries Commission, the power to adopt regulations restricting or prohibiting dredging, filling, removing, or otherwise altering coastal wetlands. However, this section is limited by the same definition of marshland set forth in Section 113-229 and therefore pocosins are excluded. Orders authorized under Section 230 can extend to land contiguous to coastal wetlands if necessary to achieve the purpose of the act. It might therefore be possible for pocosins to be covered by this section if they are continguous to wetlands. Unless the definition of wetlands is legislatively expanded to include more inland freshwater wetlands, it is doubtful that pocosins could effectively be regulated under Section 229 or 230.

The Mining Act of 1971(N.C. Gen. Stat., Section 74-49 [1971]), defines minerals as "soil, clay, coal, stone, gravel, phosphate, rock, metallic ore, and any other solid material or substance of commercial value found in natural deposits in the earth." Although peat is not specifically mentioned in this definition, it could be included under the act as a "solid material found in deposits in the earth." Peat or any other type of mining within or out of pocosin requires a permit from the Department of Natural Resources and Community Development. In applying for a permit, the applicant must submit a reclamation plan outlining methods that will be used to protect adjacent surface resources, revegetate the affected area, and restore the surface gradient for subsequent use. Some of the reasons a permit can be denied under the act include adverse effects on wildlife or on freshwater or marine fisheries, or degradation of surface or ground water quality. To the extent that mining in pocosins adversely affects these factors, it can be prohibited.

Local Regulation

In addition to regulation at the state level, local governments may have ordinances currently in effect or they may adopt regulatory tools and techniques as part of a management plan for pocosins. In developing a management plan, current ordinances such as zoning and subdivision ordinances should be examined in each locality to determine their impacts on pocosins. In general, zoning at the county level is not widespread in coastal North Carolina. Counties that do have zoning do not tend to enforce the ordinances strictly. However, it is possible for local governments to create zoning districts that correspond to the rural and conservation categories of the land classification system under CAMA. These districts can be designated as wetland, watershed, shoreland, flood plain, forest, or wildlife habitat districts (Schoenbaum and Rosenberg, 1976).

There are several drawbacks to the use of zoning as an effective management tool for pocosins. First, zoning ordinances are not a permanent solution to keeping a resource in its natural state due to the availability of variances and the ease of amending ordinances (Reitz, 1974). Often, poor administration and uncoordinated enforcement of zoning restrictions reduce their effectiveness. Another weakness of zoning ordinances is that they often are not related to regional plans. Although the North Carolina enabling legislation for zoning requires that zoning be done in accordance with a comprehensive plan, the North Carolina courts in 1970 held that the zoning ordinance itself can fulfill this requirement and that no master plan is required (*Allred v. City of Raleigh* 7 N.C. App. 602, 173 S.E. 2d 4 [1969], reversed on other grounds, 277 N.C. 530, 178 S.E. 2d 432 [1971]). In addition, there is no requirement in the North Carolina Coastal Area Management Act of 1974 that local zoning ordinances be drawn to conform to the local land use plan formulated pursuant to the act. A strong argument can be made that the statutory requirement that a zoning ordinance be in accordance with a comprehensive plan should now be enforced and that zoning should be based on the land use plans prepared under CAMA by the localities.

Localities may wish to explore the possibility of performance zoning in conjunction with traditional zoning to manage pocosins. Performance zoning sets standards for each zone based on permissible side effects of a development rather than specifically enumerating the types of uses permitted. If the prescribed standards are met, any use is allowed in the zone. Standards of permissible impact on recharge in aquifer areas, sedimentation and pollution discharge into waters, and changes in water flow or temperature are specific performance standards that could be used. Standards could be initially set for those impacts that are easier to measure (for example, destruction of vegetation or amount of runoff into waters). The performance control ordinance is designed to preserve natural processes by permitting development that is in accord with these processes rather than by banning all development in sensitive lands. Under performance controls, it is up to the developer to prove that his project is compatible with the natural processes before the project is approved. The major weakness in the use of performance zoning in coastal North Carolina is that case by case considerations of every development proposal would impose a tremendous information and work load which could only be met by a trained staff and/or sophisticated equipment. This is not a realistic expectation in the coastal area at the present time. However, this technical burden could be placed on the developer, with the local government staff or an independent agency certifying the results. Simpler applications of performance standards that do not require quantitative analysis are frequently inexpensive and do not require special data systems or staff.

Perhaps the largest threat to effective regulation of wetlands through zoning is the constitutional prohibition against governmental taking of private property without compensation. North Carolina courts have held zoning ordinances invalid if they have the effect of completely depriving the landowner of the beneficial use of his property by prohibiting all practical uses of his property or by prohibiting the only use to which the property was reasonably suited (*Roberson's Beverages, Inc. v. City of New Bern* 6 N.C. App. 632, 171 S.E. 2d 4 [1969]). Thus, a wetlands-type district that limited development within pocosins could come under attack as an illegal taking unless it left the owner with the right to make some practical, reasonable use of the land.

Two other mechanisms that the localities might pursue are worthy of brief mention. These are transfer of development rights (TDR) and local environmental impact ordinances. The basic concept underlying TDR is that ownership of land gives the owner a bundle of rights, each of which may be separated from the rest and transferred to someone else. The right to develop the land is one. Under a TDR system, an owner can sell this development right or the right to develop for a specific use to another property owner who is required by statute to obtain a specified number of development rights before developing his or her own property. Because TDR would require state enabling legislation and would require a sophisticated planning staff for administration, TDR is probably not feasible in coastal North Carolina. If these problems could be remedied, TDR could be an effective tool in guiding development in the most sensitive pocosins.

Local environmental impact statements (EIS) are currently authorized for major developments by the North Carolina Environmental Policy Act of 1971 (N.C. Gen. Stat., Section 113A-1 et seq. [1978]). These impact statements are modeled after federal impact statements. The local EIS has not been widely used in North Carolina and thus its potential for pocosin management remains untested.

TAXATION

A third control mechanism available for use in a pocosin management program is preferential tax assessment. A preferential taxation system assesses property at its current income producing capacity, rather than at its potential value in a developed state. The purpose of such a system of taxation is to remove some of the economic pressure to develop fragile resources by reducing the tax burden on them. Preferential taxation must be used in conjunction with other land use controls in order to prevent speculation.

North Carolina's preferential tax assessment statute, N.C. Gen. Stat., Sec. 105-277.2-277.7 [1979]), covers agricultural lands but does not extend to open lands or natural areas. North Carolina uses a deferred taxation system that requires that the tax assessor keep two sets of books for eligible lands, one containing the usual market-value assessment, and one containing the use-value assessment. The taxpayer pays according to the use-value assessment until the land is converted to a higher use, and the difference between the amounts he pays under use-value and the amount which would be due under a market-value system is considered deferred tax. With the termination of eligibility, all deferred taxes become due. North Carolina requires the payment of deferred tax for the five years previous to termination of eligibility.

SPENDING

Localities may be able to utilize their spending power to affect a management strategy for pocosins. The use of a capital improvements program as a schedule for extension of public services would tend to guide growth into areas more suitable for development than pocosins. Localities can also influence federal spending which would affect pocosins in their jurisdiction by use of the consistency requirement of the Federal Coastal Zone Management Act. That legislation requires that federal action in the coastal zone of a state having an approved coastal management program be consistent with the state program. Therefore, if the local plan includes a policy regarding pocosin management, federal spending must conform to the local plan.

CONCLUSION

Because pocosins have been a neglected resource, virtually no existing management strategy focuses on the resource as a whole. Without an overall strategy, drainage of pocosins will continue without regard for the effects on pocosins themselves or on the land and water surrounding them.

This paper has shown that existing regulations and techniques could be molded with little modification into a management strategy for pocosins. A stronger program might be achieved by the passage of major new legislation. It appears that progress can be made with slight changes in current regulations and some additional controls. However, to be successful, the program must have definite resource goals that are politically viable and fiscally possible. Also, the management strategy must directly focus on pocosins rather than addressing the pocosins tangentially.

LITERATURE CITED

Notre Dame Lawyer, 1977. Note: The wetlands controversy: A coastal concern washes inland. Vol. 52:1017.

Reitz, A. W., 1974. Environmental planning: Law of land and resources. North American International, Washington, D.C.

Schoenbaum, T. J. and R. H. Rosenberg, 1976. The legal implementation of coastal zone management: The North Carolina model. Duke Law Journal, Duke University, Durham, N.C.

U.S. Department of Commerce, 1978. State of North Carolina coastal zone management program and final environmental impact statement.

A Policy for Pocosin Preservation

Arthur W. Cooper

ABSTRACT

A policy is a definite course of action to guide future decisions. It is determined in light of given conditions and is selected from feasible alternatives. Policies must be legal, constitutional, and politically practical. There are four major uses of North Carolina's pocosin resource: agriculture, forestry, mining, and nonconsumptive uses such as fishing and hunting. Certain uses, such as mining and fishing and hunting, are mutually exclusive. Other combinations of uses, such as hunting and forestry, are more compatible. However, some publics benefit and some publics lose from each combination of uses.

Present policy for the use of pocosins involves the undeclared application of governmental actions which are biased toward consumptive uses of pocosins. North Carolina's interests would be served better by a public policy fostering more preservation. This policy should be based upon a full inventory and analysis of the dynamics of the pocosin ecosystem. It should involve preservation of pocosin areas that have been identified as undisturbed habitats or habitats important for the preservation of rare and endangered species.

Agencies now managing pocosins must implement integrated management plans designed to perpetuate endangered pocosin habitats and species. Exploitation of nonrenewable resources should occur only after thorough analysis of environmental and economic impacts. Agriculture and forestry should be carried out in accordance with accepted management practices developed cooperatively by government and practitioners. Mining is a consumptive use of pocosin woodlands, a renewable energy resource, and must be very carefully studied and considered in the context of a statewide energy policy before being permitted.

Key Words: agriculture, fishing and hunting, forestry, peat mining, policy, preservation

INTRODUCTION

Development of policy is one of the most difficult processes in which government is involved. Policies evolve from a balancing of technical, economic, social, and political factors. There is constant pressure for change in policy as circumstances change and as groups with interests in a policy gain or lose political influence. Nowhere are these facts better illustrated than in the field of natural resources. Here, there is a continuing tension among professional resource managers, resource exploiters, and proponents of limited use. Development of a policy for management of North Carolina's pocosin resource has all the elements of the classical debate over resource policy. In this paper, I will make use of the technical, economic, social, and political issues discussed in this symposium to develop a preservation oriented policy for management of North Carolina's pocosins.

GENERAL CONSIDERATIONS

A policy according to Webster is "a definite course or method of action selected from among alternatives and in light of given conditions to guide and determine future decisions." Three important elements of that definition need elaboration.

First, a policy is "determined in light of given conditions." In the case of natural resources, this means: (1) determining the relevant facts concerning the resource to be managed—its biological properties, the physical conditions pertaining to it, and the economic and social dimensions of its exploitation; (2) determining how use of the resource will affect those properties and the properties of other interrelated resources; and (3) determining the impacts of alternative uses of the resource on various user and interest groups. This symposium represents an integrated effort to determine the "given conditions" for pocosins. Key questions addressed in the previous sessions include: what are pocosins, where are they located, how do they function, how does development affect them and the systems that surround them, and how do the attitudes of groups with interests in the pocosin resource affect its management.

The second feature of a policy is that it is "selected from among alternatives." The policy analyst erects a reasonable set of strategies for consideration. The consequences of each alternative strategy are considered and an effort is made to predict, at some reasonable level of confidence, the outcome of different courses of action. Finally, an alternative, or course of action, is selected.

Third, a policy is "a definite course of action to guide future decisions." It consists of a single or selected set of strategies that will translate it into the desired action. The steps to be taken can be executed in a variety of ways. They may involve simple administrative directives, the development of executive orders, the drafting of regulations, and in some cases, the development of legislation. In the case of pocosins, the "definite course of action to guide future decisions" involves government actions and programs and private sector decisions which foster the goals that we specify through legislation and programs.

Government policies must be legal and constitutional, and they must be politically practical. A policy must not infringe on basic legal freedoms and it must have enough public support to be implemented.

APPLICATION TO PRESENT USES OF POCOSINS

With that general background, let's examine how these three elements of policy development relate to future management of North Carolina's pocosin resource. The pocosin resource, as characterized in this symposium, and the interests of the various groups (e.g., industry, conservationists, local government) seeking to use or preserve pocosins define the dimensions of the management problems that our policies must address.

The major land uses of pocosins, in order of decreasing impact on the environment, are mining, agriculture, forestry, and the more passive uses such as water regulation, fishing, hunting, and limited recreation. Each of these uses has its own interest group or groups, each of which is of different size and of different political influence. The interactions among users and interest groups can be illustrated by considering peat mining. Such mining has a beneficial effect on energy and mining interests. It also has a beneficial effect on agriculture because it increases the supply of available energy and makes certain mineral soils underlying the shallow peat available for agricultural use. These soils are alleged to be more productive when farmed than the peat surface overlying them (Barnes, this volume).

The relationship of peat mining to forestry is similar to its relationship to agriculture. However, as far as hunting, preservation of endangered species, commercial fishing, and recreation are concerned, mining is entirely negative (Monschein, Street and McClees, Richardson et al., this volume). Mining reduces these uses drastically and creates environmental problems that are destructive of the natural values of pocosins.

The impacts of forestry on natural values of pocosins are less severe, largely because forestry is less intensive (Campbell and Hughes, Monschein, this volume). Hunting is compatible with forestry, and even management for many rare and endangered species can be incorporated into forest management plans.

The conclusions to be drawn from such an analysis are obvious. Some uses, such as mining and hunting, are strongly antagonistic. Other relationships are more compatible as, for example, the relationships between protection of endangered species and forestry or commercial fishing and forestry.

Finally, as the policy analyst is painfully aware, some members of the public stand to benefit while some lose from each combination of uses.

In formulating a pocosin policy, we must bear in mind that there are perhaps 1 to 2 million acres of pocosin land and perhaps as much as half of that area is already modified through farming or forestry (Richardson et al., this volume). At least 100,000 acres are already publicly owned (Taggert, this volume). Some of these areas are or could be preserved and plans for their development are subject to public environmental impact review. In terms of policy development, we are concerned with what sort of change or nonchange we will encourage in those pocosins that are not yet developed or publicly owned and what sort of strategies and uses we are going to apply to the lands that have either been converted to intensive use or have been preserved.

A PRESERVATION ORIENTED POLICY

Consideration of a pocosin management policy can begin with the present situation in as much as it represents a *policy* now in force. That policy can be described as the unorganized combination of a variety of public programs, regulatory and promotional, with private initiatives. Some of the actors behind this policy are vigorously pushing development while others are vigorously pushing preservation. Regulatory programs are being applied by government agencies unevenly and without any general rules of guidance other than those developed by the agency itself on the basis of its own interpretation of its mission. Thus, the policy that exists now is neither one of development nor preservation, but one which, because of the weight of public pressure and the strength of the interest groups pushing for development, tilts toward intensive development unless some intervention occurs.

My own preference, and the one that I feel would be wisest for North Carolina, is the development by state government of a new policy that will provide opportunities for both development and preservation, but which will be more conservative than our present policy, hence tilting toward preservation. I feel this is desirable because such a policy will preserve a greater array of options for the future than will our current policy. Furthermore, my proposed policy would provide a cushion against the unknown hazards associated with development when it occurs too rapidly. Thus I will pose a policy that provides for balanced use and preservation, but one which maximizes opportunities for preservation and which preserves options for the future.

Before explaining my proposed policy, I want to stress that it is based upon existing laws, agencies, and programs and is not dependent on any new legislation. I do not feel that it would be at all wise to predicate a proposed policy on new legislation; it is highly unlikely that any such legislation could be passed. An attempt to develop new legislation clearly could create more problems than it would solve.

What should a new policy entail? The first element is a full inventory of the pocosin resource. This conference on pocosins represents a first effort to prepare such an inventory. As a digression, it is worth noting that there is a remarkable parallel between this pocosin conference and the conference on estuaries that was conducted at Sapelo Island in 1964. That conference was the first effort to organize our knowledge of estuaries and salt marshes. In a real way, it was a progenitor of coastal zone management and wetland protection programs. It began the political process by which our attitude toward management of coastal resources was changed dramatically. We probably could effect the same sort of attitudinal change toward pocosins.

In the pattern of the Sapelo Island conference, the first aspect of the inventory should be to define the pocosin system and to understand its natural values and functions. Although this conference has summarized a good deal of what we know about pocosins, much still needs to be documented. For example, the interaction of pocosins with adjacent estuaries needs to be understood. The second aspect of the inventory should be the identification of areas that are critical for preservation. What are the key habitats that are not now preserved, what are the requirements of rare and endangered species, and where are there pocosin areas that might be appropiate for preservation? The North Carolina Heritage Program has made a good beginning on such an inventory and it is important that its work continue.

We also need to obtain data on the distribution of other key natural resources such as minerals, energy, and archaeological features. We need to identify the relative values of the unmodified lands for agriculture and forestry and then make thorough economic analyses of the various use and preservation options. This conference is a good beginning on such analyses but we must push them through to completion.

The second element of the policy is implementation of a series of private and governmental actions that are consistent with the inventory data. The first necessary action is preservation, by whatever legitimate strategy, of areas of pocosins that are generally accepted as being worthy of preservation. Such efforts will involve a variety of alternatives such as regulations, private preservation, purchase, and easements (Roe, this volume). For practical reasons, the only alternative that is likely to be very rewarding is one that is clearly in the best interests of the private landowner, such as bargain sale or donation. If preservation is not in the landowner's interest, it is not likely to occur, because it is unlikely that enough public money will be available to buy all areas worthy of preservation.

Another strategy that should be considered is transfer of development rights. In this process an owner of property agrees to set aside a certain portion of that property in an undeveloped condition in return for the right to develop intensively the remainder of the property. Whether one likes the technique or not, it does represent a legitimate strategy for allocating land uses, preserving some and allowing the remainder to continue in production. Pocosins seem to be amenable to such treatment. Owners can set aside extensive buffer areas along water courses to allow drainage water to spread out and be filtered in return for the right to develop intensively other sections of the property away from water bodies. Obviously, such actions are complex, require a clear understanding of the resource, and involve intensive negotiations between property owners and government agencies.

On publicly owned pocosins, management programs must be designed to perpetuate the pocosin system, its critical habitats, and its rare and endangered species. With 100,000 acres now under some form of preservation, it seems that all but the most widely ranging of rare and endangered species, such as the black bear, likely could be accommodated within the lands that are now in public ownership. But they will not be accommodated unless the agencies managing publicly preserved lands develop coordinated plans to preserve rare and endangered plants and animals that require preservation. Such programs will involve extensive manipulation of the environment and will involve more complex actions than simply preserving and protecting lands from people. The required management will be much more than preservation.

Where there are unique nonrenewable resources such as minerals, intensive, case by case examinations must be made through exhaustive environmental impact analyses. These studies must involve coordinated efforts by government and development interests and must be carried out before any significant development of resources takes place.

Where agriculture and forestry exist on pocosin lands, or where such activities are proposed, government agencies should ensure, through regulatory programs, that public values are protected. Perhaps the best way to do this is to develop a series of accepted management practices which are designed to minimize impacts on adjacent waters, because impacts on water quality are the most immediate and serious effects of agriculture (Gilliam and Skaggs, this volume) and forestry. These practices would include: (1) the setting aside of buffer strips to absorb nutrients from surface drainage waters; (2) the regulation and management of drainage discharges; (3) guidelines for the application and timing of fertilizer and pesticide use; (4) for forestry, guidelines on harvesting and replanting; and, (5) in all cases, coordination with wildlife interests. These guidelines, once developed, should then be incorporated into any permit program, forming the basis for agriculture and forestry practices in this environment.

In light of the antagonisms that exist among government regulatory programs and the forestry and agriculture communities, development of these guidelines is likely to be difficult. This is unfortunate, because the development of guidelines should not be that difficult. Agriculture and forestry interests know what needs to be done and, in many cases, are already doing it or taking steps in that direction. I think it would be to their own advantage to step forward voluntarily and develop these standards for themselves.

A POLICY FOR PEAT MINING

I have left peat mining until last because it is a special situation. Peat mining is a one-way use of a renewable resource and, of all the uses that have been discussed for pocosins, it concerns me the most. The peat mining that is being proposed for North Carolina is different from that carried out in high latitudes, because on pocosins there is a greater potential for agriculture and forestry. Uses of our peats are not climate limited in the sense that high latitude uses of peats are limited. Furthermore, peat mining must be considered on the same basis as the mining of every other fossil fuel. We can "use it up just as fast as we can, right now, and while we are using it up we can develop another strategy." If we follow this practice, we will end up forty years from now with the peat gone and with no solution to the energy problem. Our past policies for exploitation of fossil fuels lead me to have serious reservations about peat mining.

Government policy should ensure that a series of fundamental questions is asked before peat mining is permitted. The first question involves the energetics of the mining itself. How much energy will be recovered in mined peat and how much will be used in mining? Second, what is the energy balance over time with respect to the relationship between the energy now contained in the peat versus the energy that will be needed later to drain and pump these lands once their elevation is reduced. Third, is there an opportunity for the use of natural pocosin vegetation as a source of energy. Policy makers should insist on an analysis of the energetics of harvesting and burning natural pocosin vegetation rather than burning the peat that supports it. It should be demonstrated to be infeasible before a commitment is made to removal of the vegetation and destruction of the peat. Finally, analyses should be required stressing other alternatives that might produce the same amount of energy. For example, could a public investment in solar energy be made that would produce the same, or greater, amount of usable energy in eastern North Carolina. So far, we have not seen any such analyses.

Obviously, the pilot studies for peat mining need to be executed, because that is the only way we can get some of the answers we need. At the same time, the questions that I have raised need to be impartially analyzed so when it comes time to set policy on the use of peat, the decision will be an informed one. Finally, if peat mining is ever approved by the state, it should be approved as a part of an overall state energy strategy and not as an isolated, incremental decision.

CONCLUSION

The policy I have outlined probably will not please advocates of pocosin preservation and it clearly will not please proponents of development. It is, however, consistent with pocosin ecology and is, I think, in the best interests of North Carolina. Because it makes use of existing law, regulations, and administrative machinery, it could be implemented relatively quickly. Whether it is implemented or not depends largely on the urgency that state agency officials attach to better management of pocosins. Scientists and others who feel strongly that the future quality of life of the lower coastal plain is closely tied to wise management of pocosins will probably have to develop a sense of urgency in state officials because there are powerful economic forces that will profit from maintaining the present uncoordinated, development oriented policy.

Conference Critique

An Outside Perspective on the Pocosins Conference and Suggestions for Future Work

Dennis F. Whigham

ABSTRACT

Pocosin development, primarily for conversion to agricultural and forestry uses, is progressing at a rapid rate. There is little known about the structure and function of pocosins, yet it is clear that they are important components of regional environmental stability. Major potential impacts seem to be possible degradation of downstream estuarine areas by increased freshwater runoff and use of agricultural chemicals, loss of critical habitat, conversion of the area from an atmospheric carbon sink to a carbon source, and a smaller than expected per capita increase in the regional economy. The overall social and political implications are, however, not well established and there is a definite lack of public awareness about the ecological importance of pocosin wetlands.

Key Words: economics, pocosin, drainage, estuarine degradation, social impacts, public education, habitat loss, wildlife, ecology

INTRODUCTION

This conference was viewed as a first step toward formulation of management guidelines for pocosin development. The stated purposes were to assess the current state of knowledge about the ecology of pocosin wildlands, synthesize information on current and projected uses of pocosins, attempt to characterize pocosin development and potential environmental impacts, and discuss the economic, legal, and political implications related to pocosin development and/or preservation. Because so many different topics were presented at the conference and because the audience that will examine the proceedings is equally diverse, I was asked to provide an overview of the papers. My analysis of the proceedings is from the perspective of a scientist who has been conducting research on wetland ecosystems in an area of the country that has already placed great development pressure on wetland systems: the Chesapeake Bay region.

My objectives in this chapter are to discuss problems that might arise from unorganized development of wetlands on a large-scale regional basis, present an overview of each of the conference sessions, and discuss issues that I believe must be considered if an adequate pocosin management plan is ever to emerge. When discussing the sessions, I will emphasize the relationship between the conclusions that were made and the adequacy of the data bases that were used by the authors.

REGIONAL DEVELOPMENT OF WETLANDS: WHAT ARE THE MAJOR IMPLICATIONS?

Pocosins occupy approximately 20% of the North Carolina coastal plain and any attempt to manage them should automatically require a large-scale interdisciplinary effort. Private, industrial, and conservation groups as well as local, state, and federal governmental agencies must be involved if regional problems are to be avoided and if a suitable management plan is to be developed. The purpose of any management plan should be to provide for conservation of an adequate amount of pocosin habitat as well as to meet the needs of development interests. What major ecological problems might result from large-scale regional development of wetlands? An answer to this question requires an understanding of the consequences that result from alteration of natural wetland systems.

Although the conference participants failed to agree unanimously on a simple narrow definition, it is clear that all pocosins are characterized by the presence of standing water, either continuously or periodically, and can generally be classified as a southern bog ecosystem. Development, either for small-scale residential use or large-scale agribusiness and/or forestry, requires drainage of the land. On a small scale, drainage impacts may not be severe but it is clear from the proceedings of this conference that drainage of North Carolina's coastal plain has occurred, is occurring, and will continue to occur on a large scale and at an accelerated pace. What are the major impacts of pocosin conversion?

When wetlands are ditched for conversion to residential, timber, or agricultural uses, the hydrologic cycle is modified. Runoff is quickly diverted into the ditches and a larger percentage of the annual precipitation is exported to downstream areas at a faster rate than occurred under natural conditions. In coastal regions, the impacts that large-scale hydrologic modifications would have on estuarine processes must be considered. In addition to removal of water, conversion of pocosin land into agricultural and forestry uses requires extensive site preparation which may include the use of organic pesticides and fertilizers.

A third area of concern is the impact that drainage of extensive wetland areas will have on the global carbon dioxide cycle. Undoubtedly, a large percentage of the carbon that is stored in pocosin substrates will be oxidized on site or elsewhere if significant amounts of peat are mined and exported for energy production. The coastal plain region would be converted from a carbon sink to a carbon source. An important question is whether or not the oxidized carbon will have a significant influence on regional CO_2 levels which may affect the global changes in the carbon cycle that are currently causing so much concern (Armentano, 1980).

A fourth concern would be the impact that extensive regional drainage has on groundwater quality and quantity. North Carolina has a humid climate with adequate rainfall so that irrigation would be required only infrequently. The major industrial user of water from the underlying aquifer is Texasgulf, Inc., and the long-term impact of that operation is unknown. It seems unlikely, however, that groundwater depletion will result from pocosin alteration. A major potential problem is contamination of the aquifers through the use of chemicals. In drier climates (e.g., California), conversion of productive wetland soils into agricultural uses has created not only regional water supply problems but also groundwater contamination problems.

Finally, what are the economic implications of large-scale development of a regional resource? The loss of wetland resources will have a direct negative impact on certain segments of society (e.g., hunters). Positive impacts would be the creation of jobs as well as generation of economic growth that would be directly associated with development. However, the regional economic impacts of large-scale pocosin development may not be that large even though individual developers benefit. Pocosin development is diffuse; few people are employed and little urbanization results from the utilization of vast acreages of land. Furthermore, if pocosin development results in regional water quality problems, the overall development impacts would be undesirable because of estuarine eutrophication which would have negative impacts on one of the largest economic groups in that portion of the state. In short, all of these issues need to be considered if a wise course of action is to be followed in the management and development of North Carolina's pocosins.

SESSION OVERVIEWS

Introductory Session

The overview paper by Richardson et al. demonstrated that drainage of pocosin wildlands is proceeding at an alarming rate and that there is a real need to develop an integrated plan to ensure that development of the remaining pocosin wildlands will not result in severe regional environmental problems. Richardson calculated that over 16% of the coastal plain (2.2 million acres; 914,000 ha) could be classified as pocosin and that over 50% has been totally converted or drained for development since 1962. An additional 600,000 to 800,000 acres will quite likely be totally developed during the next ten years.

Richardson and Thompson identified five groups that are, or should be, interested in pocosin development: (1) governmental agencies, (2) industry, (3) conservation groups, (4) social scientists, and (5) natural scientists. They suggested that these groups have the expertise needed to develop a management strategy that provides for the maintenance of both a healthy regional environment and economy while avoiding environmental disasters as well as confrontations that so often result when so many special interest groups are attempting to influence the decision making process.

Resource Ecology Session

The purpose of the papers in this session was to summarize information on natural features of pocosin wetlands and to provide a framework for understanding structural and functional attributes of pocosin ecosystems.

Conference participants were unable to arrive at a common definition for pocosins because of differences in interpretation of what categories of lands would be called pocosins. Most differences of opinion were due to varying interpretations of the types of plants, hydrologic characteristics, and substrate characteristics of pocosins. If there is any unifying definition, it should be found in the wetland classification system of the United States Fish and Wildlife Service (Cowardin et al., 1979). Pocosins would be classified as Palustrine *systems* and would fall into either the Scrub-Shrub (vegetation less than 6 meters) or Forested (vegetation more than 6 meters) *classes*. Other designations would be: (1) Broad-leaved evergreen, *subclass*; (2) *water regimes* that are saturated, semipermanently flooded, intermittently flooded, and seasonally flooded; (3) fresh-acid *water chemistry*; and (4) organic *soil*.

A universally acceptable definition for pocosins is not easy to resolve but, nonetheless, is central to planning because the resource must be delineated before it can be managed. Christensen et al. described four types of pocosin wetlands based on an earlier study by Woodwell (1956). Most pocosin wetlands are dominated by several species of evergreen shrubs and/or pond pine. Except for the most hydric situations, the development and maintenance of pocosin wetlands appear to be strongly influenced by fire and many areas would proceed through succession to hardwood dominated sites if fire were eliminated.

Pocosin biota includes a number of unique components although Wilbur indicated that the fauna is not as well known as the flora, either taxonomically or ecologically. Pocosins provide the last remaining habitat for a number of species including the black bear and, perhaps, panther.

Wilbur's paper is important because it introduced the issue of managing the resource on a regional basis rather than considering each wetland in a case by case approach. Central to his discussion is the proposition that reduction of pocosin habitat below some critical, yet unknown, level could result in species extinction even though some pocosin habitat would remain. He discussed components of island biogeographic theory which, in this case, is important because the coastal plain wetlands are being fragmented and the result will be the production of islands of wetland habitat that are isolated from one another in a sea of managed lands. Wilbur presented important guidelines that must be considered as management plans are being developed.

It does not appear that any animal species is currently doomed to extinction because of habitat elimination. The pine barren treefrog (*Hyla andersoni*) may, however, be endangered because of loss of habitat and change in the quality of the habitat that remains. This species has specific breeding requirements; especially important are water chemistry and water flow characteristics. Monschein indicated that although some wildlife species might increase in number as a result of pocosin development, others will surely decline; the most vulnerable species is the black bear. Wilbur suggested that although pocosins provide suitable food and cover, bear would do better in other habitats. Pocosins are used as the last refuge by bears because the more preferred habitats have been eliminated or are too small in extent to sustain a viable bear population.

At this time, very little can be said about internal functional processes such as primary production, nutrient cycling, and decomposition. Only generalities about input and output characteristics are currently available although Christensen's research in the Croatan National Forest will provide important information on many processes, especially as they are affected by fire.

Citing work by Barber et al. (1979) and Skaggs et al. (1980), Richardson showed that it seems unlikely that pocosins are able to retain phosphorus and that the use of fertilizers on drained peat substrates will likely result in increased phosphorus runoff to estuarine areas. This phenomenon has been shown for other types of peat based systems although research findings are not always clear (Tilton and Kadlec, 1979; Zoltek et al., 1979; Ewel and Odum, 1978), and much more research is needed on the movement and storage of phosphorus in peat dominated substrates. Richardson also considered the impacts of pocosin drainage on the global carbon dioxide cycle and suggested the large amounts of CO_2 have already been released from drained North Carolina pocosins.

Daniel provided important insight into the hydrologic implications of pocosin drainage. He showed that natural pocosins regulate the rate at which water is delivered to downstream estuarine areas. Much of the net annual precipitation is retained in the wetlands for a long enough period of time that most is lost to the atmosphere via evapotranspiration rather than as stream runoff. Pocosin drainage increases the runoff intensity and shifts the primary pathway of water loss from evapotranspiration to stream runoff. On a regional basis, there is evidence that this may cause salinity fluctuations in downstream estuarine areas. Daniel also indicated that ditching is likely to result in degradation of estuarine water quality but additional mass balance studies are definitely needed.

Nonindustrial Values Session

The major conclusions of the papers in this session were that an insufficient number of pocosin wetlands are owned by the public or are controlled by private conservation interests. Second, the areas that are currently protected are not evenly distributed; the northeastern portion of the coastal plain is poorly represented, given the amount of pocosin land that occurs there. Existing means are available for obtaining additional pocosin areas but a key missing element is public awareness of the importance of pocosins.

Perhaps the only aspect of pocosin wildlands that is important in the public image is their use for hunting, trapping, etc. As noted, Monschein suggested that pocosin development would result in increased numbers of some game species but others, such as the black bear, would be eliminated unless a suitable management plan is developed. How many and what should be the configuration of sizes of pocosin habitat that must be retained in order to maintain viable black bear populations in the coastal plain region? Answers to this question are not possible because there still are not enough data on the ecological requirements of the species. The paper by Wilbur is also germane to this issue.

The other papers in this session centered on the issues of ownership patterns, the role of public education in increasing information about pocosins, and means that are available for obtaining pocosin lands. Taggert, for purposes of describing the ownership patterns, divided the coastal plain into four sections. The most striking feature of his analysis was that only a small percentage of total pocosin land is currently protected and that the distribution of protected areas is not well balanced. Protected areas are especially lacking in the section of the state from the Pamlico River northward. He also noted that very few areas that are protected are using fire as a management tool. As shown by Christensen et al., in the absence of fire, many pocosins would succeed to hardwood forest which might result in the elimination of many interesting pocosin species.

An important factor that seems to be missing is an understanding of the importance of pocosins by the general public. The short-term possibility of alleviating this situation seems bleak for, as Ashton showed, there are few ongoing public education programs and most of the existing programs are poorly supported. He presented a framework for development of a plan for large-scale public education but the possibility of success seems remote because of the current economic climate. In addition, there does not seem to be any readily identifiable constituency that is willing to push for implementation of any public education program.

Industrial Values Session

This set of papers was very informative and produced, for me, the largest number of notes and potential questions about the impacts of pocosin development. Street and McClees provided information, and a warning, about one impact that may affect the economic future of the region. Coastal fisheries, both commercial and recreational, are enormous and crucial to the regional economy. Several factors threaten that resource but most important to the present discussion are those that cause deterioration of estuarine water quality. Street and McClees's analysis of the shrimp industry shows a definite decline in the resource and they suggested that one possible cause has been deterioration of water quality associated with pocosin development. They suggested that the primary pollutant, in this case, is the amount of fresh water that is delivered to the estuary because the absorptive capacity of intact pocosin wetlands has been eliminated by ditching and resultant drainage.

It is unclear if the problems may be due primarily to development of pocosin wetlands or due to increased development on the piedmont. Water quality of the coastal estuaries is certainly affected by development of upstream watersheds in the piedmont (Humenik et al., 1980) but decreased estuarine water quality, as described by Richardson, may also result from pocosin development. In Maryland, three counties that border the estuarine portion of the Patuxent River have filed suit against the state and EPA for negligence because they believe that estuarine water quality degradation has been due to the inability of the state and EPA to control development of the upstream watersheds. Most of the problems seem to be due to nonpoint runoff from agricultural lands and/or point source discharges from sewage plants. The same problems, if they aren't already present, will surely occur in North Carolina as development accelerates in the piedmont. Unlike Maryland, however, North Carolina will have the additional problem of uncontrolled development of the extensive pocosin wetlands that border the estuarine areas.

From the papers of Campbell and Hughes, and Barnes, it is clear that with proper management, pocosin lands can be used to produce high yield agricultural crops and wood products. A certain percentage of pocosin wetlands can also provide peat which can be used for several purposes including energy production. Economically, it appears that those uses can be or are currently economically profitable. Based on the number of ditches that I saw while flying over the coastal plain, it seems that development will proceed at an accelerated pace. The question remains, however, regarding the implications that development will have on the environmental stability of the region. None of the authors addressed that issue and it seems unlikely that answers could be provided at this time.

In my opinion, the following issues should be of primary concern.

1. What is the impact of peat extraction and conversion of pocosins for timber production on water quality of downstream areas? Barber et al. (1979) and Skaggs et al. (1980) show that changes can result from agricultural runoff.
2. Are the same problems associated with existing management plans for peat farming and forestry production?
3. Are impacts that result from development in the coastal plain as large as those that are or will result from development in the piedmont region?

In addition to the studies by Humenik et al. (1980), Kuenzler and his colleagues have been studying the impacts that floodplain forests have on water quality. It may be that their work will provide answers to the questions posed but it seems likely that answers will require additional research. Evidence was provided in this session that would indicate that the development industries are actively pursuing the questions of the impacts that their development has on estuarine water quality. First Colony Farms, Inc., has cooperated with scientists and it seems likely that effective cooperation could be fostered if all parties become committed to the idea of pursuing development with sound conservation practices.

Based on Barber et al. (1979), it would appear that all runoff from drained pocosin lands should be routed through additional wetlands (intact marshes) before it is permitted to enter streams that drain into the estuary. The wetlands could remove nutrients as well as suspended particulate matter. It will be necessary to determine the size and composition of the most effective buffer zones that are needed in each instance but, given the present state of our technology, the problem is not insurmountable.

Resource Economics Session

The papers in this session dealt with the economics of pocosin development. Harwood analyzed the economic potential for using peat for energy production. As also shown by Campbell, it is feasible to harvest peat from certain types of pocosin wetlands and those resources are very large. The major hurdle to using peat for energy production is that there is no current market. As other fuel prices increase, peat may become economically more competitive and a market will develop.

Lindenmuth and Vasievich performed a sensitivity analysis to determine if large-scale timber management is economically sound. They concluded, as do Campbell and Hughes, that pocosins can provide high yields of timber at a profit even though the initial investment is large. This is due to current and projected costs of timber products which have increased significantly in recent years. The data used in their analysis are, however, speculative because few silvicultural data can be found in studies of altered pocosin wetlands. Clearly, more data are needed, but it appears that conversion of pocosins into timber production is economically feasible.

Postel provided an excellent overview of the natural functions of pocosin wildlands. The preservation benefits are hunting and other related activities, maintenance of estuarine water quality, water recharge and storage capacity, flood control benefits, critical habitat maintenance, ecosystem preservation, and option demand. Because data are lacking to assess critically many of the benefits, she suggested that a conservation policy toward pocosin development is warranted until a regional development plan can be produced.

Law and Policy Session

The papers in this session identified the political realities associated with pocosin development, discussed the legal strategies that could be used to preserve pocosins, and suggested policies to bring about a proper management plan for the development and preservation of pocosins.

Heath painted a rather bleak picture for enactment of adequate pocosin protection measures because the primary development interest groups are politically very strong. He suggested that development of an effective management plan will require that the preservation support constituency demonstrate that an adequate mix of developed and nondeveloped lands is in the long-term public benefit.

Brower analyzed the methods that are currently available for perserving pocosins. He recommended that existing avenues be utilized and that these techniques be exhaused before additional legislation is sought.

Cooper presented some strategies for developing management plans. Basically, there is no current policy (local or state) for pocosin management even though pocosins clearly provide many benefits to man. Cooper suggested that any emerging policy should provide for preservation and development with a tilt toward preservation because much is unknown about the long-term consequences of pocosin development. This would provide for future options. A management policy should be drafted by all affected parties and should be based on existing legislation. He outlined the minimum planning that is needed.

THE FUTURE: WHAT IS NEEDED?

Cooper presented a succinct summary of research that is needed as well as an approach to developing a plan to assure a long-term regional stability.

The basis of his argument is that we do not know enough about the social benefits of pocosins and the management plan should be one of caution and conservation to provide for future options. My personal opinion is that the potential for avoiding problems is slight unless a large constituency is developed to champion the cause of pocosin preservation.

A number of questions need to be answered and I would suggest that several need to be addressed very soon. Although the idea is not new (Odum and Odum, 1976), there is a definite need to interface ecological and economic theory to assure a workable plan for the management of the remaining pocosin wetlands. Considerations of economic benefits are much easier than analysis of both positive and negative benefits of nondirect impacts (e.g., compare papers by Lindenmuth and Vasievich, and Postel). Postel lists nondirect benefits that are important but it will not be an easy task to complete the analysis as has been shown by the continuing arguments about the value of tidal wetlands (Gosselink et al., 1974; Shabman and Batie, 1978 and 1979; Odum, 1979).

Quantifying ecological characteristics will not be easy either. There are few data on structural and functional attributes of pocosins. An expanded research effort is definitely needed with particular emphasis being given to:

1. Performing a state inventory as a first step in planning for the maintenance of regional diversity patterns. As this conference has shown, there seems to be enough interest in this task although the position of development groups is unclear. Special attention must be focused on the establishment of additional conservation areas, especially in the northern section of the coastal plain.
2. Research on the correct mixes of natural and managed lands that are needed to minimize downstream development impacts as well as maintain suitable habitat diversity to ensure that species extinction does not occur. More specifically, research is needed to determine:
   a. The contribution of nutrients, sediments, etc., that reach the estuaries from piedmont sources versus the magnitude of the same materials from natural and altered pocosins;
   b. The role that buffer zones play in ameliorating potential runoff problems from ditched pocosin lands. Richardson cites evidence that agricultural lands will export excess nutrients but there are no data from sites altered for forestry production or peat mining. It would be helpful if water from ditched areas were routed through wetlands. I would suggest that development interests and researchers interact to determine the size and composition of buffer zones that would be most efficient.

Comments from the audience clearly showed that development of the coastal plain is entering an exponential phase and that the impacts, including bringing seemingly unwanted cultural changes to the region, are not fully appreciated in political circles. Because the public seems to be almost unaware of the importance of pocosins, enlightenment must come from researchers, conservation groups and the media. The proceedings of the conference are the first step in a process that I hope will ultimately lead to a suitable solution so that society does not lose yet another portion of the biosphere because some people failed to interact for the good of all.

LITERATURE CITED

Armentano, T. V., 1980. Drainage of organic soils as a factor in the world carbon cycle. Bioscience, 30:828-834.

Barber, R. T., W. W. Kirby-Smith, and P. E. Parsley, 1979. Wetland alterations for agriculture, pp. 642-651. In: P. E. Greeson, J. R. Clark, and J. E. Clark, eds., Wetland functions and values: The state of our understanding. American Water Works Assn., St. Paul, Minn.

Cowardin, L. M., V. Carter, F. C. Golet, and T. E. LaRoe, 1979. Classification of wetlands and deepwater habitats of the United States. Office of Biological Services, Fish and Wildlife Service, U.S. Department of the Interior, Washington, D.C. FWS/OBS-79/31, 103 pp.

Ewel, K. C., and H. T. Odum, 1978. Cypress swamps for nutrient removal and wastewater recycling, pp. 181-198. In: W. P. Wanietista and W. W. Eckenfelder, Jr., eds., Advances in water and wastewater treatment: Biological nutrient removal. Ann Arbor Sci. Publ. Inc., Ann Arbor, Mich.

Gosselink, J. G., E. P. Odum, and R. M. Pope, 1974. The value of the tidal marsh. Center for Wetland Resources, Louisiana State Univ., Baton Rouge, La. LSU-SG-70-03, 30 pp.

Humenik, F. J., L. F. Bliven, M. R. Overcash, and F. Kochler, 1980. Rural nonpoint source water quality in a southeastern watershed. J. Water Poll. Control Fed., 52:29-43.

Odum, E. P., 1979. Rebuttal of Economic value of natural coastal wetlands: A critique. Coast Zone Mgt. J., 5:231-237.

Odum, H. T., and E. C. Odum, 1976. The energy basis for man and nature. McGraw-Hill, New York, N.Y., 288 pp.

Skaggs, R. W., T. J. Sheets, and J. S. Barnes, 1980. Effect of agricultural land development on drainage waters in the North Carolina tidewater region. Report No. 159, Water Resources Research Institute of the University of North Carolina, Chapel Hill, 164 pp.

Shabman, L., and S. S. Batie, 1978. Economic value of natural coastal wetlands: A critique. Coast Zone Mgt. J., 4:231-248.

Shabman, L., and S. S. Batie, 1979. A reply to the rebuttal Economic value of natural coastline wetlands: A critique. Coast. Zone Mgt. J., 5:243-244.

Tilton, D. W. and R. H. Kadlec, 1979. The utilization of a freshwater wetland for nutrient removal from secondarily treated waste water effluent. J. Envt. Qual., 8:328-334.

Woodwell, G. M., 1956. Phytosociology of coastal plain wetlands of Carolinas. Unpublished M. A. Thesis, Duke University, Durham, N.C., 50 pp.

Zoltek, J., Jr., S. E. Bayley, A. J. Herman, L. R. Tortora, and T. J. Dolan, 1979. Nutrients from treated municipal wastewater by freshwater marshes. Center for Wetlands, Univ. of Florida, Gainesville, 325 pp.

Index